New Directions :

MW00816584

Vol. 34

Jane Eyre in German Lands

The Import of Romance, 1848–1918

Lynne Tatlock

BLOOMSBURY ACADEMIC
NEW YORK • LONDON • OXFORD • NEW DELHI • SYDNEY

BLOOMSBURY ACADEMIC
Bloomsbury Publishing Inc
1385 Broadway, New York, NY 10018, USA
50 Bedford Square, London, WC1B 3DP, UK

BLOOMSBURY, BLOOMSBURY ACADEMIC and the Diana logo are
trademarks of Bloomsbury Publishing Plc

First published in the United States of America 2022
This paperback edition published 2023

Cover design by Andrea F. Bucsi
Cover image *The New Novel* by Winslow Homer. Courtesy of the Michele
and Donald D'Amour Museum of Fine Arts, Springfield, Massachusetts,
The Horace P. Wright Collection. Photography by David Stansbury.

Bloomsbury Publishing Inc does not have any control over, or responsibility for, any
third-party websites referred to or in this book. All internet addresses given in this
book were correct at the time of going to press. The author and publisher regret
any inconvenience caused if addresses have changed or sites have ceased
to exist, but can accept no responsibility for any such changes.

Library of Congress Cataloging-in-Publication Data
Names: Tatlock, Lynne, 1950- author.
Title: *Jane Eyre* in German lands : the import of romance, 1848-1918 / by Lynne Tatlock.
Description: New York : Bloomsbury Academic, 2022. |
Series: New directions in German studies ; vol. 34 | Includes bibliographical references
and index. | Summary: "A case study in international reception, pairing
translated and adapted "foreign" material with German national popular literary
production to examine the spread and power of a romance plot promising
liberation, parity, and love"– Provided by publisher.
Identifiers: LCCN 2021040023 (print) | LCCN 2021040024 (ebook) | ISBN 9781501382352
(hardback) | ISBN 9781501382390 (paperback) | ISBN 9781501382369 (epub) |
ISBN 9781501382376 (pdf) | ISBN 9781501382383 (ebook other)
Subjects: LCSH: Brontë, Charlotte, 1816-1855. Jane Eyre–Appreciation–Germany. |
Brontë, Charlotte, 1816-1855. Jane Eyre–Influence. | German literature–English
influences. | Marlitt, E. (Eugenie), 1825-1887–Criticism and interpretation. |
LCGFT: Literary criticism.
Classification: LCC PR4167.J33 T38 2022 (print) |
LCC PR4167.J33 (ebook) | DDC 823/.8–dc23
LC record available at https://lccn.loc.gov/2021040023
LC ebook record available at https://lccn.loc.gov/2021040024

ISBN: HB: 978-1-5013-8235-2
         PB: 978-1-5013-8239-0
         ePDF: 978-1-5013-8237-6
         eBook: 978-1-5013-8236-9

Series: New Directions in German Studies

Typeset by Integra Software Services Pvt. Ltd.

To find out more about our authors and books visit www.bloomsbury.com
and sign up for our newsletters.

For Joe

Contents

Illustrations

Abbreviations of German Translations and Adaptations of *Jane Eyre*

1854	Anon. *Jane Eyre, die Waise von Lowood* (1854)
B	Borch, Marie von, trans. *Jane Eyre, die Waise von Lowood: Eine Autobiographie* (1887–90)
F	Fort, Ludwig. *Jane Eyre. Memoiren einer Gouvernante* (1850)
G	Grieb, Christian Friedrich, trans. *Jane Eyre* (1850)
H	Heinrich, A., trans. *Jane Eyre oder die Waise aus Lowood* (1854)
Ha	Hartung, Ilka von. *Die Waise von Lowood* (1911)
R	Reichard, Gertrud. *Die Waise von Lowood* (1905)
Rt	Reichhardt, Rudolf. *Jane Eyre, die Waise von Lowood* (1906)
S	Susemihl, Ernst, trans. *Johanna Ehre* [*sic*] (1848)
Sp	Spitzer, Jacob. *Die Waise aus Lowood* (1862)
Wa	Wachler, Auguste. *Die Waise von Lowood* (1882)
We	Wedding, Anna. *Jane Eyre, die Waise von Lowood von Currer Bell* (*c.* 1890)

Preface

Charitas Bischoff (née Dietrich, 1848–1925) encountered *Jane Eyre* in two German iterations on two occasions: first, sometime in her childhood in the form of Henriette Stieff's adaptation, *Johanna, oder: Durch Nacht zum Licht* (1852; Johanna, or: Through Night to the Light), and second, when she was fifteen in a German translation, titled *Jane Eyre*.[1] Both times she was swept away, prompted to imitation and empathy.[2] As a member of what Rudolf Gottschall later cleverly termed the "Proletariat des Geistes" (proletariat of the intellect), that is, the impecunious but highly literate middle classes, Bischoff embodied a kind of reader to whom, as we shall see, the romance of *Jane Eyre* particularly appealed.[3]

As young Charitas saw it, Johanna's story was her story. *Johanna* held out the possibility that a sad life—one like her own, which was marked by intermittent placement in foster care—could take a turn for the better. It was up to her to follow Jane's lead: "wenn ich nur klug genug war, das alles zu lernen, was Johanna gekonnt hatte" (if I was just clever enough to learn everything that Johanna had been able to do).[4] She resolved to dress just like her—with a plain black dress and narrow band of white around her neck and wrists—and to teach herself French. Johanna's spell, moreover, inspired her to write. Determined to find a "room of her own," she settled on the woodshed, which was available only because the family, as usual, lacked firewood. The episode ended badly with her father discovering that she had written a poem and telling her he would see to it that in the future she had no time for such foolishness. Charitas tried telling Johanna's story to other children on the village square, but to her dismay they wanted adventure stories instead. Later she became a teacher-in-training with Henriette Breymann in Wolfenbüttel. When her fellow trainees asked for a story, she was better armed than on the village square, for she had meanwhile

---

1   In *c*. 1863, Bischoff could have read one of three extant translations, Ludwig Fort's adaptation, or an adaptation of this adaptation. Since she describes the title as consisting of the, for her, unpronounceable "Jane Eyre," she may refer to Christian Friedrich Grieb's translation (1850), titled simply *Jane Eyre*.

2   Charitas Bischoff, *Bilder aus meinem Leben* (1912; repr., Berlin: G. Grote, 1914), 109–14.

3   Rudolph Gottschall, "Der Gouvernantenroman," *Blätter für literarische Unterhaltung*, no. 1 (1854): 15.

4   Bischoff, *Bilder*, 110.

met Johanna once again, this time as Jane. Now she knew the whole story. They asked for more.[5]

Bischoff's second encounter with Brontë's heroine had occurred during a stint in foster care not long after her mother, Amalie Dietrich, left for Australia on a ten-year trip to collect botanical and biological specimens. The unwitting adolescent pulled *Jane Eyre* off a bookshelf after having been told expressly not to touch these books. There she found her role model, "Johanna," once again, yet this was a different story. When *Jane Eyre* took a direction different from the pious *Johanna*, the book became so exciting that she sat there with flaming cheeks; "die übrige Welt war für mich versunken. Mit fiebernder Aufregung geleitete ich sie nach Thornfield Hall, ich sah jede Räumlichkeit, ich hörte die Stimmen der verschiedenen Personen, ich empfand all ihr Glück, all ihr Weh!" (the world fell away. With feverish excitement I accompanied her to Thornfield Hall, I saw every room, I heard the voices of the various characters, I felt all her happiness, all her pain!).[6]

Recourse to the library of others brought Charitas intense joy but also quick and harsh disapprobation. The unpleasant Funke family with whom she had been temporarily placed scolded her upon discovering what had occupied her during their daylong absence. Not only was the book inappropriate for someone her age, but by touching the books she had also disobeyed her hosts. The forlorn Charitas saw the incident as one of many in a life in which every "Lebensäußerung" was suffocated, Bischoff later reported.[7] In choosing the word "Lebensäußerung" (expression of life) with respect to an incident of intense empathetic reading, she invokes (self-)expression. She had, that is, grasped precisely what Brontë's novel models. Soon thereafter, she reports, she made yet another, if unsuccessful, attempt to set the terms of her life. Later on, she became a governess, spending two years in England. Eventually, like Stieff's Johanna, she married a pastor. Much later she became a writer. Life uncannily mimicked fiction.

* * *

The reading experience of the historical Charitas Bischoff raises many of the questions that drive the following investigation of *Jane Eyre: An Autobiography* in the German-speaking lands, 1848–1918, an era of inequality that was beginning to question that very circumstance. Bischoff's testimony confirms that the novel circulated in more than one form and could be read by the same person in more than one way and at different ages, that some considered it adult reading inappropriate for younger readers, and that it affected some readers powerfully who then wanted more of the same and others not at all. It shows that, in a time in which women's options were severely restricted, readers could find in Jane a role model and in the romance plot a happy ending, one that included writing (oneself) and the prospect of a better life made feasible by education

---

5   Bischoff, *Bilder*, 361.
6   Bischoff, *Bilder*, 329–30.
7   Bischoff, *Bilder*, 331.

and founded in a sort of parity. Like the male readers of Goethe's *Die Leiden des jungen Werther* (The Sorrows of Young Werther) who in the previous century donned Werther's signature blue waistcoat and yellow breeches, young Charitas even wanted to dress like the heroine. The Funkes' disapproval and her own feverish excitement, glowing cheeks, empathetic pain and happiness invoke the cultural valences and effects of romance. While the orphan tale affected the child, the promises of romance spoke to the adolescent.

Bischoff's autobiography was a lucky and rare find. I do not have a stack of such detailed documentation of girls' and women's historical reading of *Jane Eyre* in German. Nevertheless, ample evidence of other kinds exists for the purchase of this work during its first seventy years in German on the European continent, that is, for productive reception and multiple episodes of transmission that testify to the book's international reach and importance as a romance narrative for the times. Women's fiction and non-fiction writing, reviews, translation, abridgment, adaptation, and imitation provide clues as to how Brontë's novel was read in German in this period, how very wide its reach was, and why it flourished.

* * *

A few preliminary remarks and acknowledgments are in order before we turn to the entry of *Jane Eyre* into and diffusion in German-language reading culture. In this examination of translations, adaptations, and *Jane Eyre*-influenced novels as "episodes" of "German" transmission, the adjective German serves as a succinct designation for the domain in which this diffusion took place, one not limited to the current-day national boundaries of Germany. In 1848, a loose confederation of thirty-nine sovereign territories—including parts of the Austrian Empire—on the European continent, where German was the principal language of education and print culture and where a version of German was spoken daily, formed the base of a German-language-based book trade and reading culture.[8] As of 1871, most of these territories, reorganized as twenty-six German states, united under the aegis of Prussia as the Second German Reich. The hereditary lands, German-speaking Austria, however, followed a separate path politically as a constituent of the multinational Dual Monarchy, Austria-Hungary, and thus from the perspective of the Reich was from then on officially a foreign country. Yet the print and reading cultures of the German lands remained intertwined. I cite examples across these political borders. Therefore "German," unless otherwise indicated, applies inclusively to all thirty-nine states before 1871, the later German Reich, and to German-speaking Austria. In this vein, the eponymous "German Lands" includes all of these territories at all points in the nineteenth century. As, however, will also become clear over the course of the following

---

[8]   The Swiss Federation, with its four languages and a federal constitution dating from 1849, follows a different historical trajectory from the German-speaking territories that eventually constitute Imperial Germany and the hereditary lands of Austro-Hungary. None of the fiction, translations, prose adaptations, editions, or plays examined in this study originates in Switzerland.

chapters, Berlin, Leipzig, Hamburg, Munich, and Stuttgart figure overlarge in this account as the points of origin for the vast majority of the books, plays, editions, and reviews adduced.

I also wish to acknowledge some important precursors to the present work as well as the part that digital tools and methods have played in making it possible. First, Stephanie Hohn's foundational study of the German translations and reception of *Jane Eyre* in German, from 1848 to 1990, proved helpful to me at the start of this project.[9] In choosing to set aside most of the adaptations and to focus on a limited set of the nineteenth-century translations, Hohn, does not, however, include most of the data that figure in my investigation, for example, the many adaptations for younger readers. In the late 1990s, furthermore, she worked without the resources that have supported my own work; unsurprisingly, her study evinces some gaps despite her meticulousness, and she left puzzles to be solved.[10] My work, however, does not entirely supersede the section of her book treating the period from 1848 to c. 1910, for I have taken my interrogation of these texts in different directions from hers in keeping with my overall goal to trace the cultural diffusion of a romance formation and its impact. Focusing her comparison of nineteenth-century texts on Fort's adaptation, the Hendel edition of 1904, and four late-century translations, three of which are abridgments of mid-century translations, Hohn systematically works through their renderings of selected features of the original to uncover differences in the orientation of each. In this respect, her work remains instructive. I, by contrast, make the determination in the following chapters that despite their differences from one another and their small linguistic deviations from the original, the four major nineteenth-century translations do convey the values and valences of meaning that matter to the present study.

My first engagement with some of the ideas that drive this study appears in two essays that were significantly informed by my participation in anthologies that grew out of two conferences. *Vergessene Konstellationen literarischer Öffentlichkeit zwischen 1840 und 1885* (2016) urged the reconceptualization of the literary public sphere in the first phase that figures in the story I mean to tell about the impact of *Jane Eyre* and encouraged me to think about the mix of literature circulating in this period and the readership that it addressed. *Die Präsentation kanonischer Werke um 1900* (2017) in turn led me to bring into view the multifarious factors that buttressed the literary survival of *Jane Eyre* as a member of a translated international reading canon.[11]

---

9   Stephanie Hohn, *Charlotte Brontës Jane Eyre in deutscher Übersetzung: Geschichte eines kulturellen Transfers* (Tübingen: Günter Narr, 1998).

10 Of the adaptations for younger readers, Hohn, for example, includes only that by Gertrud Reichard. Her limited corpus obscures the much-longer and more complex history of several of the translations and adaptations she examines.

11 Lynne Tatlock, "Jane Eyre's German Daughters: The Purchase of Romance in a Time of Inequality (1847–1890)," in *Vergessene Konstellationen literarischer Öffentlichkeit zwischen 1840 und 1885*, ed. Katja Mellmann and Jesko Reiling, Studien und Texte zur Sozialgeschichte der Literatur 142 (Berlin: de Gruyter, 2016), 177–200; Lynne Tatlock, "Canons of International Reading: Jane Eyre in German around 1900," in *Die Präsentation kanonischer Werke um 1900: Semantiken, Praktiken, Materialität*, ed. Philip Ajouri (Berlin: de Gruyter, 2017), 121–46.

My investigation of German *Jane Eyre* was aided throughout by what the World Wide Web had to offer in the way of digitized texts, search engines, and access to antiquarian bookstores and libraries and other archives. The project was, furthermore, supported at Washington University beginning in 2012 by the resources of the Humanities Digital Workshop—not only by tools built by Stephen M. Pentecost that expedite linguistic comparison and calculations and aid in the management of information and texts, but also by deformance experiments that Pentecost, Douglas Knox, and student workers designed to support my investigations.

Deformance, a principle and set of procedures modeled by Jerome McGann and Lisa Samuels in *Radiant Textuality*, foregrounds alternate approaches to reading sequentially for the purpose of generating fresh interpretative insight.[12] The categories of procedures that McGann and Samuels identify—reordering, isolation (for example, selectively reading parts of speech), altering, and adding—literally involve tampering with the text.[13] Subtracting, a fifth such procedure, is implicit in both isolating and adding. Digital tools are well suited to carrying out such manipulations. In fact, some of the variations of deformance reflect what takes place in processes of adaptation.

Over the past seven years our automated textual analysis and their visualizations as graphs in experiments involving such techniques as Topic Modeling and sentiment analysis have served to de-familiarize (in the sense of deformance) not only *Jane Eyre* but also many nineteenth-century works in both German and English. This defamiliarization revealed aspects of Brontë's text and affinities between and among texts that might otherwise have escaped my notice—escaped it in part because they are familiar and thus easy to ignore. These tools also enabled me to place Brontë's novel in the context of a greater number of texts than I could actually read for the project. While in the end I elected to proceed more traditionally, digital methods and tools helped me to know where to look and when to look more closely. Computational methods in turn taught me not always to seek the rarest words but rather the more common ones in search of trends. Although this experimentation is not highly visible in the following chapters, it did change and underpin my thinking.

In the context of digital tools and digital humanities and translation studies, I would also like to mention "Prismatic Jane Eyre," a work-in-progress on global translations of *Jane Eyre* supported by Oxford University.[14] It appears that this ambitious project—with the aid of digital tools—both maps the spread of *Jane Eyre* translations around the globe and addresses questions of linguistic variation in translation under such categories as "lexical richness." To date, according to its website, the project has not yet turned to the German-speaking world. My

---

12   Jerome McGann (with Lisa Samuels), "Deformance and Interpretation," chap. 4 in *Radiant Textuality: Literature after the Word Wide Web*, by Jerome McGann (New York: Palgrave, 2001), 105–35.

13   McGann, "Deformance and Interpretation," 117.

14   An Experiment in the Study of Translation: Prismatic Jane Eyre. https://prismaticjaneeyre.org/ (accessed January 23, 2021).

investigation of translation, adaptation, imitation, and reception in a specific his-torical context will support and complement this effort in future.

The enduring import of *Jane Eyre* and *Jane Eyre*-style romance, 1848–1918, bears witness to a culture in motion. In this historical context, variations in the instantiations of *Jane Eyre* and related fiction encouraged and engendered dis-parate understandings of Brontë's romance that imagined social possibility and also undercut it. For seventy years, that is, from the year of the European March Revolutions to the end of the First World War, the year before the enactment of German and Austrian women's suffrage, multiple German *Jane Eyres* and their avatars never stopped circulating in the German-language print realm, declar-ing in many registers, "Reader, I married him"—except in the cases, when, pre-cisely as a sign of the romance narrative's potential explosiveness in the German context, the adapter intervened.

Introduction: The Survival and Diffusion of *Jane Eyre* in German

In 1855, the year of Charlotte Brontë's death, the British novelist Margaret Oliphant wrote of the "invasion of Jane Eyre" that had swept the nation.[1] This invasion had not only spawned many English imitations but completely changed romance by infusing it with ideas of equality such as had not been seen in the older courtship novel. *Jane Eyre* was "a wild declaration of the 'Rights of Woman' in a new aspect"; here a "fierce incendiary, doomed to turn the world of fancy upside down" struggled with a lover who fought her as he would a man. In turning from "pretty fictions of politeness," male "deference and respect" toward the opposite sex, *Jane Eyre* set up a brutal struggle for equality.[2] Oliphant winces in this review at a future in which love stories will consist only of "bitter personal altercations, and mutual defiance" and yet acknowledges "true revolution" in Brontë's work.[3] "Perhaps no other writer of her time," she allows, "has impressed her mark so clearly on contemporary literature, or drawn so many followers on her own peculiar path … ."[4]

Oliphant here has her eye only on the English-language world she knew well. Yet the book had long since "invaded" other lands. The German-speaking territories had from the start proved fertile ground for a plethora of translations and adaptations. Soon after its original publication, a German reviewer excitedly pronounced it one of the most gripping stories to appear in years. It was "voll jugendlicher Kraft, Frische und Originalität in märkiger Sprache, eine Geschichte der Leidenschaft, die sich bisweilen zur Höhe der Tragödie erhebt, ein Buch welches den Herzschlag verdoppelt und Wasser in die Augen treibt" (full of youthful vigor, freshness, and originality in a pithy language, a story of passion that at times reaches the heights of tragedy, a book that doubles one's heartbeat and brings tears to one's eyes).[5] By 1855 it was circulating in multiple

---

[1] Mrs. [Margaret] Oliphant, "Modern Novels—Great and Small," *Blackwood's Magazine* 77, no. 475 (May 1855): 557.
[2] Oliphant, "Modern Novels," 557.
[3] Oliphant, "Modern Novels," 560, 558 respectively.
[4] Oliphant, "Modern Novels," 568.
[5] Review of *Jane Eyre; an Autobiography*, edited [*sic*] by Currer Bell, *Blätter für literarische Unterhaltung*, no. 267 (1848): 667.

forms—as a re-publication in English; in translation; and as adaptations for adults, younger readers, and the stage. In 1855, Oliphant could not even suspect that a decade later a German popular writer, E. Marlitt, would begin to re-animate elements of *Jane Eyre*; nor could she predict that, as serializations in a popular liberal family magazine, Marlitt's novels would introduce hitherto unimagined numbers of readers to romance conversations initiated by Brontë's novel. And she certainly could not anticipate the entrance of these German novels into the English-language domain as internationally bestselling novels read alongside *Jane Eyre*; indeed, she could not know that all Marlitt's novels in the wake of *Jane Eyre* would reach what Todd Kontje terms a "global readership."[6]

Oliphant's exclusive national literary focus has by no means faded. Even in the twenty-first century, the history of *Jane Eyre* in the nineteenth-century German-speaking realm remains terra incognita for most scholars working in English—this, notwithstanding the aforementioned Hohn's work and Norbert Bachleitner's extensive studies of the import of British novels into German culture. In her fascinating account of *Jane Eyre* and English-language avatars that preserve the original's connection to "Bluebeard gothic," Heta Pyrhönen, for example, sets aside the migration of Brontë's novel across national and linguistic borders even while acknowledging that it "has trotted the globe, leaving non-English adaptations in its wake."[7] Pyrhönen's national focus, her intention to see Brontë's novel "as a test bed for analyzing the range of meaning a literary classic has invited from authors within one cultural context," thus begins with the incorrect assertion that the "European Continental tradition does not include [the] connection" of "Bluebeard gothic" and *Jane Eyre*.[8] As we shall see, however, many of the elements of Brontë's Bluebeard gothic, such as the search for knowledge in domestic space, the hidden woman, the spatialization of mental states, and the interest in the past of the Bluebeard stand-in, haunt Marlitt's stories too, fiction deeply indebted to *Jane Eyre*. One of Marlitt's earliest publications is tellingly entitled "Blaubart" (Bluebeard).

What, then, became of this British classic when it crossed the Channel in 1848 to the German-speaking lands where it was repeatedly translated and adapted and where it resurfaced in new forms in Marlitt's ten novels and three novellas? What conversations took place in German via recreated and restyled conventions of romance introduced by *Jane Eyre*? Four strands of its first seventy years in German lands play a role in this investigation: 1) four translations and their abridgments and three adaptations of *Jane Eyre* for general audiences, 2) theater adaptations of *Jane Eyre* and the responses to them, 3) nine adaptations for girls (1852–c. 1911), and 4) Marlitt's fiction (first serialized 1865–88) and its multiple adaptations. In tracing this many-branching story of the productive reception of works in conversation with their times and one another, I foreground romance as shaped by Brontë and subsequently by Marlitt as a constituent of German

---

[6] Todd Kontje, "Marlitt's World: Domestic Fiction in an Age of Empire," *German Quarterly* 77, no. 4 (Fall 2004): 408.

[7] Heta Pyrhönen, *Bluebeard Gothic: Jane Eyre and Its Progency* (Toronto: University of Toronto Press, 2010), 11.

[8] Pyrhönen, *Bluebeard Gothic*, 11, 9 respectively.

book production, literary life, and reading culture, one that especially took up questions of women's domain and agency. In so doing, I seek to look beyond the truism of the compensatory function of romance to examine the ways in which it allows for and stimulates the expression of aspiration and possibility. In this respect I will be aided by Janice Radway, Alison Light, Jackie Stacey, Lynne Pearce, Pamela Regis, and others, all of whom have pushed back against facile assumptions about the functions and contents of romance writing and the too-ready dismissal of its purchase.[9]

Literary Survival

By 1918 Charlotte Brontë's *Jane Eyre: An Autobiography* had achieved status in the German-speaking world as international literature in translation, literature at once classic and popular. Over these decades its multiple instantiations contributed variously to its status, meaning, and circulation. In the wake of the second reading revolution, with full literacy by the end of the nineteenth century and a boom in the book trade, *Jane Eyre* did not, however, establish its presence in German in the form of a stable text; as this English novel was absorbed into German culture it was in the process repeatedly altered. By the turn of the century, it was perhaps best known by the playwright Charlotte Birch-Pfeiffer's sentimentalizing renaming of it as *Die Waise aus Lowood* (The Orphan from Lowood) or by an altered version of this title, *Die Waise von Lowood* (The Orphan of Lowood) in translations, abridgments, and adaptations for a variety of audiences. This multiplication of forms not only supported the novel's diffusion but also testifies to its enduring power in this cultural domain in this historical period. These ramifying paths of transmission and diffusion form the focus of this introduction.

In *How Traditions Live and Die*, Olivier Morin maintains that "preserving information through faithful transmission" is not what makes traditions last.[10] The "persistence of traditions does not chiefly depend on the quality," he explains, but rather the quantity. Repetition, redundancy, and proliferation—because they increase quantity—better serve transmission. Mere sequential transmission is less effective on account of reduced quantity. A corollary to quantity is accessibility. In our particular case, lending libraries, reading clubs, and a flourishing print culture and book industry that made books available in a range of prices increased availability and hence accessibility.

One additional condition especially supports cultural transmission, Morin claims, namely, "intrinsic appeal" or "attraction" (usefulness and interest), the

---

9   See, for example, Janice Radway, *Reading the Romance: Women, Patriarchy, and Popular Literature* (Chapel Hill: University of North Carolina Press, 1991), and "Readers and their Romances," in *Reception Study: From Literary Theory to Cultural Studies*, ed. James L. Machor and Philip Goldstein (New York: Routledge, 2001), 213–45; Alison Light, "'Returning to Manderley': Romance Fiction, Female Sexuality, and Class," in *Feminism & Cultural Studies*, ed. Morag Shiach (Oxford: Oxford University Press, 1999), 371–94; Jackie Stacey and Lynne Pearce, "The Heart of the Matter: Feminists Revisit Romance," in *Romance Revisited*, ed. Lynne Pearce and Jackie Stacey (New York: New York University Press, 1995), 11–45; Lynne Pearce, *Romance Writing* (Cambridge, UK: Polity, 2007); and Pamela Regis, *A Natural History of the Romance Novel* (Philadelphia: University of Pennsylvania Press, 2003).

10   Olivier Morin, *How Traditions Live and Die* (Oxford: Oxford University Press, 2015), 121.

features that guarantee the participation of multiple cultural agents and increase the chances of non-sequential transmission chains.[11] Identifying this intrinsic appeal or attraction of Brontë's novel and its imitators, 1848–1918, will particularly concern us in the following chapters; as we will see, the multiple forms in which the novel circulated signal the nature of that appeal or attraction for nineteenth-century German-speaking readers.

How, then, do we account for the status and circulation of *Jane Eyre* in this era and the multitude of factors that played a role in its persistence as an important and good read and so made possible multiple chains of transmission? Alexander Beecroft has usefully proposed conceiving literary status in terms of "ecology" rather than "economy." Ecology, he explains, presupposes "complexity [as] inherent" to a system. It "understands, accepts, and insists on, the distinct and mutually interactive nature of ... various inputs, so that changes in the external environment ... can have complex and shifting impacts on the various species found in a given context."[12] Literature can thus be seen to have "an ecological relationship to other phenomena—political, economic, sociocultural, religious" and scholars can therefore usefully entertain the idea that texts and literatures "thrive in a variety of ways" via adaptation to and within a given ecology.[13] Beecroft's conception of "literary ecologies," of multiple paths to survival, speaks to the diffusion, transmission, and enduring viability of *Jane Eyre* in German reading cultures, the mixed status of German *Jane Eyre* by the end of the century as both popular and classic, and the new aspects that the novel assumed in the German cultural domain.

One result of the multiple chains of transmission, a sign of the resonance of Brontë's novel within German reading publics and a harbinger of its continued purchase in the twentieth century, is its ascent to the status of a classic and a member of an international canon. Both the terms "classic" and "canon" must for their part also be understood as products of historical processes influenced by a variety of factors. Both designations mark selections that occur within the literary public sphere via multiple agents. The label "classic," in John Guillory's terms an "honorific" as opposed to a signifier of membership in a distinct corpus, acknowledges longevity and a degree of popularity evidenced by the re-publication and re-reading of a given work over generations, often in adaptations.[14] While the classic is in effect, in Anki Mukherjee's formulation, a "singular act of literature," a canon involves "the formation of a corpus."[15] "Canon" designates an evolving body of works that has been agreed upon as valuable reading worth preserving and (re)reading. This value is determined variously within literary ecologies and based on competing criteria—aesthetic, moral,

11   Morin, *Traditions*, 138.

12   Alexander Beecroft, *An Ecology of World Literature from Antiquity to the Present Day* (Brooklyn, NY: Verso, 2015), 18.

13   Beecroft, *Ecology*, 19.

14   John Guillory, *Cultural Capital: The Problem of Literary Canon Formation* (Chicago: University of Chicago Press, 1993), 6.

15   Ankhi Mukherjee, "What is a Classic?" *International Literary Criticism and the Classic Question. PMLA* 125, no. 4 (October 2010): 1029.

social—that may even include the capacity to entertain, criteria determined by discrete social groups.

In some respects German *Jane Eyre* was a fashion, the right plot for a certain historical moment and hence potentially merely ephemeral. In others respects, as we know from the vantage of the twenty-first century, it was also on its way to becoming twentieth- and twenty-first-century "world literature" and hence was acquiring status across national and linguistic boundaries. That fact, too, played a role in its frequent publication and marketing to multiple audiences in the nineteenth century and in turn had an effect on its transmission. Formal aesthetic values were, however, by no means paramount in the determination of what literature was important in the nineteenth century, but, instead, in Morin's terms, appeal, interest, and usefulness.

"World literature" is always subject to revision. As Damrosch asserts, it "is not an infinite, ungraspable canon of works but rather a mode of circulation and of reading, a mode that is as applicable to individual works as to bodies of material, available for reading established classics and new discoveries alike."[16] Like Beecroft, Damrosch stresses the mutability, fluctuation, and permeability of the set of books considered world literature. As he also emphasizes, the understanding of world literature itself has varied. The category of world literature has, he explains, most commonly been informed by one of or a combination of three ideas, namely, world literature as an established body of classics, an evolving canon of "masterpieces," and as "multiple windows on the world."[17] All three play a role in the nineteenth-century reception of *Jane Eyre*. Especially, the third category is important for present purposes: German *Jane Eyre*, in its many guises, brought new "worlds" to its readers in a time of inequality—hence its attraction, interest, and usefulness. The following chapters will concentrate on determining the "what" of this cultural survival, transmission, and diffusion. The current chapter takes a closer look at the "how," at the proliferating and entangled chains of transmission that over seventy years yielded a multiplicity of texts and books.

Chains of Productive Reception and Transmission

It would be surprising had *Jane Eyre* not been translated into German shortly after its appearance in London in 1847. By the middle of the nineteenth century, English novels in German translation constituted a significant share of German-language reading. As Bachleitner observes of the reception of English and French novels in the German-speaking world over the course of the nineteenth century, the increasingly intertwined "national" literary markets resulting from the industrialization of literary production led to an especially extensive reception of foreign literature.[18] While Damrosch imagines world literature in terms of circulation, as "traffic in *ideas* between peoples, a literary market to

---

16   David Damrosch, *What is World Literature?* (Princeton/Oxford: Princeton University Press, 2003), 5.
17   Damrosch, *World Literature*, 5.
18   Norbert Bachleitner, *Quellen zur Rezeption des englischen und französischen Romans in Deutschland und Österreich im 19. Jahrhundert*, Studien und Texte zur Sozialgeschichte der Literatur 31 (Tübingen: Niemeyer, 1990), ix.

which the nations bring their intellectual treasures for exchange,"[19] Bachleitner understands circulation or, rather, what he calls extensive reading, materially, as driven by economic and industrial conditions. At least in the beginning, *Jane Eyre*, which as foreign literature was not well protected by the few extant treaties and regulations governing international copyright, was simply appropriated and re-packaged for the German market for the sake of profit.[20]

Conditions in the book trade—intertwined "national" markets mid-century undergirded by what Bachleitner terms "Übersetzungsfabriken" (translation factories)—facilitated (indeed, virtually assured) the entry of *Jane Eyre* in translation into German "national" reading. In fact, translations of foreign novels especially from French and English reached an all-time high in 1850, claiming 50% of the total novels published in German in that year.[21] Publishers' series, which always required new material, often prompted the initial translation and thus hastened the domestication of foreign literature.[22]

Jane Eyre was first published in the German territories in 1848, the tumultuous year of revolution, in two languages: in English in Leipzig with Tauchnitz's famous Collection of British and American Authors as a "copyright edition for continental circulation" (2nd ed., 1850) and as *Johanna Eyre* in Berlin in Duncker & Humblot's Britannia series, Englands vorzüglichste Romane und Novellen (England's Most Exquisite Novels and Novellas) (see Figure I.1).[23] As the title for this translation suggests, *Jane Eyre* in translation was, despite the series label identifying it as a foreign book, from 1848 on, always just a little Germanized.[24] The title page actually reads *Johanna Ehre*. The translator, Ernst Susemihl, replaced English Jane with German Johanna, just as he substituted Blanca for Blanche to make it more pronounceable in German. The foreign surname Eyre would remain a problem—Charitas Bischoff stumbled over the English name; satirists would later vulgarize it as "Eier" (eggs/testicles). Brontë's subtitle—"an Autobiography"—meanwhile vanished.

The year 1850 yielded a second German translation, titled simply *Jane Eyre*, by Christian Friedrich Grieb, in Franckh's Das Belletristische Ausland, Kabinettsbibliothek klassischer Romane aller Nationen (Bellestristic Literature from

---

19 Damrosch, *World Literature*, 3.

20 See Bachleitner, *Quellen*, 32–51. According to Bachleitner, at mid-century, even when some individual German states had signed agreements with France and England, these were powerless to prevent multiple unauthorized translations of French and English works. Not until 1871 did a unified copyright law come into being for the German territories. Even then it remained for the Bern Convention of 1883 to bring about more effective treaties between the Reich and France and thereafter Great Britain (1887).

21 Norbert Bachleitner, "'Übersetzungsfabriken': Das deutsche Übersetzungswesen in der ersten Hälfte des 19.Jahrhunderts," *Internationales Archiv für Sozialgeschichte der Literatur* 14, no. 1 (1989): 4–5.

22 Bernd Weitemeier, "Deutschsprachige Übersetzungsserien 1820–1910," in *Die literarische Übersetzung in Deutschland: Studien zu ihrer Kulturgeschichte in der Neuzeit*, ed. Armin Paul Frank and Horst Turk (Berlin: Erich Schmidt, 2004), 337.

23 A year later Brontë's *Shirley* was published as vols. 14–16 of Britannia; in 1853, Brontë's *Villette* appeared under its original title as volumes 26–8 of the series.

24 [Charlotte Brontë], *Jane Ehre* [sic], trans. Ernst Susemihl, 3 vols. (Berlin: Duncker & Humbot, 1848), hereafter cited in text cited as "S."

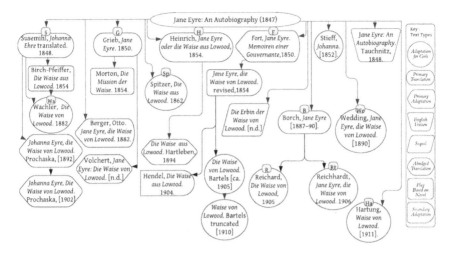

Figure I.1 Literary genealogy of German editions, translations, and adaptations.
Graphic by Grace Klutke.

Abroad, Select Library of Classic Novels of all Nations).[25] Here it took its place among 3,618 volumes published between 1843 and 1865, a cheap edition among cheap editions of important and popular French authors such as Alexandre Dumas père and fils, George Sand, Eugène Sue, and Alphonse Lamartine; English and American authors such as Thackeray, Dickens, Eliot, and Beecher-Stowe; and Danish Hans Christian Anderson.[26]

In that same year, Ludwig Fort's influential adaptation appeared with Verlags-Comptoir in Grimma and nearby Leipzig: *Jane Eyre. Memoiren einer Gouvernante* (Memoirs of a Governess).[27] It, too, belonged to a series promising cosmopolitan reading in translation, namely, Europäische Bibliothek der neuen belletristischen Literatur Deutschlands, Frankreichs, Englands, Italiens, Hollands und Skandinaviens (European Library of the New Belletristic Literature of Germany, France, England, Italy, Holland, and Scandinavia), where it was sold

25 [Charlotte Brontë], *Jane Eyre*, trans. Christian Friedrich Grieb (Stuttgart: Franckh, 1850), hereafter cited in text as "G." Franckh likewise published Brontë's *Shirley* and her *Villette*, both translated by Grieb.

26 Tony Kellen, "Einleitung: Aus der Geschichte der Verlagsbuchhandlung Franckh zu ihrem 100jährigen Bestehen, 12. Juni 1922," *Die Bücher der Franckh'schen Verlagsbuchhandlung Stuttgart* (Stuttgart: Franckh, 1922), xv; Bachleitner, "Übersetzungsfabriken," 16; Alberto Martino, *Die deutsche Leihbibliothek: Geschichte einer literarischen Institution (1756–1914)* (Wiesbaden: Harrassowitz, 1990), 672.

27 *Jane Eyre, Memoiren einer Gouvernante. Von Currer Bell*, trans. Ludwig Fort, 2 vols. (Grimma und Leipzig: Verlags-Comptoir, 1850), hereafter cited in text as "F." Although it claims to be translated from the English, Fort's adaptation is actually a translation of an unacknowledged French adaptation, Paul Émile Daurand Forgues, *Jane Eyre: mémoires d'une gouvernante* (Brussels: Alp[honse] Lebègue, 1849). For the German context, Fort registered as an original. I thank Jay Dillon for alerting me to Forgues.

alongside Brontë's own *Shirley*, designated as by the "Verfasser" (male author) of *Jane Eyre*. Although *Shirley* precedes *Jane Eyre* numerically in the series, this branding of *Shirley* nevertheless suggests that the latter served as the selling point for the former.[28]

Fort's adaptation experienced a long afterlife in German culture. Evident in the subtitle itself is a change in the understanding of the character and the plot. This title was, however, soon to be altered to conform with that of the play *Die Waise aus Lowood*. Dropping the idea of a governess's memoirs, the 1854 adaptation of Fort's adaptation circulated as *Jane Eyre, die Waise von Lowood nach dem Englischen der Currer Bell* (The Orphan of Lowood, after the English of Currer Bell). This adaptation became the key text for future adaptation in the strain originally emanating from Fort.

The year 1854 also yielded a new translation—the third German translation in six years— with the publication of A. Heinrich's *Jane Eyre oder die Waise aus Lowood*. Abridged by *c.* 20,000 words, it appeared in Hartleben's Neues Belletristisches Lese-Cabinet der neuesten und vorzüglichsten Romane aller Nationen in sorgfältigen Übersetzungen (New Belletristic Select Library of the Newest and Most Exquisite Novels of all Nations in Meticulously Executed Translations), a series whose label promised fresh quality reading and excellent translations. The golden ivy on the spines of the two volumes and the elaborate stamped vegetal design on the front and back covers of this edition present *Jane Eyre* as a member of an aestheticized collectable library. This select library included translated French, American, and British novels alongside a few works originally written in German—as in the other series, a mix of now-canonical and now-forgotten works. While, as we shall see in subsequent chapters, Heinrich's small abridgments do reduce the richness of the text, for the most part this version too reproduces the crucial elements and vocabulary of the original. Its greatest shortcoming as a translation may be its bland (mis)translation of Jane's defiantly transitive "Reader, I married him" as "Wir wurden vermält" (We were married).[29]

The titles of translations and adaptations appearing after 1853 reflect a central episode in the nineteenth-century transmission and reception of Brontë's novel. In 1853, Charlotte Birch-Pfeiffer adapted *Jane Eyre* for the stage as *Die Waise aus*

---

28   Basing his conclusion on printed reviews, Bachleitner, however, asserts that in Germany *Jane Eyre* did not really get attention until the appearance of *Shirley*. Norbert Bachleitner, "Die deutsche Rezeption englischer Autorinnen des neunzehnten Jahrhunderts, insbesondere Charlotte Brontës," in *The Novel in Anglo-German Context: Cultural Cross-Currents and Affinities*, ed. Susanne Stark, Internationale Forschung zur Allgemeinen und Vergleichenden Literaturwissenschaft 38 (Amsterdam and Atlanta: Rodopi, 2000), 181. The Verlags-Comptoir of Grimma and Leipzig also published Anne Brontë (*Wildfell Hall*, 1850) and Emily Brontë (*Wutheringshöhe*, 1851). In 1851 it published a novel entitled *Die Geschwister* (The Siblings) by a certain "Acton Currer Bell" and translated by Ludwig Fort "from the English." Acton Currer Bell combines Charlotte Brontë's pseudonym, Currer Bell, with that of her sister Anne, Acton Bell. This novel is by neither and thus appears to have been an attempt to cash in on the mid-century aggregate fame of the Brontës.

29   [Charlotte Brontë], *Jane Eyre oder die Waise aus Lowood*, trans. A. Heinrich, 5 parts in 2 vols. (Pest, Vienna, and Leipzig: Hartleben's Verlags-Expedition, 1854), 5:123, hereafter cited in text as "H."

Lowood, thus forging a German title by which the novel would be known from then on among nineteenth-century German-speaking publics. In addition to revamping Brontë's title for the German-speaking context, the play became for many the first encounter with *Jane Eyre*.

Meanwhile, adaptations for younger audiences proliferated. As the very first of these, Stieff's *Johanna* appeared in 1852 designated as for "die reifere Jugend" (more mature youth). This pious *Johanna* moved young Charitas Bischoff sometime around 1857 to change her life. A central character, in which "weibliche Würde" (feminine dignity) united with "männlicher Kraft" (masculine strength), the dutiful and pious Johanna Horst of this adaptation joyfully finds her place in life as a missionary's wife.[30] Stieff likely adapted *Jane Eyre* under the influence of Grace Kennedy's (1781–1825) religiously infused orphan story *Anna Ross: The Orphan of Waterloo* (1824). At Lowood, that is, Stieff's Helene Born (=Helen Burns) lends Kennedy's book to Johanna, and the latter quickly affirms it as resembling her own history.[31]

Ten years later in 1862, the Viennese publisher A. Pichler brought out a new version for younger readers, Jacob Spitzer's *Die Waise aus Lowood* (The Orphan from Lowood). The title page claims that it was freely adapted after Grieb's translation.[32] As Chapter 3 explores in greater detail, Spitzer's *Waise* deviates widely from the original plot and shares little language with its alleged source. Among other innovations, it transforms Jane into a good Catholic and the Lowood orphanage into a benign Catholic institution. Grieb's translation must have figured merely as the translator's access to the main pillars of the story. The prominent citation of Grieb as its source nevertheless linked the adaptation with a recognizable and reputable circulating translation. Spitzer's adaptation merited a second printing in 1867.[33] Catholic Jane did not, however, survive the 1860s. Another fifteen years would pass before Brontë's novel was again adapted for the younger set and then in at least seven variations.

Even as *Jane Eyre* rose to prominence in the German territories, Brontë's other novels fell off the horizon, as did the novels of Emily and Anne Brontë, all of which had also been translated in the 1850s. Three of the original publishers of German translations or adaptations of *Jane Eyre* (Duncker & Humblot, Franckh, and Verlags-Comptoir) had tried their luck with *Shirley* and/or *Villette*. None of

---

[30] Henriette Stieff, *Johanna, oder: Durch Nacht zum Licht. Eine Erzählung für die reifere Jugend* (Leipzig: M. Simion's Verlag, [1852]), 136.

[31] Stieff, *Johanna*, 39–40; Grace Kennedy, *Anna Ross: The Orphan of Waterloo* (London: George Routledge and Sons, n.d.).Kennedy's story was translated into German as Grace Kennedy, *Anna Ross: eine Erzählung für Kinder* (Berlin: Franklin et Comp., 1830).

[32] Inga-Stina Ewbank, "Adapting Jane Eyre: Jakob Spitzer's Die Waise aus Lowood," in *Beiträge zur Rezeption der britischen und irischen Literatur des 19. Jahrhunderts im deutschsprachigen Raum*, ed. Norbert Bachleitner, Internationale Forschungen zur Allgemeinen und Vergleichenden Literaturwissenschaft 45 (Amsterdam: Rodopi, 2000), 288; and Birgit Pargner, *Zwischen Tränen und Kommerz: Das Rührtheater Charlotte Birch-Pfeiffers (1800–1868) in seiner künstlerischen und kommerziellen Verwertung* (Bielefeld: Aisthesis Verlag, 1999), 489. See also Bachleitner, "Die deutsche Rezeption englischer Autorinnen," 185–7.

[33] Jacob Spitzer, *Die Waise aus Lowood, frei bearbeitet nach Dr. Grieb's Übersetzung* (Vienna: A. Pichler's Witwe & Sohn, 1867), hereafter cited in text as "Sp."

these translations, however, gained traction in German-language print culture. Franckh's and Duncker & Humblot's 1853 translations of *Villette* appear to be the last such nineteenth-century German-language editions of either of these two novels. Brontë's posthumously published *The Professor* appeared in Vienna in 1857 as *Der Professor* in Ludwig & Zang's Roman-Zeitung, Bibliothek der vorzüglichsen Romane des In- und Auslands (Novel-Newspaper, Library of the Most Exquisite Novels, Domestic and Foreign)[34] and in Stuttgart with Franckh who in 1858 promoted it on its title page as "Von Currer Bell, Verfasserin von Jane Eyre, Shirley, Villette u.s.w." (By Currer Bell, Authoress of Jane Eyre, Shirley, Villette, etc.). The acronym "u.s.w." implied that Brontë—by this date recognized as female—had written an entire series of novels, yet there were none to populate the promise of "u.s.w." *Der Professor* itself did not reappear in German until the second half of the twentieth century.

In short, after 1858 there is little evidence in the German publishing industry of an attempt to cluster Brontë's four novels or the novels of the Brontë sisters. Nor did the continental German domain witness the emergence of the "Brontë myth" described by Lucasta Miller, in which the reception of the story of the three ambitious sisters intertwines with the reception of their novels.[35] The sisters' slender oeuvre in German translation was soon out of print. Of Charlotte Brontë's four novels, only *Jane Eyre* persisted. The name Currer Bell/Charlotte Brontë did not therefore offer in German the serial reading of Brontë's more prolific nineteenth-century peers. Those hoping for more of the same, like Charitas Bischoff's colleagues in Wolfenbüttel, had to look to other authors.

After a lull of nearly twenty years a fresh round of new adaptations, abridgments, and translations of *Jane Eyre* commenced in the German-speaking world. Beginning in the 1880s, German and Austrian publishers made available to an array of audiences new German iterations of the novel, still identified as written by Currer Bell and usually titled with a variation of Birch-Pfeiffer's *Waise*. These new episodes of transmission emerged in the expanding and segmenting book market and took many forms. They include five new adaptations for girls, beginning in 1882 with Auguste Wachler's Birch-Pfeiffer- and Susemihl-indebted version; two new editions for girls, based on the 1854 adaptation of Fort; a sixty-two-page folk edition also from 1882, adapted by O. Berger; Hendel's popular edition from 1904, based on the adaptation of 1854; a sequel, *Die Erbin der Waise*; and abridged versions of the first three translations.[36] A fourth translation,

---

34   Zang published a "Bibliothek der vorzüglichsten Romane des In- und Auslandes" (Library of the Best Domestic and Foreign Novels) in his own *Roman- und Novellen-Zeitung* (Novel- and Novella-Newspaper). Martin Bruny, "Die Verlagsbuchhandlung A. Hartleben. Eine Monographie" (MA thesis, University of Vienna, 1995), 95. Tauchnitz published the novel in English in 1857 in its Collection of British Authors.

35   Lucasta Miller, *The Brontë Myth* (London: Jonathan Cape, 2001). Miller indicates the crucial role that Elizabeth Gaskell's *The Life of Charlotte Brontë* (1857) played in creating and sustaining the myth of the sisters and their work (57–79). Gaskell's work was not translated into German until the 1990s. It appeared in English in two editions (1857, 1859) with Tauchnitz in Leipzig.

36   *Jane Eyre, die Waise von Lowood, oder Gott führt die Seinen wunderbar. Für's Volk erzählt von Otto Berger* (Reutlingen: Enßlin & Laiblin, 1882).

Borch's new translation, *Jane Eyre, die Waise von Lowood: Eine Autobiographie*, appeared with Reclam in 1887–90, having reinstated the "autobiography" of Brontë's original title.

The widespread availability of Brontë's novel in different formats and at different prices supports Uwe Spiekermann's observation regarding the appeal of the book trade to both mass consumption and pretentious book collection. As Spiekermann notes, the industry walks a thin line when it presents mass-produced items in a form that creates the illusion of uniqueness—like luxury items—and yet makes them affordable for those with less purchasing power.[37] The recourse to older texts and translations also reflects the new publishing landscape after the Bern Convention of 1883, which led to new, enforceable laws regulating international copyright. By the end of the century, German and Austrian publishing houses could no longer mine new international literature for the purpose of translation and publication in Germany and Austria without paying for it.[38] Now the most lucrative sources for generating new book products at low prices were older literature and older translations that were no longer under copyright protection.

Reclam's *Jane Eyre, Die Waise von Lowood: Eine Autobiographie* (Jane Eyre, The Orphan of Lowood: An Autobiography) appeared in four volumes between Henrik Ibsen's *Das Fest auf Solhaug* (vol. 2375; The Festival at Solhaug) and *Gesprächsbüchlein Ulrich von Huttens* (vols. 2381–2; Little Conversation Book [1521]) and so joined an eclectic set of older and very old publications constituting a so-called "universal library." As Georg Jäger notes, this series was predicated on the idea of a canon; committed to upholding tradition, it strove to preserve and recirculate the literature of the past.[39] In its completeness, Reclam's edition of *Jane Eyre* aspires to faithfulness to the original "masterpiece" from the storehouse of the past for the purpose of present-day reading. This last and longest enduring of the four nineteenth-century translations remains available in the twenty-first century both in the form of print on demand and in a lightly edited version in hardcover and paperback.

While Borch's translation was newly commissioned by Reclam, the three additional translations circulating at the end of the century were revised, newly abridged, and unattributed versions of Susemihl's, Grieb's, and Heinrich's mid-century translations appearing with the publishers Prochaska, Franckh, and Hartleben, respectively. The version (*c.* 1912) of Grieb's 1850 translation with Franckh had been sufficiently reworked so as to be attributed to a new translator, G. A. Volchert, without reference to Grieb.[40]

---

[37]   Uwe Spiekermann, *Basis der Konsumgesellschaft. Entstehung und Entwicklung des modernen Kleinhandels in Deutschland 1850–1904*, Schriftenreihe zur Zeitschrift für Unternehmensgeschichte 3 (Munich: C. H. Beck, 1999), 581.

[38]   Bachleitner, *Quellen*, 42.

[39]   Georg Jäger, "Reclams Universal-Bibliothek bis zum Ersten Weltkrieg: Erfolgsfaktoren der Programmpolitik," *Reclam. 125 Jahre Universal-Bibliothek 1867–1992* (Stuttgart: Philipp Reclam jun., 1992), 41.

[40]   Charlotte Brontë, *Jane Eyre: Die Waise von Lowood, aus dem Englischen neu bearbeitet von G. A. Volchert*, 6th ed., Stuttgarter Ausgabe (Stuttgart: Franckh, [1912]).

Franckh branded Volchert's revision of Grieb's translation as a "Stuttgarter Ausgabe" (Stuttgart edition), a distinction that the publisher also accorded, for example, to German translations of international literature such as *The Pickwick Papers, David Copperfield, Oliver Twist, Anna Karenina, The Last of the Mohicans, The Last Days of Pompei,* and *The Three Muskateers.* The designation "bearbeitet" (adapted) on the title page coupled with the designation "Stuttgarter Ausgabe" implied quality international reading and also hinted at tailoring for a German audience. As Hohn points out, Volchert indeed took liberties with the presentation of Rochester, St John, and Jane—as Grieb had not—liberties that obscured psychological complexity and motivation to the point of making especially Jane seem inconsistent in her decisions and actions.[41]

In 1892 the Austrian publisher Prochaska made available for purchase a revised, abridged, and unattributed edition of Susemihl's 1848 rendering titled *Johanna Eyre, die Waise von Lowood.* The publisher marketed it in two different series with uniform covers that featured the book as important "world literature": Die besten Romane der Weltliteratur (The Best Novels of World Literature), consisting of eighteen volumes. In 1902, Prochaska reissued it in the series Klassische Romane der Weltliteratur. Ausgewählte Sammlung Prochaska in 32 Bänden (Classic Novels of World Literature. The Prochaska Select Collection in 32 volumes). A novel translated into "alle Cultursprachen" (all the languages of the civilized world), *Johanna Eyre* appealed to both "Geist und Gemüt" (mind and heart).[42]

The cover design of novels in the 1892 series features flowers and foliage with a crest whose interlocking parts and the indication of cords threaded through rivets lend it a mechanical look. As the dual pricing on the cover indicates, Prochaska expected to sell the book in both Germany and Austria. The uniform covers of Prochaska's second series from 1902, the Classic Novels of World Literature, strive, in turn, to address the connoisseur with covers indicating the precious and select.[43] Their gold-stamped secession design presents an underwater view of two mermaids with flowing hair, swirling seaweed, and bubbles. Sexually charged, it intimates the erotics of book collecting with its partial view of one mermaid's bare breast and the second's rump, which despite its fish scales suggests the human buttocks.

As a selection of the "hervorragendsten Romane aller Nationen" (most superb novels of all nations), the Collection Hartleben likewise promised quality reading. *Jane Eyre oder Die Waise aus Lowood* claimed a prominent place in the second year of the series, between German translations of Sand's *Confession of a Young Girl* and Flaubert's *Madame Bovary.*[44] In addition to works by Sand and Flaubert,

41 Hohn, *Jane Eyre in deutscher Übersetzung*, 113–14.

42 [Charlotte Brontë], *Johanna Eyre, die Waise von Lowood von Currer Bell*, Die besten Romane der Weltliteratur in neuen Ausgaben (Vienna: Karl Prochaska, [1892]), 3: front matter.

43 [Charlotte Brontë], *Johanna Eyre. Die Waise von Lowood*, Klassische Romane, Sammlung Prochaska, 3 vols. (Vienna: Prochaska, [1902]), cover.

44 [Charlotte Brontë], *Die Waise aus Lowood*, 3 vols. (Vienna: A. Hartleben, n.d.). Hohn dates the volume to 1894. *Jane Eyre in deutscher Übersetzung*, 106.

the series offered in uniform bindings a mix of now sub-canonical works such as Thackeray's *Henry Esmond*; well-known popular French, American, and English authors such as Dumas fils, Sue, Wilkie Collins, Bulwer-Lytton, Gaskell, and Beecher-Stowe; and now forgotten international authors. The series cover features a medievalizing vegetal design of twining ivy, a cherub, castle ruins, and a singing bird invoking a locus amoenus. A contemplative woman—flowers in her hair, a quill and a small book in her right hand, and her legs parted beneath her skirt—props her left elbow on a frame with a decorative border. Hartleben announced the set as comprising the "gediegenen Werke des eigenen belletristischen Verlages (welche meist seit Jahren vergriffen sind), die es verdienen, Gemeingut zu werden, in guten sorgfältig revidirten neuen Ausgaben" (tasteful works from its own belletristic publishing house [which for the most part have been out of stock] that deserve to become common property, in good, carefully revised new editions).[45] The publisher thus lays claim to cultural recovery in support of shared literary valuation.

These three late-century editions of earlier translations of *Jane Eyre* do present variations of the novel as a result of abridgment. At the same time, in the aggregate and alongside Reclam's new translation, they supported the stature and market presence of Brontë's novel in the German publishing context. The hardy lineage of adaptation that begins with Fort, treated in detail in Chapter 3, likewise kept the pseudonymous author and title in the public eye. The piously sentimentalizing 1854 version of Fort's adaptation, like the four translations, was in fact marketed alongside other international and domestic works with the cachet of world literature, with no indication that it was an adaptation and not a translation. In 1904 the publisher Otto Hendel published it in a new edition furnished with Brontë's portrait and information about her life, oeuvre, and the reception of the novel in Germany—as was standard for the series.[46] Touting the novel's impact and quality, the preface justifies inclusion in Hendel's Bibliothek der Gesamtlitteratur des In- und Auslands (Library of the Entire Repertoire of Domestic and Foreign Literature) as an act of historical preservation. While the front matter venerates the author and her literary product, the actual text belies the alleged aim of historical preservation. Yet even in this much-altered form, Hendel's *Jane Eyre* supported the novel's continued presence and rising status in the literary marketplace.

Publication in Series, Canon Formation, and Literary Survival

Publication in "collections," "series," and "libraries" promotes literary survival and transmission. These affiliations valorize a given work and sustain public attention.[47] Designations such as "Collection" and "Bibliothek" invoke high-end

---

45   [Brontë], *Waise* (Hartleben), 1: flyleaf.

46   E. Von Bauernfeld, *Jane Eyre, die Waise von Lowood* (Halle a. d. S.: Otto Hendel, [1904]).Given the date of the anonymous original (1854), it is possible that Hendel's adapter designation refers to Eduard von Bauernfeld, the Austrian playwright (1802–90), as the original adapter.

47   Fritz Nies, "Superlativ in Serie: Französische Buchreihen mit besonderem Wertanspruch (1875–1921)," *Romanistische Zeitschrift für Literaturgeschichte* 16 (1992): 227–36; Weitemeier, "Deutschsprachige Übersetzungsserien," 329.

book collecting; they make an impression of abundance and order as well as preciousness and enduring value.[48] Placement of *Jane Eyre* in such nineteenth- and early twentieth-century series implied selection based on evaluative criteria: descriptors such as "hervorragend" (outstanding), "best," "klassisch," "gediegen" (tasteful), and "universal" asserted *Jane Eyre*, along with the other books in the series, as exemplary and precious, worthy of collection and intensive reading. Hartleben's above-quoted contention that the books selected from its own backlists should become "Gemeingut" (common property) operates with an idea important to limiting the reach of copyright in the name of general accessibility, that is, the idea of books as public property that serves the "Gemeinwohl" (common good).

By the end of the century, Brontë's novel had indeed become German common property. While to some degree it figured in German culture as a distinct international classic, translation, adaptation, and transmediation had brought about cultural assimilation. Like all literature that leaves its culture of origination and enters another to become world literature, *Jane Eyre* changed as a result of its movement across cultural and linguistic borders. To paraphrase Damrosch, this single work of literature, a site of negotiation between two different cultures, could be used by the receiving culture "in all sorts of ways."[49] The translations, adaptations, and abridgments did, as we shall see in subsequent chapters, precisely that. In the process *Jane Eyre* became a German story that spoke to German readers of their own discontent and hope, but not always in the same register. A collection of agents generated multiple versions of Brontë's novel, variations that occupied different positions in the literary field and thus aided its transmission and diffusion. In Part Two we turn to Marlitt's single-authored serialized series and their adaptations as yet another piece of the history of the diffusion of *Jane Eyre* via multiple modalities.

The seven adaptations for girls published in the years 1882–1911 likewise functioned as links in the chains of transmission. They exemplify the miscommunications that characterize such chains yet also ensure transmission and survival. In these decades *Jane Eyre* temporarily became a part of an emergent commercially driven children's and adolescents' literary canon consisting of supposedly age-appropriate adaptations of classic adult reading.[50]

Jane Eyre as a "Secondary Classic"

In 1854, Elise von Hohenhausen (1789–1857) warmly endorsed *Jane Eyre* as one of several English novels that were useful particularly for girls who hoped to become educators.[51] The feminist Louise Otto (1819–95), moreover, asserted in 1876 more generally of novel reading that it could benefit girls who enjoyed

---

48   Nies, "Superlativ," 232.
49   Damrosch, *World Literature*, 283.
50   Bettina Kümmerling-Meibauer, *Kinderliteratur, Kanonbildung und literarische Wertung.* (Stuttgart: J. B. Metzler, 2003), 40.
51   Elise von Hohenhausen, *Die Jungfrau und ihre Zukunft in unserer Zeit* (1854; excerpt), in *Bildung und Kultur bürgerlicher Frauen 1850–1918*, ed. Günter Häntzschel (Tübingen: Max Niemeyer, 1986), 378–9.

it: such girls would find therein "Beschäftigung für ihre Phantasie, die sie gerade *ohne diese* viel eher verleitet, im Leben selbst kleine Romane zu spielen" (occupation for their imagination, which especially *without this [reading]* would otherwise induce them to play out little novels in their own lives).[52] Herself a sometime novelist, Otto advocated, furthermore, reading as aiding girls in the attainment of a moral compass and zest for the ideal. She instanced the benefit of immersing oneself in the fates of fictional characters to prevent stultifying preoccupation with local gossip.[53] In touting reading as a way of acquainting readers with the Good and the Ennobling, Otto was not, however, one to suggest bowdlerizing and simplifying books. Yet the adaptations of *Jane Eyre* that proliferated especially near the end of the century seem bent on doing just that in the name of the Good and thus withholding the moral and psychological complexity of the original.

By 1882, when Wachler adapted *Jane Eyre* for more mature youth, ushering in a late-century round of new adaptations for younger readers, the contents of a novel originally written for a general audience had come under sharper scrutiny. Market segmentation—the creation of the girl reader, as it were—had led to stricter attention to the contents of books designated "for younger readers." Especially, the near bigamy of the original plot made *Jane Eyre* suspect, even though the protagonist's determination to thwart Rochester's misguided intentions and the novel's happy ending firmly support the sanctity of marriage and domestic values more generally. We will take a closer look at the effective censorship of the novel and the struggle over meaning in juvenile adaptations of *Jane Eyre* in Chapters 1, 3, and 4.

Despite dubious contents, multiple publishers set about establishing *Jane Eyre* as classic reading for a younger audience—as what Bettina Kümmerling-Meibauer terms a "secondary classic," that is, an adaptation of adult classic reading for children and adolescents. They attempted, furthermore, to integrate Brontë's novel into an emergent canon of adaptations of other such secondary classics, including, among others, Cooper's *Leatherstocking Tales*, Defoe's *Robinson Crusoe*, Cervantes's *Don Quixote*, Bulwer-Lytton's *The Last Days of Pompeii*, Swift's *Gulliver's Travels*, and Beecher-Stowe's *Uncle Tom's Cabin*. Publishers' catalogs overlap significantly in their offerings, thus affirming a shared sense of this classic reading for younger readers. As they mined the classic repertoire, adapters refashioned these novels for the target audience in keeping with contemporary mores—often in a pedagogical vein.[54]

The multiplication of *Jane Eyre* adaptations for younger readers in these decades exemplifies processes of cultural diffusion.[55] It involved proliferation, repetition, redundancy, and appeal on several levels. These adaptations all bear

52   Louise Otto, *Frauenleben im Deutschen Reich: Erinnnerungen aus der Vergangenheit mit Hinweis auf Gegenwart und Zukunft* (Leipzig: Moritz Schäfer, 1876), 207.

53   Otto, *Frauenleben*, 207.

54   Bettina Hurrelmann, "Was heißt hier 'klassisch'?" in *Klassiker der Kinder- und Jugendliteratur*, ed. Bettina Hurrelmann (Frankfurt am Main: Fischer Taschenbuch Verlag, 1995), 9.

55   These publishers include Bartels, Globus, Jugendhort, Leo, Meidinger, Schreiter, Weichert, and Zieger.

more or less the same title and yet they deviate significantly from one another. In this regard they bear out Morin's observation of the relative unimportance of accuracy and quality in chains of transmission. Even as they relied on the reputation of *Die Waise aus/von Lowood* in their creation of a secondary classic, publishers and adapters also solidified that reputation. As both Bettina Hurrelmann and Kümmerling-Meibauer assert, secondary classics in effect enhance the standing of the originals.[56] The multiple adaptations, as additional variables in the literary ecology of *Jane Eyre*, helped to capture reader attention and to lend the novel cachet in the German-language domain.[57] As a member of a canon of secondary classics, *Jane Eyre* in German adaptation was hooked to the transmission chains of some of the great masterplots of Western literature.

The publisher Jugendhort, as one example, pursued the appeal of cultural authority and membership in a canon with Gertrud Reichard's *Die Waise von Lowood* (1905). The title page announces the book as freely adapted for the "junge Mädchenwelt nach der Reclamschen Ausgabe" (world of young girls after the Reclam edition).[58] Jugendhort thereby tied the adaptation to a specific achievement of the German publishing industry—Reclam's universal library— with its educational, democratizing mission. With a text that is about a third of the length of the original, Reichard takes considerable liberties with Brontë's novel—as described in Chapter 3—while nevertheless invoking the cultural authority of the universal library.

The back matter of the book in turn cements its authority not only through the mention of Reclam but also through affiliation with "classic" books in German for younger readers, all illustrated and available at the same price. This canon of secondary classics includes, for example, Andersen's fairy tales, *Uncle Tom's Cabin*, Cooper's *Leatherstocking Tales*, *The Last Days of Pompeii*, and Campe's *Robinson* alongside favorite German authors, such as Ottilie Wildermuth, Christopf von Schmid, and Wilhelm Hauff and works such as Grimms' fairy tales and *Reineke Fuchs* (Reynard the Fox). Eugen Hanetzog's illustrations, for their part, also invest the book with cultural significance. Hanetzog opted for Empire style for his six black-and-white illustrations and five color plates, thereby setting the story anachronistically in the Napoleonic era as if it were a historical novel. The book thus potentially resonated with other popular girls' reading that evoked the life of the beloved Queen Luise and the triumph over Napoleon, the period that occupied an over-large place in the nationalist imagination in Imperial Germany.[59]

---

56   Kümmerling-Meibauer, *Kinderliteratur*, 179.
57   Kümmerling-Meibauer sees the adaptation of *Weltliteratur* as a first step in the transfer of the idea of the classic to select literature for younger audiences, a trend that sets in toward the end of the nineteenth century. *Kinderliteratur*, 273.
58   Gertrud Reichard, *Die Waise von Lowood von Currer Bell* (Berlin: Jugendhort, n.d. [1905]), hereafter cited in text as "R."
59   On the Prussian Queen Luise as the subject of popular (nationalist) reading for girls, see Jennifer Drake Askey, *Good Girls, Good Germans: Girls' Education and Emotional Nationalism in Wilhelminian Germany* (Rochester, NY: Camden House, 2013), 143–82.

Rudolf Reichhardt's adaptation of Brontë's novel as *Jane Eyre, Die Waise von Lowood*, as a further example, also relies heavily on Borch's translation but does not acknowledge its source.[60] Here another Berlin publisher, Globus, pursued a different strategy to balance its availability as a mass-produced item with the air and appeal of artistic distinction and pretention of a classic.[61] While the adaptation is barely over a third of the length of the original, the book's heft and slightly outsized dimensions project importance. The bright red cover with its gold-stamped *Jugendstil* design featuring the profile of a young woman within a stained glass window underscores the effect. The front flyleaf of the book block cultivates pride of ownership by designating a space for the book owner's name with a prompt in all capital letters: "Dies Buch gehört" (This book belongs to). Max Wulff's five color plates secure the appeal to aesthetic connoisseurship.

German adaptations of Brontë's novel from the years 1882–1911 did not long remain in the canon of secondary classics and all but disappeared after the First World War.[62] In the end, these bowdlerized, sometimes highly improbable, even outright silly adaptations of a novel written originally for adults did not gain the traction with the younger set achieved by adaptations of such international classics as *Gulliver's Travels*, *The Last of the Mohicans*, and *Uncle Tom's Cabin*. In contrast to these adaptations, which retain the most interesting plot elements of the originals and continue to read well enough to entertain younger readers, *Jane Eyre*, as we shall see, loses what makes it most interesting—its interiority and conversations, its critical moral conflicts, its sensational episodes, and romance tied to self-formation. Without these exhilarating features, the text becomes a dull creature, often focused merely on Jane's helpless suffering. Adolescents who were good readers, of course, did not need an adaptation; they could turn to one of the translations, abridged or not, to read a story of an unprepossessing woman who arrives at self-possession and acknowledgment via romance.

Still, in the first seventy years, adaptations for younger readers played a role in the survival and general reading of Brontë's novel in the German territories. Such adaptation aids and signals the acquisition of literary status and market

---

[60] Measured by overlapping four-word sequences, it tallies more matches than does Reichhardt's adaptation. Rudolf Reichhardt, *Jane Eyre, die Waise von Lowood. Nach Currer Bell aus dem Englischen übersetzt und für die Jugend bearbeitet* (Berlin: Globus, [1906]), hereafter cited in text as "Rt."

[61] Christine Haug, "Kunst, Bibliophilie und Warenhaus. Kultur als Element professioneller Reklametechnik um 1900," in *Parallelwelten des Buches. Beiträge zu Buchpolitik, Verlagsgeschichte, Bibliophilie und Buchkunst*, ed. Monika Estermann, Ernst Fischer, and Reinhard Wittmann (Wiesbaden: Harrassowitz, 2008), 422.

[62] A truncated version of Reichhardt's adaptation with Meidinger, 128 pages in length (as opposed to the 240-page Globus edition) and furnished with illustrations featuring the fashions of the 1920s, constitutes an exception. Rudolf Reichhardt, *Jane Eyre, die Waise von Lowood, nach Currer Bell aus dem Englischen übersetzt und für die Jugend bearbeitet*, illustrated by Walter Plantikow [Berlin: Meidinger's Jugendschriften Verlag, n.d.]), copy owned by author. Klotz mistakenly lists this version as 240 pages in length, i.e., the same length as a reprint of the Globus edition appearing in the same year. Aiga Klotz, *Kinder- und Jugendliteratur in Deutschland 1840–1950. Gesamtverzeichnis der Veröffentlichungen in deutscher Sprache* (Stuttgart: J. B. Metzler, 1990–6), 4:20.

presence. As Hurrelmann observes in keeping with Morin's observations on cultural transmission, the achievement of status as a (secondary) classic work becomes visible precisely in the variety and dynamic of its instantiations, adaptations, translations, and the forms in which it appears in the media.[63] In this respect, even the ephemeral effort to make *Jane Eyre* part of a young people's canon aided its survival and diffusion in the decades before the First World War. As multiple forms of proliferation, the adaptations for younger readers in effect joined forces with the translations, the *Volksausgaben*, adaptations for adults, theater performances, and play scripts to guarantee that German *Jane Eyre* would be preserved, adapted and re-adapted, bought, borrowed, read, and re-read.

The Fictions of E. Marlitt

What, then, of productive reception in that ostensible twenty-year lull between Spitzer's adaptation for girls of 1862 and Wachler's of 1882? What of the even greater gap between the translations and adaptations of the 1850s and Borch's translation of 1887–90? Plenty of evidence exists that the novel was being read, viewed on stage, and talked about. In 1869, for example, Franz Hirsch framed his review of new English novels with reference to "Currer Bell" as having established a genre or direction with her "Gouvernantenroman" (governess novel) that competed with the French "Sensationsroman" (sensation novel). The reviewer simply assumed German readers' familiarity with Brontë's novel, never mentioning it by name, but referring merely to its impact.[64]

The persistent appeal of the governess novel, as Gottschall maintained in his 1854 review of Brontë's *Villette*, likely had to do with the gap between the "Bewußtsein geistiger Selbständigkeit und Unabhängigkeit und äußerlicher Abhängigkeit und Unselbständigkeit" (consciousness of intellectual autonomy and independence and external dependency and lack of autonomy) characteristic of the social and cultural positioning of the governess. Viewed in these more abstract terms, the predicament of Jane Eyre, the orphan and governess, becomes visible in literary constellations that more generally feature intellectually strong and independent heroines forced into positions of dependency.[65] Among others, Wilhelmine von Hillern's *Ein Arzt der Seele* (1869; A Physician of the Soul), as we shall see in Chapter 4, evinces affinities to *Jane Eyre* in narrating a romance involving a highly intelligent woman thwarted in her efforts to pursue science by her dependency on both her male guardian and the male scientific establishment. *Jane Eyre* had, in short, in subtle and not so subtle respects, informed popular German-language literary discourse on female selfhood in a period in which the questionable status of women was coming ever more under scrutiny even as women made scant progress toward improving it.

From 1865 to 1888, E. Marlitt, the star fiction writer of the premiere German family magazine of the age, *Die Gartenlaube*, published a series of novels that

---

[63]   Hurrelmann, "Was heißt hier 'klassisch'?" 10.
[64]   Franz Hirsch, "Neue englische Romane," *Blätter für literarische Unterhaltung*, no. 28 (1869): 441–5.
[65]   Gottschall, "Gouvernantenroman," 15.

were also *Jane Eyre* surrogates. Whatever its shortcomings, Marlitt's fiction constituted a significant and enduring path of cultural transmission and diffusion of *Jane Eyr*ish romance, its first-time publication falling into the lull in *Jane Eyre* translations, adaptations, and new editions. Her fiction was in turn quickly translated into multiple European languages to become strong sellers in the receiving cultures, the translation sometimes commencing even before the serialization was complete. The United States in particular became an important market for these books in English. Meanwhile, in the German territories, Keil reissued Marlitt's fiction regularly; by the new century other publishers were printing it and selling it at various price points.

The *Gartenlaube* and its publisher-editor Ernst Keil published Marlitt's work not only during a hiatus in new German versions of *Jane Eyre*, but also during one in new English-language imitations, as made visible by a gap in a recently assembled bibliography of principally English-language imitations and adaptations: the bibliography lists no new publications between Rhoda Broughton's *Cometh Up as a Flower* (1867) and Henry James's *The Turn of the Screw* (1898).[66] This list is to be sure incomplete or, rather, too strictly conceived to include all possible candidates—it does not, for example, contain Louisa May Alcott's *The Inheritance* (written *c.* 1852, published posthumously in 1997), *Behind a Mask* (1866), *Moods* (1865), or her *Little Women* (1868–9), for example, which, as John Seelye and Christine Doyle, among others, have shown, all evince traces of Brontë.[67] Nor does it include Augusta J. Evans's *St. Elmo* (1866), which explicitly references Brontë's novel. But the addition of even these works only narrows but does not close the gap that the list reveals. Given that the first-time publication of Marlitt's fiction falls into this bracketed time, the possibility arises that, as internationally bestselling popular literature, it served as an equally or even more important chain of transmission than original English-language fiction in perpetuating, adapting, and revitalizing features of *Jane Eyre* to tell new (and yet familiar) stories in the context of the changing conditions of the last decades of the nineteenth century in Europe and North America.[68] There is evidence that international publishers published and international readers read Marlitt's

---

[66]   Amber K. Regis and Deborah Wynne, *Charlotte Brontë: Legacies and Afterlives* (Manchester: Manchester University Press, 2017), 283.

[67]   John Seelye, *Jane Eyre's American Daughters: From The Wide, Wide World to Anne of Green Gables; A Study of Maginalized Maidens and What They Mean* (Newark: University of Delaware Press, 2005), esp, ch. 6, 139–61, and ch. 7, 162–90; and Christine Doyle, *Louisa May Alcott & Charlotte Brontë: Transatlantic Translations* (Knoxville: University of Tennessee Press, 2000), esp. ch. 2, 23–76.

[68]   Bachleitner, by contrast, argues for two novels by Amely Bölte as the more important examples of productive reception in German of *Jane Eyre*: *Elisabeth oder Eine deutsche Jane Eyre* (1873; Elisabeth or a German Jane Eyre) and *Das Forsthaus* (1855; The Forester's House). While I by no means dispute that both evidence the influence of *Jane Eyre*, their ephemerality renders them dead ends in transmission chains. Neither novel saw more than one edition and neither was ever translated. Furthermore, the very novel that names *Jane Eyre* in the title shows little indication of comprehension and reworking of the interest in intelligibility, sympathy, emotion, and conversation. Bachleitner, "Die deutsche Rezeption englischer Romanautorinnen," 189–94.

fiction within a *Jane Eyre* complex, possibly even as a surrogate for *Jane Eyre*. Two examples may serve here to underscore that possibility.

In 1876, in response to a "prize question" circulated by *The Publishers' Weekly*, thirty-nine United States publishers ranked novels according to their "salability." They were told to discount works by Bulwer-Lytton, Dickens, Eliot, Scott, and Thackeray, since the journal considered these authors to "stand at the head of standard novelists" and believed they would easily outpace the others. *Publishers' Weekly* subsequently reported the ranked results for 203 books, most of which were written originally in English, that received from thirty-seven votes to a single vote. *Jane Eyre* ranked second on this list with thirty-five votes, after Miss Mulock's *John Halifax Gentleman*, which received thirty-seven.[69] These thirty-nine American publishers also identified as salable all of Marlitt's novels then available in translation, namely, *The Old Mam'selle's Secret* (No. 23 with twenty votes), *The Second Wife* (No. 27 with nineteen notes), *Gold Elsie* (No. 50 with twelve votes), *The Little Moorland Princess* (No. 95 with seven votes), and *Countess Gisela* (No. 114 with five votes). Only Mary Jane Holmes and James Fenimore Cooper, a perennial nineteenth-century favorite, surpass Marlitt with six titles each in the top 119.

The other novels on the list suggest the ways in which Marlitt's fiction met the taste of the era. Of the top 119 titles (titles with five votes or more), sixty-eight of the titles are by women. Sixty-nine of the top 119 had, like Marlitt's novels, first appeared in the decade 1866–76. Many of these ephemeral titles have obvious female appeal. Brontë's *Shirley* and novels by Susan Warner, Julia Kavanagh, Dinah Craik (Miss Mulock), Mary Elisabeth Braddon, Rhoda Broughton, Louisa May Alcott, and August J. Evans, all of whom were influenced by Brontë, also claim prominent positions on this list. This contest provides one indication of the international reading world in which Marlitt circulated with a high profile.

Circulation data from the Muncie Public Library in Muncie, Indiana, provide further evidence of the status of Marlitt's fiction as prominent international reading and its association with *Jane Eyre*.[70] According to library records from November 5, 1891–December 3, 1902—with a year-and-a-half hiatus from May 28, 1892–November 5, 1894, on account of a smallpox epidemic—Marlitt was the tenth most-read author in the library. These transactions involved twenty-three books and eleven different works (all her novels and the shorter "Blaubart," translated as "Over Yonder"). Her five top-circulating novels include *Gold Elsie*, *The Old Mam'selle's Secret*, *The Second Wife*, *The Lady with the Rubies*, and *The Little Moorland Princess*; these works tally more borrowings *per title* than Alcott, Dickens, or Mulock. At 265 checkouts by 235 patrons, *The Second Wife*, a work highly reminiscent of *Jane Eyre*, as outlined in Chapter 8 below, was the most

---

[69]   "The Prize Question in Fiction," *The Publishers' Weekly*, 1876, no. 127: 633. It includes 204 titles with one duplicate title ranked by votes.

[70]   The origins, contents, and structure of the Muncie database are described in Frank Felsenstein and James J. Connolly, *What Middletown Read: Print Culture in an American Small City* (Amherst: University of Massachusetts Press, 2015), 261–8.

borrowed of Marlitt's novels; these transactions far surpass the 116 involving *Jane Eyre* itself.[71]

The preferences of women and girls, who checked out similarly woman-centered novels, drive these numbers. The median age of borrowers of both *Jane Eyre* and Marlitt's fiction, for whom demographic information is available, is twenty-four. Of those Marlitt readers whose gender is documented, 75% were female; of borrowers of *Jane Eyre*, 73%. Moreover, 56.57% of the checkouts of *Jane Eyre* correlate with at least one checkout of a Marlitt novel. At *c.* 188,100 words, *Jane Eyre* is nearly a third longer than even the longest of Marlitt's five most-borrowed novels, *The Little Moorland Princess* (*c.* 129,800), and much longer still than the other four. The coincidence of median age and gender of the borrowers; the affinities of the novels in plot and motif, which this study will explore in detail; the difference in pretention and in length; and the far greater circulation of Marlitt's novels in translation suggest that in offering similar but lighter reading pleasure, Marlitt's fiction displaced *Jane Eyre* with ordinary readers in Muncie. The details of the international marketing and reading of *Jane Eyre* alongside Marlitt's fiction lie beyond the scope of this study. I nevertheless here invoke this dimension to emphasize that German and Austrian "national" reading took place in an international context.[72] The German context, that is, was also a way station in the broader global diffusion of romance in the manner of *Jane Eyre*.

Even though German contemporaries clearly recognized the link, my pairing of German versions of *Jane Eyre* with Marlitt's derivative popular novels pursues a course nearly unthinkable in scholarship undertaken before the impact of second-wave feminism, media, and cultural studies, and the influence of impulses from English literary studies on German literary scholarship especially beginning in the 1980s. In earlier decades, Marlitt routinely and cavalierly received the label "trivial" to be deemed unworthy of the kind of attention that I accord it here. Newer scholarship, however, exists that takes respectful account of Marlitt's strength as a storyteller and her importance to those who read her. The new millennium has yielded important books by Erika Dingeldey (2007), Caroline Haas (2009), and Manuela Günter (2015), not to mention a spate of insightful essays by other scholars.[73] Kirsten Belgum, for one, strenuously makes

---

71 "What Middletown Read," Center for Middletown Studies, Ball State University Libraries, https://lib.bsu.edu/wmr/search.php#keyword (accessed August 13, 2021).

72 For the US reception of Marlitt and the link between the American reading of *Jane Eyre* and Marlitt, see Lynne Tatlock, "Romance in the Province: Reading German Novels in Middletown, USA," in *Print Culture Beyond the Metropolis*, ed. James J. Connolly, Patrick Collier, Frank Felsenstein, Kenneth R. Hall, and Robert G. Hall (Toronto: Toronto University Press, 2016), 304–30; Lynne Tatlock, "The One and the Many: *The Old Mam'selle's Secret* and the American Traffic in German Fiction (1868–1917)," in *Distant Readings: Topologies of German Culture in the Long Nineteenth Century*, ed. Matt Erlin and Lynne Tatlock (Rochester, NY: Camden House, 2014), 229–56. On Marlitt's general popularity in nineteenth-century America, see Lynne Tatlock, *German Writing, American Reading, 1866–1917* (Columbus: Ohio University Press, 2012).

73 Erika Dingeldey, *Luftzug hinter Samtportiere: Versuch über E. Marlitt* (Bielefeld: Aisthesis, 2007); Caroline Haas, *Eugenie Marlitt—eine Erfolgsautorin des 19. Jahrhunderts* (Leipzig: Edition Hamouda, 2009); Manuela Günter, *Im Vorhof der Kunst. Mediengeschichten der Literatur im 19. Jahrhundert* (Bielefeld: transcript, 2008), 238–61.

the case for reevaluating "reader fantasy" as an element of realism and thus Marlitt's versions of women's experience of desire as the counterpart of male narratives.[74] My intention is, however, not merely to offer yet another account of the unrecognized virtues of Marlitt's work—and these are many—but rather to uncover the crucial role that her work, as widely read popular literature, played in the transmission and diffusion of the aesthetic valences and social messages of refashioned romance and of *Jane Eyre* in particular as world literature and a formative book for its time and beyond. Indeed, Marlitt's fiction, served in the nineteenth century as links in the transmission chains of *Jane Eyre*; it circulated in the same reading world and addressed many of the same reader needs and pleasures of the era. Like *Jane Eyre*, it offered romance plots to the disempowered in a time of inequality—not just escapist and compensatory outcomes (though it may well have figured as such for some readers). Rather, alongside *Jane Eyre*, Marlitt's fiction unleashed serial imaginings that pushed the parameters of possibility—at least a little.

Dingeldey labels her book on Marlitt *Luftzug hinter Samtportiere* (Puff of Air Behind a Velvet Doorway Curtain). While she never mentions Brontë, her title image brings to mind the opening pages of *Jane Eyre* as the eponymous heroine reads on a windowsill behind the curtains. This connection once entertained, Dingeldey's title serves to evoke the world of private reading depicted in *Jane Eyre* where rebellion, empathy, and hope come to be, when through reading one comes to think what one is not (yet) and so to undertake the labor of self-formation and fashioning.[75] From 1848 to 1918, in an era of limited possibility but new aspiration, Brontë and Marlitt offered their readers, in multiple languages, narratives that pleasurably freed the imagination.

The sojourn, transformations, and productive reception of *Jane Eyr*ish romance within the German-speaking world—especially Marlitt's literary production—to a degree reinforce Franco Moretti's observation (with A. L. Kroeber) of "the growing sameness of European literary taste," his sense, that is, of diffusion as "the great conservative force."[76] He sees the spread of the novel, "this most European of forms," as depriving "most of Europe of all creative autonomy."[77] German-language print culture did indeed receive and reproduce Brontë's novel in multiple forms and in imitation. With Marlitt's fiction, it, moreover, generated bestselling fiction that for its part flourished in the international market and supported the spread of *Jane Eyr*ish fiction. In this respect, German production certainly labored under the literary formation instigated by the English novel.

---

[74] Kirsten Belgum, "E. Marlitt: Narratives of Virtuous Desire," in *A Companion to German Realism, 1848–1900*, ed. Todd Kontje (Rochester, NY: Camden House, 2002), 259–82. As a countervoice, Christof Hamann rather quickly concludes that Marlitt works the territory of the normative and the normal or average. *Zwischen Normativität und Normalität: Zur diskursiven Position der "Mitte" in populären Zeitschriften nach 1848*. Diskursivitäten 18 (Heidelberg: Synchron, Wiss.-Verl. der Autoren, Synchron Publishers, 2014).

[75] Wolfgang Iser, *The Implied Reader: Patterns of Communication in Prose Fiction from Bunyan to Beckett* (Baltimore, MD: The Johns Hopkins University Press, 1974), 293.

[76] Franco Moretti, *Atlas of the European Novel 1800–1900* (London: Verso, 1998), 190.

[77] Moretti, *Atlas*, 186.

The following chapters do not, however, worry over the lack of generic inno-vation or large-scale creative literary autonomy or original authors that preoc-cupy Moretti. Instead, they relish smaller movements and changes, the multiple ramifications of a single English novel in the German publishing and reading context—its productive reception—that testify to widespread creative invest-ment in romance by a multitude of German cultural agents—not just original authors—as new ideas of women's freedom and equality topped the horizon and sought a home in the German middle classes. An array of German-speaking translators, adapters, publishers, imitators, fiction writers, and readers them-selves did things with and to this book; their activity makes visible the energies of a certain kind of romance in a particular historical period. The period under scrutiny began with the failed March revolutions; at the end of this era, after a catastrophic war, German and Austrian women got the vote. Meanwhile, multi-ple chains of transmission during these seventy years ensured the survival and spread in German of Brontë's angry novel of freedom, equality, selfhood, love, passion, possibility, and hope into the new era.

This study falls into two parts as it investigates the durability of *Jane Eyr*ish romance in the German cultural sphere and the forms in which it circulated in something like a swarm rather than as a single book. In so doing it uncovers the formative and liberating possibilities that this novel in its German translations, adaptations, and imitations promised readers in this time of inequality—or withheld from them.

The first part identifies durable aspects of romance that form the particu-lar appeal of *Jane Eyre* in this historical period and the ways in which the four nineteenth-century translations preserve these. Positing adaptation as a form of reception and sign of the power of the original, it also traces the manner in which most adaptations for younger readers refashion or eliminate the features that bespeak agency, equality, unsanctioned language and emotion, in short rela-tional self-formation. It locates these iterations of *Jane Eyre* in the broader print culture that both reinforced social limitations and entertained new possibilities for girls and women. Part One also examines Charlotte Birch-Pfeiffer's theater adaptation, *Die Waise aus Lowood*, as a crucial node in the transmission of *Jane Eyre* within the German-speaking lands and also internationally in English-speaking domains. Since many German and Austrian contemporaries encountered the play before they read the book, the play figures as a quintessential historical case of "upended priority."[78] The reception and impact of the play, especially in the German-speaking cultural domain, in turn testifies not only to the play's popu-larity but also to fissures in the literary field, marked by inequalities of gender, class, and ethnicity, on the one hand, and, on the other, to the interrelatedness and interdependency of international and domestic literary production.

Part Two turns to Marlitt's novels, their editions, and their adaptations as juvenile fiction, popular theater, and early films as a multi-branched conduit of transmission and sign of the enduring power of the schema of

---

[78]   Linda Hutcheon with Siobhan O'Flynn, *A Theory of Adaptation*, 2nd ed. (London: Rout-ledge, 2008), 122.

romance-cum-self-formation plotted in *Jane Eyre*. As will become clear, Marlitt's novels, although less complex, retain many of the features and sometimes much of the power of *Jane Eyre*; on the other hand, most of the adaptations of Marlitt's novels evidence weakening and misapprehension of the signature romance dynamic. Yet even as pale renditions they served to extend Marlitt's reach in their own time; in our time, in turn, they testify to the widespread popularity and reception of Marlitt's *Jane Eyre*-flavored fiction. Marlitt's novels, as serial productions, provide variations on Brontë's original that in the aggregate offer some surprising innovations. Sometimes they project an even more generous and progressive social vision, yet one with its own historical limitations.

The epilogue reflects on the longer-term historical implications of reading *Jane Eyre* or its surrogates in German, of being released via reading in a time of inequality from the dulling claims of the real to imagine an otherwise. One effect, as will become clear over the course of this investigation not only through the principal example of Marlitt but also the cases of Else Ury, Hedwig Courths-Mahler, and Emma Goldman, was the impetus to write a romance of one's own.

Part One: German *Jane Eyre*s: Translation and Adaptation as Transmission and Reception

As *Jane Eyre* and *Jane Eyre*ish romance make visible, if woman's inevitable destiny was marriage, then the process by which one arrived at that union was paramount in shaping happiness within it. German women's writing on the subject of marriage in the second half of the nineteenth century brings into focus what such fictions of romance addressed when they worked within the convention of marriage as destiny, yet offered their own thrilling take on it. By resisting the claims of realism, the dreary economic marriages enforced by the practically minded, they could, that is, imagine the possibility of a union resulting from individual disposition, desire, and mutuality.

According to the popular German writer Ottilie Wildermuth (1817–77), marriage was the "Heimat der Frau" (homeland of the woman), where she dwelled at the side of the man to whom she was wed with God's blessing.[1] When she published an anthology with precisely that title in 1859, Wildermuth examined three bad marriages, the worst of which ended in divorce followed by the wife's remarriage and subsequent abandonment by her second husband. All these bad marriages resulted from hasty, wrong-headed decisions. The respective heroines had little idea of the merits and deficits of the husbands they chose, of appropriate expectations for them, or even of their own needs. The titles of the three novellas speak volumes: "Heimkehr" (Return Home), "Verfehlte Wahl" (Wrong Choice), and "Daheim" (At Home). Proposing the choice of husband as the most important decision any woman will ever make, each story follows its female protagonist through her marital misery. Two of them, essentially plots of remarriage, involve reconciliation that makes possible living amicably in a normative marriage with the (wrongly) chosen husband. None of the novellas imagines an acceptable life outside the responsibilities of even a bad marriage. Nevertheless, while the first story proves the foolishness of a heroine who is carried away by her wish for intellectual stimulation and passion, the final one suggests that successful marriage does require the bloom of romance. Here a happy ending more in harmony with that of *Jane Eyre* is not reached until the couple's love

---

[1]   Ottilie Wildermuth, *Die Heimat der Frau* (Stuttgart: Union Deutsche Verlagsgesellschaft, 1859), v.

experiences the renewal signified by a completely new "Brautzeit" (engagement period).[2]

Sentimental assertion of marriage, embroidered by love, as woman's home-land hardly places Wildermuth among the progressives of her historical period. Yet her emphasis on marriage as woman's destiny is in line with much of the writing on marriage by both conservative and progressive women even when their writing exhibits awareness of new opportunities for women. These opportunities are largely configured in terms of economics and not as fulfilling alternatives to marriage; while the more progressive among these writers begin to advocate for women's right to education and work, they generally frame these rights with reference to marriage, thus confirming its enduring centrality in the (bourgeois) social imaginary.

In the new introduction to the second edition of her passionate defense of women's education and right to work, originally inspired by John Stuart Mill's *The Subjection of Women* (1869), Fanny Lewald (1811–89), for example, keeps marriage and the family front and center. Here she strategically couches the benefits of women's work in terms of better marriages in which both partners support the family financially: "die Frauen versittlichen, sie für den Erwerb geschickt machen, heißt die Möglichkeit richtiger Ehebündnisse, und das Gedeihen der Familien in allen denjenigen Ständen befördern, in welchen des Mannes Arbeit allein die Mittel für die Bedürfnisse einer Familie nicht zu beschaffen im Stande sein würde" (to improve women morally, to make them able to earn a living, means furthering the possibility of proper marital bonds and the flourishing of families in all the classes in which the man's work alone could not provide for the family's needs).[3]

Louise Otto, Anna Klapp (b. 1840), and Amalie Baisch (1859–*c.* 1904) likewise take up questions of women's education and women's work outside the home. They stress the need of single or widowed women to support themselves financially, yet they appear to operate with the assumption that every woman who can marry will marry. In 1892, Klapp's *Unsere jungen Mädchen und ihre Aufgaben in der Gegenwart* (1892; Our Young Girls and their Tasks in the Present) opens in a vein similar to Lewald's with a meeting of two twenty-something schoolmates. The recently engaged Agnes forcefully brings home to the happily married Bertha the fact that women cannot count on marrying and thus must find a means of earning their living. While she is now prepared to give up her teaching career for a man she truly loves, Agnes insists that she would never marry someone she did not care for under the duress of social pressure. In this opening gambit Klapp stops just short of intimating that some women might wish never to marry; instead, she suggests simply that many will be disappointed and so need to be prepared. Pedantically pedagogical and practical, Klapp's advice book speaks to the truth of women's vulnerability and reviews many options for supporting oneself as a single woman, but the story she tells musters none of the

---

2   Wildermuth, *Heimat der Frau*, 343.
3   Fanny Lewald, *Für und wider die Frauen. Vierzehn Briefe. Zweite durch eine Vorrede vermehrte Auflage* (Berlin: Otto Janke, 1875), v.

delight of romance narrative to propose work and financial independence as a joyful alternative to marriage.[4]

Two decades earlier, in 1869, Caroline S. J. Milde (1830–1903) had by contrast invoked the exhilarating idea of self-formation in her advice book, *Der deutschen Jungfrau Wesen und Wirken* (The German Maiden's Essence and Effect), even as she pushed girls to marry in conformity with social expectation. Here she emphasizes individual nature, declaring that education and upbringing should not place obstacles in the path of the free unfolding of a girl's inborn disposition, her talents and inclinations. Girls therefore need not all be educated in the same way. Yet she posits an overriding educational goal that coheres in a conservative idea of home, and family. Goethe imagined the male subject becoming a public person, socialized so as to play a role in national institutions and national life; Milde formulates the culmination of female *Bildung*, however, as "Schönheit und Hoheit" (beauty and lofty ideals), both terms calibrated to the domestic sphere.[5] Insisting on both the practical and the ideal, she proceeds to describe women's education and self-formation largely in terms of interior spaces and social and family obligations under the rubrics "heart," "mind," "house," and "world." The destination of women's self-formation was marriage. Twenty years later, Baisch too continued to imagine woman's development and happiness largely within domesticity.

Situated between tradition and change, Baisch's *Aus der Töchterschule ins Leben* (1889; From the School for Young Ladies into Life) promises to restore to German women what the pressures of modern times and emulation of male "Geistesbildung" (education of the intellect) have lost sight of, namely, the "Herzens- und Gemütsbildung" (education of the heart and soul).[6] Nothing should supersede these imperiled treasures of the inner life, Baisch maintains. Part 1 focuses on the social and private spaces, institutions, and activities that shape and normalize middle-class girls' lives. Part 2 of the book appears to change direction, for here, like Klapp, Baisch urges readers to conceive of a broader field of action, including professions formerly closed to women. This section delivers an argument in favor of girls' education similar to Klapp's: girls need a fallback profession in case they do not have the opportunity to marry or are widowed. The review of possible professions and sources of income for women does bespeak a society in motion. Yet the essays in part 2 also urge girls not to overestimate their talents and remind them that because society is always judging their behavior they must carefully regulate it. They, moreover, promote marriage as preferable to being out in the world. In the end grandmother's voice prevails. Lina Morgenstern's (1830–1909) letters from a grandmother to her granddaughter, which open the second part, assert the abiding truth that domestic duties are paramount in women's lives.

---

4   A. Klapp, *Unsere jungen Mädchen und ihre Aufgaben in der Gegenart* (Berlin: L. Oemigke, 1892).

5   Caroline S. J. Milde, *Der deutschen Jungfrau Wesen und Wirken* (Leipzig: C. F. Amelang, 1869), v.

6   Amalie Baisch, *Aus der Töchterschule ins Leben. Ein allseitiger Berater für Deutschlands Jungfrauen*, 5th ed. (Stuttgart: Deutsche Verlags-Anstalt, 1890), 9.

Still other essays discourage readers from entering the masculine-coded professions, such as medicine or the arts, since only the most talented and truly exceptional women succeed. Baisch is positively vitriolic on the subject of writing and publishing, while also claiming that women hope most of all to pursue this profession. Chapter 13, "Die Schriftstellerin" (The Woman Writer), insists on the hard truth that whatever illusions women may have about their little stories, most of their trivial efforts belong in the trash.[7] If given the choice between belletristic pursuits and a "good man," women should choose the latter.[8] Chapter 14, "Der wissenschaftiche Beruf" (The Scientific Profession), cautions against competition with men, which likely ensures that a woman will never be loved, let alone marry; men seek in the woman not their equal but their complement.[9]

This same chapter calls on the medical doctor Franziska Tiburtius (1843–1927), one of the first of two women admitted to the profession, to outline the hurdles confronting women who wish to pursue scientific study. Tiburtius rehearses the difficulties of women succeeding in scientific fields, especially medicine, and concludes by asserting that girls age sixteen to nineteen should not be in school. Instead, in the period in which their bodies are achieving the maturity required for fulfilling the demands of their "weiblichen Lebensberuf" (female life calling), that is, puberty, girls must devote themselves to the serene cultivation of the domesticity that constitutes a blessed female existence.[10] Indeed, nature *and* culture have made the home woman's own special domain of activity.

Morgenstern, in her own three-volume *Frauen des 19. Jahrhunderts* (1887–8, 1993), keeps a steady eye on the domestic sphere as a woman's realm, even as she touts women's roles in public life. This collection of biographical sketches of important women and their achievements includes those of famous writers, poets, musicians and composers, doctors, dentists, scientists, and activists. Some of the women Morgenstern presents are non-conforming and single, but her text repeatedly calls attention to good marriages, good mothers, and good housekeepers. Repetitions of "häuslich" (domestic) and the laudatory "echt weiblich" (genuinely feminine) abound. Although she begins the work with a description of German women crossing the domestic threshold into public life during the Wars of Liberation, the women of her biographical sketches never abandon the values of the space once bounded by that threshold. A feminist activist who recognized the social significance especially to the poor of women's disposition over food, Morgenstern brings the domestic sphere into public life, insisting on the importance of keeping house and rearing children and good pay for both, when one labors as a domestic or a governess. In describing the best marriages, she repeatedly employs the word "gleich" (equal), by no means in the sense of shared responsibilities, but to indicate marital relations shaped by intellectual and emotional parity and something akin to equal authority within the home. In the view of social arrangements that prevails in this anthology, a good marriage (particularly in the middle classes) reads as the universally desirable outcome.

---

[7]   Baisch, *Töchterschule*, 409–16.
[8]   Baisch, *Töchterschule*, 416.
[9]   Baisch, *Töchterschule*, 417–28.
[10]   Baisch, *Töchterschule*, 427.

How those good marriages came to be in these historical cases remains largely a mystery.

In fact, it is the feminist Louise Otto who comes closest to entertaining the need for romance when she writes of women's lives in the new empire. "Gleiches Recht für Alle! Gleiches Recht auf Entwickelung der eignen Anlagen, auf Bethätigung der Kraft, keine Schranken für die selbständige Entfaltung!" (Equal rights for all! The equal right to develop one's own talents, to activate one's powers, no barriers to independent development!), the progressive Otto insisted in 1876.[11] Invoking, like the conservative Milde, the Goethean idea of *Bildung*, she by no means exhorts women in her *Frauenleben im deutschen Reich* (Women's Lives in the German Empire) to forgo matrimony in asserting their right to self-formation, but rather imagines that they could accomplish it in a manner compatible with marriage. In emphasizing self-formation and self-sufficiency Otto cautions, moreover, not against marriage per se but rather marriage contracted without mutual love. As a sign of the materialistic times, girls exhibit, in her view, "viel seltner die Sehnsucht nach einem gleichgestimmten Herzen, nach Sympathie der Seelen und Liebesglück als vielmehr nur den Wunsch der Eitelkeit, zu gefallen und Freier zu finden, die Sehnsucht nach einer 'vortheilhaften Partie'—das entspricht dem herrschenden Zeitgeist, denn 'der Profit regiert die Welt'!" (much less often the longing for a kindred heart, sympathy of souls and the bliss of love than instead only vanity's wish to please and to find suitors, the longing for an "advantageous catch"—that corresponds to the prevailing spirit of the times, for "profit rules the world").[12] Otto's evocation of what girls should long for—a kindred heart, sympathy of souls and the bliss of love—sounds very like what Brontë's *Jane Eyre* offered readers.

Nineteenth-century literary narratives of male self-formation are realized through quest plots that end in social and/or national integration as attempted in Goethe's seminal *Wilhelm Meisters Lehrjahre* (Wilhelm Meister's Apprenticeship).[13] In *Jane Eyre*, by contrast, female self-formation finds literary expression in plots that link the female protagonist's personal development to the romance of identifying and attaining the right partner no matter what hindrances impede arrival at the destination of marriage, the female variant of social integration.[14] In telling this slowly unfolding story in which individuals make a free choice based on attraction, disposition, and sympathy and not, first and foremost, propriety or property, *Jane Eyre* invests heavily in scenes of looking and seeing. Neither Jane nor her surrogates are overtly looking to marry—they even refuse to marry when presented with a partner not of their choosing—but their stories

---

11 Otto, *Frauenleben*, 48.
12 Otto, *Frauenleben*, 206.
13 See, for example, Tobias Boes, *Formative Fictions. Nationalism, Cosmopolitanism and the Bildungsroman* (Ithaca, New York: Cornell University Press, 2012), 7.
14 On one such female counterpart, see Lynne Tatlock, "Zwischen Bildungsroman und Liebesroman: Fanny Lewalds *Die Erlöserin* im literarischen Feld nach der Reichsgründung," in *Der Bildungsroman im literarischen Feld. Neue Perspektive auf eine Gattung*, ed. Elisabeth Böhm and Katrin Dennerlein, Studien und Texte zur Sozialgeschichte der Literatur (Göttingen: de Gruyter, 2016), 221–38.

do involve attaining relational selfhood configured in the nineteenth-century context *as* marriage. While literary convention pressures happy endings in marriage, in a well-told romance readers come to desire and believe in that outcome. Brontë enabled nineteenth-century readers to desire and believe in Jane and Rochester's marital conversation like none other through a plot that opens with longing for intelligibility.

A central point of this study will be that the four principal nineteenth-century German translations and the novel's most important German productive reception in the form of Marlitt's fiction testify precisely to the fact that *Jane Eyre* as romance did speak in German in this modern, hopeful register—and, moreover, that it mattered. While the occasions for misunderstandings and deliberate redirection were many in the chains of transmission—and we shall explore some of these variations—these four translations offered historical readers the risky strangeness and pleasures of a pairing of equals in intellect, imagination, and perception, thereby suggesting what might be. They conveyed the regime of mutual looking that shapes and affirms Jane and Rochester's tentative steps toward mutual intelligibility—at least in the free space of reading.

One Looking for Sympathy and Intelligibility

To say ... that there is no helpmeet prior to language amounts to saying that there is no human desire without the capacity to make oneself intelligible; so it amounts to saying that there is no human desire without the imagination of one to whom one may be intelligible ... .[1]

What might Marie von Borch have thought as she prepared her German translation of *Jane Eyre* for Reclam's *Universalbibliothek* (1887–90) and her rendering of Ibsen's *Et Dukkehjem* (A Doll's House) for publication in Samuel Fischer's *Nordische Bibliothek* (Nordic Library) in 1890? As she puzzled over adequate German words with which to express Nora's incisive farewell to her uncomprehending husband, she might have recalled the disembodied voice that called Jane back to Thornfield and Jane's self-confident "Reader, I married him."[2] She might have asked herself why a happy marriage turns out to be impossible in Ibsen's play and entirely possible in Brontë's novel.

Two works, written just over thirty years apart—a novel by an Englishwoman, in effect a plot of remarriage with Gothic affinities,[3] and a play by a Norwegian man with elements of melodrama—could by the end of the 1880s both boast a lively reception history in the German-speaking world, one that included mitigating adaptations that undermined precisely the interrogation of the status of women and marriage that informs the English and Norwegian originals. In the former, a highly self-aware autobiographical narrator ultimately returns to her morally and physically maimed ex-fiancé to put her faith in marriage and a life with him *a second time*, while in the latter a disillusioned wife realizes that she

---

I thank Muriel Cormican and Jennifer M. William for the opportunity to join the seminar that they organized for the German Studies Association, 2018, which focused on Cormican's coinage "The Tender Gaze." Participation significantly aided me in conceptualizing this chapter. Their follow-up anthology is available as Muriel Cormican and Jennifer Marston William, eds., *The Tender Gaze: Compassionate Encounters of the German Screen, Page, and Stage* (Rochester, NY: Boydell & Brewster, 2021).

[1]   Stanley Cavell, *Contesting Tears: The Hollywood Melodrama of the Unknown Woman* (Chicago: University of Chicago Press, 1995), 37.

[2]   Charlotte Brontë, *Jane Eyre: An Autobiography*, ed. Deborah Lutz, Fourth Norton Critical Edition (New York: W. W. Norton & Company, 2016), 399, hereafter cited in text.

[3]   For plots of remarriage, see Stanley Cavell, *Pursuits of Happiness: The Hollywood Comedy of Remarriage*. (Cambridge, MA: Harvard University Press, 1981).

has been nothing but a purblind plaything for the men in her life and that her husband is not the man she took him for. Nora leaves with a slam of the door and little prospect of a second chance for this marriage.

When Jane transcends her disillusionment to act on her desire for Rochester after all, a hard-won mutual intelligibility makes intimate conversation and harmonious living together possible. At the end of Ibsen's play, by contrast, conversation seems impossible. Yet even Nora has an inkling of a life together called marriage that might be desirable, one that contrasts with life as she has actually experienced it. Such a way of living together would be possible for Torvald and herself only in the unlikely event that "det vindunderligste," "das Wunderbarste," the "greatest miracle of all," came to pass, if they were to "transform."[4] For Nora it would begin with education. Ibsen leaves his audience with open questions: in the words of Toril Moi, "What will count as love between a man and a woman in a world where women too demand to be acknowledged as individuals: What will it take for two modern individuals to build a relationship (whether we call it marriage or, simply, a life together) based on freedom, equality, and love?"[5]

If Borch, who knew these two texts intimately, considered their import, then she must have recognized that in both the female protagonist wishes to be acknowledged as an individual with needs and wants. Nora asserts in the final scene, "I believe that before all else I'm a human being, no less than you—or anyway, I ought to try to become one."[6] She is not the inert doll that Torvald and the society she lives in make of her. Jane protests in related language in response to Rochester's verbal torment, "Do you think I am an automaton?—a machine without feelings? ... Do you think, because I am poor, obscure, plain, and little, I am soulless and heartless? You think wrong!—I have as much soul as you,—and full as much heart!" (227). As we shall see, these words reverberate through the German transmission chains and in so doing sound the central promise of *Jane Eyr*ish romance, a marriage for modern individuals who become intelligible to one another, one in which that "most wonderful thing" comes to pass. Romance plays a vital role in these literary reshapings of the marriage held to be woman's destiny.

* * *

Aside from character names, the most frequently occurring noun in *Jane Eyre* is "eye," followed by "face." The translations retain this relatively high

---

4   Henrik Ibsen, *Et Dukkehjem: skuespil i tre akter* (Copenhagen: Gyldendal, 1879), 180; Henrik Ibsen, *A Doll's House*, in *The Complete Major Prose Plays*, trans. and intro. Rolf Fjelde (New York: Farrar Straus Giroux, 1979), 196; Henrik Ibsen, *Ein Puppenheim*, trans. Marie von Borch (1890; Berlin: S. Fischer Verlag, 1901), 105.

5   Toril Moi, *Henrik Ibsen and the Birth of Modernism* (Oxford: Oxford University Press, 2006), 247.

6   Ibsen, *A Doll's House*, 193. In Borch's German: "Ich glaube, daß ich vor allen Dingen Mensch bin, so gut wie Du—oder vielmehr, ich werde versuchen es zu werden." Ibsen, *Ein Puppenheim*, 100.

frequency of both (*Auge, Gesicht*). Still more telling, *Jane Eyre* stands out among nineteenth-century novels in general for the relative frequency of the word "eye."[7] Both the nouns "eye" and "face" flag the watching, looking, and reading of facial expressions, that is, the reliance on the practice of physiognomy that informs Brontë's novel. The signature word "eye," that is, serves as a synecdoche for the looking practices that play crucial roles in a romance plot that begins with inequality of social station, wealth, gender, age, and experience and ends in a semblance of parity.

Jane Eyre tightly interweaves looking with the desire to know, connect, and empathize with the Other. As I unpack this narrative economy in this chapter, it will become clear that the four important nineteenth-century translations— Susemihl, Grieb, Heinrich, and Borch—despite light abridgments in the first two and somewhat heavier elision in the third, reproduce it. The four translators struggled with Brontë's vocabulary, sometimes generating clumsy text and alternate meanings or missing the subtlety of the original. With respect to appearance and speech, the English adjective "plain," as one example, presented problems. Still, for all their minor flaws and deviations, these four translations do convey the disruptive, liberating, and joyful effects of gazing and talking that constitute this romance plot.

The first section of this chapter examines the dynamics of gazing, empathy, intelligibility, and conversation in the original and in German translation. The second interrogates the diminishment of these elements in German adaptation. These *Jane Eyre*s tell different stories that in effect censor the original. Just as with Ibsen's alternate audience-friendly ending for early German and Austrian productions of Ibsen's *A Doll's House*, in which Nora after looking once more at her children decides after all not to leave, the deviations in German-language adaptations of *Jane Eyre* point to the broader public's uneasiness with emancipatory elements.[8] Indeed, the dampening of looking and talking confirms precisely their disruptive potential.

* * *

The art historian Hans Belting asserts of the gaze as an analytical category, "in the singular the gaze is understood only as a collective term for a *contradictory*

---

[7]   I thank Stephen Pentecost and Tomek Cebrat who in the spring of 2018 under the auspices of Washington University's Humanities Digital Workshop undertook the computations and analysis that yielded these data. They compared *Jane Eyre* to a database of 1,102 English-language novels gleaned from Project Gutenberg and present in the Public Library of Muncie, Indiana, 1892–1902 and created in the workshop. I also employed the computational tools available online at https://voyant-tools.org/.

[8]   Christian Janns, "When Nora Stayed: More Light on the German Ending," *Ibsen Studies* 17, no. 1 (May 2017): 3–27. From the earliest productions in Flensburg, Berlin, and Vienna, German and Austrian audiences were treated to this alternate ending, urged upon Ibsen by, among others, Heinrich Laube, the theater director of the Vienna Stadttheater. Laube presents a point of convergence between Brontë and Ibsen reception, for Laube also directed Birch-Pfeiffer's adaptation of *Jane Eyre* with firm ideas about the appropriate ending.

spectrum of practices of looking [my italics]."[9] His conception of the gaze as a "contradictory spectrum" supports and is confirmed by the multiple practices of looking that inform *Jane Eyre*. The gaze that Brontë "pictures" through writing is not monolithic or the property of either gender. It matters to the plot, the genres in which it operates, character development, and the novel's epistemology and philosophical outlook. Sometimes it objectifies, freezes the object; sometimes it figures and serves the imagination and so liberates, transforms, sets things in motion. In this second vein, the gaze in this romance narrative seeks and facilitates connection and attachment; it overcomes distance in a plot that culminates in an animated conversational union.

The set of practices crucial to a happy ending in this particular kind of marriage entails 1) a searching gaze that seeks to read the soul or character of the other, 2) an empathetic gaze that is able to imagine and acknowledge the mind, feelings, and sufferings of the other, and 3) a transformative gaze that transcends, and even rewrites, outer appearance otherwise judged plain or ugly as the gazer sloughs off social convention and comes to apprehend self and other as mutually intelligible. All three modes of looking and seeing ultimately bolster the confidence of future spouses in one another, enabling what Rochester terms the "kindly conversation" of marriage and social bonding more generally (274). Brontë's novel necessarily mediates gazing via language and therefore we will take some time with its vocabulary in English and in translation. Reading as a form of picturing, moreover, also constitutes an act of mediation, and we will therefore also address the potential effects of accounts of gazing on reading.

For all its interest in romantic transformation via the gaze, Brontë's novel also represents looking as objectification, as a means of cementing social hierarchy and difference. We therefore begin with objectification. The autobiographical narrator Jane exercises discrimination and power over the narration of such practices. While her account reveals their damaging effects, the young Jane herself indulges in them. Indeed, from her inferior social position, Jane painfully and overtly objectifies women—both herself and others—in a manner consistent with social convention. In her above-cited demand to be seen as a human being with feelings, for example, she also asserts that had she had "some beauty and much wealth" she would have made it hard for Rochester to leave her. Inexperienced, all-too practical, and skeptical, she—and not Rochester—will for a time resist the liberating possibility engendered by sympathy, intelligibility, and quality of mind.

Chapters 16–19, which recount Rochester's protracted house party, involve some of the most sustained and overtly featured looking in the novel. Watching from the margins, Jane, the social outsider, judges herself and others as Rochester's guests perform their superior social status and Rochester and Blanche Ingram seem to carry on a courtship. Attention to appearance commences even before the arrival of the guests. Upon hearing the rumor that the yet unseen

---

9   Hans Belting, "The Gaze in the Image: A Contribution to an Iconology of the Gaze," in *Dynamics and Performativity of Imagination. The Image between the Visible and the Invisible*, ed. Berndt Huppauf and Christoph Wulf (New York: Routledge, 2009), 113.

Blanche will marry Rochester, Jane disciplines herself with a look in the mirror. She then sketches the "Portrait of a Governess, disconnected, poor, and plain" (146) for comparison with an idealized portrait of Blanche, an exquisite minia- ture that she paints from her imagination: "Blanche, an accomplished lady of rank" (146).

Jane here connects her alleged physical plainness to her low social rank and lack of means. As the guests arrive, she, in a voyeuristic scenario, stands to one side, screened by a curtain so that she can see without being seen. Expressing fear of a lack of mutuality, she declares (wrongly) that Rochester has made her love him *"without* looking at me" (my italics; 158). As she observes and shrinks from the "spectacle" of Rochester and Blanche, she reiterates, "I have told you, reader, that I had learnt to love Mr. Rochester: I could not unlove him now, merely because I found that he had ceased to notice me" (167).

All four translators reproduce these dynamics, yet they struggle with Brontë's vocabulary, especially the labels Jane proposes for her portraits of two differ- ently disposed women—"disconnected," "plain," and "accomplished."

S: Portrait einer armen und einfachen Erzieherin ohne Verwandte und Freunde. (2:16; portrait of a poor and simple instructress without relatives and friends)
   Blanca, eine vollendete Dame hohen Ranges. (2:16; a consummate lady of high rank)

G: Portrait einer Gouvernante ohne Verwandte, ohne Vermögen, ohne Schönheit. (1:251; portrait of a governess without relatives, without means, without beauty)
   Blanche, eine vollendete Dame von hohem Range. (1:251; a consummate lady of high rank)

H: Bildniß einer armen, häßlichen Erzieherin von niedriger Herkunft. (2:106; portrait of a poor, ugly instructress of low birth)
   Blanche, eine vollendete Dame von Rang. (2:106; a consummate lady of rank)

B: Porträt einer armen, alleinstehenden, häßlichen Gouvernante. (249; portrait of a poor, single, ugly governess)
   Blanche, eine liebenswürdige und schöne Dame von Rang! (250; a charming and beautiful lady of rank)

Susemihl tries here to cover the field in a literal social sense when he translates "disconnected" as "without relatives and friends," while Grieb narrows discon- nectedness to "relatives." Heinrich understands "disconnected" broadly to refer to a low social station, whereas Borch simply uses a word meaning "alone in the world" and commonly used to describe marital status. While they all convey a form of social difference, the respective narrators characterize Jane's precarious social status variously and thus the gap that will eventually be bridged by a love based on sympathy and intelligibility.

The descriptor "plain," insofar as it points to a central problem of this romance, presents still more challenges. Heinrich and Borch figure Jane as down- right ugly in her own eyes and those of others. Grieb here softens Jane's critical view of herself with the words "without beauty," and better approximates one meaning of "plain," whereas Susemihl picks up on plain as "simple," a sense that other occurrences of "plain" do underscore, but probably not the dominant meaning in this passage. Meanwhile Blanche, as a social ideal that young Jane in effect accepts when she paints her portrait, is "liebenswürdig" (literally, worthy of love; charming) for Borch and "vollendet" (completed/consummate) for the other translators. "Vollendet" pictures the society lady as a construct; "liebenswürdig," on the other hand, speaks to society's response to its own construction, but conceals the social effort. Neither option quite grasps the idea that Blanche herself has sought "accomplishments" to meet social expectation.

In Jane's afore-quoted protest that she is not a machine but a human being with feelings, the four translators again struggle with "plain" as they try to convey the multiple ways in which Jane perceives her disadvantage. They interpret the clause "because I am poor, obscure, plain, and little" alternatively as

S: weil ich arm, ohne Verbindungen, einfach und klein bin (2:138–9; because I am poor, without connections, simple and small)

G: weil ich arm, klein, und weder von hoher Herkunft bin, noch auf meine Gestalt stolz sein kann; (2:80; because I am poor, small, and not of high birth and cannot be proud of my form)

H: weil ich arm, von geringem Stande, nicht hübsch und unansehnlich bin (3:99; because I am poor, of lowly station, not pretty, and unattractive)

B: weil ich arm und klein und häßlich und einsam bin. (402; because I am poor and small and ugly and desolate)

For all its clumsiness, Grieb's "cannot be proud of my form" most incisively calls attention to the difficulty of rendering a dubious self-assessment (plain) that, as the text at other points makes clear, is subjectively determined and liable to change.

The interpretive aspect of translation of a text that itself thematizes interpretation becomes visible in these word choices surrounding gazing and appearance. In the original, the narrator repeatedly uses the word "plain" with regard to young Jane's appearance, language, clothing, social station, and address to the world. None of the translations fully reproduces her subtle deployment of it in its several meanings and none has found a single German word to cover the breadth and variety of its meanings. The translators also try out "unschön" (unlovely), "mittelmäßig" (mediocre), "gewöhnlich" (common), "schlicht" (simple), "ohne Schönheit" (without beauty), "nichts weniger als schön" (certainly not beautiful), "unbedeutend" (insignificant), or even describe Jane as a woman "die so viele Leute häßlich finden" (that many people find ugly). Her "plain" speech is, by contrast, "offen" (frank), and "deutlich" (clear), and, as these adjectives indicate, a virtue. The question as to what Jane might be in the eyes of other characters (excluding Rochester) as well as Jane herself persists. How much imagination does it ultimately take to make Jane as beautiful as Rochester believes her to be? While Borch's consistent rendering of Jane's "plain" appearance as "häßlich" misapprehends the English, it perhaps makes it all the more wonderful when Rochester finds Jane beautiful.

The valences of plain are critical, for indeed Jane (and the reader) must believe in the feeling and insight that fuel Rochester's declaration: "You are a beauty in my eyes, and a beauty just after the desire of my heart,—delicate and aërial" (232).

S: Du bist eine Schönheit in meinen Augen, eine Schönheit gerade nach dem Wunsche meines Herzens—zart und ätherisch. (2:146)

G: Sie sind in meinen Augen eine Schönheit und zwar eine Schönheit ganz nach dem Wunsche meines Herzens,—zart, ätherisch. (2: 290)

H: In meinen Augen sind Sie eine Schönheit, und eine Schönheit nach dem Wunsche meines Herzens: zart und luftig. (3:109)

B: In meinen Augen bist du eine Schönheit, und gerade eine Schönheit nach meinem Herzen;—zart und elfengleich. (412)

As the uniformity in the above translations signals, "beauty" (Schönheit) presents no problem; nor does the idea of desire (Wunsch [wish]) and subjectivity (in meinen Augen [in my eyes]). Therefore even if German word choices cannot convey the capacity and ambiguity of "plain," none of the texts loses sight of the transformative power of sympathy and imagination. Borch deviates from the other translations in substituting "elfengleich" (elf-like) for ethereal, thus invoking the magic—the most wonderful thing—that courses through the novel.

This subjective looking, based on sympathy, bespeaks the imagining of intelligibility necessary to desire, as Stanley Cavell formulates it in this chapter's epigraph. Both Jane and Rochester, upon first beholding one another, think of "fairy tales" (112); from the start their looking sets reciprocity of imagination into motion. Yet while imagination matters crucially to this romance, it operates in a tense relationship to the Real, sometimes labeled the plain. Jane's inability to put her faith in Rochester's raptures relates to her own struggles with her "mind's eye" and prosaic reality. Her story uncovers tension between the imagination and the real, tangible, and visible.

From her banishment to the red room, at Gateshead, Jane long remains ambivalent about the force of both her own and later Rochester's imagination, yet active, imaginative looking plays a crucial part in learning to know herself. Her glimpse of her mirror image—"like one of the tiny phantoms, half fairy, half imp" that appears to travelers (16) anticipates the fairy tales informing the couple's first meeting. When Rochester later asks to see her watercolors, she is quick to disparage them as "nothing wonderful" (115). Whereas she had *pictured* her subjects vividly, she had only been able to produce "a pale portrait of the thing [she] had conceived" (115). Yet Rochester intuits their force.

Jane's narration of her childhood at Gateshead sets up both dependency on and resistance to the conventional eye of the Real. Here the plain, unloved orphan contrasts unfavorably (in Mrs. Reed's eyes) with the pretty but nasty Reed children. Jane voices her wish to become intelligible in synesthetic language involving sound and sight connected to feeling. As a "*discord* in Gateshead Hall" that "was *like* nobody there" and had "nothing in *harmony*" with its inmates, the orphaned child was sorely tormented, dehumanized. Her relatives were not "bound to *regard* with affection a *thing* that could not *sympathise* with one amongst them; a *heterogeneous thing*, opposed to them in temperament, in capacity, in propensities; a useless *thing*, incapable of serving their interest, or adding to their pleasure; a noxious *thing*, cherishing the germs of indignation at their treatment, of contempt of their judgment" ([my italics]; 17). Years later on her deathbed, Mrs. Reed retains her judgmental regard: "her stony eye— opaque to tenderness, indissoluble to tears ..." (208). To the end, the Reeds see Jane as merely an irritating foreign object and eventually eliminate her from the household. With the repetitions of the objectifying "thing," the narrator names a central problem of the novel to be overcome by another kind of looking, one that imagines and acknowledges the mind, sensibilities, and sufferings of others.[10]

Although differing in word choice, the four translations convey the princi- pal components of Jane's characterization of herself as a disturbing presence at Gateshead in several modes:

> *Sound*: "Dissonanz" (G 1:15), "Mißton" (H 1:16; B 17), "nichts Übereinstimmendes mit" (S 1:16), "nicht harmoniren" (S 1:16; G 1:15), "nicht übereinstimmen" (S 1:16; H 1:16)
> *Sight*: "betrachten" (S 1:16; G 1:15); "blicken" (B 17)
> *Inequality and difference*: "ungleich" (S 1:16), "himmelweit von ihnen verschieden" (G 1:15; H 1:17), "*keine* Gemeinschaft mit" (B 17); "heterogen" (S 1:16); "heterogenes Geschöpf" (B 17); "Gegenteil" (B 17)
> *(Lack of) sympathy*: "übereinstimmen" (S 1:), "sympathisi[e]ren" (G 1:15; H 1:17; B 17).

Heinrich offers a small variation when he opts for feeling ("sich fühlen"; H 1:17) instead of regarding. They render "thing" as "Geschöpf" (B 17; creature) or "Wesen" (S 1:16; G 1:15; H 1:17; being), retaining the disparagement of the unkind regard but losing the suggestion of reification. Nevertheless, like the original, all four articulate the principal problem of sympathy and recognition that romance will solve and they set up the contrast with Rochester who recog- nizes and animates.

Jane's attachment to conventions of gender-appropriate beauty persists longer than it should given her insight into the subjectivity of beauty. When commissioned to paint a miniature of Rosamond Oliver, Jane, once again enthralled by beauty, thrills with "artist-delight at the idea of copying from so perfect and radiant a model" (329). Suspecting that St John loves Rosamond, she seeks with this "well-executed picture" (332) to flush out his true feelings. In her efforts to take charge of herself and others, she again misapprehends people and situations as she did initially the power of Blanche's beauty over Rochester.

St John knows himself better than Jane does. Later, when she chides him for not looking after his health, he dismissively employs the same words she speaks

---

[10] In this formulation I take a cue from Moi's analysis of *A Doll's House* in which she invokes Wittgenstein's deliberations over the human body as "the best picture of the human soul." Moi, *Henrik Ibsen*, 238. As Moi explains, Torvald, as spectator, fails in a key scene to recog- nize Nora's pain, for he is unable to comprehend that bodily self-expression also consti- tutes an expression of her "will, intentions, problems." Moi, *Henrik Ibsen*, 240.

to Rochester when she determines to leave Thornfield—"I care for myself ..." (284)—to express his self-sufficiency, self-love, and autonomy (337). All four translations render these words so as to leave no doubt that St John knows what he wants (S 3:115; G 2: 287; H 5:3; B 60).

Here St John shrinks from Rosamond's portrait and its delightful appeal to the senses, protesting that what it offers is not for him: even if he loves Rosamond "wildly," she would not make him a good wife. Marrying her would lead to suffering, for she "could sympathise in nothing" he aspires to (334). While readers may find it difficult to empathize with the frosty St John, the episode establishes his self-knowledge and acknowledges his personal disposition, the same self-knowledge and personal disposition that Jane will claim for herself to return to Thornfield and that Rochester had, for better or worse, long since asserted. St John, in his fashion, reminds the intradiegetic Jane of what the narrator Jane has in the meantime assimilated, namely, the critical role in marriage of the detection and embrace of a sympathy that transcends and transforms, even defies outward appearance and convention while asserting the needs and rights of individual makeup.

Sympathy must be detected by looking and verified and performed in conversation. Objective, socially sanctioned beauty, as in the case of Rosamond and St John, plays little part in these operations, even impedes them. As the narrator insists, if Rochester had embodied the "beauty, elegance, gallantry, fascination" that she revered "in theory," she "should have known instinctively [upon their first meeting] that they neither had nor could have sympathy with anything in me, and should have shunned them as one would fire, lightning, or anything else that is bright but antipathetic" (104). Once deceived by spectacle, Rochester, too, has long since been wary of external beauty as a promise of sympathy. He rejects the befuddlement of the senses that accompanies gazing at the obviously beautiful female body even as he asserts his prerogative and ability to judge women's quality of mind and feeling by observing and conversing with them.

"Do you think me handsome?" Rochester asks Jane soon after meeting her. Her blunt "No, sir" leads him to apprehend the timid woman he sees before him, whose eyes are occasionally "directed piercingly to my face" (120). Jane's apologetic follow-up—"Sir, I was too plain"—blurs appearance and speech. The translators default to bluntness of speech: S 1:171: "zu einfach" (too simple); G 1:203: "meine Meinung zu offen gesagt" (expressed my opinion too frankly; H 2:56: "zu offenherzig" (too candid); B 202: "zu deutlich" (too clear/forthright). In posing this abrupt question, Rochester invites Jane to reflect the common gaze, as she does indeed by saying no. Yet he also raises the possibility that her piercing gaze may lead her to change her mind and she does.

"Beauty is in the eye of the gazer," she observes from the margins of the house party. Rochester is not beautiful "according to rule," but more than beautiful to her (158). While visiting her moribund aunt shortly thereafter, she begins sketching, only to have another flattering portrait emerge from her imagination. She takes special care to reproduce Rochester's brilliant black flashing eyes and reports triumphantly: "There, I had a friend's face under my gaze ..." (210). In short, the novel does valorize a subjective beauty created by the feelings, imagination, and disposition of the gazer through the act of gazing itself, a beauty that emerges from sympathy and its detection. At age eighteen, however, Jane is not ready to accept this lover's gift for herself even if Rochester is all-too ready to bestow it.

In the days before the first wedding, Jane resists what she experiences as Rochester's oppressive subjectivity: she does not want to wear the jewels and rich fabrics he wishes to procure for her. Wearing them, "I shall not be your Jane Eyre any longer, but an ape in a harlequin's jacket ..." (232). When Rochester praises her "radiant hazel eyes," although her eyes are green, the narrator archly notes, "for him they were new-dyed, I suppose" (231). In response to young Jane's playful questioning, furthermore, a rapturous Rochester attempts to articulate what earns his constancy. Not a pleasant face that masks the lack of soul or heart, but "the clear eye and eloquent tongue, ... the soul made of fire, and the character that bends but does not break" render him "ever tender and true" (233). Jane is this one and only person, and he finds her beautiful. He has never met her "likeness"; she has pleased, mastered, thrilled, influenced, and conquered him (234).

These extravagant words, although presented with a touch of prim skepticism, speak to her earlier-expressed wish for beauty. Jane does not wish to be plain when she dresses for dinner; she is "obliged to be plain" by circumstances (91). Indeed, pages earlier, it seemed that she had accepted the lover's gift. Filled with hope after accepting Rochester's first proposal of marriage, even she judges herself beautiful, for a brief moment sharing Rochester's vision. She "feels" that the face in the mirror is "no longer plain" (231). It glows with hope and life. If she has previously often been unwilling to look at Rochester because she feared he could not be pleased at her "look," she now believes she might lift her face to his "and not cool his affection by its expression" (231). She then dons a "plain" summer dress. On her first wedding day, another look in the mirror pivots from this beautifying hope to "almost the image of a stranger" (257). The real gap in age, experience, rank, wealth, and gender, not to mention the yet-to-be-revealed impediment of a living wife, does not bode well for marriage to Rochester. For the sake of parity and reciprocity, Jane must bring more to the marriage than she can muster at this juncture.

The four translators again struggle with Brontë's play with multiple meanings of "plain." All four call upon the third-person singular subjunctive "sei" of the verb "sein" (to be) to underline that the narrator here evokes the intradiegetic Jane's opinion of her appearance. Susemihl's Johanna believes her face is no longer "einfach" (S 2:144; simple, ordinary). Susemihl, however, omits "plain" as a descriptor of her dress. The other three translators employ "einfach" (simple, without ornamentation) to describe the dress (G 2:87; H 3:106; B 409), but employ other words to describe Jane's transformed face. With Grieb, Jane's face is no longer "schlicht" (G 2:87; artless, unassuming). Heinrich and Borch select "häßlich" (ugly; H 3:106; B 409) for Jane's face consistent with their previous word choices.

As these passages evidence, Jane and Rochester's gazing involves interpretation, insight, and imagination, seeing beneath surfaces, fathoming and communing with those essential qualities that engender sympathy between ostensibly disparate individuals. The translations do convey this. Outward appearance may predict sympathy but, once established and verified, sympathy may refashion that same exterior in accordance with desire for what lies beneath the skin. Sympathy renders Jane's plainness beautiful, because she is intelligible to Rochester and vice versa.

While the resolution of the romance plot requires intelligibility, Brontë's protagonists, in keeping with Gothic conventions, also have secrets that disable them and retard the resolution of the plot. Jane literally and figuratively hides herself from the gaze of others, for example, in the opening chapter when she seats herself behind a curtain and then later on when she remains for a time incognito as Jane Elliot with the Rivers siblings. Once shamed by being made an object of derision to be stared at by the girls at Lowood, Jane avoids becoming the object of others' real or metaphorical looking. She figuratively hides herself by concealing her thoughts and emotions beneath an exterior that because of its unprepossessing plainness might be expected to be transparent, but is not.

Rochester, too, has secrets and hides them, though not always well—his mad wife's gurgling laugh threatens repeatedly to reveal her presence to the inhabitants of Thornfield. Prior to his confession of his past, he habitually pursues stealth: in a scopophilic scenario parallel to Jane's watching of him, he observes Jane. Undetected as a secret voyeur, he falls in love with her. Apparently unsure of the truth of what he sees, he then devises elaborate ruses to force a confession of love from her without tipping his own hand. Both Jane and Rochester undertake interrogative watching and looking and conversing in their mutual search to know the other.

Rochester believes to have quickly detected in Jane "much of the good and bright qualities, which [he has] sought for twenty years" (129). Describing his earliest encounter with Jane, he asserts his ability to recognize affinity by observing a face: "I *saw* it in your eyes when I first *beheld* you: their expression and smile did not ... strike delight to my very inmost heart so for nothing. People talk of natural sympathies ... there are grains of truth in the wildest fable" (197). None of the translators fail to pick up on the idea of "natürliche Sympathien" as the thing to be perceived. Nor do they fail to convey nuances of perceiving and interpreting. Susemihl, Grieb, and Borch employ "erblicken" for "beheld" and "sehen" for "see" (S 1:198; G 1:236; B 235) to suggest small nuances in looking (as opposed to Heinrich's who uses "sehen" for both; H 2:91) and thus deftly capitalize on the extra force of the prefix "er" to indicate thoroughness or completion. All four convey that Rochester reads her eyes, that he could detect in their expression (*Ausdruck*) a quality emerging from within (S 1:198; G 1:236–37; H 2:91; B 235).

In his confession of his past to Jane, Rochester again expresses his longing "only for what suited" him (278). In Jane he encountered a woman who, when he addressed her, as he tells her, "lifted a keen, a daring, and a glowing eye to your interlocutor's face: there was penetration and power in each glance you gave"; he is convinced that she felt "the existence of sympathy" between them despite his "cross" exterior (281). And as he rightly perceived, she was also observing him: "you watched me, and now and then smiled at me with a simple yet sagacious grace I cannot describe. I was at once content and stimulated with what I saw ..." (281). As in this passage, on the rare occasions when she employs the words "penetration" or "penetrating," which potentially invoke phallic power, the female narrator does so with regard to the intradiegetic Jane's powers of vision, mind, and language, not Rochester's.[11]

Again the four translators display understanding in their word choice for the mutual operations of looking and interpreting that Rochester describes, though Heinrich as usual strives to compact Brontë's expansive prose. All four express the connection established through looking as "Sympathie" (B 501; sympathy): "Vorhandensein der Sympathie" (S 3:28; existence of sympathy), "Band der Sympathie" (G 2:181; bond of sympathy), a "sympathischen Band" (H 4:46; sympathetic bond). They render Brontë's choice of "penetration" for Jane's powers of mind (reading) less felicitously as "Scharfsinn" (S 3:28; G 2:181; perspicacity) or "Unterscheidungsgabe" (B 501; power of distinguishment). Heinrich apparently understood the importance of penetration: each of these looks "drang durch Mark und Bein" (4:46; [literally] penetrated marrow and bone). In this instance, too, the four versions do convey power of mind and spirit even when they lose phallic connotations.

If mutual intelligibility of mind, imagination, and feeling—sympathy—ultimately unite the couple, the text has problematized all these operations. It has furthermore made the couple's unity real, first through gazing and then through language, especially conversation. But even then the text requires something wonderful to realize the "grains of truth in the wildest fable." Gazing per se, which has served its purpose, recedes to be superseded by sound and hearing. When Rochester calls out, "Jane, Jane, Jane," Jane responds to something unseen, "I am coming: wait for me" and then asks, "Where are you?" to be heard in turn by the blinded Rochester. At long last, her (other) senses are "summoned and forced to wake" (374). In the end, once united with Rochester, Jane must impress "by sound on his ear what light could no longer stamp on his eye" (401).

All four translations reproduce the voice that calls in the night and Jane's verbal and physical response to it. Three of them allow it to remain mysterious, even if not a miracle—"It is the work of nature," Jane asserts. "She was roused, and did no miracle—but her best" (374). Heinrich, however, does not leave it to "nature doing her best" but instead psychologizes it. In his interpretation the voice is an "Ausfluß meines Innern.—Es war erregt und bewirkte, wenn auch kein Wunder, so doch eine Rückkehr zu mir selbst" (H 5:78; emanation of my inner being. It was roused and effected, even if not a miracle, nevertheless a return to myself). Heinrich here thinks with the text; his reading, although deviating from the letter of the text, hews to the values of a romance consistently concerned with powers of mind and self-formation.

---

[11]   Kirilloff, Capuano, Frederick, and Jockers have, in a recent analysis of gendered pronoun pairs, noted that in *Jane Eyre* "Jane, as 'I,' performs typically male actions ... . She 'does', 'found', 'got', 'gets', and 'leaves' at a rate that almost doubles what we would expect based on a corpus of males 'doing', 'finding', 'getting', and 'leaving.'" Gabi Kirilloff, Peter J. Capuano, Julius Fredrick, and Matthew L. Jockers, "From a Distance 'You might mistake her for a man': A Closer Reading of Gender and Character Action in *Jane Eyre*, *The Law and the Lady*, and *A Brilliant Woman*," *Digital Scholarship in the Humanities* 33, no. 4 (2108): 826, https://doi-org.libproxy.wustl.edu/10.1093/llc/fqy011.

In this novel mutual intelligibility and equality ultimately require relinquishing mutual gazing and even blinding Rochester. But Jane must also stop looking at herself.[12] The happy ending involves no glance in the mirror to confirm self-possession, but instead dialogue, in essence the gift of "relational selfhood" that romance scholar Lynne Pearce formulates as the special feature not of nineteenth-century romance but of some twentieth-century romance novels. In Pearce's words, this is "an on-going exploration of the other's unique difference and peculiarity," a "refined version of self-actualization" that is also relational.[13] The first German review of Brontë's novel in fact noted something of the kind when it falsely quoted Rochester as saying to himself, "Es thut Einem wohl sie zu sehen und zu hören" (It does one good to see and hear her) to explain his "life-long" (lebenslang) passion for a woman who is not beautiful but rather "originell" (novel) and "pikant" (piquant).[14] As the reviewer recognizes, she is neither an eyesore nor a discord.

A year older and sorely tested, better educated, independently wealthy with family of her own, Jane can meet Rochester as an equal. In the final scenario, newly founded and reconfigured family stands in for imagined intelligibility and "the incorporation of the unfamiliar into [one's] own range of experience."[15] In a novel regarded as a "female bildungsroman,"[16] Jane has established a household to her own liking in which she is her "husband's life as fully as he is mine" (401). The spouses, who converse all day long and are "precisely suited in character," live in "perfect concord" (401). For a time Rochester literally cannot see Jane, but within their intimacy the two are transparent, indeed, intelligible, to one another, nearly identical. Jane has become, in two senses of the expression, the "apple of his eye" (401), as Susemihl, Grieb, and Borch carefully convey with the words "der Apfel seines Auges" (S 3:214) and "Augapfel" (G 2:405; B 722). In describing their wedded bliss, the narrator projects a collapse of the subject-object division that "otherwise is a prerequisite for all knowledge and all observation,"[17] a division that theretofore figured in their tentative searching for mutual intelligibility and acknowledgment.

---

12   Antonia Losano, pursuing a different line of investigation, comes to a similar conclusion, namely that blinding Rochester forces him "to enter into a verbally based mode of perception rather than a visual mode," for Jane has throughout the novel been threatened by the gaze of others. In Losano's view, Jane can finally "look freely" at the end of the novel while not being looked at. "Reading Women/Reading Pictures: Textual and Visual Reading in Charlotte Brontë's Fiction and Nineteenth-Century Painting," in *Reading Women: Literary Figures and Cultural Icons from the Victorian Age to the Present*, ed. Janet Badia and Jennifer Phegley (Toronto: University of Toronto Press, 2005), 48.

13   Pearce, *Romance Writing*, 153, 154. Pearce formulates this idea in her analysis of Jane Rule's *Desert of the Heart* (1964), which tells the story of two women who fall in love.

14   Review of *Jane Eyre*, *Blätter für literarische Unterhaltung* (1848): 668. The words attributed to Rochester are distilled from his account of meeting Jane and watching and listening for her. They do not correspond verbatim to Brontë's text, not even in translation.

15   Wolfgang Iser, *Implied Reader*, 291.

16   See, for example, Susan Fraiman, "Jane Eyre's Fall from Grace," in *Unbecoming Women: British Women Writers and the Novel of Development* (New York: Columbia University Press, 1993), 88–120.

17   Iser, *Implied Reader*, 292.

This repurposing of Wolfgang Iser's famous description of the reading process to characterize Jane's story proposes that Brontë, in narrating an updated and revitalized romance based in mutual sympathy, imagination, and intelligibility and resulting ultimately in the suspension of the subject-object division, approximates through human romance the relationship of author and reader that comes to be through reading: in Iser's words, "the thoughts of the author take place subjectively in the reader, who thinks what he is not."[18] Should we, however, think that Jane or readers in general are submerged, silenced, or paralyzed in the alien thought and experience of the Other (be it the romantic partner or the text or the author), Iser also recognizes that the act of reading leads "to something formulated in us," formulated in a dialectical relationship of self and text: "The need to decipher gives us the chance to formulate our own deciphering capacity," Iser maintains. Brontë's novel confirms that this is so; the very act of narrating her story as an autobiography from a position within her harmonious marriage realizes the "possibility that we may formulate ourselves and so discover what had previously seemed to elude our consciousness."[19]

German *Jane Eyre*s for Girls

Jane Eyre in the original English-language publication was subject to different readings in its own time and place, some of which perplexed Brontë herself. Varied reception stems in part from the mixed signals of Brontë's capacious text itself. As Jerome Beaty has shown, the "generic voices incorporated by the intertextuality of *Jane Eyre*" reveal why this novel has always been subject to multiple interpretations, to what he terms "misreadings." A novel written "on the cusp of the Romantic and the Victorian," Beaty maintains, "because of its psychological negotiation between passion and reason; and because of its intense realization of the powerful tension between individual desire and social restraint" perforce incorporated multiple voices and "ideologemes that were transforming the rebellious Romantic and aristocratic Regency world into the bourgeois Victorian world."[20] Adaptation and imitation actively and unapologetically participate in such (mis)reading, as we shall see here and in the following chapters. Furthermore, as Pamela Regis has shown, romance itself is inherently flexible and protean and is thus amenable to re-vision.[21] In short, *Jane Eyre* was always already primed for rewriting and (mis)reading in multiple directions when it entered the German language domain. What, then, of seeing and conversing, of sympathy and intelligibility, in the transmission chains that uncoil via adaptation and imitation?

* * *

---

[18]   Iser, *Implied Reader*, 293.
[19]   Iser, *Implied Reader*, 294.
[20]   Jerome Beaty, *Misreading* Jane Eyre: *A Postformalist Paradigm* (Columbus: Ohio State University Press, 1996), 218–19.
[21]   Regis, *A Natural History*, 85. Regis provides a useful overview of critical takes on the genre and form of *Jane Eyre* (85–91).

Fort's *Memoiren einer Gouvernante* from the start registers losses with regard to seeing and conversing. As chapter 3 details, this Jane no longer speaks to an unknown imagined reader, but rather to her friend, Elisabeth. In recounting her story, she tends to summarize and over-explain her feelings and motives and to dispense with scenic presentations of gazing and conversing. The text therefore forgoes the slow unfolding of the romance through these operations. While it does not lose sight of love, it does largely elide the emergence of sympathy and intelligibility, the drawing together of individual dispositions through looking and watching.

The text additionally reduces not only Rochester's strength and magnetism, but also his quest to know Jane. Fort, for example, abridges and summarizes in *Jane's voice* Rochester's lengthy confession, which appears in the original as quoted text. Without this confession, the reader never learns of his wary and interested watching of Jane or his family's past deception of him through spectacle. Rather than taking a moment to empathize with Rochester's suffering, Fort's Jane simply expresses her determination not to become one of his dalliances. Fort's narrative thus operates more in the register of earlier novels of seduction and reformed rakes and much less in that of the epistemological drama of Brontë's novel in which (searching) vision is paramount and sympathy its goal. Elisabeth in fact—and thus also the reader—already knows that Jane became Rochester's wife (2:184). And since the outcome is always already known, interrogative uncertainty cannot factor significantly and convincingly. Narration does not constitute a suspenseful process of tentative and interested watching, looking, and thinking.

Juvenile fiction evinces still greater deviation. German-language adaptations for younger readers exhibit undisguised discomfort with elements of the original and avoid narrating the slowly unfolding, highly charged romance. Gazing and the intimate conversation of marriage fall by the wayside.[22]

Each of these adaptations for the younger set diminishes and alters gazing in at least one of three principal ways. First, two of them—Wachler (1882) and Reichard (1905)—tell the story in the third person, thereby reconfiguring the subjectivity of gazing overall. Second, these adaptations are all significantly shorter than the original, usually less than a third of the length of the latter. As a result of abridgment, in most of the adaptations gazing has all but vanished, as has interiority, the moment of reflection on looking and seeing. Usually accompanying such abridgement is the third principal way in which gaze behaviors and conversation are changed, repurposed, or truncated, namely, alterations in the plot, some of which are extreme. In Reichard's version, for example, Rochester dies in the fire at Thornfield and Jane lives happily ever after with the three Rivers cousins. In Stieff's version Rochester is missing to begin with. Spitzer's adaptation, as we will see in Chapter 3, devotes little attention to the love story. Only Wedding, Wachler, Hartung, and Reichhardt preserve a skeleton romance,

---

[22]   I here omit Spitzer's and Stieff's adaptations; these deviate so wildly from the original that a comparative examination of the deployment of the gaze in them is unproductive for present purposes. I address both of them in Chapters 4 and 5.

with only Hartung preserving Rochester's mysterious call to Jane in the night. A closer look at these four reveals considerable variation in gazing and the engendering of sympathy.

Wachler relies on both the novel (probably Susemihl's translation) and Birch-Pfeiffer's play for its major plot elements.[23] Recounted in the third person, this version forgoes Jane's (self-)reflection and the practices of looking that thereby become visible. Its refashioning (in keeping with Birch-Pfeiffer) of the social encounter with Rochester's guests, for example—Jane's cousin Georgine replaces Blanche as Rochester's potential bride—eliminates Jane's comparison of herself with her beautiful rival. Descriptions of the soirées with the Ingrams (here the Reeds) are not focalized through Jane. Thus Jane does not function as the quiet observer at the margins of the social space. Instead, she becomes the object of the gaze. Mrs. Reed, who hopes to marry off Georgine to Rochester, sharply observes Jane, whom she nevertheless does not recognize. Fearing a deeper understanding between Rochester and Jane, she proceeds to speak ill of all governesses with an unmistakable reference to Jane herself that immediately renders the latter the object of interested social scrutiny. Subsequently, dramatic revelations and Jane's vindication again turn the attention of the assembled guests to the title character, making the act of looking a form of melodramatic social valuation. We will return to this mechanism in the following chapter when we take up Birch-Pfeiffer's play.

Romance also pales in Reichhardt's adaptation as a result of the attenuation of gazing and conversing. After Bertha has conveniently slipped on the stairs and broken her neck, Rochester reveals his wish to marry Jane. Each time he asks her whether she is happy, she dutifully answers "Ja, ja," concluding that God has been provident (Rt 238–9). While Reichhardt does grant the couple conversation all day long and untroubled mutual trust, his adaptation reproduces little of the looking and watching necessary to reaching this happy state. Readers must accept the ending without the pleasure of gazing, thinking, and talking to get there.

Ilka Hartung's *Die Waise von Lowood* (1911) mitigates some of the harsher facts of the plot—the word bigamy is, for example, never uttered—yet it stands out among the adaptations for its faithfulness to the basic plot. Still, abridgment results in the loss of gazing and reflection on it. Furthermore, although it does include dialogue as an element of the unfolding romance, the final description of the marriage omits "conversation all day long" and the idea of "audible thinking." In merely emphasizing closeness and harmony, it loses sight of the perceptive intelligence and spirit that animate Brontë's idealized marriage.

The vision of the intimate and animated conversation of marriage—the end point of the watching and looking—recedes even more sharply in Anna Wedding's adaptation (*c.* 1890). Words fail the narrating Jane after she recounts how Rochester comes to fetch her from the West Indies where she has been living with her uncle; she simply cannot find words for the "Seeligkeit der Gegenwart"

---

23   Auguste Wachler, *Die Waise von Lowood. Für die reifere Jugend erzählt* (Leizpig: Carl Ziegler, 1882), hereafter cited in text as "Wa."

(bliss of the present).[24] At this point a new voice interrupts the narrative, referring to Jane in the third person and exhorting the book's girl readers—despite the fact that at their young age they must have been inexperienced in love—to consult their own feelings for a fuller picture of Jane's happiness than Jane's pen can paint. This narrator then affirms Jane's choice to fall silent, "denn für das höchste Glück giebt es keine Worte!" (We 215; for there are no words for supreme happiness). In not talking, this Jane neither realizes nor expresses that "something formulated in us" through the dialectic of self and other; nor do readers have the opportunity to formulate their own deciphering capacity.

In these divergent adaptations, the characters never see what Brontë's original characters saw and needed to interpret; in fact, there is often little or nothing left to interpret. The texts instead favor surface reading for the plot. When they do venture into thinking and feeling, they do not so much invite readers to interpret faces and actions through active observation alongside the narrator as simply tell readers what to think and feel. In the meantime, the heroine attains neither selfhood nor a meaningful relationship with the Other. As their textual interventions indicate, these adapters were in the end "ideal readers" in Alberto Manguel's ironic sense. They divined the book's politics, that is, and therefore altered the original, censoring its liberating impulses with specific audiences in mind.[25]

As will become still clearer in the following chapters, especially Jane's relationship to Rochester and the culmination of their romance in a companionate marriage were subject to change—both subtle and extreme—in German adaptation. In these texts the construction of the "individual's value" "in terms of … essential qualities of mind" and "subtle nuances of behavior" so crucial to sympathy in Brontë's original frequently gives way to normalizing assertions of gender-prescribed virtue.[26] While these adaptations tended to elide gazing and conversing, these aspects of Brontë's narrative of sympathy and intelligibility found sturdier pathways into a broader German reading culture through Marlitt's imitative fiction, which as a result of its serialization in *Die Gartenlaube* was from the start available to the whole family. As we shall see in Chapter 5, Marlitt's *Geheimnis*, for one, testifies eloquently to the enduring energies of seeing, looking, and hearing akin to Brontë's first imaginings.

---

[24] Anna Wedding, *Jane Eyre, die Waise von Lowood von Currer Bell. Aus dem Englischen für die reifere weibliche Jugend bearbeitet*, 5th ed. (Berlin W: Leo, n.d.), 215, hereafter cited in text as "We."

[25] Alberto Manguel, *A Reader on Reading* (New Haven: Yale University Press, 2010), 153. Manguel adduces "Pinochet, who banned Don Quoxote because he thought it advocated civil disobedience" as Cervantes's ideal reader.

[26] These formulations are Nancy Armstrong's and pertain to domestic fiction in general. Nancy Armstrong, *Desire and Domestic Fiction: A Political History of the Novel* (Oxford: Oxford University Press, 1987), 4.

Two "Upended Priority": The Orphan on Stage

In 1853 the national-liberal magazine *Die Grenzboten* pronounced Birch-Pfeiffer's *Die Waise aus Lowood* the most popular play of the season, a well-deserved honor in light of the play's felicitous combination of all those things that affect the "gute Herz des Deutschen" (good heart of the German). Its success was predicated on a "gequälte aber starke Unschuld, ein finstrer aber tugend-hafter Lord, grausiger Hintergrund, und ein erhebender Schluß, in welchem die Tugend erhört, die Brutalität bestraft, der grausige Hintergrund sich als ganz unschädlich erweist" (tormented but strong innocent, a dark but virtuous lord [*sic*], a frightening background, and an uplifting ending in which virtue is heard, brutality punished, the frightening background proves harmless).[1]

Waise indeed became one of the enterprising playwright's greatest hits, and an evening in the theater with Jane Eyre became a widely shared experience across German-speaking Europe in the following decades. From 1853 to 1895, the Vienna Burgtheater alone tallied 102 performances of the play.[2] The Austrian writer Marie von Ebner-Eschenbach attended productions of *Waise* at the Burgtheater twice in the 1860s alone. In 1870s Germany, Theodor Fontane, twice reviewed the play for the *Vossische Zeitung*.[3] At the turn of the century, it was still going strong: from September 1, 1899, to August 31, 1903, *Waise* tallied 168 performances on German stages.[4] It had meanwhile become available in print in several editions and remained so until *c.* 1920. In the early twentieth century, it could even be bought for one Mark as a script for amateur actors, categorized as "dramatisch, gemütvoll" (dramatic, warm-hearted) and furnished with diagrams of the stage set and blocking and a pronunciation guide to the English

---

1   "Theater," *Die Grenzboten* 12, no. 2, part 2 (1853): 518.
2   Inga-Stina Ewbank, "Reading the Brontës Abroad: A Study in the Transmission of Victorian Novels in Continental Europe," in *Re-constructing the Book: Literary Texts in Transmission*, ed. Maureen Bell, Shirley Chew, Simon Eliot, Lynette Hunter, and James L. W. West III (Aldershot: Ashgate, 2001), 93.
3   Theodor Fontane, "Königliche Schauspiele," *Dritte Beilage zur Königl. privilegirten Berlinischen Zeitung*, no. 251, October 26, 1876; Theodor Fontane, "Königliche Schauspiele," *Vierte Beilage zur Königl. privilegirten Berlinischen Zeitung* no. 117, May 21, 1878. The reviews refer to performances Fontane saw on October 24, 1876, and May 19, 1878, respectively.
4   By this time, *Waise* was one of only three plays of the dozens that Birch-Pfeiffer wrote that had survived. Else Hes, *Charlotte Birch-Pfeiffer als Dramatikerin, ein Beitrag zur Theatergeschichte des 19. Jahrhunderts*, Breslauer Beiträge zur Literaturgeschichte, n.s., 38 (Stuttgart: J. B. Metzler, 1914), 223.

names.[5] Yet for all its success with the general public, professional reviewers of the play could be viciously dismissive.

An unfriendly review of a performance of *Waise* in Pest with (Edwina) Viereck as Jane sums up the general fate of Birch-Pfeiffer's plays: being panned by the critics and loved by theatergoers even when they recognized their weaknesses. As the reviewer elaborates, actors relished the juicy roles and the theater managers were more than glad of the full houses; the playwright herself did not worry about quality since, after all, she only cared about profits.[6] In this same vein, a snide caricature from 1853 depicts Birch-Pfeiffer gleefully collecting a sack full of royalties for *Waise*.[7] Gottschall, too, wrote of "Currer Bell" stuffing Birch-Pfeiffer's purse with royalties and supplying the material to unleash a flood of tears in the theater and money in the theater cash boxes.[8] Birch-Pfeiffer in fact needed the money. When she died in 1868, she had accumulated no wealth; she had spent her profits to aid her husband's projects, her siblings, and others in need, and in particular to support the acting career of her daughter, Wilhelmine, and, later, Wilhelmine's expanding household.[9]

Yet some contemporaries did recognize her talent. The theater historian Eduard Devrient, for example, offered an appreciation of Birch-Pfeiffer's theatrical acumen. She had a good sense for what worked on stage—effects and structures—and a nose for adaptable material.[10] The theatrical talent that Devrient recognized comes sharply into focus in the performance and reception history of *Waise*. The role of Jane became a reliable favorite of many a German actress. In Berlin, the playwright herself reaped applause as a performer when she alternately played Judith Harleigh (her version of Mrs. Fairfax) and Mrs. Reed in early stagings of the play.[11] *Waise* played alongside works from the nineteenth-century classical repertoire, such as Goethe's *Faust*, Schiller's *Maria Stuart*, Shakespeare's *Romeo and Juliet*, and others, with the same actress playing the respective female leads.[12] In that vein, a farce recounting a performance of

---

5   Charlotte Birch-Pfeiffer, *Die Waise aus Lowood. Schauspiel in 4 Akten (2 Abteilungen)*, ed. A. Ziegler, Danner's Volksbühne 26 (Mühlhausen i. Th.: G. Danner, [1913]).

6   Alexander von Weilen, *Charlotte Birch-Pfeiffer und Heinrich Laube im Briefwechsel, auf Grund der Originalhandschriften dargestellt*, Schriften der Gesellschaft für Theatergeschichte 27 (Berlin: Selbstverlag der Gesellschaft für Theatergeschichte, 1917), 79.

7   A. Brennglas [Adolf Glassbrenner]: *Komischer Volks-Kalender mit vielen Illustrationen von Jul. Peters für 1853* (Hamburg: Verlags-Comptoir, 1853), 121.

8   Rudolph Gottschall, "Gouvernantenroman," 15.

9   Gisela Ebel, *Das Kind ist tot, die Ehre ist gerettet* (Frankfurt am Main: tende, 1985), 228.

10   Eduard Devrient, *Geschichte der deutschen Schauspielkunst*, ed. Rolf Kabel and Christoph Trilse (Munich/Vienna: Langen Müller, 1967), 2: 355–6.

11   "Königliches Theater," *Erste Beilage zur Königl. Privilegirten Berlinischen Zeitung*, no. 261, November 8, 1853, 6; "Königliches Theater," *Erste Beilage zur Königl. Privilegirten Berlinische Zeitung*, no. 274, November 23, 1853, 5.

12   Margarete Rubik cites an article that appeared in the *Neues Fremden–Blatt* on August 31, 1867, that lists Jane Eyre among the best-known female parts, including Luise from *Kabale und Liebe* and Käthchem from *Das Käthchen von Heilbronn*. Margarete Rubik, "Jane Eyre on the German Stage," in *Anglo-German Theatrical Exchange: "A sea-change into something rich and strange?"* ed. Rudolf Weiss, Ludwig Schnauder, and Dieter Fuchs (Leiden/Boston: Brill/Rodopi, 2015), 298.

Birch-Pfeiffer's play imagines the actress playing Jane rushing to end the play for fear of not being able to perform in Friedrich Schiller's *Jungfrau von Orleans* (Maid of Orleans) the following night.[13]

The actress Marie Seebach may serve as a case in point. Recalling her debut as Jane at the Hamburg Thalia Theater on June 8, 1853,[14] Seebach evokes the acclaim reaped by the play's tenth performance attended by Birch-Pfeiffer herself: after the first act a laurel wreath was thrown from the front orchestra seats onto the stage; when Birch-Pfeiffer herself was called to the stage, flowers and adulatory poems were tossed her way.[15] As the Leipzig *Illustrirte Zeitung* gushed on July 16, 1853, Seebach played Jane so movingly that the theater director Heinrich Laube who saw the performance immediately rushed to make her a handsome offer to join the Burgtheater in Vienna.[16] The role soon became a standard in Seebach's repertoire alongside such parts as the eponymous Maria Stuart and Gretchen in *Faust*. A considerably older Seebach later debuted as Jane with her German company in New York City at the Fourteenth Street Theater on October 6, 1870, in a German-language production accompanied by a bilingual edition of the play.[17] A nearly three-month-long tour followed, in which *Waise*, alongside *Faust* and *Maria Stuart*, numbered among the three plays she most often performed.[18] Seebach

---

13   Anon., "Die Waise von Lowood, ein wunderbor schönes Stück von de Birch-Pfeiffer," in *Die Waise von Lowood* (Berlin: Eduard Bloch, n.d.), 119 [Staatsbibliothek zu Berlin, Call No. 20 ZZ 202], hereafter cited in text.

14   Gensichen correctly refers to Seebach's debut in Hamburg as the very first performance of the play. Otto Franz Gensichen, *Marie Seebach—Memoiren* (Charlottenburg: Max Simson, n.d.), 83. Previous scholarship exhibits some confusion with regard to the play's premiere and the actors playing Jane. Pargner incorrectly cites the premiere at the Königliche Schauspiele in Berlin with Zerline Gabillon as Jane as the first. Birgit Pargner, *Charlotte Birch-Pfeiffer (1800–1868): Eine Frau beherrscht die Bühne* (Bielefeld: Aisthesis Verlag, 1999), 32; Pargner, *Zwischen Tränen und Kommerz*, 489. Stoneman, in turn, cites Catherine Anne Evans, "Charlotte Birch-Pfeiffer: Dramatist," PhD diss., Cornell University, 1982, 235–6, to document the premiere of the play as taking place in Vienna, even though Evans notes that the play had played previously in Berlin with success. Patsy Stoneman, *Jane Eyre on Stage, 1848–1898: An Illustrated Edition of Eight Plays with Contextual Notes* (Aldershot: Ashgate, 2007), 141, 141n9. When, however, the Berlin premiere occurred on November 5, 1853, *Waise* was playing in several German cities, having premiered in Hamburg five months earlier. A. Heinrich, ed., *Deutscher Bühnen-Almanach*, vol. 18 (Berlin: Leopld Lassar, 1854), 40, 92, 136, 147, 149, 152, 162, 172, 182, 183, 194, 196, 231, 232, 254, 265, 272, 285, 312, 334, 367, hereafter cited as DBA by volume number, year, and page number. The premiere at the Burgtheater in Vienna on December 10, 1853, occurred over a month after the Berlin premiere. Zerline Würzburg Gabillon did compete successfully with Seebach for the role at the Burgtheater. Ludwig Hevesi, *Zerline Gabillon: Ein Künstlerleben* (Stuttgart: Adolf Bonz & Comp., 1894), 108.

15   Gensichen, *Marie Seebach*, 85.

16   Gensichen, *Marie Seebach*, 90–1.

17   *The Outlook* confirms that Seebach performed in German. "A French Theater in New York," *The Outlook*, no. 104, May 24, 1913, 135.

18   "Home Notes. Mme. Seebach's Farewell Performances," *New York Times*, January 1, 1871, 4. The *New York Times* reported that audience favorites in the tour were *Maria Stuart*, *Faust*, and *Jane Eyre*, which had seen "twenty, nineteen and eighteen performances" respectively. Seebach stood out in St. Louis for her performances as Prinzessin Eboli in Schiller's *Don Carlos*, as Louise in *Kabale und Liebe* (Intrigue and Love), and Jane Eyre in *Waise*. Ernst D. Kargau, *St. Louis in früheren Jahren. Ein Gedenkbuch für das Deutschthum* (St. Louis: self-published, 1893), 248.

was not alone in performing Jane regularly. Lina Fuhr (Caroline Fuhrhaus) who played the lead in the Berlin debut of November 5, 1853, summarized her career as 334 performances in classical roles versus 327 in non-classic roles. Of the latter, fifty-three were as Birch-Pfeiffer's Jane.[19]

The play followed its own trajectory on the German and the international stage. The latter included not only international performances in German, but also at least two different English translations, and also Slovenian, Hungarian, and Danish translations.[20] At the same time, it had a far-reaching impact on the broader German reception and (mis)reading of the English original. Even as it was playing in February 1854 in Berlin, the *Vossische Zeitung* carried advertisements for Brontë's novel, advertisements that leveraged the popularity of the play to sell the book. It promoted "Jane Eyre, die Waise von Lowood ... Prachtvoll eingebunden mit Goldschnitt" (splendidly bound in gold leaf) as an exquisite gift for a lady. The item in question was a re-titled edition of Grieb's 1850 translation. The notice cements the connection between the novel and the popular play, when it asserts that the play is based on this "höchst interessanten Roman" (highly interesting novel).[21] Meanwhile the play was for some actually displacing the novel.

The play's role in the transmission of *Jane Eyre* exemplifies Linda Hutcheon's sense of the upending of priority and originality that may occur as a result of adaptation: "For unknowing audiences," Hutcheon writes, "adaptations have a way of upending sacrosanct elements like priority and originality." In other words, the novel itself became for some audiences, in Hutcheon's terms, "derivative and belated," the one experienced "second and secondarily."[22] One indication of this phenomenon is the aforementioned titling after 1853 of all

---

[19]   Lina Fuhr, *Von Sorgen und Sonne. Erinnerungen, bearbeitet von Heinr[ich] Hub[ert] Houben*, 2nd ed. (Berlin: Berlin Behr, 1908), 252–3.

[20]   Stoneman identifies the first German performance as taking place in 1854 in New York and lists the following English translations: *Jane Eyre, or, The Orphan of Lowood*, trans. Clifton Tayleure (1871); *Jane Eyre*, trans. Mme. Heringen von Hering (1877). Stoneman, *Jane Eyre on Stage*, 257, 260. She conjectures that Heringen von Hering may have known Birch-Pfeiffer's play through a Danish translation of it as *Et Waisenhuusbarn* (An Orphanage Child; *Jane Eyre on Stage*, 203). An additional copyrighted but unpublished English translation is held in the US Library of Congress: "The Orphan of Lowood a Play in two Parts and 4 Acts dramatized from Charlotte Bronte's Novel 'Jane Eyre'/ written and adapted from the German by John Schlesinger," US Library of Congress, PS635 Z99 S44 (Drama Deposits). For the reception of *Waise* on the Viennese stage, see Rubik, "Jane Eyre on the German Stage," 283–304. For a partial list of performances in the United States and Great Britain, 1848–1997, see Philip H. Bolton, *Women Writers Dramatized: A Calendar of Performances from Narrative Works Published in English to 1900* (London: Mansell, 2000), 75–94.

[21]   Advertisement for *Jane Eyre, Die Waise von Lowood. Aus dem Englischen des Currer Bell*, *Zweite Beilage zur Königl. privilegirten Berlinischen Zeitung*, no. 48, February 25, 1854, 3. An advertisement placed by the Stuhr'sche Sortiments-Buchhandlung approximately three weeks earlier, by contrast, promoted a translation titled "Jane Eyre, Roman von Kurrer Bell" that was now in stock and reminded the public that Birch-Pfeiffer's play was based on this "ausgezeichneten Roman" (excellent novel). *Zweite Beilage zur Königl. Privilegirten Berlinischen Zeitung*, no. 31, February 5, 1854, 4.

[22]   Hutcheon with O'Flynn, *Adaptation*, 122.

translations, abridgments, and adaptations. Birch-Pfeiffer's play title persisted well into the twentieth century. In 1926, Kurt Bernhardt's film adaptation hewed to this convention when it circulated as *Die Waise von Lowood*, even though it was not based on Birch-Pfeiffer's play.[23] Furthermore, Robert Stevenson's 1943 film version of *Jane Eyre* carried the title *Die Waise von Lowood* when it was released in Austria and Germany after the Second World War in a dubbed German version.[24]

Birch-Pfeiffer's alterations also endured in subsequent adaptations. The American Thanhouser Company's *Jane Eyre*, released on May 6, 1910, perpetuates a number of these, from naming Rochester "Lord Rochester" to refashioning Bertha as Rochester's sister-in-law and Adele as his niece.[25] Some adaptations for the younger set likewise invoke the play as a touchstone. They highlight the orphan theme to the neglect of other aspects of the original as if prompted by Birch-Pfeiffer's pathetic title. As mentioned above, Wachler especially relies on Birch-Pfeiffer's play to tell the story of the governess who marries *Lord* Rochester, borrowing episodes that Birch-Pfeiffer invented, such as Jane tying Georgina's shoe during a soirée. Wedding's *Jane Eyre, die Waise von Lowood*, too, takes cues from Birch-Pfeiffer's play by making Bertha Mason (here named Aimée) Rochester's mad sister-in-law rather than his wife.[26]

Reichhardt addresses this "upended priority" in the preface to his adaptation. Our young reader will be familiar with this name, he supposes, "vielleicht hat er ihn schon auf einer Theaterankündigung gelesen oder das Schauspiel dieses Namens im Theater selbst gesehen. Obwohl es schon vor fünfzig Jahren zum ersten Male gegeben wurde, hat es bis auf unsere Zeit an Zugkraft nichts verloren ..." (perhaps he has read it already on a theater bill or even seen the play with this name in the theater. Although it was put on for the first time over fifty years ago, it has lost nothing of its draw right up to our own time ...). The preface to Hendel's 1904 edition, too, remarks on the importance of Birch-Pfeiffer's play, adducing the theater adaptation as a reason for *Jane Eyre* becoming the best known of Brontë's works in Germany.[27] In fact, this publishing house itself trafficked in upended priority by publishing an edition of the play in 1890 well before its 1904 edition of the novel.[28]

Reichhardt's and Hendel's invocations of the play as a point of reference for their adaptations of the book also support the general findings of nineteenth-century book historians concerning theater adaptations, which explain such upended priority. As William St. Clair and Annika Bautz maintain of stage

[23] Even a recent revised translation of Borch's translation retains Birch-Pfeiffer's designation, just as Borch had originally: Charlotte Brontë, *Jane Eyre: die Waise von Lowood. Eine Autobiographie*, rev. translation by Martin Engelmann (Cologne: Anacanda, 2012).

[24] "Jane Eyre (1943)," International Movie Database, https://www.imdb.com/title/tt0036969/releaseinfo?ref=ttdtdt#akas (accessed August 13, 2021).

[25] Karen E. Laird, *The Art of Adapting Victorian Literature, 1848–1920: Dramatizing Jane Eyre, David Copperfield and The Woman in White* (Surrey, UK: Ashgate, 2015), 49, 58.

[26] Rochester tells the tale of his relations with "Aimée" in chapter 17 (We 176–86).

[27] Bauernfeld, *Die Waise von Lowood*, 3–4.

[28] Charlotte Birch-Pfeiffer, *Die Waise aus Lowood. Schauspiel in zwei Abtheilungen und vier Aufzügen* (Halle a. d. S.: Otto Hendel [1890]).

versions of Bulwer-Lytton's *The Last Days of Pompeii*, in the nineteenth century, even in the case of this international bestseller, theater performances could muster audiences far surpassing in numbers the readers of the book in a given period.[29] However, the book, unlike ephemeral theater performance, had by virtue of its materiality an inherent form of longevity. In the case of *Jane Eyre*, theater production and print culture conspired to ensure *Waise* a long run and support the literary survival of Brontë's novel in German.

In catering to the taste of theater audiences of the time and conforming to the dramatic conventions of the "Rührstück" (sentimental play) or melodrama, Birch-Pfeiffer reconfigured *Jane Eyre* with somewhat different emphases from the original. Birch-Pfeiffer's title itself already invokes a type, the orphan—and thus the sentimentality associated with the figure—in contrast to the emphasis on the eponymous unique individual of the novel. It thus primes potential readers, theatergoers, or filmgoers for a different experience. In emphasizing Jane's status as an orphan, it returns *Jane Eyre* to the soil from which, as Beaty shows, it emerged in all its originality, that is, to contemporary types, genres, themes, and tropes.[30]

Recourse to melodrama was neither unwarranted nor unprecedented. As scholars have noted, Brontë's novel itself operates at times within that emotional register. Both Peter Brooks and Carolyn Williams have demonstrated, moreover, that works of major nineteenth-century novelists, including, for example, George Eliot, Balzac, and Henry James, generally display a kinship with melodrama in techniques such as the tableau and excess of emotion and in their concern with seeing, revelation, virtue, and innocence.[31] Staging *Jane Eyre* using conventions of melodrama did not in 1853, that is, constitute an artistically far-fetched or historically singular undertaking.[32] Much is lost in Birch-Pfeiffer's staging of the novel. Nevertheless, as this chapter outlines, in adapting the play for contemporary theater, she retained—even amplified—Brontë's Jane's statements of independence, her righteous anger, her vivid imagination, and her demands to be acknowledged. More broadly, the play made visible, if simplistically, the injustices of power and the fragility of family; it ensured that these elements of the original novel were revived upon each performance for audiences prepared to empathize.

---

[29]   William St. Clair and Annika Bautz, "Imperial Decadence: The Making of the Myths in Edward Bulwer-Lytton's *The Last Days of Pompeii*," *Victorian Literature and Culture* 40 (2012): 374–5. This calculation presumably changes if one substitutes magazine publication for book publication.

[30]   Beaty, *Misreading Jane Eyre*, 218–19.

[31]   Carolyn Williams, "Moving Pictures: George Eliot and Melodrama," *Compassion: The Culture and Politics of an Emotion* (New York and London: Routledge, 2004), 105–44; Carolyn Williams, "Melodrama," in *The Cambridge History of Victorian Literature*, ed. Kate Flint (Cambridge, UK: Cambridge University Press, 2012), 193–210; Peter Brooks, *The Melodramatic Imagination: Balzac, Henry James, Melodrama, and the Mode of Excess* (1976) (New Haven, CT: Yale University Press, 1995).

[32]   As Stoneman has shown, the English stage saw at least eight different adaptations of *Jane Eyre*, 1848–98 (*Jane Eyre on Stage*, 5).

Melodrama

Waise assuredly owed its success to its ability to tap into the emotions of its audiences, "das gute Herz des Deutschen," as the *Grenzboten* put it. Theatergoers attended the play with the expectation of being moved. An undated satire, which appears to operate somewhat in the vein of late-century Berlin *Jargon* theater, lampoons precisely this dynamic. Featuring the responses of the Jew Schmul Katz and his wife and daughters to a mediocre performance, it pokes fun at the emotional appeal of the play and the audiences that succumb to it. When sixteen-year-old Jane "Eier" (eggs/testicles) furiously talks back to Mistreß Reed in the first act, the audience, as Katz recounts in Yiddish-flavored German, goes wild:

Do ist ein Beifall losgebrochen,	(Then applause broke out,)
Ein wohrer Sturm,	(A veritable storm,)
Aus Freide, daß der getretene Wurm,	(Out of joy, that the crushed worm,)
Sich hot mit soviel Kouroge gekrimmt,	(Writhed with so much courage)
Und's ganze Haus—mer waren	(The entire house—we did too—)
auch dobei—	
Hot angestimmt	(Sounded)
Ein Jubelgeschrei:	(A jubilant cry)
"Brovo! Bovo! Schön! Schön!	(Bravo! Bravo! Good! Good!)
So mies, wie auch ihr Ponum aussieht,	(As miserable as her face appears)
De Waise hat doch ein Gemieth	(The orphan actually has a soul)
Voll Muth und Chehn:	(Replete with courage and charm:)
Heraus! Heraus! Jane Eier heraus."	(Curtain call! Let Jane Eier come out!)
(112–13)	

At one point Katz's wife and daughters sob so loudly that other audience members ask the police to silence them. Katz's naively frank description of the performance makes its deficits obvious, yet at the end of the evening he and his family clap enthusiastically along with the rest of the audience. In closing, Katz warmly recommends the play to everyone: "Se werden sich wundervoll amusiren" (120; You'll be highly entertained).[33]

A cursory glance at the play may tempt a critical reader to side with the satirist and to dismiss the play as overwrought, clichéd, and especially flawed in its marked deviation from Brontë's original rather than considering the

---

[33] Marline Otte makes the case for *Jargon* theaters in the late-century Berlin theater scene as belonging "to an urban middle-class amusement scene in which Jews constituted an important part." Such theaters, which specialized in satire and mockery in which Jewish performers sometimes "embraced, problematicized and even satirized their own Jewishness," were "yet another one of the manifold ways in which German-Jewish entertainers sought to shape the cultural canon of Imperial Germany." *Jewish Identities in German Popular Entertainment, 1890–1933* (Cambridge: Cambridge University Press, 2006), 126, 125, respectively. This witty, biting (and for our modern ear condescending) sketch probably functioned in a similar way. Its publisher, Eduard Bloch (1831–95), who was himself Jewish and wrote farces for the theater, may be the author.

historical valences and functions of nineteenth-century melodrama.[34] In her comprehensive study of Birch-Pfeiffer in the context of the popular theater of the mid-nineteenth-century German territories, Birgit Pargner too slips into this mode, stressing the intellectual and artistic impoverishment and feckless sentimental messages of Birch-Pfeiffer's plays in general, the playwright's hard-headed expedience, and the credulity and intellectual and political shallowness of contemporary audiences; in effect she sides with Birch-Pfeiffer's harshest nineteenth-century male critics. Pargner sees her resort to sensation and sentimentality as the mark of the bankrupt descendent of the eighteenth-century stage, when sentimentality actually served a moral and cultural purpose. Her plays no longer educate audiences but instead merely entertain them.[35]

In making this sharp division between entertainment and serious literature, Pargner does not engage with the scholarly inquiry that informs my own examination of Birch-Pfeiffer's theater adaptation of *Jane Eyre*. Re-evaluations of "the melodramatic imagination" and of nineteenth-century melodrama in particular, as well as studies of emotion of the last two decades, prompt me to consider in the following that Birch-Pfeiffer's *Waise*, in its own fashion and within its limitations, did address matters that deeply concerned its historical German-speaking and international audiences. Pargner understandably expresses skepticism toward studies that too readily explain away the deficiencies of the plays in the interest of rehabilitating Birch-Pfeiffer as a proto-feminist. Still, the expression of gender in these plays and the appeal to emotion need not be dismissed out of hand as mere sensation for sensation's sake. At the very least *Waise* and its long-lived popularity provide insight into the *mentalité* of the decades during which it, alongside the book *Jane Eyre* and, later on, Marlitt, repeatedly found audiences, the decades after the March revolutions of 1848, after the Austrian defeat in 1866, after unification in 1871, and beyond.[36] It is worth pondering what these nineteenth-century audiences took home from an evening of weeping, laughing, and clapping at the fortunes of an abused orphan and why they sought such experiences.

Pleasure taken in this play's happy ending could simply bespeak attachment to deceptive fantasies of a good life that is unreachable or unsustainable outside the free space of the theater and thus detrimental to one's wellbeing, what Lauren Berlant in a different context has termed "cruel optimism."[37] On the other hand, given that it focused more on suffering than happiness, the play may have tapped into an unacknowledged and still ineffable well of dissatisfaction and

---

[34]   For discussions and summaries of the deviations, see Rubik, "Jane Eyre on the German Stage," esp. pp. 284–97; Stoneman, *Jane Eyre on Stage*, 10–12, 120, 152, 205; and Ewbank, "Adapting Jane Eyre," 289–91.

[35]   Pargner, *Zwischen Tränen und Kommerz*, 466.

[36]   In her study of the first two English-language stage adaptations of *Jane Eyre*, first performed 1848–9 and both melodramas, Laird notes the strong tendency of these dramas to focus on social inequality as a reaction to the revolutionary times. These two plays, which never achieved the currency of Birch-Pfeiffer's play, are J. Courtney, *Jane Eyre, or The Secrets of Thornfield Manor* (London, 1848) and John Brougham, *Jane Eyre* (New York, 1849). Laird, *The Art of Adapting Victorian Literature*, 17–18.

[37]   Lauren Berlant, *Cruel Optimism* (Durham, NC: Duke University Press, 2011).

pain; it may have spoken to the as-yet personally unformulated wish for something better and different, and thus helped audience members to formulate it for themselves as the tormented orphan moved over the course of an evening to the acknowledged center of the staged social imaginary.

Martha Vicinus's work on melodrama underscores this second possibility. In her reassessment of nineteenth-century melodrama as a popular art form, Vicinus points out the necessity of recreating "a sensibility attuned to the psychological truths of sentiment and melodrama" in historical studies of nineteenth-century Great Britain.[38] In exploring (and not immediately judging) Birch-Pfeiffer's evocation of and appeal to emotion as offering some truths to its contemporary public, I follow Vicinus's lead in the German context. In so doing, I will make visible one avenue and its accompanying ramifications through which Brontë's novel spoke anew to German audiences of precarious social arrangements and inequality.

To create a play that moved audiences, Birch-Pfeiffer intensified the anger and domestic violence of the original; she put Jane's mistreatment by the Reeds front and center in the first part (*erste Abtheilung*) and maintained it as a central conflict to the very last scene. She thus reinvested in a plot thread of the novel that ends abruptly when Jane returns to Mrs. Reed's deathbed, a key event to which Chapter 4 of the present study returns. While Brontë dispatches Mrs. Reed in chapter 21 with seventeen chapters still to unfold, Birch-Pfeiffer by contrast picks up on the rich promise of her cruelty for creating dramatic conflict and spectacle and returns her to the stage at Thornfield.

In the first act of Birch-Pfeiffer's play, a patriotic Jane attempts to read Hume's once popular history of England to educate herself about her "Vaterland"—and not Thomas Bewick's *A History of British Birds* as in the novel. We soon learn that the Reeds have confiscated Jane's books and that John Reed once chased and then struck the defenseless Jane with a hammer (and not a book as in the novel). The play thereby sets the stage for more violent abuse.

Mistreß Reed presents herself from the start as Jane's chief tormentor and remains an active villain to the final act when she must, to her chagrin, live to see Jane engaged to Rowland Rochester—Birch-Pfeiffer named her male protagonist Rowland after Brontë's protagonist's older brother; she in turn named the older brother Arthur. The confrontations between Jane and Mistreß Reed offer Jane repeated opportunity to protest her abuse.

Susemihl—as indicated by linguistic overlap, likely Birch-Pfeiffer's chief source—renders the words of the trembling Jane in her emotional face-off with Mrs. Reed in chapter 4 of the novel as "Ich bin froh, daß Sie keine Verwandte von mir sind; ich will Sie nie wieder Tante nennen, so lange ich lebe; ich will Sie nie besuchen, wenn ich herangewachsen bin ..." (14:45; I'm happy that you're not my relative; I'll never again call you aunt as long as I live; I'll never visit you when I'm grown ...).[39] Birch-Pfeiffer amplifies this retort to make Jane even

---

38   Martha Vicinus, "'Helpless and Unfriended': Nineteenth-Century Domestic Melodrama," *New Literary History* 13, no. 1 (1981): 128.

39   Charlotte Birch-Pfeiffer, *Die Waise von Lowood*, in *Gesammelte Dramatische Werke* (Stuttgart: Philipp Reclam jun., 1876) 14: 45, hereafter cited in text.

angrier. In Mistreß Reed's presence, this Jane speaks vehemently to Blackhorst (Brocklehurst) of her tormentor, referring rudely to her in the third person:

> Ich verabscheue nichts auf der Welt so sehr wie diese Frau, deren Blicke Dolche, deren Worte Stacheln für mich waren, seit ich zu denken und zu fühlen begann; ich juble darüber, dieses Haus zu verlassen, diese Frau und ihre bösen Kinder nicht mehr sehen zu müssen, und welche Zukunft mir auch bestimmt sei, ich werde nie zu ihr zurückkehren und sie nie wieder "Tante" nennen, und wenn ich alles Glück der Welt mit diesem einen Wort erkaufen könnte! (14:52–3)

> [I despise nothing in the world as much as this woman whose looks have been daggers, whose words thorns for me since the time I began to think and feel; I rejoice to be leaving this house, never again to be forced to see this woman and her evil children, and whatever the future has in store for me I'll never return to her and never again call her "aunt," even if I could purchase all the happiness in the world with this single word.]

Mistreß Reed's glances and words perpetrate violence, Jane protests. The actress playing Mistreß Reed can reproduce this violence in voice and gesture with each line she utters.

As Vicinus observes, melodrama "always sides with the powerless," "the weak and unappreciated," and orphans in particular are suited to carry these plots.[40] This play is no exception. Laube described the playwright's success with her orphan in precisely this vein, as stemming from the appeal she made to "Gefühl" (feeling): everyone is ready to go along "mit den Schicksalen einer gemißhandelten Waise" (with the turns of fortune of a mistreated orphan).[41]

The first act draws battle lines between the Reeds and a sixteen-year-old Jane—not the ten-year-old child who opens Brontë's novel, but a nearly grown woman. This sixteen-year-old lashes out not so much with the fury of a naive and rebellious child but with the righteous anger of a girl on the verge of adulthood who painfully perceives and chafes at her low social station and the Reeds' disdain. The stage directions note that the same actress should play both the younger and older Jane; they thus emphasize that this figure is not a child, but an adolescent. As Margarete Rubik reports, this idea did present problems for those who imagined young Jane as a child in this scene and did not grasp that Birch-Pfeiffer had an older person in mind.[42]

---

40   Vicinus, "'Helpless and Unfriended,'" 130.

41   Hes, *Charlotte Birch-Pfeiffer als Dramatikerin*, 65. Hes cites *Heinrich Laubes ausgewählte Werke in zehn Bänden*, ed. Heinrich Hubert Houben (Leipzig: Max Hesses Verlag, [1906]), 5:40.

42   Rubik ("Jane Eyre on the German Stage," 289–90) adduces a review that took issue with a mature actress playing the young Jane, namely, Rev. of Carltheater, *Blätter für Musik, Theater, und Kunst*, August 2, 1872, 226, and herself subscribes to the reviewer's position. While there is a certain illogic in sending a sixteen-year-old, who at that age could be put into service, to an orphanage, for Birch-Pfeiffer's purposes, the first act needs to be played not so much as a childish rebellion but as a justified protest against oppression. Aging Jane serves not so much to tone down the shock of a child uttering such words, as Rubik suggests, but rather gives the words more force in service of the play's central conflict between virtue and its villainous oppressors.

The satirical account of Schmul Katz's reactions to the play in fact provides evidence that audiences did understand the Jane of the first act to be a teenager and not a child: Katz grumbles that an actress who looks forty is playing a fifteen- or sixteen-year-old (107). In making young Jane a teenager and nearly twice as old as in the novel, Birch-Pfeiffer pursues a dramatic conception, whereby Jane can, beginning in the first act, speak for herself. She in fact supplies her in this act with her longest speeches, longer than in the love scene at the far end of the play. Through her speech, Jane establishes herself at the outset as a worthy opponent of the nasty Mistreß Reed and her allies.

Birch-Pfeiffer's dramatization of Mistreß Reed's mistreatment of Jane in the first act borrows from the sojourn of Brontë's Jane at Lowood where a child named Julia incurs the wrath of Reverend Brocklehurst. In so doing she again heightens Mistreß Reed's villainy while also making Jane the only victim in the play, standing in for all of Brontë's victimized children who, without scenes in the orphanage, do not figure in this stage adaptation at all. In the novel, the Reverend Brocklehurst pillories as a religious-moral affront Julia's naturally curly hair, which will not submit to the tight braiding prescribed for all the inmates of the institution. The orphan girls are supposed to become the "children of Grace" (60) and renounce all vanity. He orders the offending curls cut off. Birch-Pfeiffer's Mistreß Reed, for her part, perceives Jane's curly hair as a violation of the boundaries and privileges of social rank. Doesn't Jane remember that she has been forbidden to curl her hair? Doesn't she know that Georgina won't tolerate it? "Diese Frisur paßt nur für Töchter großer Häuser, wie meine Georgine, die zum Befehlen, nicht für solche, die zum Dienen bestimmt sind wie Du" (14:43; This hairdo is suitable only for the daughters of rich families like my Georgine who are meant to command, not for those, like you, who are meant to serve). Jane responds by dreamily running her fingers through her curls and pointing out that she cannot prevent her unruly hair from curling. Mistreß Reed, upon hearing the word unruly (*widerspenstig*) angrily pronounces Jane's hair the emblem of her character (14:44).

Such baseless denigration of Jane's character serves to outrage an empathetic audience, but it also solidifies a central theme of the play (and the genres on which it draws), namely, the injustices of power in the wrong hands. In Mistreß Reed's thinking, some, like herself and her daughters, are destined to rule; others, like the orphaned and destitute Jane, are destined for servitude. The Reeds have the power; Jane suffers.

By the end of the first part of the play, Jane has talked back to her tormentor at length, detailing the Reeds' villainy and easily securing the audience's sympathy. Gottschall wrote appreciatively in 1858 of this first act, posing the rhetorical question, "Wer hätte nicht die Entrüstung der armen Waise am Schlusse des ersten Acts getheilt?" (Who wouldn't have shared the outrage of the poor orphan at the end of the first act?).[43] Ultimately, Jane's conflicts with the Reeds claim nearly as many scenes as Jane's interactions with Rochester—Rochester and Jane do not even appear on stage together until act 1, scene 5 of the second

---

[43] Rudolf Gottschall, review of *Die Waise von* [sic] *Lowood*, etc.," *Blätter für literarische Unterhaltung*, no. 2 (1859): 32.

part—with Jane's longest and most stirring speech occurring in the preliminary act when she enumerates Mistreß Reed's misdeeds to Mr. Blackhorst after learning that she is to be sent to an orphanage.

In his review from October 26, 1876, Fontane proves susceptible to the force of the young Jane of the first part. He judges her "meisterhaft gezeichnet" (masterfully drawn) in all her contradictions; the audience was "ergriffen" (moved), he reports. As soon, however, as the curtain rose for the second time, he recounts, the play began to distract viewers with a rather dull romance and the hint of dark secrets in the home, which proved to be a red herring. During the performance he saw, the appreciative applause for the opening part diminished over the course of the three acts of the second, "indem die psychologische Aufgabe theils diesen äußerlichen Dingen, theils einer Durchschnitts-Liebesgeschichte das Feld räumte, schwindet die Hauptgestalt immer mehr in sich zusamen, statt vor unseren Augen zu wachsen" (when the psychological task made way in part for these external matters, in part for a mediocre love story, the protagonist dissolved ever more into herself instead of growing before our eyes).[44] Fontane the critical reviewer desires something different from the generically dictated obvious externality of melodrama. In his second review he admires the actress playing Jane, who has moved him more deeply than better-known actresses playing the same part. Yet here, too, he expresses dissatisfaction with the overwrought performance. He seeks a variety of registers in the play—and certainly not continuous emotional excess.[45]

If Fontane had had access to the playscript (or had seen Birch-Pfeiffer's many other plays), he could have expected precisely the unrelenting emotional volubility of the performance. This highly prescriptive playbook precedes most lines with parenthetical indications of the emotion or action that should shape the utterance.[46] These attitudes run the gamut from joy to terror and are usually extreme; they guarantee that the actors both show and tell their feelings. In the short fourth scene of the first act alone, the script instructs actors to regard one another with a look "voll Abscheu" (filled with disgust), "mit einem drohenden Blick" (with a menacing look), "mit einem scharfen Blick" (with a sharp look), "erstaunt" (astonished), "durchbohrend" (piercing), "mit funkelnden Augen" (with glittering eyes). Jane "sieht sie [Mistreß Reed] groß an" (Jane looks at [Mistress Reed] in surprise) (14:41–5). In scene 6 of the same act, the stage directions demand a rising tide of emotion, beginning with Jane's trembling and Mistreß Reed's speaking coldly. By the end, Jane's rebellion has caused Mistreß Reed to be "überwältigt von Staunen und Schreck" (overcome with astonishment and shock) as Jane continues to speak "leidenschaftlich, bis fast zu Thränen" (passionately, practically in tears) Mistreß Reed is "unfähig sich länger zu halten, entsetzt" (can't contain herself any longer, horrified). Jane is "außer sich" (beside herself) and refuses to allow herself to be interrupted. She then departs in fury

44   Fontane, *Königl. privilegirte Berlinische Zeitung*, October 26, 1876.
45   Fontane, *Königl. privilegirte Berlinische Zeitung*, May 21, 1878.
46   Devrient maintains that these practical instructions spare directors and actors the work of interpretation, thus making it easy for performers of all kinds to produce a passible staging of the play. Devrient, *Geschichte der deutschen Schauspielkunst*, 2: 355.

and Mistreß Reed "sinkt zitternd in das Sofa und verhüllt ihr Gesicht" (sinks trembling onto the sofa and covers her face), a gesture she repeats in the final scene of the play (14:48–54).

In addition to stage directions that demand increasing emotional intensity, Birch-Pfeiffer's parenthetical instructions are, as Hes points out, often paired as opposites in adjacent speeches.[47] Part 2, act 2, scenes 6 and 7 (14:70–8), for example, punctuate most of Jane and Rowland's dialogue with stage directions. While Jane is "ruhig" (calm), Rowland is "kurz angebunden" (brusque). Rowland is "finster" (dark) and Jane responds "heiter" (brightly). Meanwhile, over the course of these two scenes Jane talks to herself "humoristisch" (humorously) and is variously "ruhig," "bescheiden" (modest), "ohne Furcht" (unafraid), "heiter" (cheerful), "ernst" (serious), "schmerzlich berührt" (embarrassed), "verwundert" (amazed), speaks "trocken" (drily), and so forth. Rowland "sitzt in Gedanken" (sits [deep] in thought); he is "kurz" (brusk), "frappiert" (astonished), "trocken," "mißtraurisch" (mistrustful), "finster" (somber), "bedauernd" (regretful), etc. He looks at her "nicht ohne Wohlgefallen" (not without appreciation). Contrastive pairings as well as the general insistence on communicating fluctuating emotion from line to line and gesture to gesture set up a given scene as a series of sharp reactions, heightening the impact and import of even innocuous lines.

The parenthetical directions, just as much as the contents of the actors' lines, dictate the staging of character and conflict and thus shape audience reaction and interpretation. They reveal Birch-Pfeiffer's insistent reliance on displayed affect, that is, interiority exteriorized on stage. Monologues and asides furthermore help to externalize the characters' emotions and feelings.[48] But affect does not predominate here merely for its own sake. It supports revelation and the message thereby delivered. It is no surprise, then, to read—in addition to instructions indicating emotional responses, such as "entsetzt" (horrified), "frappiert," "bitter," "spöttisch" (mocking), and "zornig" (angry)—stage directions involving seeing and looking, such as "sieht ihn groß an" (stares at him in surprise), "sie scharf anschauend" (intently staring at her), "hat sie mit Staunen betrachtet" (observed her with astonishment), and "sieht sie überrascht an" (looks at her with surprise); nor is it unexpected to encounter a key scene near the end of the play in which overhearing a revealing conversation crucially paves the way for rescue, and vindication.

Virtue Revealed

Vicinus maintains of melodrama, "Much of the effectiveness of melodrama comes from making the moral visible,"[49] thus formulating what historians of melodrama repeatedly assert: the chief gesture of the emotional appeal of melodrama is revelatory, a gesture it shares with the nineteenth-century novel and later with film. Summarizing the common themes and functions of the novel

---

[47]   Hes, *Charlotte Birch-Pfeiffer als Dramatikerin*, 199–200.
[48]   Hes points to both the monologue and asides as characteristic of Birch-Pfeiffer's plays. *Charlotte Birch-Pfeiffer als Dramatikerin*, 200–202.
[49]   Vicinus, "'Helpless and Unfriended,'" 137.

and melodrama around 1850, Carolyn Williams maintains, furthermore, "melodrama works with similar fundamental questions of social, ethical, and epistemological recognition." While "the public externality of melodrama has often been contrasted with the privacy of novel reading," both launch "debates about civic virtue." Both the novel and the melodrama involve looking as they explore "the range of attitudes—from credulity to skepticism—about whether outer, visible appearance can be interpreted correctly to reveal inner, psychological or ethical truth."[50]

In his influential *The Melodramatic Imagination* Peter Brooks elucidates the nature of revelation in melodrama. The melodramatic mode, he explains, exists in large measure "to locate and to articulate the moral occult," that is, the battle between good and evil that lies beneath the surface of the social world "where every gesture, however frivolous or insignificant it may seem, is charged with the conflict between light and darkness, salvation and damnation ...."[51] Melodrama, Brooks therefore contends, "is centrally about repeated obfuscations and refusals of the message and about the need for repeated clarifications and acknowledgments of the message. The expressive means of melodrama are all predicated on this subject: they correspond to the struggle toward recognition of the sign of virtue and innocence."[52] Melodrama thus turns on "virtue's right to exist qua virtue," that is, not so much on virtue rewarded as virtue revealed.[53]

Virtue is indeed revealed in Birch-Pfeiffer's *Waise* and also rewarded: Jane is delivered, as it were, when the play handily delivers up *Lord* Rowland Rochester to her. The re-titling of Brontë's country gentleman to make him a member of the peerage supports the trajectory of a play in which the mistreated orphan is outwardly vindicated by realizing a sizable and namable leap in social standing.[54]

While Jane's social ascent is steeper in the play than in the novel, her desire for Rowland Rochester, by contrast, remains somewhat pale and surprisingly does not drive the plot. Rather, Rowland's recognition of her virtues and talents, *his* growing desire for *her*, and her conflict with the Reeds serve that function. Revelation depends in large part on Rowland's perceptions; in the end, Rowland also bestows the reward. These mechanisms to a degree also drive the original novel, but the play has lost sight of the passionate mutuality of a love story told by the female protagonist.

The pallor of the romance in *Waise*, furthermore, bears out Brooks's view of the mechanisms of melodrama, namely, that romance, when present, indicates "virtue's right to reward," but does not constitute the central concern of the drama.[55] While melodrama is structured around "blockage" and the victory over that blockage, he explains, "what is being blocked in melodrama is very

---

50   Williams, "Melodrama," 217.
51   Brooks, *Melodramatic Imagination*, 5.
52   Brooks, *Melodramatic Imagination*, 28.
53   Brooks, *Melodramatic Imagination*, 32.
54   The matter of Rochester's rank testifies to cross-cultural confusion. In the original Rochester is "Mr. Rochester," not "Lord Rochester." This misapprehension of rank is widespread in the nineteenth-century German reception of the novel and certainly fueled by the play.
55   Brooks, *Melodramatic Imagination*, 32.

seldom the drive toward erotic union." Rather, "[w]hat is blocked, submerged, endungeoned is much more virtue's claim to exist qua virtue."[56] In other words, romantic union can serve as a sign of victory, but does not constitute the victory itself. Gottschall's description of Jane on stage suggests precisely the way in which she epitomizes virtue under attack: "dies edle trotzköpfige Ding, dies Ideal aller Gouvernanten mit dem verkannten Menschenrechte im Busen" (this noble contrary thing, this ideal of all governesses with unrecognized human rights in her bosom).[57]

Birch-Pfeiffer's retention of the episode in the original novel in which Rochester examines Jane's artwork as a means of coming to know her, of penetrating the plain exterior, operates in this revelatory vein; it serves to make the existence of virtue visible. Here, as in very few other scenes in the play, Birch-Pfeiffer's text at first reproduces language from Susemihl's translation of *Jane Eyre* verbatim.[58] Rowland asks whether Jane was happy when she made these drawings, Jane expresses her frustration at not being able to realize her inner vision, Rochester praises the drawings nonetheless. While Brontë's Rochester shows interest in them, Birch-Pfeiffer's Rowland, who earlier referred to Jane as a "verwünschte häßliche Hexe" (14:67; a cursed ugly witch), now seems completely smitten by her exquisite artwork: "Sie sind voll Poesie!" he exclaims, "... was kocht in Ihnen, daß Ihr Gehirn solche Blasen wirft?" (14:77; They are replete with poetry ... what boils within you that your brain throws off such bubbles?) These last lines are Birch-Pfeiffer's words, not Brontë's or Susemihl's. And to ensure that spectators understand what the novel more subtly intimates as the protagonists tentatively find their way to one another, the stage directions specify exaggerated reactions: "Er hält plötzlich inne, wie über sich selbst erschreckend, sein Ton ändert sich augenblicklich, er schiebt die Blätter von sich" (14:77; He suddenly pauses as if startled at himself, his tone immediately changes, he pushes the sheets away from him). After striking these poses, Rowland voices his fear that the drawings will penetrate his dreams and render him sleepless. The scene both accelerates the developing romance—visibly on Rowland's part—and reveals yet another of the heroine's virtues, namely, her powers of mind.

By making such powers a virtue and explicitly revealing that virtue through Rowland's histrionic reaction, the play exchanges Brontë's mutual search for sympathy of mind and feeling for a stage convention of "virtue revealed." At the same time Birch-Pfeiffer, in keeping with the original, also defies the commonplace by which a woman's exterior beauty, in harmony with her virtue, dictates her power and instead substitutes mental capacities in harmony with virtue. This substitution required a different approach to the visual regime of the stage to win sympathy for her heroine; hence the importance of the artwork. As Russell West points out, it represents "the world of Jane's imagination which is

---

56   Brooks, *Melodramatic Imagination*, 32.
57   Gottschall, review of *Die Waise von Lowood*, 32.
58   Rubik's mention of Birch-Pfeiffer's reproduction of the original text "verbatim" gives a false impression of the author's heavy reliance on the language of the original when quite the opposite is true. "Jane Eyre on the German Stage," 285, 293.

the motor of her independence and mobility."[59] Later scenes (act 2, scenes 9–11) compensate for the substitution of mind for beauty by making Rowland over-eager to have his guests share his enthusiasm for Jane's talent, that is, to garner public recognition, which also becomes vital to the play's resolution.

Waise crams the resolution of the love story, to which it has hitherto devoted relatively few scenes, into the penultimate scene after Rowland has overheard Jane acquiesce to Mistreß Reed's demand that she leave, followed by the latter's refusal to give Jane her blessing. Jane expresses her utter despair, "wie erstarrt und schaudernd, in wilder Verzweiflung ausbrechend" (14:136; as if petrified and shuddering, bursting into wild despair) when mercifully Rowland steps forward from the shadows. The exchange between the two of them that follows borrows more language from the original as translated by Susemihl than any other scene in the play.[60]

Even as she turns to the text of the translated novel to bring about union and to assert Jane's equality, Birch-Pfeiffer again makes the language more emphatic and more explicit through accumulation and repetition. Her Jane imagines their equality at the conclusion of a lengthy speech: "unsere Seelen ständen sich *gleich*, wie sie sind, zu den Füßen Gottes!" (144; our souls would stand equal as they are at the feet of God!). Rowland paraphrases it: "*Gleich*, wie wir sind!" (14:144; equal as we are). In Susemihl's translation, as in the original text, "gleich" is merely implied in Rochester's response, which is simply "wie wir sind" (2:139; as we are).

In its passionate assertion of independence and social equality based on sympathy, intellect, and soul, Jane's lengthy speech in this scene combines language from two different episodes from Brontë's novel. It includes up front the most memorable articulation of her right to have feelings from Brontë's garden scene:

> Halten Sie mich für einen Automaten, für eine Maschine ohne Empfindung, die sich den Tropfen lebendigen Wassers, nach dem sie lechzt, von den Lippen nehmen läßt, ohne zu zucken? Glauben Sie, weil ich arm und klein, einfach und verlassen bin, ich hätte deshalb kein Herz, keine Seele?—Sie irren sich in Ihrem Hochmut, ich habe so viel Seele wie Sie, und ebenso viel Herz! (14:144)

> [Do you think I'm an automaton, a machine without feeling, which allows every drop of living water for which it thirsts to be taken from its lips without flinching? Do you think because I am poor and small, plain and forsaken I have no heart, no soul? You deceive yourself in your arrogance; I have as much soul as you and just as much heart.]

---

59   Russell West, "English Nineteenth-Century Novels on the German Stage: Birch-Pfeiffer's Adaptations of Dickens, Brontë, Eliot and Collins," in *Beiträge zur Rezeption der britischen und irischen Literatur des 19. Jahrhunderts im deutschsprachigen Raum*, ed. Norbert Bachleiter (Amsterdam: Rodopi, 2000), 305.

60   I thank Stephen Pentecost for creating a tool to expedite these calculations and comparisons.

The play's addition of the verb "lechzen nach" (thirst for) amplifies the drama and emotion of the scene. The speech then borrows from Jane's observation during Blanche's sojourn at Thornfield in the original that the guests are not of his kind, but that she is: "ich fühle etwas in Kopf und Herzen, in Blut und Nerven, was mich mit Ihnen verwandt macht, was mich geistig mit Ihnen vereint!" (14:144; I feel in my head and heart, in my blood and nerves, what makes me like you, what unites me spiritually [intellectually] with you). It then moves back into the declaration in the Thornfield garden: "Und wenn Gott mich mit Schönheit und Reichtum gesegnet hätte—so sollte es Ihnen gewiß ebenso schwer werden, mich gehen zu sehen, als es mir ist, Sie zu verlassen" (14:144; and if God had blessed me with beauty and riches, I would have made it just as hard for you to see me leave as it is for me to leave you). It continues, "es ist mein Geist, der Ihren Geist anredet …" (14:144; it is my spirit that addresses your spirit). The collapse of these declarations into a single speech amplifies the theme of equality, based on Jane's virtues, entitling the humble orphan to become Lord Rowland Rochester's wife.

Where, then, does the emotive Jane's leap in social rank land? John Schlesinger's English translation, submitted for U.S. copyright and deposited on August 17, 1863, in the U.S. District Clerk's Office Southern District New York, ends the play on a romantic high.[61] It, like the translation published by Grau for Marie Seebach's performance at the Fourteenth Street Theater in 1870, does not include the final scene in which Rowland makes the impending marriage public, instead concluding with only Jane and Rowland on stage, intimate and private, as Rowland extends his hand to Jane. Schlesinger's version thus more or less corresponds to one extant German version of Birch-Pfeiffer's play which concludes with the protagonists' embrace and Rowland's words "Und ich will dich ewig halten!" (14:147; And I will hold you forever).

A second version, as documented by two additional English translations and several German print versions, ends the play differently with a closing thirteenth scene.[62] This alternate version of Birch-Pfeiffer's play overtly retreats from the individualism of Brontë's romance by ending the play with a social configuration on stage. Birch-Pfeiffer herself insisted on the importance of this social embeddedness when Heinrich Laube thought to cut the fifth act (=fourth act of the second part) of the very first version of the play: "Es fehlt da der

---

[61]   "The Orphan of Lowood a Play in two Parts and 4 Acts dramatized from Charlotte Bronte's Novel 'Jane Eyre'/ written and adapted from the German by John Schlesinger," US Library of Congress, PS635 Z99 S44 (Drama Deposits), n.p.

[62]   The version published in Reclam's *Gesammelte Dramatische Werke* (1876) includes this final scene in full with no indication that it could be left out (147). By contrast, it does not appear in the Reclam edition of 1899. Charlotte Birch-Pfeiffer, *Die Waise aus Lowood. Schauspiel in zwei Abteilungen und vier Aufzügen. Mit freier Benutzung des Romans von Currer Bell von Charlotte Birch-Pfeiffer*, Universal Bibliothek 3928. (Leipzig: Verlag von Philipp Reclam jun. [1899]). Other publishers' editions include it in square brackets (as they do other parts of the play) with the idea that the play could be performed omitting this material. Hendel's popular series, for example, does so. Charlotte Birch-Pfeiffer, *Die Waise aus Lowood. Schauspiel in 2 Abteilungen und 4 Aufzügen*. Bibliothek der Gesamtlitteratur des In- und Auslands 1229 (Halle a/S.: Otto Hendel [1899]). On the other hand, Danner offers the truncated version in what it labels "9. Scene." Birch-Pfeiffer, *Die Waise aus Lowood*, Danner [1913]).

Schlußakkord, und viele sind nicht zufrieden, daß die Gesellschaft nicht Zeuge dieser Verlobung ist" (The final chord is missing there and many people are not satisfied that society is not witness to this engagement).[63] The prompter's book from 1853, held in Gotha, fortunately preserves the last few pages of that excised fifth act, from which the significant thirteenth scene of later versions derives, and thus provides evidence of the importance to the playwright of this thirteenth scene.[64] Precisely the emphatic inclusion of the social in that scene reveals the play's kinship with melodrama in its messaging.[65]

This thirteenth and final scene concludes the play with Jane, Rowland, Francis, Georgine, Lord and Lady Clawdon, Clarisse, Judith, and Mistreß Reed gathered on stage. Its stage directions indicate careful blocking that calls upon the melodramatic device of the tableau or at least gestures in that direction. The tableau punctuates the action on stage, as Williams describes it, "with sudden stasis (and sudden movement)," "balletic movement between movement and stillness, speech and silence."[66] The effect of sudden "composed stillness," Williams explains, serves to interrupt and park the action "calling for the audience to be likewise arrested yet all the while to be actively feeling and interpreting."[67] Birch-Pfeiffer's final scene unfolds as follows.

Rowland proclaims to the assembled that Jane is his bride-to-be. Upon hearing this public announcement, "Alle (in starrem Staunen)" (All [in petrified amazement]) exclaim "Seine Braut!" (His bride!) presumably producing the frozen tableau of melodrama. This frozen astonishment is then released into movement by Mistreß Reed's "Ich wußte es!" (I knew it) and then she herself freezes: "sie verhüllt das Gesicht und bleibt unbeweglich" (she covers her face and remains motionless). Rowland resumes speaking to summarize the conclusion and strikes a pose trusting that God will bless their union: "... Gott, der die verlassene Waise durch die Hand des Hasses an das Herz der Liebe führte, wird zwei Seelen schützen, die nichts zu ihrem Glück bedürfen als sich selbst—und (er legt die Hand auf Janes Haupt und streckt den Arm zum Himmel) seinen Segen!" (God, who led the abandoned orphan through the hand of hate to the heart of love, will protect two souls who need nothing for their happiness but themselves—and [he lays his hand on Jane's head and raises

---

63   Charlotte Birch-Pfeiffer to Heinrich Laube, November 24, 1853, quoted by von Weilen, *Charlotte Birch-Pfeiffer und Heinrich Laube im Briefwechsel*, 78, 78n112. Von Weilen notes that the critic G. Birnbaum also pleaded for the fifth act, which was later excised, because he believed that more justification was required to make believable the eccentric decision of a lord to marry an orphan. Gustav Birnbaum, "Die Waise aus Lowood," in *Dramaturgische Blätter aus Oesterreich* (Vienna: Prandel & Meyer, 1857), 39–42.

64   Charlotte Birch-Pfeiffer, *Die Waise aus Lowood. Schauspiel in fünf Akten, mit freier Benutzung des Romans von Currer Bell; Als Manuscript gedruckt und Eigenthum der Verfasserin* (Berlin: Druckerei von F. W. Gubitz, 1853), 123–4.

65   Both the anonymous and abridged translation of *Die Waise aus Lowood—Jane Eyre or The Orphan of Lowood* (1867) and Mme. Hering's *Jane Eyre, or the Orphan of Lowood*, translated from the aforementioned Danish version, include a version of this thirteenth scene. Stoneman, *Jane Eyre on Stage*, 135, 264–5.

66   Williams, "Moving Pictures," 109.

67   Williams, "Moving Pictures," 105.

his arm to the heavens] his blessing). After this speech, the playbook indicates "allgemeine Gruppe" (general group/tableau), presumably meaning that a new tableau forms in reaction to Rowland's appeal for God's blessing. The characters then resume motion to express their varied responses. Meanwhile Jane folds her hands in prayer for the purpose of the final tableau and the fall of the curtain. While Jane does not have the final word in either version, the second version does allows her this explicit mime of prayer, a gesture directed not toward Rowland but God.[68] The social context, marked simply by the presence of other bodies on stage and the staging of the reactions of all present, makes visible the significance of their union as not so much the fulfillment of desire as the public and social vindication of the poor orphan.[69]

When she called upon Birch-Pfeiffer's play to aid her in her adaptation of the novel for girls, Wachler adhered to the message of this scene—social recognition rather than perfect harmony or conversation all day long as in the original novel. After the couple has determined to adopt Adele because Jane does not want to see any more orphans around her, Jane asks Rowland, "Und wenn die Welt Dich fragen sollte, Rowland, wer ist Deine Gattin? Was wirst Du antworten?" (And if the world should ask you, Rowland, who is your spouse? What will you answer?). Rochester, in keeping with the final line of the play, responds, "So werde ich mit gerechtem Stolze ausrufen: Die Waise von Lowood!" (Wa 253; Then I will announce with justifiable pride: the orphan of Lowood).

In the end, Schmul Katz's creator knew what he was doing when he twice put the Yiddish word "Chehn" in his ebullient narrator's mouth. The naively appreciative Katz speaks of both the play and the homely Jane Eier as having "Chehn," meaning "charm." "Chehn" derives from the Hebrew חֵן; in its original religious context, it means "grace."[70] Those who went to the theater to see *Waise* could over the course of the evening experience the operation of grace in the form of simple revelation and vindication as the virtuous orphan looks forward in the final scene to a happy and secure future as the wife of a lord. When the curtain falls, Jane's final attitude with hands folded in prayer bespeaks grace from God, virtue and innocence restored before the entire company, or

---

68   All text quoted in this paragraph appears on p. 147. Rubik's view that "the conflict is a personal, not a social one" ("Jane Eyre on the German Stage," 287) misses the point that in melodrama the personal is social, even if not clearly articulated as social critique.

69   Patsy Stoneman, in her discussion of Charlotte Thompson's performances of Birch-Pfeiffer's play in translation, hypothesizes that Thompson added a final scene for her 1873 performances in the United States. Her account suggests that the actress perceived the importance of the final scene, which had been omitted in some English translations. An "etched scene" of this last scene as performed at Union Square Theatre, New York, 1873, reproduced by Stoneman, shows Jane and Rowland on center stage with groupings of the seven other characters present on stage to acknowledge Jane's new status. It appears to correspond to the thirteenth scene as written by Birch-Pfeiffer. Stoneman, *Jane Eyre on Stage*, 147–9.

70   "The Yiddish word is "taken from the Hebrew חֵן, which would transliterate today as 'chen' or 'hen.' In its original, religious context, it means 'grace.'" Hillel Kieval, Professor of Jewish Studies, Washington University in St. Louis, email to author, August 26, 2018.

as *Die Grenzboten* phrased it, the play offers an uplifting conclusion in which virtue is *heard*.

Jane and Rochester

On February 9, 1854, Harry Morton's *Die Mission der Waise* (The Orphan's Mission) premiered at the Friedrich-Wilhelmstädtisches Theater in Berlin.[71] For a while, this rival adaptation played in Berlin and elsewhere regularly and simultaneously with *Die Waise aus Lowood*—not only in the same cities but also sometimes at the same theaters.[72]

Birch-Pfeiffer and Morton offer two different takes on Brontë's novel. Birch-Pfeiffer's adaptation takes many liberties with the original with an eye to theatrical effect, setting aside key features and both eliding episodes and inventing new ones. Morton, by contrast, retains many of the most memorable elements of the original—including the madwoman (renamed Bertha Antoinette Slender), the near bigamy, and the strange voice calling to Jane—as well as restoring the Rivers cousins to the plot. He also allows a morally flawed Rochester to be blinded at the end of the play.

Birch-Pfeiffer principally mined chapters 1–4, 11–23 of the novel and relied largely on Susemihl's translation. Morton, who, as language overlap indicates, had probably turned to Grieb's translation, opened his play with material from chapter 25, and, although he too took many liberties, he followed the rough outlines of the original plot to its conclusion in chapter 38.[73] This not particularly successful dramatization of key elements of the original led the reviewer for the *Vossische Zeitung* to the conclusion that the play was more interesting for those "welche sich die Lektüre bisher ersparten" (who had hitherto spared themselves reading [the novel]).[74]

Scholarship, most recently Rubik, has termed Morton's play a sequel or a continuation.[75] Advertisements for the play in the *Vossische Zeitung* and the printed

---

71   "Königstädtisches Theater," *Zweite Beilage der Königl. Privilegirten Berlinischen Zeitung*, no. 32, February 7, 1854, 2; Liselotte Maas, *Das Friedrich-Wilhelmstädtische Theater in Berlin unter der Direktion von Friedrich Wilhelm Deichmann in der Zeit zwischen 1848 und 1860* (Berlin and Munich: Dissertations-Druckerei Charlotte Schön, 1965), 96.

72   Morton's version was performed five times at the Friedrich-Wilhelmstädtisches Theater in Berlin and then in many other venues, both regional and international, through 1856 (DBA 19 [1855], 49, 52, 90, 98, 119, 144, 204, 206, 235, 242, 272, 287, 292, 312, 314, 330, 346; 20 [1856], 177; 21 [1857], 63, 211, 393). A review from the *Spenersche Zeitung* (2/3, no. 1, 1854) called the "Terrain der ernsten und düsteren Charakterzeichnung" (territory of serious and gloomy depiction of character) in Morton's play unusual for this theater venue. Maas, *Das Friedrich-Wilhelmstädtische Theater in Berlin*, 96, 220.

73   A comparison of Birch-Pfeiffer's play with Susemihl's and Grieb's translations with regard to the number of matching four-word sequences reveals 273 and 225 matches with Susemihl and Grieb respectively, suggesting Susemihl as the more likely source. Morton's overlap with Susemihl is, by contrast, 371 as compared with 451 with Grieb, suggesting Grieb as his more likely source. I thank Stephen Pentecost for constructing a tool for the purpose of undertaking and automating such comparison.

74   "Wilhelmstädtisches Theater," *Erste Beilage zur Königl. Privilegirten Berlinischen Zeitung*, no. 36, February 11, 1854, 7.

75   Rubik, "Jane Eyre on the German Stage," 298.

playbook support that idea. Playing off Birch-Pfeiffer's success while also indicating that the later play offered something more, the printed playscript explicitly advises theaters producing Morton's play to advertise it on the theater bill as treating the second half of the novel.[76] The *Vossische Zeitung*, however, rightly termed the label "Fortsetzung" (sequel) a "ganz unzutreffende Bezeichnung" (completely inaccurate designation).[77] The play in no sense connects neatly with Birch-Pfeiffer's *Waise*; even the names of its central characters differ.

As Rubik notes, Birch-Pfeiffer's adaptation makes of Rowland Rochester a one-dimensionally virtuous protagonist.[78] Despite having been betrayed by Harriet (=Bertha) and his elder brother, he sees to it that she and her daughter, Adele, are cared for. Bigamy does not threaten Jane's happiness, and Rowland can invoke his moral and social capital to step in at the end of the play to make everything right, almost as if God worked miracles through him. The play embodies a reading of Brontë that capitalizes on the heroine's strength, yet ensures that she asserts it within carefully delimited patriarchal confines.

Morton, for his part, accepts the premise of near bigamy and then must deal with the conundrum of Jane's decision both to marry a morally compromised man who deceived her and to refuse the marriage proposal of the virtuous missionary, St John. Brontë's novel reaches for complexity. It solicits empathy with Rochester's sufferings, allows him to repent, and also drastically punishes and purifies him by fire while clearly showing readers that St John's ruthless and unyielding missionary zeal, though intended to serve God, fails to acknowledge the humanity of the differently disposed. Morton's different take on Jane's relationships with Rochester and St John is adumbrated in the word "Mission" in the title.

Act 4, scenes 8–12, and act 5 dramatize Jane's return to Wellfield, which has meanwhile burned down, and her reunion with "Lord" Rochester at Elton—we note that Rochester's estate has changed names from the menacing Thornfield to the happy Wellfield, that Ferndean is now Elton, and that Morton's Rochester is, following Birch-Pfeiffer's lead, also a member of the peerage. In this version, St John, still seeing himself as Jane's protector, tails her as she sets off in search of Rochester (52). Not until act 5, scene 9, do Jane and the blind Rochester speak to one another again. Jane declares that she has returned to him, rich and with a new family. She wishes to be his caregiver, his companion in his loneliness; she will read to him, care for him, and take walks with him. If the audience continues to wonder why, an explanation is forthcoming. Jane retells their personal history as a fairy tale, transforming Rochester's transgression into mere misfortune: "Ich liebte einen sehr edlen Mann, recht innig, wahr und rein—und er liebte mich auch und machte mich zu seiner Braut. Aber ein schreckliches Unglück trennte uns—ich mußte von ihm gehen, ob wir uns auch über alle Maßen liebten. Nun hat sich seitdem Manches geändert, Sir,—meine Liebe aber ist noch

---

[76] Harry Morton, *Die Mission der Waise: Schauspiel in 3 Abtheilungen und 5 Akten* (Berlin: [C. Lindow], 1854), title page, hereafter cited in text.

[77] "Wilhelmstädtisches Theater," 7.

[78] Rubik, "Jane Eyre on the German Stage," 293.

stärker, heiliger geworden ..." (55; I loved a very noble man, quite passionately, truly and purely—and he loved me too and made me his fiancée. But a terrible misfortune separated us—I had to leave him, even though we loved one another beyond all measure. In the meantime some things have changed, Sir—my love, however, has become stronger, more holy).

If the fairy tale did not suffice to explain Jane's wish to be his nursemaid, St John generously weighs in with a letter. In contrast to the novel where he never explicitly grants Jane forgiveness for refusing him, he writes here that, now knowing everything, he understands and forgives her; he asks her not to think of him in anger. The play has tamed Jane's passionate return to Rochester triggered by a preternatural occurrence so as to make it acceptable even to this pious missionary who had other plans for her.

Jane invokes a quasi-religious domestic mission as her destiny at the end of the fourth act as she prepares to seek out Rochester. St John too acknowledges that calling as he departs for his own. The play closes as Jane again invokes her mission: "Du kennst jetzt meine Mission, ich kenne sie auch—(sich an Rochester schmiegend) und werde sie erfüllen!" (55; You know my mission now, I know it now too—[nestling against Rochester] and will fulfill it).

What had become of the spirited and self-sufficient Jane on the German stage, of a character able to find a path through the social mores and restrictions of her rural English social setting to attain her heart's desire, to find a life partner, flawed and externally inappropriate yet suited to her disposition? And what made the new stage versions of Rochester appropriate marriage material and, in Birch-Pfeiffer's play, even a suitable redeemer? In his short-lived play, Morton reproduces Jane as a moral subject who will neither agree to bigamy nor capitulate to the pressure of entering a marriage without love for the purpose of serving God. Morton's unfailingly virtuous Jane even empathizes with the madwoman, declaring that it is not her fault that she is insane, and she also insists on the nobility of Rochester's character despite everything. While morality requires her to begin a new life far from Wellfield, the play deploys virtue to clear a path for her return. In the end, it frames her marriage to the older man of her choice as a moral imperative, the much younger wife's duty as helpmeet to her older impaired husband. While both plays temporarily untether Jane only to reinscribe her within religiously inflected social norms in the process of revealing her virtue, Birch-Pfeiffer's much longer-lived play ultimately speaks to greater possibility as its angry heroine vehemently speaks her mind.

Birch-Pfeiffer's final two scenes of acknowledgment, first, by the male lead and then by society as a whole, that is, were not necessarily all that viewers took home from an evening at the theater. Spectators after all heard Jane declare, "Ich bin ein freies Wesen mit unabhängigem Willen" (14:145; I'm a free creature with an independent will) and then repeat the sentiment in the face of Rowland's dark threat of violence (he could break her like a reed): "meine Seele is mein!" (14:145; my soul is mine!). They then saw Rochester capitulate and give himself up completely to her: "du hast meine Seele mit zauberhafter Gewalt an dich gerissen, sie ist dein, mein Herz ist dein, was ich bin und habe, ist dein—nimm auch noch das Geringste, was du übrig ließest, meine Hand!" (14:145; you have torn my soul to you with a magical force, it is yours, my heart is yours, what I am and have is yours—take the most paltry thing you have left me, my hand!). Scholars who overlook this last line or the thrill of Jane's repetitious assertions of freedom and instead focus on the distasteful dark threats and images of capture that issue from Rowland miss the point of the verbal fencing match between the two characters.[79] Jane, not Rowland—at least for the moment—has come out on top and violently pulled him to her ("gerissen" [torn] in the language of ravishment), not the other way around. Over the course of revealing virtue, the play momentarily toys with inversion, with "topsy turvy."

The mechanism of topsy turvy, performance of gender reversal, is always both potentially liberating and potentially restorative and conservative: liberating insofar as it violates sex/gender norms and conservative insofar as its effects depend on the recognition of these norms and thus potentially prompt their reinstatement. Indeed, it is often deployed precisely for the purpose of reaffirming order in the face of disorder. As, however, Natalie Davis concludes in her now classic essay on female unruliness in Early Modern Europe, "Woman on Top" (1975), the almost inevitable conservative restoration need not erase the effects of the resistance that preceded it: "the woman-on-top renewed old systems, but also helped change them into something different."[80] As Williams observes, furthermore, melodrama qua genre itself pushes in contradictory directions, "both actively inculcating yet also pressing against normative social expectations, both conditioning and constructing elements of the public sphere."[81] The play and its performances thus in and of themselves, with their contradictory impulses, made a variety of responses and understandings available to audiences.

The very existence of two adaptations generated within a year of one another in any case provides an index and testimony to contemporary interest in Brontë's novel and the appetite of the general public to *see* it as well as *read* it. A review of *Waise* in *Deutsches Museum* confirms the prominence of Brontë's novel when it explores the feasibility and advisability of adapting it for the stage: "Der Roman ist so bekannt und so beliebt, daß ich überhoben bin, über das Sujet ein Wort zu sagen ..." (The novel is so famous and so popular that it is superfluous for me to say a word about its subject matter ...). While he praises the psychological development of the two protagonists, the reviewer recoils from certain

---

[79] Susanne Kord sees this scene as a contradiction that Birch-Pfeiffer fails to resolve when she forces the happy ending; she does not acknowledge Rowland's surrender. Susanne Kord, *Ein Blick hinter die Kulissen: deutschsprachige Dramatikerinnen im 18. und 19. Jahrhundert*, Ergebnisse der Frauenforschung 27 (Stuttgart: J. B. Metzler, 1992), 75–6. Rinske van Stipriaan Pritchett, also offended by the language of the scene (a mash-up of Brontë's original text), raises the, in my view, doubtful possibility that Birch-Pfeiffer is exercising critique and laying bare the unlikelihood that anyone would accept "this fallen Byronic hero as a husband." Rinske van Stipriaan Pritchett, *The Art of Comedy and Social Critique in Nineteenth-Century Germany: Charlotte Birch-Pfeiffer (1800–1868)*, North American Studies in 19th-Century German Literature 35 (Oxford: Peter Lang, 2005), 24.

[80] Natalie Zemon Davis, "Woman on Top," *Society and Culture in Early Modern France* (Cambridge, UK: Cambridge University Press, 1975), 151.

[81] Williams, "Melodrama," 217.

dubious aspects, declaring the story of the insane "Lady Rochester" and the novel's catastrophe "abstoßend und widrig" (abhorrent and repugnant). If the novel was to be staged at all, in other words, this staging required alterations to make the material presentable, for, as the review also implies, public collective viewing is potentially more disturbing than private reading.[82] Birch-Pfeiffer had certainly made some dramatic changes, and the reviewer was only too ready to condemn all of them as well as the taste of the "Köchinnen und Scheuerfrauen" (cooks and cleaning women) who allegedly loved the play. While making the novel stageworthy and reducing what the reviewer considers the repugnant elements, Birch-Pfeiffer had unleashed the heroine's anger; for this reviewer, Jane had become a "widrig streitsüchtiges, keifendes 'Mädchen für alles' ... eine wahre Kratzbürste" (disgustingly truculent, scolding maid of all work ... a genuine shrew).[83]

Parody and Satire

In Berlin, the stage Janes prompted several mocking responses in addition to Schmul Katz's account. As these satirical pieces indicate, the more critical among Berlin literati had within a matter of months had a surfeit of *Jane Eyre* and yet could not stop talking about the material. As will shortly become clear, each of these pieces evinces gendered differences in taste and reception.

On February 25, 1854, two weeks after the premiere of Morton's *Mission* at the Friedrich-Wilhelmstädtisches Theater, A. C. Görner's *Die Waise aus Berlin, oder: Ein Mädchen für Alles, parodistische Faschingsposse mit Gesang* (The Orphan from Berlin, or: a Maid of all Work, Parodistic Carnival farce with Songs) also premiered there.[84] This "belustigende Karnevalsschwank" (amusing Carnival farce)[85] played widely in the German territories—for about a year—sometimes at the same theaters as both Birch-Pfeiffer's and Morton's plays.

Görner, who was serving as a visiting director at the Friedrich-Wilhelmstädtisches Theater,[86] proceeded in the vein of the Berlin farce to turn Jane into a comic figure. With the classic sauciness of the servant or the Berlin gamine and masculine strength and affect, Görner's leading lady, played by the popular Otillie Genée, famous for her trouser roles, has marriage to the leading man on her mind. In a send-up of Birch-Pfeiffer's opening scene, Jane, now Hanne Eier (eggs/testicles), first appears in a pantry among laundry hung up to dry, standing before a crude, unframed picture of her deceased Uncle Pietsch. With bread and butter in one hand, she stations herself behind the wash to read Scheibler's cookbook (not Hume's history of England and not Bewick's *Birds*) in order to

[82] "Correspondenz. Aus Berlin," *Deutsches Museum: Zeitschrift für Literatur, Kunst und öffentliches Leben* 4, no. 1 (January 1, 1854): 42.
[83] "Correspondenz. Aus Berlin," no. 1 (1854): 42.
[84] "Friedrich-Wilhelmstädtisches Theater," *Zweite Beilage zur Königl. Privilegirten Berlinischen Zeitung*, no. 48, February 15, 1854, 2.
[85] "Friedrich Wilhelmstädtisches Theater, Berlin," *Wiener Zeitung*, March 3, 1854, 578. The *Pest-Ofner Localblatt* reports two days later that the play was received "beifällig" (with approval). *Pest-Ofner Localblatt*, March 5, 1854.
[86] DBA 18 (1854), 54.

enjoy the cuisine of her Fatherland.[87] In place of a heroic, darkly mysterious, and irresistible Rochester or an impossibly virtuous one, Görner makes of the male protagonist the blustering and coarse master tanner Rosch, who first appears in act 2, scene 2, relentlessly pursued by women. In act 2, scenes 13 and 17, his female admirers play cards with the idea that the winner will marry him. He refuses to cooperate.

Potentially gender-bending elements of Birch-Pfeiffer's play and Brontë's novel serve comedy in Görner's play. After Hanne's vociferous rebellion in the first act, Aunt Pietsch sends her off to become a "Waisenjunge" (orphan boy). We never catch sight of her as a *Waisenjunge* per se—just as we do not see Jane at Lowood in Birch-Pfeiffer's play—but this formative sojourn leaves its mark on Hanne. She enters act 3, scene 15, carrying a saber and pistols after having vanquished all of Rosch's enemies. Similarly, in act 2, after calling the fire department when she discovers that Rosch's straw mattress is on fire, she shoves a fireman aside, takes the hose and his helmet, shouting, "Mein ist der Schlauch und mir nur kommt er zu!" (269; The hose is mine and I'm the only one who should have it). The double entendre of her words marks her usurpation of male authority. The firemen admire her work: "Die hat Courage!" (269; She's got courage). A discomfited Rosch, for his part, repeats his mantra "Nur Charakter" (Show character!) to maintain his distance from this disturbingly zealous and assertive woman.

A tough Hanne has meanwhile made clear that she finds Rosch irresistible on account of his unparalleled "Grobheit" (268; coarseness). In the end, after Hanne has twice rescued him, Rosch finally declares his love for her, and the company congratulates them both. Still he has no intention of marrying her: "Ihr denkt, die Geschichte muß wie in der Waise von Lowood mit einer Heirath enden?— Fällt mir gar nicht ein!" (294; You think the story has to end with a marriage as in the Waise von Lowood? I wouldn't dream of it.) Since the two of them have tormented one another far too much, he believes, they should become brother and sister and he should make her his heir. His use of the verb "cujoniren" (bully) to characterize their verbal exchanges, given its derivation from Latin "coleus" (testicles) and thus vulgar tone, again makes Hanne one of the boys. When she declares that she would still rather be a master tanner's wife, he holds out the hope that a marriage might still come to pass under the pressure of the original plot: "Ich werde hoffentlich bald das Bedürfniß verspüren, blind zu werden, und dann werden mir hoffentlich wohl die Augen aufgehen" (294; hopefully I'll soon feel the need to become blind and hopefully then my eyes will be opened). After an evening of music, hijinks, and silliness, spiced with puns and contemporary references, from *Faust* to *Kladderadatsch* to Fanny Lewald to the Spanish

---

[87]   C. A. [Karl August] Görner, "Die Waise aus Berlin, oder: Ein Mädchen für Alles, Parodistische Posse mit Gesang in 2 Abtheilungen und 3 Akten," *Possenspiele* (Altona: Verlags-Bureau, 1862), 226, hereafter cited in text. On the cast, see "Wissenschaftliche und Kunst-Notizen," *Erste Beilage zur Königl. Privilegirten Berlinischen Zeitung*, no. 52, March 2, 1854, 5, and "Genée, Ottilie," *Ludwig Eisenberg's großes biographisches Lexikon der deutschen Bühne im 19. Jahrhundert* (Leipzig: Verlagsbuchhandlung Paul List, 1903), 316–17.

dancer Pepita de Oliva, who in the years 1853–7 gave guest performances at the Friedrich-Wilhelmstädtische Theater,[88] the farce concludes by ridiculing the very premises of the novel and the two plays: it refuses romance, redemption, grace, morality, and feminine virtue.

The reception of the farce was a "sehr lebhafte, theilweise enthusiastische" (very lively, at times enthusiastic one), the *Vossische Zeitung* reported. Nevertheless, to appreciate the fun of the play one needed to be able to contrast it with Birch-Pfeiffer's original. The newspaper therefore advised theatergoers first to see the original at the Königliches Schauspielhaus (where it was currently playing) and then to see Görner's play at the Friedrich-Wilhelmstädtisches Theater.[89] *Deutsches Museum*, in turn, seized the occasion of the premiere of this "burlesken Parodie" (burlesque parody) to pronounce a verdict on Birch-Pfeiffer's play. The journal hoped that the laughter the farce generated would last long enough to enable it to expiate the "sinnlose Greinen, womit man die Birch-Pfeiffer'sche Rührspeise verschlungen hat!" (witless whining with which people had gobbled up Birch-Pfeiffer's sentimental fare).[90]

As theater-lovers flocked to the play adaptations and the parody, the Berlin satirical magazine *Kladderadatsch* seized the opportunity to join in the ridicule of Birch-Pfeiffer's play. *Deutsches Museum* in fact credited the magazine with turning the tide from uncritical praise to condemnation on behalf of "good taste."[91] On November 27, 1853, approximately three weeks after the Berlin premiere of *Waise*, the satirical magazine published a fictitious letter to the playwright from "Friederike Badeker, Hausmädchen beim Rentier Einsam" (housemaid at the rentier Einsam's [the surname means lonely]).[92] This naively sincere letter, heavily peppered with Berlin dialect, purports to be written late at night in a cold kitchen while the maid's master sleeps—only at night does she have the peace and quiet to compose a letter. Like the account in the voice of Schmul Katz, Friederike's letter provides the occasion for condescension to audiences characterized in terms of a marginalized group, marked by dialect, for the sake of a laugh.

As a servant and as a woman, Friederike applies for a favor to Birch-Pfeiffer whose play, she believes, indicates sympathy with women of her social station. Her fiancé promised to take her to the theater to see *Waise*, she informs Birch-Pfeiffer, and her employer pronounced the play really worth seeing and urged them to have a good time. Friederike then proceeds to describe her reactions to the performance. The first act leaves her cold, but then things change.

88   Maas, *Das Friedrich-Wilhelmstädtische Theater in Berlin*, 263–4.
89   "Wissenschaftliche und Kunst-Notizen," 5.
90   "Correspondenz. Aus Berlin," *Deutsches Museum* 4, no. 12 (March 16, 1854): 436.
91   "Correspondenz. Aus Berlin," no. 1 (1854): 42.
92   "Die Waise von Lowood. Offner Schreibebrief an Frau Charlotte Birch-Pfeiffer hierselbst," *Kladderadatsch* 6, no. 55 (November 27, 1853): 218. The letter appears on a single page. All references to this text refer to this single page. By the time of its appearance, *Die Waise aus Lowood* had been performed eight times at the Königliche Schauspiele. DBA 18 (1854), 40–2.

During the second act when Jane has become a governess Friederike begins to warm to the play—anyone who knows what it is like to have to take care of children will empathize with the protagonist, she declares. When Jane stands trembling before Rowland for the first time, Friederike improbably asserts, "Dies ist aus dem Leben jegriffen und erinnert so an die Wirklichkeit …" (This is taken from life and in this way recalls reality). Shivers run down her spine; tears run down her face. But then when Jane shows Rowland her artwork in act 1, scene 10, and the actress declares in an aside, "Edler Mann—das wußt' ich wohl!" (Noble man—I really knew it),[93] Friederike, completely smitten with the play, repeats these words and begins sobbing noisily—just like Katz and his family. Her wailing precipitates an argument with her fiancé. He finds her ridiculous; she accuses him of lack of sensitivity. The noise attracts the attention of a policeman who removes them both from the theater. Poor Friederike! She has no idea as to what happens in acts 3 and 4. Preoccupied with wondering and worrying about the outcome of the play, she is sleepless in Berlin. She asks Birch-Pfeiffer for a ticket to see the play once more, in consideration of what she shares with the orphan, promising to conduct herself according to the "Moral aus Ihrer Feder" (morality [flowing] from your pen). The piece mocks the playwright at the expense of the humble Friederike, who as a serving girl apparently (in the view of the anonymous author) embodies the naive audiences most receptive to the petty morality of the play.

In a similar vein, a Carnival play in a special Carnival issue of *Kladderadatsch* (February 22, 1854), takes the opportunity to ridicule Birch-Pfeiffer's play, Morton's *Mission*, and Brontë's novel and others who were profiting from this story.[94] In the anonymous very short rhymed three-act farce, Rochester, characterized as a "blinder Grobian" (blind boor), sets the tone by declaring that he and Jane must stop serving as the vehicle for others, namely Bell (Brontë) and Birch(-Pfeiffer) and the Berlin theaters, namely the Königliche Schauspiele, invoked by his mention of (Botho von) Hülsen (head of the theater) and the Friedrich-Wilhelmstädtisches Theater (where *Mission* was playing), referenced by the naming of (F. W.) Deichmann, head of the Friedrich-Wilhelmstädtisches Theater.[95] All four of them are reaping profits by attracting the masses to the theater or selling books. Rochester and Jane ought to be able to profit from their own story. Well aware of current tastes for sensation ("Wer heut Gedanken hat, der schreibt nicht für die Bretter" [Nowadays those who have thoughts don't write for the boards]), Rochester wants to invent a new plot and torment Jane even more to produce an "Effekt": "Als Weib hast du nur Recht zu dulden und

---

93   The aside to which the fictional Friederike refers does not appear in the print versions of the play.
94   "Die Waise von Lowood. Dritter Theil. Fastnachtsspiel in 3 Acten. Frei nach dem noch ungedruckten Manuscripte aus dem Englischen bearbeitet von Hans Sachs dem Jüngeren," *Carnivals-Scherz des Kladderadatsch* 5 (February 22, 1854): 6. The farce appears on a single page; all quoted text may be found on this page.
95   The mention of the Wilhelmstädtisches Theater may allude to both *Mission* (premiere February 9, 1854) and *Die Waise aus Berlin* (premiere February 25, 1854).

zu schweigen!" (As a woman you only have the right to suffer and be silent!) he declares in a crude display of masculine authority and then throws her out.

Rochester, accustomed to tears and tragedy, grumbles over his newfound happiness. After initiating a new plot, he returns in the third act as the leading man he wished to become. At this point in the farce, however, he presents as even more of a physical wreck, presumably as a device for increasing the pathos of the new plot. This time he is not only blind and maimed, but also lame and deaf. After some stage business in which another woman nearly usurps Jane's place, he lasciviously gropes the real Jane's body and recognizes her by the shape of her hips. The two gleefully determine to go to Berlin where they will find the cure for all that ails him. They enumerate the various cures that await them, concluding that if none of them work, they will simply drink hard cider! They embrace. As the stage directions specify with a sneer, the curtain falls overcome with emotion.

Kladderdatsch, it seems, could not cease expressing vitriol over the play's success. In the same Carnival edition a twelve-line poem, playing with repetitions of the homonyms "Waise" (orphan) and "Weise" (wise, wise person, manner) once again scorns Birch-Pfeiffer's canny ability to make money with her orphan by writing in a way that pleased the public but did not measure up to the German greats.[96]

These satirical pieces, all of which appeared in Berlin, may appear to hit the mark when they mock Birch-Pfeiffer's theater adaptation, which by any measure falls short of the complexity and force of the original novel. In ridiculing the idea of the dark, mysterious hero as love object; the unprepossessing, long-suffering Jane's ostensible submissiveness as governess to her rough master; the happy ending in marriage; and the very idea that the virile male protagonist should end up dependent on his former female employee and future wife, they point to aspects that trouble some readers of the novel up to the present day. Still, there is reason not to accept these criticisms as the last word. In their mockery, none of these satirical treatments take seriously what, alongside the play's deficits, is also in plain sight, namely, the breaching of the social order on behalf of the downtrodden orphan and others like her, that aspect of the play, which, as the condescending caricature of the fictitious Yiddish-speaking Katz in effect shows (regardless of the satirist's original intention), repeatedly struck a responsive chord among second-class subjects in a time of inequality, including the "cooks and cleaning women" invoked in the above-cited review.

The enduring success of *Waise* with mixed audiences for over half a century and the marked hostility of many contemporary male cultural pundits toward the author and the play prompt a closing reflection on the gender bias of the Berlin satirical press in particular, a bias that rather too obviously underpins the scorn heaped upon the play and that perhaps deflected these skeptical contemporaries from recognizing the truths articulated and functions fulfilled by

---

[96]   "An Frau Charlotte Birch-Pfeiffer bei der fünfundzwanzigster Aufführung der 'Waise von Lowood,'" *Carnivals-Scherz des Kladderadatsch*, 5 (February 22, 1854): 7.

even "bad art," that is, what contemporary readers and spectators also sought in romance.

Upon the Berlin opening, the *Vossische Zeitung* did try to formulate the special appeal and success of the play: "Aus dem Roman einer Verfasserin ist dies Schauspiel einer Verfasserin entstanden, man darf sich also bei zwei geistigen Schwestern nicht darüber verwundern, daß im Urtheil die Weiblichkeit nothwendig bedacht werden muß" (This play by a woman author emerged from the novel by a woman author; one shouldn't be surprised, then, given two spiritual sisters, if in an assessment [of the play] femininity has to be considered).[97] This femininity, the review proposes, supports the "Innerlichkeit" (inwardness) of the play, its riveting "Spannung" (suspense), which enables theatergoers to overlook its lack of plot and general illogic; perceived "femininity," that is, marked *Waise* from the start in the Berlin context. That femininity may have also made it especially vulnerable to ridicule even as it enabled affective identification with the virtuous orphan and thereby enchanted audiences.

In 1824, just four years before Birch-Pfeiffer's own debut with her first two plays, Gotthilf August von Maltitz, also located in Berlin and known for his satires, published a mocking eight-verse poem entitled "Die Dichterin" (The Poetess) in the Berlin journal *Der Gesellschafter, oder Blätter für Geist und Herz* (The Companion, or Leaves for Mind and Heart).[98] Calling on well-known tropes of the bluestocking, the poem enumerates the domestic failings of the "poetess"— her children run around naked, her wash will not dry (and she seldom bothers to do it), the kitchen maid ridicules her, she does not know how to spin, and her chemises are full of holes. In short, he rhymes, her "edler Dichter-Leib" (noble poet-body) lacks the "Weib" (woman). With this poem he embodies attitudes toward women writers that, as Ruth-Ellen Boetcher Joeres has demonstrated at length, constituted a norm in nineteenth-century German letters. The so-called bluestocking, the intellectually ambitious woman, the woman writer, presented an easy target for the (male) satirical pen.[99] Men who "made the rules" were ever ready to label and dismiss the work of women writers as merely popular and the women themselves as deviant.[100] Mary Lee Townsend likewise remarks on the proliferation of jokes about "authoresses" and the emancipation of women particularly in the late 1830s in Berlin, jokes reflecting uneasiness with the idea of the changing status of women. In the years before and after the revolution of 1848, she observes, "jokes continued in the same vein: women should not mix in politics, but stay home to take care of their men and children."[101]

---

97 "Königliches Theater," *Erste Beilage zur Königl. Privilegirten Berlinischen Zeitung*, no. 261, November 8, 1853, 6.

98 G. A. v Maltitz, "Die Dichterin," *Der Gesellschafter oder Blätter für Geist und Herz* 8, no. 43 (March 15, 1824): 209.

99 Ruth-Ellen Boetcher Joeres, *Respectability and Deviance: Nineteenth-Century German Women Writers and the Ambiguity of Representation* (Chicago: University of Chicago Press, 1998), 1–35.

100 Joeres, *Respectability*, 31.

101 Mary Lee Townsend, *Forbidden Laughter: Popular Humor and the Limits of Repression in Nineteenth-Century Prussia* (Ann Arbor: University of Michigan Press, 1992), 94.

Benefiting from the gender inequality that shaped social arrangements, the moderately talented men of the press, were, as copious examples evidence, ever ready to instrumentalize women to make a political point. At mid-century the satirical press was, in short, unapologetically misogynous; scornful of women interested in public life, women writers, and women's taste; and implicitly and explicitly committed to maintaining the status quo in gender relations even when they held progressive views in other respects. In the interest of maintaining high literary standards, this same press also often quarreled with the taste of the general public, which it saw as largely determined by women's (uneducated) preferences. In other words, male pundits routinely feminized and then ridiculed popular taste and the, in their view, concomitant inability to appreciate what came to be understood as highbrow literature.

The above-mentioned caricature of Birch-Pfeiffer reaping profits published by Adolf Glassbrenner, the "Vater des Berliner Witzes" (the father of Berlin wit), provides a case in point. Glassbrenner, who elsewhere labeled Birch-Pfeiffer the "große dramatische Heuschrecke" (great dramatic locust) was married to the actress Adele Peroni-Glassbrenner (aka Anna Elisabeth Adelheid Mraseck, aka Adele Peroni).[102] While Adolf sneered at Birch-Pfeiffer's success, Adele wrote joyfully on December 18, 1853, to their mutual friend (and her favorite acting pupil) Zerline Würzburg Gabillon to congratulate her on her debut as Jane Eyre in Vienna. No one was as overjoyed as she was at her success: "Mit Zittern und Zagen sah ich der ersten Nachricht entgegen, denn dieser Wurf war zu entscheidend, um ihn mit Gemütsruhe erwarten zu können ... Gottlob, daß meine Hoffnung mich nicht getäuscht hat!" (I anticipated the first news with trembling and hesitation, for this cast of the dice was too crucial for [me] to await it calmly ... Thank goodness my hopes didn't deceive me!)[103] As a female theater professional, acting teacher, and former leading lady, who knew full well the meaning of good parts for the working women of the theater, Adele applied standards different from those of her famous husband.

Görner, Schmul Katz's anonymous creator, and the anonymous authors of the three *Kladderadatsch* pieces reproduce in their satires, lampoons, and parodies a general mindset of their times. They rehearse now well-recognized gestures of male pundits and cultural elites vis-à-vis popular culture, those (especially women) who produced it, and those (especially women and outsiders like Katz) who consumed it. In the process they dismiss as "trivial" work that, whatever its shortcomings, at some level powerfully addressed the wishes, fantasies, and pleasures of women (and also men) who in their quotidian reality, in the second half of the nineteenth century, negotiated a social imaginary shaped by social and political inequality and injustice, women (and men) whose desires were, in the Real, in Brooks's words, "blocked, submerged, endungeoned."

Literature, even simple, shallow literature, potentially addresses and provides access to such blocked or submerged desires. Eric Bentley's defense of

---

[102] Quoted by Helene Bettelheim-Gabillon, *Im Zeichen des alten Burgtheaters* (Vienna: Wiener Literarische Anstalt, 1921), 93, 162.

[103] Bettelheim-Gabillon, *Im Zeichen des alten Burgtheaters*, 108.

melodrama recognizes just that point: in labeling the tears shed at a Victorian melodrama a "good cry," he imagines melodrama as the "poor man's catharsis" and thus tears as the salutary objective of popular melodrama.[104] In his defense of melodrama against what he sees as the reigning Naturalism of the tastes of the 1960s, moreover, Bentley claims for the genre, as the "lower form" of tragedy, the ability to produce the same empathetic effects as does tragedy, namely, Aristotle's fear and pity. "Melodrama," he asserts, "belongs to this magical phase [childhood], the phase when thoughts seem omnipotent, when the distinction between I want to and I can is not clearly made, in short when the larger reality has not been given diplomatic recogniton."[105] He concedes the immaturity of the fantasies conjured by melodrama, but he nevertheless grants them the right to exist and recognizes them as widely present where we might not expect to find them. In his defense of melodrama, he insists that there is "a melodrama in every tragedy"; in his view, Naturalism—and not tragedy—"tries to exclude childish and melodramatic elements."[106]

In defending the romance genre, Alison Light likewise supports the ability of entertainment literature to satisfy real needs while also providing pleasure. As she presciently observes with reference to *Rebecca*, a *Jane Eyre*-indebted novel, romance grants women "uncomplicated access to a subjectivity which is unified and coherent *and* still operating within the field of pleasure."[107] The need for such access, as indicated by the popularity of romance with women especially, Light explains, can be seen as symptomatic of the difficulty of fulfilling the demands and promises of femininity in real life. Advocating a more complex and less judgmental understanding of the consumption of popular literature, Light advocates recognizing readers' active seeking and suggests, furthermore, that reading for happy endings and romantic pairings, while perhaps not politically progressive and often even politically incorrect, can still have transgressive effects or meanings in the context of readers' realities, that is, realities that withhold what literature delivers. Light's observations challenge us to recognize that the popularity of Birch-Pfeiffer's play may speak to the failures of lived historical realities.

At a historical moment when most women had few alternatives, when for most middle-class women marriage was the only way out of the family home, it is hardly surprising if the collective imagination obsessed over that path and sought comfort and pleasure in literature that romanticized and dramatized it. Moreover, in a time of more general social inequality and recently disappointed hope for change, it is hardly surprising if plots that now seem to be women's stories for some men stood in for their stories, too. Indeed, in his history of contemporary German literature (1859), Robert Prutz, though condescending in tone by modern standards, proposed that women who suffered more than men from contemporary social conditions might have a keener eye for certain ills

---

[104]   Eric Bentley, *The Life of the Drama* (New York: Atheneum, 1965), 198.
[105]   Bentley, *Life of the Drama*, 217.
[106]   Bentley, *Life of the Drama*, 218.
[107]   Light, "'Returning to Manderley,'" 391.

in contemporary social relations, particularly "gewisse dunkle Flecken in den Herzen und der Bildung unserer Männer" (certain dark spots in the hearts and social and intellectual formation of our men) and "gewisse Tragödien des häuslichen Lebens" (certain tragedies of domestic life), and thus be better positioned to write about them.[108] As Townsend, moreover, demonstrates in her study of Berlin wit in the Vormärz and beyond, while Berlin produced its fair share of misogynous humor, the "jokes and caricatures about family and sexual relations were extremely varied and complex"; they had political dimensions now not readily apparent but "obvious to contemporaries."[109] In the mind of contemporaries, that is, the family was intertwined with the state; misogynous jokes about husbandly tyranny sometimes carried a subversive message against the restrictive state.[110] The "daily laughter" that Townsend describes, in short, could give voice to a broad (and justified) political complaint, yet did so at the expense of women. Plays such as *Waise*, at the other end of the affective spectrum, likewise carried the potential to tap into male as well as female discontent—and could do so in a story of a mistreated and redeemed female orphan who is the heroine and not the butt of a joke.

In sum, the German *Jane Eyre*s that populated the theatrical scene—and especially Berlin—in the 1850s responded variously to Brontë's novel, sometimes as mediated by Birch-Pfeiffer's play. With *Mission*, Morton offered a version that returns to Brontë's novel and its then more problematic and shocking aspects, ultimately to offer a traditionalist interpretation of the concluding union that plays down transgressive desire and plays up the idea of woman as helpmeet. Görner and *Kladderadatsch*, in turn, ridiculed and delegitimized the cardinal premises of Birch-Pfeiffer's play, and thus indirectly the novel and its romance plot. In the end, of these dramatizations and parodies, only Birch-Pfeiffer's *Waise* maintained broader international currency into the new century side by side with the novel *Jane Eyre*.

Far from being frightened of sentiment and sentimentality, *Die Grenzboten* praised Birch-Pfeiffer's play as appealing to the German heart and thus as a play that both men and women could love. Five years after the failed revolution of 1848, some German men were apparently also avidly reading Brontë's novel and enjoying Birch-Pfeiffer's *Waise*. The Berlin parodists and satirists, in their withering ridicule, underestimated the force and significance of the play and the German public's need for what it delivered over the course of an evening. Yet by attacking the play, they also acknowledged its power. As entertainment, that is, *Waise* entailed both emotional release and, in Williams's formulation concerning melodrama in general, "social, ethical, and epistemological recognition."[111] Whatever Birch-Pfeiffer's pecuniary motivations may have been, her play put virtue on display and through romantic union asserted the right of that virtue to

108   Robert Prutz, *Die deutsche Literatur der Gegenwart: 1848 bis 1858* (Leipzig: Voigt & Günther, 1859), 253.
109   Townsend, *Forbidden Laughter*, 87.
110   Townsend, *Forbidden Laughter*, 96.
111   Williams, "Melodrama," 217.

persist in a hostile social imaginary. As we shall see in the following two chapters, the histrionic language and amplified emotion of the play do have something to do with the original appeal of the novel. For all its artistic faults and deviations from the original, it transmitted an aspect of Brontë's *Jane Eyre* that historical readers, international and national, relished and some pedagogues and cultural authorities wished to dampen.

Three The "Erotics of Talk"

In her now-classic essay entitled "Girl Talk: *Jane Eyre* and the Romance of Women's Narrative," Carla Kaplan proposes what she terms "girl talk" as coming closer than does heterosexual coupling to fulfilling Jane's true desire, the desire for an ideal listener.[1] In examining the dynamic of *Jane Eyre* in terms of an "erotics of talk," the "desire for discursive intimacy," Kaplan understands "conversation as the 'paradise of union'" (8). She cites textual evidence that, she maintains, reveals that Jane and Rochester's conversation "all day long" has provided neither this intimacy nor this paradise. In her view, *Jane Eyre* thereby offers a transparently false utopian ending that by its very inadequacy makes visible the strictures under which Brontë wrote and within which her character operated: in mid-century England, namely, Jane's longing for a "conflict-free intersubjective exchange" remained unrealizable (10). In making visible this unrealizability, Kaplan contends, "Brontë inserts a pause into the inevitable machinery of this compensatory formula [the fulfillment of romance], both projecting and questioning this kind of poetic justice." By extension, the novel undercuts compulsive heterosexuality to replace it with a notion of sisterhood (7). While uncovering the irresolution of the happy ending, Kaplan observes that "Jane's most compelling description of ideal human interactions and satisfaction of her desires for contact is offered not in terms of Rochester, but … in terms of her exchanges with Diana and Mary Rivers, exchanges that recall Jane's friendship with Helen Burns and Miss Temple" (18). In the end, Kaplan, however, resists substituting a romance of girl talk to characterize the communication of author/narrator with the desired reader (imagined as female) for the romance of "conversation all day long" with Rochester, a line of thinking raised by a "strand of feminist criticism" (26). Still she entertains girl talk, as represented *in* the text, as closer to providing what Jane really wants—"intimacy, recognition, a change in her gender and class position and in the meanings attached to such categories" (27).

However illuminating the idea of girl talk may be to a modern understanding of this text, literal valorization of women's conversation apart from men does not generally carry a progressive valence in German adaptations of *Jane Eyre*, especially not in a historical moment that relegated men and women to separate, unequal spheres. Nevertheless Kaplan, in calling attention to the conversation

---

[1]   Carla Kaplan, "Girl Talk: Jane Eyre and the Romance of Women's Narrative," *Novel: A Forum on Fiction* 30, no. 1 (Autumn 1996): 7, hereafter cited in text. This essay is included under "Criticism" in the Fourth Norton Critical Edition of *Jane Eyre* as one sign of its present currency.

of female interlocutors and juxtaposing it with the conversation that forms the novel's resolution, suggests a useful entry into nineteenth-century German adaptations and transmission of Brontë's novel. As we shall see, imagining girl talk as a structure of intimacy proves in German adaptation not to insert a pause that opens up new possibility. Rather, girl talk tends to foreclose it. Neither Reichard's happy ending for girls where Jane finds a permanent home in the feminized space of Moor House where she can talk to her female cousins all day long while mothering Adele, nor Spitzer's idyllic picture of the sojourn at the all-girl orphanage as a happy time in Jane's life, nor the Fort strain of adaptation that locates Jane's entire telling of her story within intimate female conversation enacts a critical disruption in the romance narrative that serves a revelatory purpose. They instead tame the potential of romance conversation per se; their omissions and circumlocutions indicate that nineteenth-century contemporaries saw in the coupling and conversation that conclude the original novel radically enticing possibility. As we shall also see, valorizing a certain kind of "girl talk" significantly reduces the "boy talk" of Brontë's original text and thus its power. In the nineteenth century, this boy talk opened up an expressive alien world of experience, one that temporarily liberated readers from the proprieties of the prevailing social imaginary.

"Girl Talk"

With the word "Memoiren," Fort's *Jane Eyre. Memoiren einer Gouvernante* shifts the book's generic affiliation from autobiography to memoir. It thereby promises not so much self-formation as titillating recollections of the heroine's life and times in the homes of the upper classes. In so doing, it brings Jane's account closer to precisely the genre snubbed by the disdainful Blanche Ingram when she sneers at "the memoirs of all the governesses extant" (161). This adaptation in fact excises this episode, thus avoiding a disdainful reflection on the very genre in which the adaptation repositioned Brontë's novel.

As an adaptation, Fort's *Memoiren* offers a story somewhat distant from the original. Yet from its first appearance through the first decade of the twentieth century, it, like Birch-Pfeiffer's theater adaptation, proved to be a viable and salable alternative to the four more-or-less faithful translations, especially in the form of its subsequent adaptation of 1854. This later version bore a title all but indistinguishable from the several translations and adaptations that circulated simultaneously with it—*Jane Eyre, die Waise von Lowood*—and so outwardly blended in with the translations.

The Fort strain of transmission gentled Jane Eyre's story via girl talk. As we shall see, the adaptations belonging to this line fail to deliver fiery elements of the original, those components that supported the imagining of new possibilities for women through an account of female self-formation tied to romance. Yet, as in the case of Birch-Pfeiffer's play, these alternate versions helped to keep the novel *Jane Eyre* in circulation and thereby contributed to its long-term survival and circulation in German reading culture in the period 1850–1918.

Memoiren is just over a third of the length of Borch's nearly complete German translation for Reclam. This curtailed version of Brontë's novel launches the fiction that Jane writes her story for a woman friend, Elisabeth, who has requested it. Jane periodically asks her "liebe/teure/werthe/verehrte/beste Freundin" (dear/dear/valued/honored/best woman friend) for empathy and understanding as she carefully selects which episodes Elisabeth needs to hear in full.[2] While Brontë's Jane, in the four German translations, continues to address an impersonal general reader—in German the universal, masculine-gendered "Leser" (reader)—Fort's adaptation and all the subsequent adaptations that rely on it transform this narrative situation into an intimate exchange between two women. As becomes clearer over the course of the novel, Elisabeth, whom Jane addresses with the formal "Sie" (you), already knows the outcome of the story. The narrating Jane supplies the missing details, reframing the story with this female interlocutor in mind.

Throughout Fort's adaptation, Jane appears eager to assure her friend of her motives and her virtue:

> Meine Bedenklichkeiten könnten Manchem als übertrieben, ja vielleicht als kindlich erscheinen, aber Sie, meine verehrte Freundin, werden sie erklärlich finden bei einem zugleich liebenden und stolzen Herzen, dem in einer so ganz besonders schwierigen Lage darum zu thun ist, die Neigung, welcher es sich hingibt, vor jedem Verdacht und jedem Rückhalt zu bewahren. (F I:182)

> [Some might find my concerns exaggerated, indeed, perhaps even childish, but you, my honored friend, will find them understandable in a heart that is both loving and proud, one that in an especially difficult situation is concerned to preserve from every suspicion and every reserve the affection to which it yields.]

This Jane writes in keen awareness of social scrutiny and generally remains more overtly socially determined than Brontë's fierce individualist. Since she has taken the daring step of confessing her long-hidden passion, she must now protect her feelings from any and every evil construal. She worries especially that she will appear to have sought social position and wealth: "... es durfte nicht den Anschein gewinnen, als ob eine feile Berechnung der Beweggrund meines Verfahrens sei, das, wie ich sehr gut wußte, ein Gegenstand des Spottes und Tadels für die Welt sein würde" (F I:182; I had to keep it from appearing as if venal expediency motivated my actions, which, as I well knew, would become for the world the object of scorn and blame).

Precisely the fear that Elisabeth and others might impute mercenary motives to her were she to marry Rochester leads Fort's Jane to contact her uncle in Madeira. In this telling, that is, she cannot afford to wait for the lucky happenstance of the original in which, despite Mrs. Reed's machinations, the inheritance from her unknown uncle finally catches up with her. In her efforts to preserve

---

[2]   These epithets are repeated either modifying Elisabeth or "Freundin." Examples of each may be found on the following pages: "liebe" (F 1:98); "theure" (F 1:17); "werthe" (F 2:134); "beste" (F 2:186); "verehrte" (F 1:182).

her reputation, this Jane becomes a more active character, but at the cost of the narrative's interiority and searching uncertainty, those aspects that distinguish the original and make of the character an unforgettable individual coming to be and not merely a literary type.

Fort's narrator bonds with her female interlocutor most explicitly in her wish to ensure that the latter's daughter should experience nothing like what has befallen her. While Elisabeth, as a married woman, is safe, her single daughter may be vulnerable to the sorts of trials and tribulations that Jane has had to weather:

> Möchten ihre Augen niemals die bitteren und heißen Thränen zu vergießen nöthig haben, die aus einem gebrochenen Herzen kommen! Möchte sie nie Ursache haben, mitten unter Angst und Schmerzen, welche denen des Todeskampfes gleichen, hoffnungslose Gebete gen Himmel zu senden! Möchte sie endlich nie die Befürchtung, die grausamste von allen, zu empfinden haben, für den Mann, den sie mit aller Kraft ihrer Seele liebt, ein Werkzeug des Unglücks und der Verzweiflung zu werden! (F 2:55)

> [May her eyes never need to spill the bitter hot tears that flow from a broken heart! May she never have cause, amidst fear and pain, which resemble those of mortal agony, to send hopeless prayers heavenward! Finally, may she never have to experience the fear, the cruelest one of all, of becoming a tool of misfortune and despair for the man she loves with all the might of her soul!]

Jane's story reads here as a cautionary tale. In the original, however, as translated by Susemihl, Grieb, Heinrich, and Borch, when she directly addresses "the reader," Jane makes no explicit mention of women or girls in need of protection and instruction.

This adaptation includes many additional formal changes. It replaces Brontë's minute depictions of episodes, reproduction of dialogue, and staging of dramatic confrontation with narrative summarizing. This substitution for the first-person speech of others and for dialogue pulls the adaptation toward the mode of narration expected of autobiography more generally. Meanwhile, the voices of others go silent. The resultant omissions include key moments in the plot replete with emotion. The adaptation eliminates, for example, such scenes as Brocklehurst's humiliation of Jane at Lowood School and Bertha Mason's ripping of Jane's bridal veil. As these examples show, summarizing significantly diminishes the oft-remarked theatrical scenic aspect of Brontë's novel and its effects on readers. Furthermore, as will be evaluated in detail below, the substitution of Jane's sober summary for Rochester's tormented first-person account of his marriage to Bertha Mason leads to the loss of a voice that, in its emotional and intellectual expansiveness, can matter deeply to a female reader.

In Brontë's original, the first-person narrator routinely permits the speech of others—despite the fiction of an autobiography—to be heard through dialogue. Its scenic, dramatic, and dialogic accounts allow the plot to unfold minute by minute as originally experienced by Jane herself, as also signaled by recurring temporally significant words rendered in German translation as "Augenblick," "Stunde," "Uhr," "Abend," "Morgen," "endlich," and "gerade" (moment, hour, clock/o'clock, evening, morning, finally, just). Summarizing in Fort's account puts this temporality in abeyance; the adaptation loses the immediacy, contingency, and accompanying affect of the original.

As yet another result of the curtailment of description, the infamously charged spaces of Thornfield (in Pyrhönen's terms "external stages" on which the protagonists project their mental distress[3]) also recede, as does articulated interior space generally with its thresholds, vestibules, trapdoors, doors, windows, curtains, staircases, fireplaces, and vantage points. As articulated domestic space disappears, Fort's narrator also devotes fewer words to the crucial gazing and listening across it. Later adaptations of Fort truncate the description of domestic space still more, reducing the narrative to plot events.

Fort's rendering of the important scene early at Thornfield when Jane climbs a ladder through a trapdoor to the roof exemplifies the reductiveness of summarizing. It does not reveal how Jane gained her vantage in the first place and condenses the experience as follows: "Die Aussicht von den Dächern war in der That reizend und ich gewann schon eine richtigere Ansicht, als ich bis jetzt gehabt hatte, von der Ausdehnung dieses schönen Landgutes, das, meiner Meinung nach, von seinem undankbaren Besitzer viel zu sehr vernachlässigt wurde" (F 1:49; The view from the roofs was indeed charming and I gained a better view than I had heretofore had of the expanse of this beautiful estate, which in my opinion was much too neglected by its ungrateful owner). The moment of expansive and joyous imaginative possibility becomes in this version merely a moment of assessment and moralizing. The "bright," "velvet," "green," "sunlit" aspect of the original has vanished. In 1848, the German translator Susemihl had, by contrast with this terse judgmental summary, painstakingly hewed to every detail of the original, including Jane's ascent and descent. His text follows her up the narrow staircase to the attic from where a ladder leads to the trapdoor of the mansion, reproducing the original nearly word for word so that one sees into the ravens' nests and the area "spread out like a map" (98; *wie eine Karte* [S 1:138]) articulated with mossy paths, quiet hills and populated with trees, churches, and gates in the "Sonne des Herbsttages ruhend, den Horizont von einem heiteren Himmel begrenzt, und nur hier und da mit perlenhellem Weiß marmorirt" (S 1:138; sunlight of the autumn day, the horizon separated from the bright sky and marbled here and there by a bright pearly white [98]).

As in the original, Susemihl's rendering follows Jane back down the ladder as she returns to the interior of the house. Heinrich and Borch likewise reproduce this incident in full while Grieb, as an exception to his overall practice, includes it only in condensed form.

In short, in contrast to the four translators, Fort's narrator regularly condenses, encapsulates, distances, and diffuses both the delight and the potential peril of these past events from the superior, settled, and removed perspective of the present time of Jane's writing. The narrating Jane repeatedly declares,

---

[3]   Pyrhönen, *Bluebeard Gothic*, 24.

as in the following passage referring to the days following her departure from Thornfield, that she means to spare Elisabeth (and herself) the sordid details of certain episodes: "Ich fühle, liebe Freundin, daß alle diese Einzelnheiten Sie ermüden werden, denn jetzt, während ich sie Ihnen erzähle, finde ich selbst noch einen Theil von dem Abscheu und der Demüthigung in meinem Herzen, welche ich damals empfand. Ich will daher Ihre Qual und auch die meinige abkürzen" (F 2:65–6; I feel, dear friend, that these details will weary you, for, now, as I recount them for you, I myself still find in my heart some of the disgust and humiliation I felt back then. Therefore I will abbreviate your torment and also my own).[4]

Fort's narrator strives to bring the story well under control and to get emotions well in hand—and succeeds insofar as the happy outcome is from the start never in doubt. The question is rather how Jane managed to reach the point from which she in the present can assure her "beste Freundin" (best friend) concerning this "eigenthümliche Ehe" (peculiar marriage), namely, that it has made her the happiest woman she knows (F 2:186).

Memoiren reads like a fairy tale with a moral and a guaranteed happy ending. Its opening scenario elicits precisely such generic expectations:

> Herr Reed hatte zwei Töchter und einen Sohn. Jene waren schön wie Engel, weiß und rosig, wirkliche Taschenbuchgesichter mit kindlichen Herzen voll lieblicher Jugendfrische, Koketterie und Unschuld; dieser, mein abscheulicher Cousin, John Reed, von dem ich Ihnen wohl zuweilen schon Einiges gesagt habe, war der ächte Typus eines werdenden Dandys … . (Fort 1:4)

> [Mr. Reed had two daughters and a son. The former were like angels, white and rosy, with faces like the pictures one finds in those little ladies books, with childlike hearts replete with the charming freshness of youth, flirtation, and innocence; the latter my loathsome cousin John Reed—I've already told you some things about him—was the true type of the soon-to-be dandy … .]

Fort's narrator likewise frames the entrance of her rival, here named Blanca Ingram, as a fairy tale: "zehn Meilen von Thornfield-Hall wohnte ein schönes Mädchen, welche die Natur mit allen ihren Gaben überschüttet und die das Alter erreicht hatte, in welchem die vierzig Jahre Mr. Rochesters sie nicht mehr erschrecken konnten und in dem sein Vermögen ihr ganz besonders lockend erscheinen mußte" (F 1:105; ten miles from Thornfield Hall there lived a beautiful girl whom nature had showered with all her gifts and who had reached the age at which Mr. Rochester's forty years could no longer frighten her and at which his wealth had to appear to her especially tempting).

The fairy-tale motif returns in Fort's rendition of Rochester's raptures in anticipation of the first wedding. Picking up on the original text's interweaving

---

4   Hohn too notes the summary phrases with which Fort dispenses with Jane's soul searching after the discovery of Rochester's secret. *Jane Eyre in deutscher Übersetzung*, 93–4.

of folk tales and superstition, *Memoiren* creates a Rochester who recalls the beast of "Beauty and the Beast." In a departure from the original, he promises to grant Jane three wishes, "ganz so wie in den Feenmährchen" (just as in fairy tales). And just as in fairy tales he sets a condition: "Nur hüte Dich, Jane, nichts Unmögliches zu fordern, denn ich würde es ganz bestimmt versuchen" (F 1:178; But beware, Jane, of asking for the impossible, for I would certainly attempt it). Once invoked, the moralizing fairy tale exerts generic pressure. Pedagogical and predictable, the familiar formula also mitigates shock.

The narrator in fact lessens the harshness of the narrative from the start. Instead of beginning in medias res with a presentation of her cruel abuse at the hands of her cousin John, Jane presents the episode briefly as epitomizing her childhood suffering and then quickly turns to the next phase of her life (F 1:5). In lieu of sensation and individualization, Fort promotes an unambiguous moral reading of the story and thus subjectification.[5] Among other things, the adaptation sidesteps the ethical dilemma that arises when, in the original, St John tries to coerce Jane to marry him to support his missionary aspirations by simply omitting this event. Without this dubious episode, Fort's version can confidently conclude with a prediction of St John's good death without lingering doubts about his character.

While Fort's adaptation does fixate intensely on Rochester to tell the love story, it blunts the ideas of equality and gender blending that inform the original by omitting, for example, a key scene in chapter 37. Here the maimed Rochester gives his watch to Jane because he can no longer use it and reveals that he has been wearing Jane's pearl necklace beneath his masculine attire; the characters remain attached to the cross-gender objects. By contrast, the watch does not figure in Fort's version at all. In this version Jane merely asks Rochester to return the necklace that she left behind (and that he has been wearing), thus restoring it to the appropriate gender. The concluding chapter, moreover, emphasizes their harmony but omits the crucial conversation of companionate marriage of the original and so forgoes the notion of parity based in dialogue.

Over the decades, new versions of this adaptation deviated still more from the original.[6] The 1854 adaptation, *Jane Eyre, die Waise von Lowood*, retains a female interlocutor as the recipient of Jane's story, but removes the opening paragraph explaining that Jane is telling her story at the request of her particular friend, Elisabeth. Jane's interlocutor thus remains anonymous and the narrative situation underexploited. At the same time, this adaptation of an adaptation tames the story still more, rendering it even more sentimental. Two added poems fuel that sentimentalization. The first of these, a paean to marriage from the happy bride's point of view, appears in the text shortly before Jane learns that Rochester already has a wife. This religiously informed poem, echoing Friedrich Schiller's

---

5   My use of the terms "subjectification" and "individualization" relies on Ute Frevert, "Defining Emotions: Concepts and Debates over Three Centuries," in *Emotional Lexicons: Continuity and Change in the Vocabulary of Feeling 1700–2000*, ed. Ute Frevert et al. (Oxford: Oxford University Press, 2014), 5.

6   *Jane Eyre, die Waise von Lowood. Nach dem Englischen der Currer Bell*, 2 vols. (Altona: E. M. Heilbutt, 1854), hereafter cited in the text as "1854."

"Würde der Frauen" (1796; Dignity of Women) in its use of the term "Frauen-würde" (1854 2:4; women's dignity), assigns husband and wife gender-specific attributes and praises marriage as a gift from God, "ein sel'ges Loos" (1854 2:4, 6; a blessed lot), a "Lebenssegen" (1854 2:4; life blessing), a "herrlicher Beruf" (1854 2:6; glorious profession), a blessing from a "Vaterhand" (1854 2:4; father's hand), for which God created her. While this poem could serve to generate narrative irony, given that Jane will soon learn that she is about to become a party to big-amy, the text provides no signal that Rochester's deception of Jane undermines the sentiment of the poem. I will address the second of these poems shortly.

An impulse to control the reception of the story becomes evident in this adap-tation in the segmenting of the novel into chapters with headings that offer clear steps forward in the plot and that can be taken in at a glance. Unlike the origi-nal in which the plot seems contingent and thus a happy ending not necessar-ily guaranteed even if readers hope for it, this adaptation enables readers to anticipate and in retrospect recall the shape of a plot that culminates generically in "der Waise Vermählung" (1854 2:127; the orphan's marriage). The chapter headings relentlessly repeat the word "Waise," emphatically figuring Jane as the orphaned heroine of a sentimental rags-to-riches story. Hohn claims that these new divisions result in suspenseful endings that urge the reader to read the fol-lowing chapter.[7] Yet these moments constitute at most a simulacrum of suspense and not the real thing; rather the revelatory chapter headings dull whatever sus-pense the chapter divisions create by announcing the trajectory of each. These titled chapters, which are retained in both later editions with Bartels that target girls, enable readers to take in the entire plot at a glance and also impose a way of both experiencing and understanding Jane's story.

The general tendency of the 1854 adaptation of Fort's adaptation to soften the story also shapes its conclusion, which deviates both from Brontë's original and Fort's *Memoiren*. Here Rochester has the manor house rebuilt, and he and Jane leave the unhealthy climate of Ferndean to raise their family at "Thornfield-Hall". This conclusion overall fends off loss and insists on wholeness: not only is the manor restored, but Rochester himself is also "vollständig wieder erholt" (1854 2:131; completely recovered) and soon attains "vollständigen Besitz seiner Seh-kraft" (1854 2:131; complete possession of his eyesight). Since he has not lost his left hand in this version, complete restoration is possible. Jane closes her story revealing that she now has a family of "fünf lieblichen Kindern" (1854 2:132) These "five charming children," three of whom are boys (Brontë mentions only a first-born, who is a boy), unmistakably signal a dominant mid-century idea of a successful middle-class marriage reflected in fertility—the number of children and particularly the three boys secure the family's future, line, and property. While the spouses are always together in this harmonious marriage, the narrator makes no attempt to define this harmony in Brontëan terms as emotional, intel-lectual, and spiritual.

The 1854 conclusion, moreover, places St John elsewhere where he is fulfilling his noble destiny as a missionary, but, in contrast to the original, he is not expected

---

7   Hohn, *Jane Eyre in deutscher Übersetzung*, 85.

to die soon. Thereby free to omit Brontë's puzzling and somewhat melancholy closing in which the autobiographical narrator goes silent after quoting St John's presentiments of his own death and hopes for eternal salvation, this text instead turns to platitudes. Turning its back on the fictitious female interlocutor, the text addresses instead a community of implied readers of both sexes—"Ihr alle ... Leserinnen und Leser" (1854 2:132; all of you, female and male readers)—with the exhortation to learn from Jane's story: true happiness lies within, suffering and persecution are easier to bear when they are undeserved, and a spotless life is the greatest good humankind can achieve and must be fought for. A concluding poem has aided Jane, as she confides, in her trials and tribulations. It seven times issues a command in the singular familiar form of "you"—"Weine nicht" (1854 2:133–4; don't cry)—and exhorts readers to remain virtuous and look heavenward for solace—blithely ignoring the fact that Jane (not so virtuously) returns to Thornfield in this version neither as a result of a compelling cry in the night nor as a result of having gained knowledge of Bertha's death.[8] This closing consolatory poem is the second of the above-mentioned two poems inserted in the adaptation, both of which render the material more sentimental and pious, the marriage more conventional, and the story as a whole more exemplary than individual.

This adaptation was so "sittenrein" (morally pure), as the introduction to Hendel's popular edition of it later deemed it, that Bartels published abridged versions of it packaged especially for girls—as if it had been revised for that audience from the very start.[9] A Bartels edition from around 1905 touting pastels by [Martin] Ränicke and [H.?] Pasedach absurdly offers illustrations depicting sentimental domestic scenes that do not correspond to episodes in the story. The frontispiece, for example, depicts a woman in white in a high-necked dress, with two children on her lap and one child on the ground playing with chickens. No such scene occurs in the novel or the adaptation.[10] These ostensibly random illustrations graphically incorporate the domestic message that the volume apparently was to impart, one cogently expressed by the first of the two poems.

In yet another Bartels book for girls, this same adaptation of an adaptation of an adaptation appeared in a single volume with *Aus der Pension ins Leben* (From Boarding School into Life), a story by the well-known author of girls' fiction Marie von Felseneck. A plate inserted between pages 144 and 145, of a woman playing with a small child next to a baby carriage, with an adult man greeting two children in the background, has nothing to do with the

---

8   Fort refers only to an "unbeschreibliches Gefühl" (indescribable feeling), one less thrilling than the original "elektrische Schlag" and the following cry "Jane! Jane! Jane!" (F 2:142). In the revised version of Fort, in a chapter entitled "Sehnsucht nach Thornfield-Hall" (Longing for Thornfield Hall), Jane simply begins to wonder after a year has passed what has become of Rochester (1854 2:101).

9   Bauernfeld, *Jane Eyre, die Waise von Lowood*, 4.

10   Anon., *Die Waise von Lowood, Erzählung von Currer Bell*, illus. Ränicke und Pasedach (Berlin: Bartels, [c. 1905]), copy held by the Staatsbibliothek zu Berlin (Westhafen), signature B VIII, 22597.

episode recounted on the surrounding pages of *Waise*, but instead the reunion of Frieda with Georg Roneg in chapter 18 of Felseneck's story.[11] *Waise* itself appears in this edition in truncated form. Eliminating the second half of the story, this version ends with Jane leaving Thornfield after learning the secret of the madwoman upstairs. In an apparent effort to keep the material book from becoming outsized, the publisher dispensed with the happy ending, respecting neither the conventions of the romance genre nor the plot of the original. One can only speculate on the effect on readers who upon coming to the end of the volume read only Jane's sad farewell after she has avoided Rochester's outspread arms: "'Lebe wohl' rief mein zerrissenes Herz, als ich ihn so allein zurückließ. Und tausend Stimmen wiederholten in meinem Innern: 'Lebe wohl auf ewig!'" ("Farewell," my shredded heart cried as I left him so alone. And a thousand voices repeated within me: "Farewell for ever!").[12] Especially if they had seen the stage play or heard others tell of the novel, readers must at the very least have started at this unexpected lethal turn of events and dashing of hope for romantic union.

Girl Talk for Girls

In featuring girl talk, the iterations in the Fort strain ever more spoke to girls in an ever-more pedagogical and conventional tone, especially as they adapted the original adaptation for the particular audience of the "older girl," deemed not ready for the real thing but nonetheless conceived of as an eager reader of somewhat more mature literature. The adaptations emerging from Fort were not alone in valorizing girl talk. Reichard's *Die Waise von Lowood* and Spitzer's *Die Waise aus Lowood* similarly feature female bonding.

Reichard's adaptation borrows heavily from Borch's translation, but quickly deviates radically from the original plot ultimately to tell a story of sisterhood rather than romance. Its departure from Brontë begins with skewed emphasis on the orphan's suffering. It then proceeds to eliminate not only Bertha and her keeper, Grace Poole, but also the entire romance plot and the moral dilemma it presents to the heroine. While Brontë and Borch's Janes each name Rochester 371 times, his name appears only fifty-two times in Reichard's un-romantic version as but one indication of his diminished importance.

The adaptation likewise reduces the significance of Thornfield, which figures as the setting of the weighty center of the original novel, Brontë's chapters 11–20, 23–6. In Reichard's version Jane's return to a ruined Thornfield occurs immediately after her sojourn at Gateshead Hall to visit the dying Mrs. Reed instead of following her time with the Rivers. The reunion of the couple at Ferndean, chapters 36–8 of the original, in turn never takes place, for there is no romance to begin with and Rochester is dead. In short, the center of the original, 17 of 38

---

[11]   Anon., *Die Waise von Lowood. Erzählung von Currer Bell*, in *Aus der Pension ins Leben. Erlebnisse dreier Backfische. Dem Leben nacherzählt von William Forster* [Pseud. of Marie von Felseneck] [Berlin: Bartels, n.d.], 94–5, edition owned by author.

[12]   Anon., *Die Waise von Lowood* (Bartels [c. 1910]), 224.

chapters, takes up only four (10–13, 15) of twenty chapters in the adaptation, having shrunk from 45% of the total chapters to 20%.

In Reichard's adaptation, moreover, an anonymous narrator tells Jane's story in the third person and thus from the start dampens the female protagonist's voice. Jane's thoughts and feelings become audible only in dialogue, the use of free indirect speech, or simple omniscient narration in the historical past tense. As a result of the narrator's mediation, readers experience Jane from a greater distance; they see her through the eyes of an Other rather than through narrative intimacy established through self-reported interiority. Reichard's anonymous narrator furthermore imagines a different audience for the story. Rather than constructing a narrative situation involving the original Jane's address to a generic reader (in Borch's translation "mein lieber Leser" [my dear reader]) or a female interlocutor as in the adaptations deriving from Fort, Reichard renders the narrative instead a conversation between a third-person narrator—her own surrogate—and this narrator's female reader, her "liebe Leserin," whom she addresses with the intimate "du" (R 181; dear female reader, you). In its overt gendering of readers as female, this adaptation resembles Fort's; it renders the telling of the story a female conversation.

On the very first page, the narrator who has up to that point reproduced Borch's translation nearly verbatim, interjects a titillating question and a response: "Wer war jenes Kind, und weshalb saß es so einsam dort? Nun, meine liebe Leserin, ich will deine Wißbegierde gleich befriedigen" (R 5; Who was that child and why was it sitting there so lonely? Well, my dear female reader, I mean to satisfy your curiosity immediately). This interpellated "liebe Leserin" is of course the stand-in for the imagined target audience, the "junge Mädchen-welt" (doubly feminized with the word "Mädchen" [girl] and the feminine noun "Welt" [world]) of the title page. The narrator invokes her "liebe Leserin" five more times to secure that dear girl reader's interest, empathy, and understanding for the life lessons to come.

Reichard's version especially deserves attention at this juncture. In featuring girl talk, it transforms the original narrative from romance and heterosexual coupling to surrogate motherhood in a feminized and sexless familial configuration. In this era, in the German domain, that is, its turn to extradiegetic female conversation between the narrator/author and the implied audience withheld the excitement of romance and circumscribed Jane's story within tightly constricted propriety. In this case the conversation does not even allow for the solid bourgeois marriage that the adaptations in the Fort strain envisage but keeps Jane in latency.

Reichard's adaptation amplifies moments from the original that encourage female friendship, investing most particularly in Jane's friendship with Helen Burns. One of the narrator's six direct addresses to the "liebe Leserin" speaks of this friendship, which it describes as strong, tender, and respectful; it has moved her as no other feeling ever has: "Wie hätte es denn auch anders sein können, wenn Helen zu allen Zeiten und unter allen Umständen Jane eine ruhige und treue Freundschaft bewiesen hatte, die keine böse Laune je verbitterte, kein Streit jemals störte?" (R 96; How could it have been otherwise, when Helen at all times and under all circumstances had shown Jane a calm and true friendship that no bad mood ever embittered, no quarrel ever troubled?). Abridgment makes the Helen Burns episode the focal point of the five chapters that take place in Lowood, which themselves constitute a quarter of the total chapters of the adaptation. In Reichard's telling, the evocation of the social imaginary of the orphanage requires one more chapter than the sojourn at Thornfield.

Jane never wearied (*niemals überdrüssig geworden* [R 96]) of Helen Burns's company, the narrator reports, even if she is also spending time with Mary Ann Wilson. Reichard here relies on Borch's translation, where the formulation "niemals überdrüssig" (B 117) anticipates Jane's later description of her happy marriage to Rochester, whose company "ermüdet mich niemals" (B 721; never wearies me). But Reichard's Jane never experiences this companionate marriage. Instead, the romance with Helen Burns moves homosocial bonding to the center while Rochester falls off the narrative horizon.

When, for example, Reichard's Jane, filled with anticipation, returns from Mrs. Reed's deathbed to Thornfield on a summer's day she is not thinking of Rochester, for she had developed no romantic feelings for him before her departure for Gateshead. Instead she happily anticipates female companionship, recalling Mrs. Fairfax's friendly smile and imagining her reunion with Adele. The beautiful weather does not herald the sensual scene in the garden with Jane's declaration of her feelings and Rochester's marriage proposal, but instead masks the terrible sight Jane will soon behold: the charred ruins of Thornfield. As she soon learns, Rochester has died in a catastrophic fire set by a vengeful band of thieves whom he had earlier turned over to the police. He heroically rescued a servant only to be brought low by the fatal crash of a burning beam directly thereafter. Since the manor housed no compromising secrets, Rochester can die a paragon of virtue.

Jane's departure from Thornfield thereafter thus occurs not as the result of a moral decision, for there is none to be made, but instead dire necessity, for she no longer has employment or a home. The narrator notes her sorrowful state of mind as she contemplates what she has lost: "Die neue Heimat, die lieben Menschen, die Ruhe und der Frieden war wie ein Hauch in der Luft entschwunden, wie eine Fata Morgana—wie ein Nichts" (R 183; The new home, the dear people, the calm and peace had vanished like a puff of air, like a fata morgana—like a nonentity). Rochester has no part in this lament. As she thereafter wanders, destitute, from town to town, Reichard's protagonist, unlike Brontë's Jane, never gives Rochester a second thought.

While Reichard withholds romance, she does allow Jane ample suffering and persecution throughout. The arduous journey from Thornfield to the vicarage unfolds with the full detail of the original novel, as does Jane's sojourn at Lowood where she is placed on a chair to be pilloried by Mr. Brocklehurst and scorned by the inmates of the orphanage. Reichard in fact sees to it that Jane suffers from the start; the opening chapter hews closely to the original, though narrated in the third person and slightly condensed. The narrator almost appears to relish recounting John's cruelty. "Es gab Augenblicke, wo der Schrecken, den er ihr einflößte, sie ganz besinnungslos machte, denn sie hatte niemanden, der sie gegen seine Drohungen und seine Tätlichkeiten verteidigte ..." (R 8: There were moments when the terror that he inspired rendered her senseless, for she had no one who would protect her from his threats and his brutality …).[13]

After eliminating romance from Thornfield, Reichard sees to it that no thought of coupling or moral ambiguity troubles the sojourn at Moor House either. Jane reveals her true identity from the start, for she has no reason to conceal events at Thornfield. St John, for his part, betrays no romantic feelings for the daughter of Mr. Oliphant, the local factory owner (Rosamond Oliver in the original), who, remaining without a first name, quickly becomes Jane's friend instead of St John's secret crush. Nor does St John show any trace of missionary religious zeal, and without this calling, he has no need or wish to make Jane his wife.

Reichard truncates this section of the original with the news of Jane's inheritance and the revelation that she and the Rivers are cousins, and then proceeds to a happy ending at Moor House. Jane enthusiastically embraces the new familial configuration: "Ich liebe Moor-House, und in Moor-House will ich wohnen. Ich liebe Diana und Mary, und bei Diana und Mary will ich mein Lebelang bleiben" (R 225; I love Moor-House and I want to live in Moor-House. I love Diana and Mary, and I want to live my whole life long with Diana and Mary). The news of family is "Reichtum für ihr Herz!" (R 223; riches for her heart). When St John tries to talk her out of her generosity toward her newfound cousins after she inherits, she insists that he cannot imagine her longing for "schwesterlicher und brüderlicher Liebe" (R 226; sisterly and brotherly love). Although she plans to live at Moor House, Jane does not intend to give up her teaching position in Morton. In pursuing a profession commonly restricted to single middle-class women around 1900, she in effect again expresses a wish not to marry.

As in the original, Jane frees Diana and Mary from the yoke of labor as governesses and goes to extraordinary lengths to refurbish the vicarage in preparation for her reunion with her female cousins. Thus she prepares a happily-ever-after in which sexual desire plays no disturbing role: Jane finds herself in "wohlhabenden Verhältnissen, in geachteter Stellung und im Kreise lieber Verwandten" (R 230; wealthy circumstances, in a respected position, and in the circle of dear relatives).

And what of St John Rivers? While Brontë's first-person narrator names him 128 times, Reichard's third-person narrator utters his name only thirty-nine times as a sign of his reduced role. After curtailing his plot with its religious zeal and conflicting desires, the text remains ambiguous as to whether St John, whose vicarage is in Morton and whom Jane at the end of the adaptation still addresses as "Mr. Rivers," will take up residence with Jane and his sisters in his father's house. After he reluctantly expresses his approval of the innovations at Moor House, he simply disappears from the page.

---

[13]   Brontë's text reads, "every nerve I had feared him, and every morsel of flesh in my bones shrank when he came near. There were moments when I was bewildered by the terror he inspired, because I had no appeal whatever against either his menaces or his inflictions …" (12).

The tranquil female utopia of life with Diana and Mary removes Jane from heterosexual desire and marriage. Nevertheless, the text generates the requisite reproductive moment of nineteenth-century happy endings. Jane brings the orphaned Adele to Moor House and becomes her surrogate mother. In this—to borrow a term used by M. Susan Elizabeth Bonifer in her study of orphan narratives—"rematriation" as the joyous conclusion to an orphan's story, Jane has a "besondere Liebespflicht" (R 230; special obligation of love) to fulfill and she devotes herself to it "mit gerade mütterlicher Zärtlichkeit" (R 230; with downright motherly tenderness). As Bonifer points out, rematriation entails a "reconciliation with the mother's role as defined by the patriarchal culture."[14] Such reconciliation can hardly be considered a progressive outcome of girl talk in Kaplan's sense.

Nevertheless, as preposterous as this resolution may sound to readers familiar with the original plot, Reichard did in fact follow the logic of what turns out to be a blind alley in the original to imagine this feminized happy ending. In the original, the elaborate cleaning and redecorating of Moor House could appear to promise a happy ending there, were it not for Jane's enduring desire for Rochester and St John's determination to enlist Jane in his own passion, his religious cause. It thus figures as a temporary holding zone for the three female cousins, all of whom eventually marry. Fissures in this paradise soon make themselves visible when St John is unable to share in the joy of reunion and quickly exploits this new familial intimacy to impose his grand missionary plans on Jane.

Reichard's narrator tells a story devoid of such cross-purposes. While the book contains no explanatory preface, the announcement of its girl target audience on the title page signals that this version keeps its imagined girl readers securely circumscribed within the girl talk of latency. Forty years earlier, Spitzer likewise found ways of favoring girl talk in his adaptation and thus of deflating romance.

As Inga-Stina Ewbank wittily observes, "instead of a love life, Jakob Spitzer's Jane has a geographical life."[15] Indeed, this surprisingly mobile Jane, whose story is situated explicitly within the manufacturing economy around Manchester rather than the moors and the homes of the landed gentry of the original, makes a number of journeys over the course of the novel. Although called *Die Waise aus Lowood* after Birch-Pfeiffer's play, Spitzer's German-language adaptation especially for girls claims on its title page to be freely adapted after Dr. Grieb's translation. A comparison of Spitzer's adaptation with the then six extant versions of the novel (three translations, Fort's adaptation, the 1854 adaptation, and Stieff's rewrite) confirms the greatest linguistic overlap with Grieb. Nevertheless, these overlaps remain relatively few and also largely insignificant. As Ewbank also notes, Spitzer quickly departs from his source text. The citation may have served simply to lend authority to Spitzer's version.

---

14   M. Susan Elizabeth Bonifer, "Like a Motherless Child? The Orphan Figure in the Novels of Nineteenth-Century American Women Writers, 1850–1899," PhD diss., Indiana University of Pennsylvania, 1995, iv.

15   Ewbank, "Adapting Jane Eyre," 290.

As signaled by the frontispiece, which depicts Jane's departure for Lowood, Spitzer's *Waise* is most concerned with orphanhood, not the orphanhood of "Jane Eyre" but of "Jane Reed." The first half of the 198-page text (two of its four chapters) supplies the back story of the death of Jane's parents, her arrival at Gateshead, her torment there especially at the hands of her cousin John Reed, her departure for Lowood, and the happy time she spent there. A third-person narrator recounts the sad story of Jane's loss of her parents. With only the unprepossessing signal of a centered line between paragraphs, the third-person narrative perspective switches on page 19 to the first person, when Jane begins a graphic account of her travails at Gateshead.

The second half of Spitzer's *Waise* takes place mostly at Thornfield (apart from trips to Manchester and London) where Jane establishes herself as a sober-minded teacher of the orphaned Adele. No Bertha Mason sets Thornfield on fire, but it does burn down as a result, the text implies, of arson committed by two vagrants whom Rochester had treated harshly. The Rivers plot has vanished, but when Jane receives her inheritance, three friendly cousins pop up with co-claims to a portion of it.

On the very last page, the narrator reports that she became Rochester's wife and retired to Thornfield where she passed the "glücklichsten Stunden an der Seite meines Gatten" (Sp 197; the happiest hours at the side of my spouse). Despite this invocation of marital bliss, repetitions in the text of words with the root "Glück" (happiness) point the reader in a different direction, namely, toward the orphanage, the Lowood of the title. Here her "Glück" was "vollkommen" (Sp 90; complete), Jane declares. Gateshead, by contrast, is the locus of "Unglück" (unhappiness), as fifteen repetitions of the words Unglück/unglücklich (unhappiness/unhappy) in this section (as opposed to seven in the entire rest of the novel) make clear. This edifying account needs a depiction of her unhappiness to light the way to happiness. As the unnamed third-person narrator of this section of the novel piously maintains, "Das Maß ihrer Leiden mußte voll werden, damit auch für sie wieder das Licht des Glückes zu dämmern beginne, und ihr eine bessere Zukunft in Aussicht stelle" (Sp 10; The cup of her sorrow had to be filled so that the light of happiness would begin to dawn for her and give her prospects for a better future). As it turns out, Jane's move to Lowood signifies precisely that beginning. Indeed, the pedagogically minded adapter takes full advantage of the single-sex setting of the orphanage to afford Jane a moral education that offers yet another conservative variation of girl talk and also succeeds in undermining romance.

Brontë's novel tells a tale of socially determined suffering that persists from Gateshead to Lowood to Thornfield. Spitzer's adaptation takes the narrative in a different direction, starting with Lowood. His account of Jane's time there anticipates later nineteenth-century German-language boarding school stories for girls, the most famous of these being Emmy von Rhoden's *Der Trotzkopf* (The Contrary One), which we will examine in Chapter 4. These stories portray all-female education as positively formative for girls who, of course, after this period of latency will soon reach the safe haven of matrimony.

Unlike Jane Eyre, Spitzer's Jane Reed experiences no unwarranted shaming and no privation at Lowood. She finds an untroubled friend in Helene [*sic*] Burns who teaches her arithmetic and in the head teacher, Miss Temple, who looks after her throughout her time there. Unlike the bigoted Brocklehurst, the abbot who oversees the school proves to be well intentioned. Reflecting on the years at Lowood, which had passed in such an "angenehme Weise" (pleasant fashion), the narrator has only happy thoughts of the loving headmistress and the just principal and female teachers. Moreover, she had in Helene a friend, "die mir mit wahrhaft schwesterlicher Liebe zugethan war; und somit war mir der Aufenthalt in Lowood zu einem freundlichen und angenehmen Asyle geworden, das ich um keinen Preis der Welt mit Gateshead vertauscht haben würde" (Sp 90; who was attached to me in truly sisterly love, and thus the sojourn at Lowood had become a friendly and pleasant asylum for me; I wouldn't have exchanged it with Gateshead for any price on earth). Later, after she has worked for three years as a teacher at Lowood and even after Miss Temple has been replaced by an unpleasant successor, Jane remains reluctant to leave Lowood. She senses that it is time to go, but cannot be certain that doing so would improve her situation or make her happier and more content. She declares yet again that she is happy at Lowood and thanks her maker in her daily prayers for this asylum (Sp 99).

Her final visit to lay flowers on her beloved Helene's grave makes the point once again. In this version, Helene has not died of tuberculosis; rather she and Jane, in their extended symbiosis, fell ill simultaneously. But while Helene died, Jane survived. Kneeling at Helene's grave, Jane, overcome with grief, again evokes the paradise of Lowood—the fourth reference to the orphanage as an "Asyl" (Sp 101; asylum). Shedding copious tears, she cries out to Helene, "warum mußtest Du mich verlassen, nachdem sich unsere Herzen kaum gefunden hatten?—Beide haben wir Lowood, das glückliche Asyl unserer Jugend verlassen; doch wie verschieden sind die Wege, die wir wandeln!'" (Sp101; why did you have to forsake me when our hearts had hardly found one another?—We have both left Lowood, the happy asylum of our youth; but the ways that we wander are different!). Signaling her departure from Eden, death makes its presence known in the form of the heavy hand of the gravedigger on Jane's shoulder; it is time to leave, he tells her.

With female friendships and feminized spaces at the center of the first half of this short adaptation, Rochester and romance pale by comparison. As the "Herr dieses Schlosses, der Besitzer der Herrschaft Thornfield, Eigenthümer mehrerer Fabriken in London,—mit einem Worte—ein steinreicher Mann" (Sp 107; lord of this castle, the owner of the demesne Thornfield, proprietor of several factories in London—in a word—a man as rich as Croesus), Rochester is certainly a good catch. A trip to Manchester affords Jane the opportunity to become acquainted with still more of his properties. Mrs. Fairfax, with whom Jane has formed a fast friendship, furthermore reports on his character in glowing terms. Besides his general goodness, it turns out that he is also a connoisseur of art, a person of "Ordnung und Pünktlichkeit" (114; order and exactingness) who knows how to show his gratitude.

After this build up, Jane finally meets him in the manor house. Spitzer omits the romance of the first meeting on the road and instead Rochester arrives with bruises sustained from a fall that Jane has not witnessed. He treats her kindly during their first meeting and speaks solely of his wishes for Adele's education, stressing especially the importance of religion. Jane becomes his reader. Thereafter the text offers little indication of a budding romance between the two and instead enmeshes Rochester in worries about his property and his ward, as Jane tends to her duties as governess. Rochester expresses his readiness to come to her aid, but shows no sign of desire or affection for her. He has nothing of the flashing falcon eye and the noble forehead or the angry and stern moodiness of Brontë's Rochester; in fact, readers learn next to nothing about his feelings or his appearance. The succinct closing of the novel, which matter-of-factly recounts that the couple wed, implies not a passionate marriage founded on conversation all day long, but rather a sensible arrangement resting on a solid financial footing.

Girl talk as configured in all these adaptations distracts from or tempers romance and sometimes curtails it altogether to replace it with stories of sober and sensible choices. As a result, Rochester becomes less interesting in Spitzer's version and in Fort's strain; Reichard's adaptation promptly eliminates him. The curious nineteenth-century reader longing to find in books what her limited life experience had hitherto withheld from her likely put down these books with a feeling of disappointment. There is no incitement to rebellion, no temptation to transgress, no protracted and titillating movement from utter social outsider to dearly beloved insider, no tentative seeking of intellectual and emotional sympathy, no imagining of a new life. One of the most telling alterations in such accounts is the depiction of Rochester per se. Changes in the handling of this character significantly diminish the excitement and possibility of Jane's own story.

Boy Talk

When in *Mellas Studentenjahre* (1892; Mella's Student Years), Bernhardine Schultze-Smidt's fifteen-year-old Mella sighs on her fifteenth birthday over her book with the "düsteren Lord [*sic*] Rochester" (gloomy Lord Rochester), she also has the good sense to hide it along with her diary in a secret compartment of her desk to guard it from her vigilant mother who is particular about her daughter's reading[16] (see Figure 3.1). The worn book, which she has borrowed from a friend, signals that she is by no means alone in this experience; her heart pounding, she immerses herself in the trials of the unfortunate Jane. Like Charitas Bischoff, this fictional reader identifies with Jane, even wishes to resemble her physically. Yet as a result of the novel's "feminine" pedagogy, by the end Mella has banished thoughts of Rochester and Jane and also her own creative writing to allow herself only furtive play with the dolls she must also soon give up. Schulze-Smidt's pedagogical story of Mella's inappropriate sighing prompts a consideration in the final section of this chapter of Rochester and his "boy talk" as a then-dubious element of Brontë's novel and its resultant fate in the German adaptation for girls.

---

16   Bernhardine Schulze-Smidt, *Mellas Studentenjahre* (Bielefeld and Leipzig: Velhagen & Klasing, 1892), 3–4, 7–8, 15 (with respect to reading *Jane Eyre* passionately and secretly), and 4 (with respect to Mella's mother's views), hereafter cited in text.

„Mella starrte über ihr Buch mit dem düsteren Lord Rochester
hinweg ins Leere." . . . . .

Figure 3.1 "Mella reads *Jane Eyre* and sighs over Rochester." Bernhardine
Schulze-Smidt, *Mellas Studentenjahre* (Bielefeld: Velhagen & Klasing, 1892).

The fictive Mella's mother was not alone in her suspicion of this novel. Elise Polko's advice book *Unsere Pilgerfahrt* (Our Pilgrimage; 5th ed., 1874) recommends reading for girls, including novels from abroad.[17] *Jane Eyre*, although circulating in the German-speaking world in 1874 in three translations, two adaptations in the Fort chain, and two adaptation for girls and performed repeatedly on stage, is conspicuously absent from Polko's list. Meanwhile the ostensibly tamer Marlitt, whose fifth novel was serialized in that same year, did make the grade.[18] Rochester was likely part of the problem.

In the present day, Rochester is often subjected to critical scrutiny, even stripped of his power in modern rewrites, as, for example, in Jojo Moyes's best-selling *Me Before You* (2012; German: *Ein ganzes halbes Jahr*, 2015). In this rewrite, Moyes takes up the theme of disability, allowing the charming Rochester figure to die and set Jane free. Yet books of this ilk have hardly displaced the original *Jane Eyre*, which remains steamy teen reading to which adult women return. Proving Rochester's enduring allure, Cary Joji Fukunaga's 2011 film remake cast the handsome Michael Fassbender as Rochester.

In this vein, in 2008 upon the occasion of the 2007 BBC adaptation of the novel with Ruth Wilson and the conventionally handsome Toby Stephens, Tanya Gold wrote a puff piece for *Daily Mail on Sunday* titled "Is Jane Eyre the Sexiest Book Ever Written?" Gold relishes Rochester as the quintessential object of desire of romance fiction, "the tender brute from Barbara Cartland, Mills and Boon," "clever, tortured, besotted." "He is the man in every film, book or TV series you ever wanted; the dark darling you can save from himself."[19] However much Gold means to exaggerate, scholarship has noted Rochester's affinity to the dangerously attractive Bluebeard—Jane herself compares a corridor at Thornfield to one in a Bluebeard castle (98)—or, in his ugly guise, to the irresistible fairy-tale beast. Nineteenth-century readers obviously also thrilled to his greater (sexual) experience—as has also often been observed—but as I will outline below, also to his license to say certain things with impunity, his "boy talk." The rewriting, softening, and effective censoring of precisely this aspect of the story for younger nineteenth-century German-speaking readers signals the perceived attraction of the language of the original text.

Of course, the near bigamy, engineered by Rochester, in itself rendered the novel suspect for a younger audience.[20] Both Wedding and Reichhardt anticipate in their respective forewords objections to their adapting *Jane Eyre* for girls, but do not name specifics. As Reichhardt declares, "In seinen romanhaften Zügen

[17] Elise Polko, *Unsere Pilgerfahrt von der Kinderstube bis zum eignen Heerd. Lose Blätter* [1865], 5th ed. (Leipzig: C. F. Amelang, 1874), 138.
[18] Polko, *Pilgerfahrt*, 76.
[19] Tanya Gold, "Is Jane Eyre the Sexiest Book Ever Written?" *Daily Mail*, September 28, 2008. https://www.dailymail.co.uk/femail/article-407404/Is-Jane-Eyre-sexiest-book-written.html (accessed May 25, 2019).
[20] Ilka von Hartung, *Die Waise von Lowood, Eine Erzählung von Currer Bell, Aus dem Englischen übersetzt und für die refere Jugend bearbeitet* (Berlin: A. Weichert, [1911]), hereafter cited in text as Ha.

konnte [der Roman] der Jugend natürlich nicht geboten werden; diese sind bei der Bearbeitung ausgeschaltet" (Rt 6; naturally [the novel] could not be offered to adolescents in its sensational [novelistic] registers; these have been eliminated in the adaptation).[21] Nevertheless, as he also emphasizes, his adaptation retains "was unsere Kinder an der Waise von Lowood mitfühlen und miterleben, das, was auf ihr Herz und Gemüt belehrend, unterhaltend und erziehend wirken kann ..." (Rt 6; what our children can empathize with and experience vicariously with the orphan, what is instructive for their hearts and minds, entertaining and educational). Since the "romanhafte" aspects of the story occur in the "last sections"—as he claims—he has shortened and reworked these parts. He has, however, retained Jane's awful experiences at Gateshead and Lowood, "dem Kindesalter so naheliegenden Jugenderlebnisse" (Rt 6; youthful experiences so pertinent to childhood). Later on, in this version, Jane herself refers to the backstory of Rochester's first marriage as "romanhaft" and "schauerlich" (Rt 199; sensational, dreadful).

In a foreword addressed to "meine lieben, jungen Freundinnen" (my dear young female friends) Wedding in a similar vein recalls her childhood frustration at being denied permission to read certain books (We iii). While, as an adult, she recognizes that young people, because they lack experience, are not ready to encounter certain contents, she has nevertheless found that parts of these adult books are suited to pedagogical purposes alongside entertainment: they can spur readers to the development of the good that slumbers in them and suppression of their inherent faults (We iii–iv). She goes on to make clear that she has turned to *Jane Eyre* in particular because it holds up a mirror to readers in which they will recognize themselves, an act that must take place for the sake of their own wellbeing and salvation. Yet for all her hints that she has censored the novel, Wedding does allow her Jane a version of the flawed hero and also permits her the unconventional thoughts that will occupy us shortly.

In fact, young Wedding's frustration was fully justified: as some cultural pundits recognized, literature for girls failed to deliver, indeed blocked, what many girl readers sought in their reading—access to the grownup conversations and adult world of desire and social and sexual coupling found in the original. Hermann Schlittgen's "In der Leihbibliothek" (In the Lending Library), which appeared in the satirical magazine *Fliegende Blätter* in 1889, offers a facetious take on the prudery of literature for girls; the cartoon

---

[21]   In identifying the need to censor the novel for younger readers, Reichhardt shared the concerns of English contemporaries. Phyllis Bentley (b. 1894) reports in her autobiography on the relative freedom she had to select her reading; her mother "did once mildly demure about Jane Eyre, which had been forbidden reading to her in her teens." Phillis Bentley, "O Dreams, O Destinations": An Autobiography (1962), 42–3; qtd. by Kate Flint, *The Woman Reader 1837–1914* (Oxford: Clarendon Press, 1993), 198. Ten-year-old Annabel Huth Jackson (b. 1870) was "terribly frightened" c. 1880 by the episode in which Bertha tears Jane's bridal veil. Meanwhile, her mother was horrified to learn that her daughter had read the book. Jackson, *A Victorian Childhood* (1932), 58, quoted by Flint, *The Woman Reader*, 218.

laughs at its tendency to withhold from young female audiences what they actually want:

> Commis (einer "höheren Tochter" Bücher vorlegend) "Vielleicht dieses hier: Geschichten für die reifere Jugend."
> Backfisch (erröthend): "Haben Sie nicht etwas für noch reifere Jugend?"[22]
> [Clerk (putting books in front of a daughter from a good family): "Perhaps this one: stories for mature adolescents."
> Young Girl (blushing): "Don't you have something for even more mature adolescents."]

Rochester, as Schulze-Smidt's narrator inadvertently admits with Mella's sighing, potentially provided that "something for even more mature adolescents."

In the original, Brontë's narrator carefully sets up the moonlit first encounter with the animated and animating Rochester. A few pages before they meet, she articulates the desire of her younger self for a particular kind of story, one that is about to begin: Jane wishes to open her "inward ear to a tale that was never ending—a tale my imagination created, and narrated continuously; quickened with all of incident, life, fire, feeling, that I desired and had not in my actual existence" (101). Speaking then in the present tense, the narrator chafes at women's limited social roles and insists that women like men suffer when they lack action, variety, and purpose:

> Women are supposed to be very calm generally: but women feel just as men feel; they need exercise for their faculties, and a field for their efforts, as much as their brothers do; they suffer from too rigid a restraint, too absolute a stagnation, precisely as men would suffer; and it is narrow-minded in their more privileged fellow-creatures to say that they ought to confine themselves to making puddings and knitting stockings, to playing on the piano and embroidering bags. It is thoughtless to condemn them, or laugh at them, if they seek to do more or learn more than custom has pronounced necessary for their sex. (101)

While the adaptations omit these preparatory and foundational passages, the four translators carefully render them and thus prepare the reader for a tale that will contrast with dull social prescription.

After declaring at this juncture that women suffer as much as men do, that they feel as much as men do, Brontë's narrator apparently needs to let Rochester speak in order to free her own tongue, to say the things that the "custom" she invokes here prohibits her from saying. After all, as she reports in the first chapter, when she was a child, Mrs. Reed instructed her, under threat of punishment, not to ask questions or express her emotions, especially anger. Pejoratively labeled a "fury" (13), the same epithet applied to Bertha, Jane attacks her male adversary, John Reed—also like Bertha. Bertha expresses her anger in unintelligible growls,

---

[22] Hermann Schlittgen, "In der Leihbibliothek," *Fliegende Blätter* 90, no. 2285 (1889): 165.

grunts, screams, and laughter. Jane, however, matures through autobiography into language and story. As a female narrator she can, however, sometimes speak more effectively by putting words in Rochester's mouth. His speaking allows her to utter what propriety otherwise forbids her—the "life, fire, feeling" the young Jane misses and seeks.

Boy talk, representing Rochester's emotional life, enters the novel liberally as quoted speech—recorded as dialogue or reported and preserved by the female narrator. This racy language, shaped and circumscribed by Jane's girl talk, marks the novel and contributes to its allure. In this vein, Rochester's very first utterance consists of a mild oath: "What the deuce ..." (103). The four translators faithfully and variously render it: "Was zum Henker" (S (1:146), G 1:172 (literally) What the hangman) and "Was der Teufel" (H:2:25 What the devil) and "Was zum Teufel" (B 172; What the devil). Rochester repeats the oath eight more times in the original, presumably as an attempt on the part of the author/narrator to imitate and access male discourse. As the scene unfolds, the narrator remarks, "I think he was swearing, but am not certain; however, he was pronouncing some formula which prevented him from replying to me directly" (104). Swearing or not, Rochester soon reveals himself to be an aggressive interlocutor, and he and Jane begin the verbal dueling that structures many of the episodes. His angry, expressive language in this scene anticipates emotion-laden speech to come.

In addition to reproducing his linguistic fencing and aggressive questioning, Jane the narrator allows Rochester to speak at length at two critical junctures in the novel—first in his recapitulation of Céline Varens's betrayal and the origins of his ward, Adele, and second, in his account of his ill-fated marriage to Bertha, her madness, his transport of her to England, and his subsequent travels during which he gave himself over to the pleasures of the flesh. In the second instance, as he agitatedly recounts his harrowing story, the enthralled reader presses on to learn that Rochester failed to find solace with the French Céline, the German Clara, and the Italian Giacinta, and finally hears his narrative of his meeting and falling in love with Jane. This account, in English consisting of *c.* 5,000 words, is interrupted only intermittently by Jane's questions urging him to continue his story and supply more information. It concludes with his frantic pledge of fidelity and his demand that Jane do the same. By any measure, this story of male suffering and error contains the most turbulent emotional vocabulary of the entire novel. As such it provides access to experience beyond the ken of most readers, foreign especially to the life experience of girls and women in the nineteenth century. Fort's Jane merely summarizes both of these instances but in the first summation she does allow that Rochester's story of betrayal in Paris opened a new world for her, arousing her curiosity (F 1:88). Without actually supplying linguistic access to it, Fort alludes here to a world previously alien to Jane.

Rochester's arresting countenance piques curiosity and makes of an allegedly ugly man an object of female curiosity and desire, thus fortifying his passionate speech. In fact, words describing his appearance do not depict an ugly man; rather, he comes across as energetic, animated, intelligent, angry, and assertive. Jane variously describes him as having a "falcon-eye" (245); "heavy brow," broad chest, and "dark face," (104); dark hair, square forehead, athletic build, "broad chested and thin flanked" (110); "sable waves" of hair (120). He scowls; his eyes flash. After their first encounter, Jane herself sets attraction in motion with her own thoughts of his appearance; she ponders the impression that this "new face," "dissimilar to" all the others in her "gallery of memory"—"masculine," "dark, strong, and stern"—has left on her (106). Her reflection builds up Rochester, as it were, and he moves to the narrative center that he will occupy for the next fifteen chapters. If he were to forfeit the charisma and expressive power that she assembles for him, then her story too would become less compelling and she herself diminished. In short, the unfolding of the romance requires his expressive masculine speech supported by his appearance. Ultimately, Rochester must also hold up his end in the marital conversation achieved at the conclusion of the novel; boy talk and girl talk, in the vision of this novel, must reach equilibrium and integration.

The German adaptations, however, put the question of Rochester's function to the test when they eliminate or abridge his extended speeches and dialogue; remake him as unambiguously virtuous and mild; curtail physical description, especially of the physiognomy that expresses Rochester's vitality, fire, and emotionality; or reduce Jane's reflections on him. Especially the adaptations for girls struggle with his charisma, generally hovering somewhere between admitting his appeal and blocking it. Not surprisingly, the result is a blander story, one that Schlittgen's "more mature adolescent" would surely have rejected in favor of the original. The narrative maiming of Rochester sets in early.

Beginning in 1850, the adapters set about reducing in various ways the emotionality that swirls around Rochester as well as his masculine language, thus missing his vital function in Jane's story. Fort's adaptation, for example, characterized as it is by girl talk, permits Rochester merely the expletive "verwünschte Geschichte" (1:54; cursed affair) upon his tumble from his horse, but otherwise keeps him from swearing. It also prevents him from speaking at length. Fort's Jane substitutes her own sober summation for Rochester's account of his history with Céline and his rescue of Adele as she does as well for his recitation of his marriage to Bertha and its consequences. Fort's text thereby robs the character of his thrilling linguistic expressivity.

Some adaptations for girls simply put Rochester himself on the chopping block. Stieff, in her markedly pious adaptation for this audience, omits Rochester altogether. Here the German Johanna's employers are the Polish Count and Countess R. "R" is the only allusion in the text to the Rochester of the source text. The involvement of this couple in the Polish revolution leads to their destruction. As we saw above, Reichard's version in effect acknowledges his dangerous allure when it kills him prematurely, while Spitzer's adaptation takes steps to elide his dark appeal. The other adapters follow this last strategy to varying degrees. In so doing, they undercut the vital functions and values of this character and thus curtail readers' opportunity to imagine (and experience vicariously) the individualization and joyful liberation that romance potentially delivers.

Yet even as they diminish him, most of the adaptations for girls do allow their Rochester at least a hint of his original fiery allure. Occasionally they permit him to express his anger in colorful language. The rendering of Jane's first meeting with him may again serve as a case in point. Despite many alterations,

Wedding's version, for example, evokes his "dunkles Gesicht, mit strengen Zügen und dicken Brauen" (We 117; dark face, with severe features and heavy eyebrows). This text even names Rochester's passionate nature for its girl readers when it renders "his eyes and gathered brows looked thwarted and ireful" (104) as "sein Blick verriet Zorn und Leidenschaft" (We 117; his glance revealed anger and passion). Wedding also permits him the oath, which he repeats five times over the course of her version. Her Johanna reflects on the impression this face has made on her—"männlich," "ernst," "streng" (We 119; masculine, serious, stern). While retaining his emotional masculinity and dark attraction, Wedding finds other ways of taming the plot. She spares this passionate man any hint of bigamy and instead makes of him the benevolent and long-suffering guardian of his insane sister-in-law and first love, Aimée, who abandoned him for his brother.

Reichhardt, too, permits Rochester to swear a mild oath five times and thus, as in Wedding's version, his language is somewhat saltier than the other adapted Rochesters. The text adheres almost to the word to Borch's translation in its description of his appearance in this iconic scene. Reichhardt, however, largely omits text addressing the impression that this face—masculine, dark, strong, stern—in Borch's translation "männlich," "düster," "streng," "ernst" (B 177; manly, gloomy, severe, serious)—has made on Jane. He eliminates the threat of bigamy, and makes sure that there is nothing to thwart or delay the pairing and thus stir the passions.

Hartung, in her general tendency to adhere to the original—more faithfully than all the other versions for girls—reproduces the eyebrows and the angry flashing eyes. She, however, allows Rochester no cursing in the moonlit encounter and describes his face as "mürrisch" (Ha 55, 69; grumpy, sullen) rather than "streng" (stern); in its several repetitions, "mürrisch" becomes, in Hartung's telling, the face of the world that thwarts the heroine, yet the Reeds also perceive Jane herself as "mürrisch" (Ha 7). Hartung's sullen Rochester does not recount his libertine adventures with Céline, Giacinta, or Clara and abridges his history with Bertha. On her way back to Thornfield after this first meeting, Johanna, as in the original, reflects on the face she has seen. Yet this Johanna has not displayed any of the restlessness of Brontë's Jane: the narrator does not report what she sees when she looks out over the grounds from the rooftop and she does not recount her boredom and wish for change. Nor does the text include the narrator's reflection on gendered custom, which sets up the meeting with Rochester. In retaining the bare bones of the plot, which she appears to have gotten from Borch, Hartung delivers up Rochester to satisfy her readers. Nevertheless, she curtails his speech and Jane's thoughts about him with the final effect of downplaying the push toward gender parity as realized in marital conversation.

Wachler's Rochester shouts the oath as rendered in Susemihl, one of her source texts: "Was zum Henker ist jetzt zu thun?" (Wa 137). Her text thereafter permits him no further cursing, but it does offer readers a look at the arresting features of the dark hero—"leicht gebräunt" (tanned), "streng" (stern), "sein Auge blickte unwirsch" (his harsh glance), "finsteren Ausdruck" (dark expression), and eyebrows grown together (Wa 138). Still, Jane returns to Thornfield with no further reflection on this striking man and so does not cue readers to pursue such thoughts either. Following Birch-Pfeiffer, she instead keeps Jane's trials (and not her ruminations on Rochester) at the narrative center.

Although she omits his cursing and ultimately dispatches him altogether to bring about Jane's happy ending with her cousins, even Reichard (also following Borch nearly word for word) in this first meeting grants Rochester his dark face, serious features, high forehead, and heavy brow. Narrating the story in the third person, however, she elides Jane's reflection on her lack of experience with men and surprising ability to trust this strange man upon first meeting as well as the mention of restlessness, desire for action, and change that precedes the encounter. The narrator notes no lasting impression. There is simply not going to be a romance in Reichard's telling. Rochester becomes instead Jane's moody employer. As a sign of the tendency of this adaptation overall to privilege femininity, the word "männlich," which appears three times in Borch's translation, is never uttered.

While in most of the adaptations Rochester does retain his narrative role as Jane's matrimonial destination, his function as Jane's own mouthpiece is largely in abeyance in these books. With a diminished Rochester, Jane's life writing overall lacks the stirring emotionalism and intelligent reflection of the original. The first-person autobiographical narrator Jane or the third-person narrator—as in Wachler, Reichard, and Stieff—does not recount "unfeminine" things, because their pale versions of the errant, emotional, and sexy Rochester have never done or said certain things in the first place. Without this deeply flawed and charismatic Rochester, furthermore, Jane herself cannot admit and give expression to emotions that women were not supposed to experience, not even in novels. Yet this expression of strong emotion in fittingly strong language is critical to the narrator's formation (*Bildung*). Through narration, she recapitulates, absorbs, sublates, and, in effect, appropriates this "boy talk."

The gendered conventions shaping these adaptations overall tend to circumscribe the unsettling material offered by the original within approved models for girls. Yet Rochester proves hard to manage if any semblance of romance is preserved. When the adaptations retain even remnants of the passionate, commanding, and angry man created by Brontë's narrator, they perforce make room for the expression of emotion, behavior, and language inappropriate to middle-class femininity but permissible for men of the same social class. From our vantage, Mella's inappropriate sighing over Rochester might then be understood less as a desire for Rochester as a lover and more as a desire to inhabit him, a desire to know that dark "masculine" world of language and experience otherwise denied her, the experience that in a time of inequality was prized above that of others.

Conversant Happy Endings

What, then, do Jane and Rochester talk about when they talk all day long? How exactly did the alluring boy talk and the verbal sparring that propelled the romance plot turn into harmonious mutuality, into marital conversation that amounts to audible thinking as if one were thinking the thoughts of the other? Brontë's narrator does not share that information, but embedded in the very idea of talk as it is presented throughout the novel in dialog is continued negotiation, negotiation through conversation that can in the end take place on an equal footing. The couple are "precisely suited in character—perfect concord is the result" (401). The word "result" in what may seem a description of stasis bears scrutiny since it points lightly to the processual.

Susemihl, Grieb, and Borch, who typically adhere closely to the English original, attend here as well to the full text. All other German versions of the novel (including Heinrich's translation), if they reproduce it at all, alter these concluding words. Tellingly, they omit the central idea of conversation as shared audible thinking, deferring instead to the simpler notion of perfectly matched character, perfect harmony, never tiring of one another's company, or as in Hartung's adaptation—"Unsere gegenseitige Nähe ersetzt uns die ganze Welt" (Ha 238; our mutual intimacy replaces the entire world for us). The more radical idea that happiness—as a "result"—might still need to be negotiated through thinking and talking as equals so that the two genders come to think the thoughts of the other never crosses the page in adaptation but remains available in translation.

* * *

When she articulates her happy ending, names and ponders positive feelings, and so formulates herself, Brontë's narrator invokes, through their pointed absence, the negative emotions that the harmonious marriage has banished or at least holds in check: "To be together is for us to be at once as free as in solitude, as gay as in company," she declares. "I know no weariness of my Edward's society" (401). These words, presented as an achievement, suggest a human condition in which one is more typically sad, sometimes bored and lonely, sometimes unharmonious and angry. Over the course of her autobiography Jane puts these negative emotions on display and by narrating them or presenting them in dialogue transforms them into feelings to be contemplated and dealt with. The trajectory of romance in the manner of *Jane Eyre* is thus intimately intertwined with expression of negative emotion and its integration or sublation as articulated feeling.

The following chapter returns to the anger that Rochester expresses so noisily, anger that suffuses the original and then fluctuates in German translation and adaptation. It includes not just renderings of Jane and Rochester but also Mrs. Reed, St John, and Bertha. It, furthermore, addresses a second unsanctioned emotion, sadness or melancholy, and the boredom or rather weariness that accompanies it, an emotion that dogs not only the emotive Rochester, but also and especially Jane. The adapters and translators wrestle with Brontë's treatment of negative emotion: while some meticulously seek equivalents for her English turns of phrase, others simply elide and introduce alternate ideas of Jane's and Rochester's affective life and what it therefore means for them to marry. To ferret out why these negative emotions for some German cultural agents proved too hot to handle and why, for others, they were essential to the powerful effects of the novel and indeed readers' joy in the ending, we must also eventually return to Mella's reading and writing.

Four   Anger and Sadness: Unsanctioned Emotion, Articulated Feeling

Rochester is not alone in his anger. Intensive and extensive textual analysis, both close and distant reading, of *Jane Eyre* yields the not entirely surprising finding that this novel engages deeply with anger, its expression, origins, nuances, effects, and remedies. Jane the child is angry, Jane the adult is angry, Jane the narrator is angry. But so too are Bertha Mason, Reverend Brocklehurst, John Reed, and St John. Mrs. Reed's anger poisons Gateshead, making it the special locus, as it is expressed in German translation, of "Wut" and "Zorn"—and not merely her own, but the rage of her unwanted niece; her son, John; and the servants who must deal with these detestable children. Anger pervades Lowood, Thornfield, and Moor House as well. Even writing from her supposed state of marital bliss at Ferndean, the autobiographical narrator summons a strident, if tensely controlled, voice to tell her story. The awful truth of Brontë's original seems to be that anger dogs human relations, presenting a source of suffering for those who experience it either as a sentient subject or as its unwitting, inappropriate, or even rightful object. Modern readings and treatments of *Jane Eyre*, not the least of which is Gilbert and Gubar's now-classic feminist *The Madwoman in the Attic* (1979), have teased out and savored the rebellious anger that courses through the novel.[1] The celebrated musical theater adaptation of 2014, one that according to *The Mail on Sunday* "captures the beating heart of the novel. And then some," stages a heroine who spectacularly speaks defiant anger.[2] Yet nineteenth-century Christian-inflected norms repudiated anger, especially that of women. Jane was by any measure out of line.

But anger is not the only unsanctioned emotion that shapes this novel. Sadness, a hopeless world-weariness, belongs to the very warp and woof of its

---

[1] Sandra M. Gilbert and Susan Gubar, *The Madwoman in the Attic: The Woman Writer and the Nineteenth-Century Imagination* (1979; New Haven, CT: Yale University Press, 1984), esp. 336–47. As an index of this generally recognized aspect of the novel, two recent novels invoke the anger (madness) of Bertha Mason and Gilbert and Gubar's feminist take on it with female protagonists who are outwardly "normal": Catherine Lowell, *The Madwoman Upstairs* (New York: Touchstone, 2016) and Claire Messud, *The Woman Upstairs* (New York: A. Knopf, 2013).

[2] Publicity for productions of the play typically include this quotation, for example, online publicity for *Jane Eyre*, a co-production of the National Theatre with Bristol Old Vic, September 26–October 21, 2017, https://www.nationaltheatre.org.uk/shows/jane-eyre (accessed January 11, 2020).

romance narrative. While anger may register more forcefully as one reads *Jane Eyre*, a pervasive sadness quietly accounts for a greater percentage of the whole. It maintains its presence from episode to episode, even as the reader presses on in the dogged hope of happiness—because, after all, it is a romance.

"Crucially," as Pascal Eitler, Stephanie Olsen, and Uffa Jensen assert, "the act of reading is now also acknowledged to engage and engender feelings; texts are not just interpreted, but also 'felt.'"[3] Writers, translators, and adapters and their readers have, of course, long known this. In the German language domain the presence and force of both anger and sadness fluctuated in the transmission of *Jane Eyre*. The ebbing of both emotions in adaptations for girls offers insight into the inflammatory aspect of Brontë's novel and its potential effects on readers. If juvenile literature concerns itself generally with "emotional learning," then these adaptations conformed with this idea in seeing to it that these two emotions were either unlearned or suppressed altogether. While some do present less normative ideas of feminine behavior, allowing for some expression and integration of anger and sadness and thus individualization, most invest in gentling Brontë's heroine or making her stupidly happy; they also set about reining in or simply eliminating the presence of other characters who are at the mercy of their unexamined emotions, among them Mrs. Reed and Bertha. As this chapter will show, anger and sadness matter to the rebellious and redemptive power of this romance narrative; their mitigation undermines it. Apparently German adapters and their publishers knew it and were prepared to do so at the risk of a duller story.

Anger

Anger was male territory. Historian of emotion Ute Frevert points to the belief generally held in the nineteenth century that men were "conquered more by rage, fume and fury."[4] If rage was "an affect of annoyance in its manly vigorous expression," she explains, it had to be inaccessible to women. Yet it was also thought that women, who by nature lacked self-control, could succumb to their own brand of "affects of annoyance," especially a range of angry emotion directed toward inappropriate and mundane objects.[5] Henriette Kühne-Harkort, for example, declared in 1878 regarding petty anger, "Ärger ist der Frauen schlimmster Feind" (anger is women's worst enemy) and offered the unromantic recommendation that women develop a sense of duty (*Pflichtgefühl*) to overcome it.[6] In listing attitudes that prevent girls from being "liebenswürdig"

---

3   Pascal Eitler, Stephanie Olsen, and Uffa Jensen, Introduction, *Learning How to Feel: Children's Literature and Emotional Socialization, 1870–1970*, ed. Ute Frevert et al. (Oxford: Oxford University Press, 2014), 6.

4   Ute Frevert, *Emotions in History—Lost and Found* (Budapest and New York: Central European University Press, 2011), 110.

5   Frevert, *Emotions*, 91. Frevert references the *Allgemeine deutsche Real-Encyklopädie für die gebildeten Stände*, 7th ed. (Leipzig: Brockhaus, 1827), 12: 548.

6   Henriette Kühne-Harkort, "Der Ärger: Vortrag, gehalten im Frauen Gewerbsvereine in Dresden," *Die Dioskuren* 7 (1878): 159, 160. I thank Kaitlin Cruz for bringing this essay to my attention. The most famous pedagogical literary treatment of young women's and girls' anger in the Anglophone domain is of course Louisa May Alcott's *Little Women* (1868/9).

(amiable, lovable), as they should be, the advice book author Johanna von Sydow cited, among other things, insolent speech, contrariness, cantankerousness, nervous irritability, bad moods, arrogance, stubbornness—all qualities suggesting anger. Above all, indulgent "Selbstliebe" (love of self), which permitted such emotion, was the enemy of "Liebenswürdigkeit" (amiability).[7] In discussing anger (*Zorn*), Caroline Milde cautioned against "Ausbrüchen, die der weiblichen Würde zuwider sind" (outbursts that are repugnant to feminine dignity) and thus eschewed both the emotion and the words, in effect, the "boy talk" examined in the preceding chapter.[8] Angry affect, in short, thwarted women's "natural decency and delicacy" and thus endangered the social order.[9] In creating a furious heroine and her furious counterpart Brontë ventured into gender-inappropriate territory.

Pedagogues had anger on their minds in the decades when the Woman Question came prominently into public discourse and when Germans and Austrians were reading German *Jane Eyres*. The same book trade that supported the multiplication of versions of *Jane Eyre* also fueled a burgeoning traffic in advice books such as Sydow's that aimed to enforce cultural norms for the social classes that counted or wanted to count, in particular those social groups that put their faith in upward mobility within a new economic order in which noble birthright per se mattered ever less than access to capital and education.[10] As the proliferation of advice books implies, middle-class girls and women, insofar as they presided over social life, required particular attention. Even as their social roles were naturalized according to the ideology of domesticity and separate spheres and attendant prescriptions for social intercourse, common opinion also held that they were naturally wild and in need of cultural conditioning for both their own and the social good. The emotional vicissitudes of adolescence presented cause for concern, for previously docile girls could suddenly present as angry, defiant, and rude—according to the advice books and fiction of the time. Emmy von Rhoden's (Emmy Friedrich [1829–85]) long-enduring and subsequently much-imitated book, *Der Trotzkopf: Eine Pensionsgeschichte für erwachsene Mädchen* (The Contrary One: A Boarding School Story for Grown-up Girls), may serve as a salient example of then current social norms.[11]

7   Johanna von Sydow, *Behalte mich lieb! Mitgabe beim Eintritt in die Welt und das gesellschaftliche Leben*, Quellen und Schriften zur Geschichte der Frauenbildung 5 (1881; repr., Paderborn: M. Hüttemann, 1989), 117–18.
8   Milde, *Der Deutschen Jungfrau Wesen und Wirken*, 81.
9   Frevert, *Emotions in History*, 110.
10 On German advice books, see Daniela Richter, *Domesticating the Public: Women's Discourse on Gender Roles in Nineteenth-Century German* (Oxford: Peter Lang, 2012).
11 An edition dated 1891 announces itself as the tenth, providing one indication of the popularity of a book that has remained in print in the twenty-first century. Emmy von Rhoden, *Der Trotzkopf. Eine Pensionsgeschichte für erwachsene Mädchen*, 10th ed. (Stuttgart: Gustav Weise, 1891). As one of several present-day publishers of von Rhoden's book, the Belle Époque Publishing House recommends its product for the 12–15 year age group. Emmy von Rhoden, *Der Trotzkopf: Gesamtausgabe* (Dettenhausen, Germany: Belle Époque Verlag, 2015), Produkt Information, https://www.amazon.com/Der-Trotzkopf/dp/3945796415 (accessed January 10, 2020).

Rhoden's novel treats adolescent anger at length. Its title refers to a recalcitrant, sulky fifteen-year-old girl, a character that Franz Hirsch in his introduction to the second edition calls an "ungebändigtes Kind," a child who requires taming, as the English translation of the book title—*Taming a Tomboy*—formulates it.[12] The book invites readers to relish Ilse Macket's silly temper tantrums and her forays into gender- and class-inappropriate behavior; it provides enjoyment via passing liberation from norms. Yet, as it puts Ilse through many social trials, the text does not conceal its pedagogical intent. Hirsch, who apparently believed in its clever pedagogy, declares it "psychologisch wahr" (psychologically true) and capable of enthralling (*fesseln, packen*) youthful hearts and minds.[13]

The all-girl boarding school, not unlike the all-girl orphanage Lowood, provides the setting for repeated shaming. In Rhoden's fictional world, however, shaming brings the heroine's passionate nature under control while preserving her charm.[14] At the same time Ilse forms lasting bonds with the other girls that motivate her to recognize and accept social norms and also to feel empathy. The book presents the boarding school, in the vein of Spitzer's adaptation of *Jane Eyre*, as a benign pedagogical institution, not as the locus of deprivation and unwarranted punishment. Fräulein Güssow, Ilse's most important mentor at the school, bears some resemblance to Brontë's Miss Temple, including the fact that both texts allow their respective pedagogical mothers to marry and move happily from the enforced spinsterhood of the teaching profession to wedded life— and presumably physical motherhood somewhere beyond the book's horizon.

By the conclusion of *Der Trotzkopf*, Ilse has learned to ask for forgiveness, in particular, to ask it of her kind and loving stepmother toward whom she had earlier behaved abominably. She welcomes her new baby brother into the world without a hint of sibling rivalry, and she has, moreover, become sufficiently refined to catch the eye of a class-appropriate marriage partner. The text thus imagines that boarding school has conditioned her for the suppression of ego that marriage and childrearing require.

Sequels provided by von Rhoden's daughter, Else Wildhagen, namely, *Trotzkopf's Brautzeit* (1892; The Contrary One's Engagement) and *Aus Trotzkopf's Ehe* (1895; [Scenes from] the Contrary One's Marriage) make clear that Ilse's spunkiness can still quickly transform into anger and that her inability to manage anger presents an ongoing obstacle to her fulfillment of her proper gender roles. Her quarrel with her fiancé in *Brautzeit* concludes with her again acknowledging and executing the need to ask for forgiveness. The *Trotzkopf* series in the end has it both ways: it provides the reading pleasure of vicariously experienced transgressive anger while it also enforces norms that seek to prevent such emotion.

The original *Jane Eyre*, too, although in a far more complex manner than *Trotzkopf*, allows for anger as an aspect of individualization while at times also enforcing religious and social mores that require mastery of temper and

---

12   Franz Hirsch, Introduction to the 2nd edition (1885), in *Der Trotzkopf*, 10th ed., vi.
13   Hirsch, Introduction, vi.
14   *Mellas Studentenjahr* indicates that contemporaries conflated *Jane Eyre* with boarding school narratives when Mella eagerly seeks out and reads "Pensionsgeschichten" (boarding school stories); *Jane Eyre* numbers among the examples listed (147).

willfulness and thus entail subjectification. Yet Brontë's romance deviates from books of a pedagogical-moralizing bent. While not openly repudiating norms militating against women's anger and effectively accepting men's anger, this romance plot allows its heroine to escape from gender-normative conciliatory behavior. It enables Jane to slough off her failed attempt at a conventional morally dictated reconciliation with Mrs. Reed requiring mastery of anger as she joyously returns to Thornfield. In the subsequent garden scene, it musters anger to allow the heroine to voice her love. Much later, through Rochester's call in the night, romance frees Jane from St John's righteous anger and her inclination to acquiesce to it.

As Coral Ann Howells has observed of Brontë's handling of affect in general, "the novel is very much concerned with exploring feelings and finding the words to describe them precisely, however odd the feelings may be."[15] Howells employs the term "feelings" here rather than "emotions." In linking feelings to words, she invokes a distinction that will serve the investigation of unsanctioned emotion in this chapter: through narrative, by "finding words," Brontë's Jane raises to consciousness what is raw and involuntary, that is, emotion, and makes of it feeling. Howells's evocation of D. H. Lawrence's sense of writing as a "struggle for verbal consciousness," an analytical attempt "to know and to understand even what is happening in himself," further supports distinguishing between emotions and feelings.[16] While the inarticulate Bertha is denied that possibility and thus remains (gender-)inappropriately furious and thus pure emotion, the novel grants the articulate Jane (and her readers) a luxurious sojourn in developing female subjectivity. Subjectivity begins when emotion is expressed in language and reflected upon as *feeling*. Bringing emotion into language, of course, also subjects it to social conditioning—and the novel struggles with that fact.

Jane's response in the book's opening pages to the illustrations in Bewick's *A History of British Birds* registers the oddness and dis-ease of unarticulated emotion: "Each picture told a story; mysterious often to my undeveloped understanding and imperfect feelings" (11), the narrator reports, naming the two capacities that will figure importantly in her future—understanding and feeling—and that she will ultimately be able to describe. The narrator thus from the start invokes her need to activate her imagination, to name and express emotion as feeling. This need informs her narration of her romance.

Jane twice explicitly insists on the existence of her feelings—and thus her personhood—in angry moments when, so it appears to her, others cannot imagine that she has them. "You think I have no feelings" (35), Jane protests to Mrs. Reed. "Do you think I am an automaton?—a machine without feelings?" (227) Jane later asks Rochester. Brontë's text not only makes room for experiencing anger but also ultimately describes and manages it. It liberates its heroine and articulating subject (and the reader) by bringing it to expression and then controls, organizes, and integrates this emotion as feeling through language in

---

15   Coral Ann Howells, *Love, Mystery, and Misery: Feeling in Gothic Fiction* (London: Athlone Press, 1978), 162.
16   Howells, *Love, Mystery*, 161.

autobiography and conversation in marriage. German adaptations for girls, however, display discomfort and awkwardness with anger and find an array of narrative solutions for handling it, many of which deviate from the tenor of the original English and some of which involve eliding this emotion altogether.

Jane is, of course, not merely a subject who expresses anger but also its suffering object. To consider both positions as pertinent to the purchase of romance, we turn to three auxiliary characters—Mrs. Reed, St John, and Bertha Mason. Jane's relationship to all three makes visible the compelling structures of romance as they allow for anger, but also provide liberation from it, a way to diffuse this emotion and recalibrate social positioning. An examination of German adaptations for girls will reveal, in turn, how adapters (as opposed to translators) handled anger differently and thus reconfigured Jane in keeping with social norms.

As Jane's perhaps most unpleasant and intentional tormentor, Mrs. Reed does not invite reader sympathy. The character, nevertheless, deserves a closer—even sympathetic—look in our context, for she, like Bertha, whom literary criticism has accorded ample revisionist readings, suffers to her dying day from anger. Although Jane does attempt a reconciliation with her, the text paints a harsh picture of Mrs. Reed, one that emerges from her inability to love her niece as she does her own children, her failure overall at motherhood, and her unchecked penchant to pour out her wrath on the vulnerable Jane. Although in some respects hewing to the fairy-tale cliché of the wicked stepmother, the original novel in the end renders Mrs. Reed in rich detail to accord her a more complex role in Jane's emotional life than first meets the eye.

The deceased Mr. Reed took in his sister's child and commanded her to care for her as if she were one of her own. Not only this circumstance but also her prejudice against this child of a misalliance and her anger toward her husband for not sharing it fuel Mrs. Reed's cruelty. Even its chief victim, Jane, rationalizes it as a form of tribalism:

> but how could she really like an interloper not of her race, and unconnected with her, after her husband's death, by any tie? It must have been most irksome to find herself bound by a hard-wrung pledge to stand in the stead of a parent to a strange child she could not love, and to see an uncongenial alien permanently intruded on her own family group. (17)

While the events of the first chapter—rendered in melodramatic tones—establish this character in her villainous role as a furious, ill-tempered woman and as a foil to implied social ideals, grown-up Jane is later prepared to forgive her.

Chapters later, Jane, in harmony with that same (Christian) ideal, returns to rationalizing Mrs. Reed's behavior. Recalling the incident that led to her being banished to the red room, she muses, "Yes, Mrs. Reed, to you I owe some fearful pangs of mental suffering, but I ought to forgive you, for you knew not what you did: while rending my heart-strings, you thought you were only uprooting my bad propensities" (20–1). But she also remembers that her every attempt to please Mrs. Reed and her careful obedience were "repulsed and repaid" by angry misplaced criticism (33). These mixed feelings are straightforward enough, and in keeping with Mrs. Reed's surface function in the story, they support a social norm that dictates forgiveness. This portrait of an angry woman, however, fig-ures in the romance narrative in more complex ways. Among other things, it exhibits parallels to the portrait of Rochester. These merit closer consideration.

In the novel's opening scene, Mrs. Reed is the same age as is Rochester when Jane first meets him—thirty-six or thirty-seven. Mrs. Reed shares his strong square build; moreover, "she had a somewhat large face, the under jaw being much developed and very solid; her brow was low, her chin large and promi-nent, mouth and nose sufficiently regular; under her light eyebrows glimmered an eye devoid of ruth; her skin was dark and opaque, her hair nearly flaxen; her constitution was sound as a bell ..." (34). While her hair is fair, her large-featured masculine face is dark—as is Rochester's face.

Upon the arrival years later of Blanche Ingram at Thornfield, Jane notes a resemblance to Mrs. Reed: "She had, likewise, a fierce and a hard eye: it reminded me of Mrs. Reed's; she mouthed her words in speaking; her voice was deep, its inflections very pompous, very dogmatical,—very intolerable, in short" (155-6). But Jane also believes Blanche and Rochester perfectly physically matched—not physical opposites as she herself and Rochester are. What she finds intolerable in Blanche (and by extension in Mrs. Reed), attracts her in Rochester.

The narrator describes the face of the moribund Mrs. Reed: "stern, relent-less as ever—there was that peculiar eye which nothing could melt, and the somewhat raised, imperious, despotic eyebrow. How often had it lowered on me menace and hate! and how the recollection of childhood's terrors and sor-rows revived as I traced its harsh line now!" (207). This strong face, the harsh, stern, imperious, despotic brow so capable of menace, anger, and hate—one has seen this unattractive face elsewhere in the novel. Refashioned, desiring and acknowledging, and placed atop a differently gendered body, it is Rochester's face and has long since become an object of fascination.

The narrative affirms an affinity between Jane's nemesis and her true love when, after viewing Mrs. Reed on her deathbed, she begins idly sketching:

> Soon I had traced on the paper a broad and prominent forehead and a square lower outline of visage: that contour gave me pleasure; my fingers proceeded actively to fill it with features. Strongly-marked horizontal eyebrows must be traced under that brow; then followed, naturally, a well-defined nose, with a straight ridge and full nostrils; then a flexible-looking mouth, by no means narrow; then a firm chin, with a decided cleft down the middle of it: of course, some black whiskers were wanted, and some jetty hair, tufted on the temples, and waved above the forehead. Now for the eyes: I had left them to the last, because they required the most careful working. I drew them large; I shaped them well: the eyelashes I traced long and sombre; the irids lustrous and large. (210)

Mrs. Reed and Rochester are certainly not identical, but they are proximate, two sides of a coin. Mrs. Reed offers only a "stony eye," a mortifying stare, when Jane attempts reconciliation, while Jane thrills to Rochester's vivifying gaze in the "lustrous" eyes she depicts here. It does not require a revisionist sentimen-tal understanding of Mrs. Reed to recognize that gender shapes the narrator's judgment of anger—it reads as strongly negative in Mrs. Reed, Bertha Mason, and Jane's younger self and as attractive in male characters (both Rochester and St John).

At Lowood, Helen Burns presciently observes that Mrs. Reed has had a profound impact on Jane. While one might expect her to encourage forgiveness, the pious Helen instead urges Jane to forget Mrs. Reed, thus pointing to a psychological problem rather than a moral one. Jane's two principal relationships—to Mrs. Reed and to Rochester—in fact exhibit structural similarities. Like Mrs. Reed, Rochester submits Jane to questioning; he issues commands that Jane, eager to please, obeys with her humble "yes sir." Immediately after Mrs. Reed's death and Jane's failure to receive Mrs. Reed's forgiveness and upon Jane's return to Thornfield, Rochester again indulges in tormenting Jane to test her feelings. As in the above-mentioned early scene with Mrs. Reed, when sufficiently goaded, Jane again bursts out in anger, protesting that she has feelings. The romance thus initially seems fated to reproduce childhood structures. Language and the self-awareness it facilitates, however, take it in a different direction. In the end, Jane talks back and is not judged, but heard.

Both the anger of others and her own shape Jane's social relationships and that structure matters to her subject formation—the arc of the text makes this clear. Rochester's angry address to the world catches her attention upon their very first meeting, and her admiration and fear of St John's (self-)righteous anger plays no small role in her protracted inability to refuse his marriage proposal. Romance plotting eventually and importantly enables Jane to free herself from her too-ready submission to the anger of others and allows her legitimately to express her own. After she does what she can and should at Mrs. Reed's deathbed, the text quickly drops the idea of duty and proceeds to the marriage proposal in the garden. There Jane in effect follows Helen's dictum to forget Mrs. Reed while recalibrating her address to the world via heterosexual desire. Yet anger will shortly explode again in Bertha, in Rochester's revelations, and St John's coercion.

An easy way to keep the anger that courses through the original from younger readers is to avoid it. As one example of avoidance, the anonymous adaptation based on the 1854 adaptation of Fort that appeared with Bartels eliminates the deathbed scene. Here, a black-bordered envelope arrives to inform Jane of Mrs. Reed's death. It also contains John Eyre's letter and, as Jane observes, proof that Mrs. Reed disliked her to the end. Still this Jane finds mitigating circumstances for Mrs. Reed's bad behavior in the latter's misfortune. Mrs. Reed's feelings toward Jane, the narrator supposes, stem from her suffering on account of the actions and early death of her adored son. With this supposition, the narrator quickly dispatches her and moves on. Mrs. Reed's death provides the occasion neither for the potentially salutary return to the primal scene of anger and torment, as in the original, nor for the sentimental reconciliation that several adaptations for girls favor.

On the whole, German adaptations for younger readers render Mrs. Reed less incurably angry; they soften or eliminate confrontational scenes with her, thereby obscuring the dynamics of self-formation and liberation that inform the romance of the original. Wachler, following Birch-Pfeiffer, for example, has the

Reeds turn up at Thornfield, but John Reed—and not his mother—assumes the role of chief villain in this episode. John's bad behavior reaps reproach even from his mother. Ultimately, Jane and Rochester tactfully come to Mrs. Reed's financial aid as a sign of reconciliation.

These adaptations, on some level, in fact seek to reunite Jane with her aunt and thus tend toward a regression that deflates the angry power of the romance. The deathbed episode again is a case in point. Spitzer and Wedding reconcile Jane and the dying Mrs. Reed. Spitzer's Catholic Jane invokes her religion, which teaches that the dying, whatever their sins in life, deserve comfort in death: "die arme verlassene und verstossene Waise soll Kindespflicht an einer sterbenden Mutter üben, die von ihren eigenen Kindern verlassen und selbst des Trostes beraubt ist, von denselben betrauert und beweint zu werden" (Sp 153; the poor abandoned and outcast orphan ought to do her filial duty to a dying mother who has been abandoned by her own children and is robbed of even the comfort of being mourned and bewept by them). Their reunion becomes a protracted account of regret and forgiveness in which Mrs. Reed seems as much a victim as a perpetrator. The episode ends with Jane praying with Mrs. Reed in her arms until the latter dies. Mrs. Reed's change of heart preserves the heroine from rehearsing her own earlier anger and she thus quits Gateshead, pious and good.

Wedding likewise enacts reconciliation. The sight of Mrs. Reed's white hair moves Jane immediately to call her "aunt" once again: "Mein Herz wurde weich bei dem Anblick, alle schrecklichen Erinnerungen, welche sich für mich an dieses Antlitz knüpften, gingen in dem innigsten Mitgefühl unter ..." (We 191; my heart softened at the sight, all the terrible memories that I associated with this countenance faded in the most fervent sympathy), the narrator reports. In their final encounter, Mrs. Reed's face has changed and assumed the mien of the kind woman she should have been: as she strokes Jane's cheek, "ihr sonst so strenges Auge blickte so milde, wie ich es nie zuvor gesehen" (We 195; her once such stern eyes assumed such a kind expression as I had never before seen them do). Mrs. Reed fears meeting her husband in the afterlife since she broke her promise to him to care for Jane as if she were her own. When she confesses that she has withheld John Eyre's letter with news of her inheritance, Jane is temporarily overcome with "Entrüstung und Erbitterung" (We 197; outrage and bitterness). Wedding, however, quickly moves the episode along to make it the occasion of Jane's overcoming of anger and subsequent reconciliation with her oldest tormentor. Upon seeing the countenance of her aunt, which was suffused with fear, and her arms, which were outstretched with longing, the narrator can do nothing after all but embrace and forgive her. Although invoking anger, the episode enacts a triumphant overcoming of it: "Du wirst es begreifen, lieber Leser, wenn ich Dir sage, daß ich dort hart mit mir zu ringen hatte, um allen Groll, alle Bitterkeit in mir niederzukämpfen, welche die Enthüllungen meiner Tante in mir wachgerufen hatten, aber ich kämpfte tapfer und gewann den Sieg ..." (We 197; You'll understand it, dear reader, if I tell you that I had to struggle with myself there to fight back all the anger, all the bitterness in me that the revelations of my aunt awakened in me, but I fought bravely and won ...). Standing before Mrs. Reed's corpse, Wedding's virtuous Jane notes that suffering has softened the angry lines of her face and, reconciled, she kisses the dead woman's hand. This conflict resolved, Wedding abandons any attempt at psychological depth and proceeds to the happy ending via a geographical detour. Jane departs for Madeira to do her duty and tend to her sick uncle until Rochester fetches her there.

Reichard, for her part, retains the bitterness of Mrs. Reed's death, borrowing in this scene verbatim from Borch's translation: "leidenschaftlich, aber nicht boshaft" (R 175; passionate but not malicious). While there is no hint of turning the other cheek, the narrative thereafter tidily puts the theme of anger aside by omitting Bertha, St John's holy mission, and Rochester as love interest. Reichhardt and Hartung, by contrast, retain the bitterness of the death scene and the circulation of anger in the critical unfolding of the romance plot that immediately follows.

While Reichard does render her heroine slightly more conciliatory, as in the original, Jane remains dry-eyed in the face of Mrs. Reed's death. For her part, Hartung, who overall remains the truest of the girls' adapters to the plot and the liberatory values of the original, also leaves little room for reconciliation. Yet this Jane manages her earlier anger perfectly. As in the original, standing at Mrs. Reed's deathbed, she perceives that her own hatred has softened with the passage of time: her heart knew nothing more of the old rancor: "Ich fühlte Mitleid mit dem großen Leid, das ihr Sohn über sie gebracht, ich hegte das innige Verlangen, alles Unrecht zu vergeben, mich mit ihr auszusöhnen, an Stelle der alten Feindschaft Freundschaft treten zu lassen" (Ha 111; I felt sympathy with the great suffering that her son had brought upon her, I cherished the fervent desire to forgive everything, to reconcile with her, to allow friendship to replace the old enmity). When, however, she realizes that Mrs. Reed's feelings have not changed, she painfully experiences a resurgence of anger only swiftly to repress it; she resolves to conquer Mrs. Reed's stubbornness through kindness (Ha 112). But even in allowing that sentimental gesture, Hartung, like Reichhardt, thereafter conforms with the original in employing the return to Thornfield and Rochester's marriage proposal in the garden to dispel any lingering thoughts of past social obligation.

Only Hartung and Reichhardt, who have allowed the bitterness of the death scene, also include the proposal in the garden. They thereby reproduce the possibility aired in the original that adult desire may show the effects of childhood suffering from the anger of others but also sublate them. In the original, Jane says of herself, "I know no medium: I never in my life have known any medium in my dealings with positive, hard characters, antagonistic to my own, between absolute submission and determined revolt. I have always faithfully observed the one, up to the very moment of bursting sometimes with volcanic vehemence, into the other ..." (357). Without Jane's angry protest in the garden, we have no repetition of the tense opposition between submission and revolt; without revolt, we lose Jane's articulation of the conversation of equals as the principal difference between her troubled relationship with Mrs. Reed and her amorous one with Rochester.

It is not a sentimental deathbed scene that frees Jane from past anger but rather the modulation of Jane's angry outburst in the garden to the declaration

"I have talked face to face with what I reverence; with what I delight in ..." (227). Both Hartung and Reichhardt and three of the translators preserve this declaration in minute detail:

> S 2:138: Ich habe von Angesicht zu Angesicht mit dem geredet, was ich verehre, woran ich Freude empfinde;
> G 2:79: Ich habe von Antlitz zu Antlitz mit dem gesprochen, was ich verehre; mit dem, was mir Entzücken macht.
> B 401; Rt 237: Ich habe von Angesicht zu Angesicht mit dem reden können, was ich verehre;

Even having just labeled Rochester her "Gebieter" (master), Hartung's Jane too speaks of conversation face to face: "Ich habe von Angesicht zu Angesicht zu ihm reden dürfen" (124; I was allowed to speak to him face to face). And while Heinrich does not quite manage to express the idea of parity in his paraphrase "Ich konnte mit einem Manne sprechen, den ich verehrte" (3:98; I could speak with a man whom I revered), his rendering—like the other three—nevertheless retains the idea of speaking to the object of desire as it displaces the binary of submission to or revolt against angry others. The victory is, however, only temporary.

Jane's near acquiescence to St John further on in the text again illustrates the enduring power of the anger of others and the power of romance to release its couple from it. St John of the chiseled face and righteous male anger proves hard to resist. Nevertheless, while Jane the narrator admires his sense of mission, she also enables readers to perceive the noxiousness of the obdurate anger that sustains it and leads him to subordinate the feelings and needs of others to accomplish it. Jane appears on the verge of falling into old patterns of obeying and trying to please when she finds herself on the verge of submitting to his insistence that she marry him to support his missionary work. In lending him a handsome, hard face, the text makes visible the attraction of righteous anger when located in a powerful male character. For a character structured in a binary fashion as Jane claims to be—either absolute submission or revolt—revolt, it seems, must be prompted from without to block socially dictated, internalized obedience. For this reason, the nocturnal voice is crucial; it calls Jane from without to abandon submission and turn to conversation, life, love, sex, and procreation.

St John's anger, while located in the "proper" gender—as opposed to Mrs. Reed's and Bertha's—receives varied treatment in German adaptation. These adaptations often tone down or elide his anger or eliminate the character altogether, resulting in a less psychologically complex narrative. By discounting or eliminating St John, they avoid depicting the questionable dynamic of his coercive anger and in most cases make Rochester Jane's only possible destiny.

Spitzer omits the section with the Rivers, as do Wachler, Reichhardt, Wedding, and the truncated Bartels version. Reichard, as we have seen, rewrites the ending to keep Jane at Moor House with no thoughts of St John or India whatsoever and certainly none of anger. Bartels's uncut edition retains the St John episode, but deviates from its source text, the adaptation of Fort of 1854. It enables Jane to refuse his proposition in firm and sober language while it omits the voice that calls her name in the night. By eliding her struggle to keep from submitting to St John's anger, it bypasses the disruption and liberating possibilities of romance. Stieff's adaptation, for its part, significantly alters the story to make St John, here called Johannes, the heroine's only and unproblematic choice. Johanna does not need to be coerced to marry her cousin and the two joyfully set off for Calcutta.

Of the adaptations marketed to girls, Hartung alone remains true to Brontë via Borch's translation. She retains the socially and psychologically disruptive power of romance when her adaptation allows Jane to hear Rochester's voice calling her name in the night, which liberates her from St John's spellbinding zeal. By also retaining St John's pious farewell note, which in effect communicates that he knows that desire has kept her from submitting to his plan—"Der Geist war willig, aber das Fleisch blieb schwach" (Ha 216; The spirit was willing, but the flesh remained weak)—Hartung underscores for her girl readers the attraction of the alternative to obedience to the will of angry others, that is, romantic coupling based on parity.

And what of the "fury," the famously angry Bertha? Scholarship has highlighted the contrastive pair of the articulate narrator and marital conversation and the inarticulate madwoman and lack of "kindly conversation." It is now well understood that the two represent two sides of the same angry coin. Bertha's anger becomes especially pertinent to a consideration of the treatment of Brontë's unsanctioned emotion in German adaptations for girls because of the tendency, similar to that described above in the treatment of Mrs. Reed and St John, to eliminate her from the story or to make her less angry and more human or to rewrite her altogether.

Five adaptations either completely elide Bertha (Stieff, Spitzer, Reichard) or soften her by making her Rochester's sister-in-law instead of his wife (Wachler, Wedding). They thereby erase the link of the angry voice of the narrator to a madwoman, both of whom are labeled furies in the original, a double designation retained only by Reichhardt (Rt 12, 195). As Rochester's sister-in-law, the character becomes far less dangerous to the couple's happiness; her presence in the castle bears witness not to Rochester's flaws but his virtues in caring for a sister-in-law whom he himself had once loved. If Aimée (Beloved) remains mad in Wedding's adaptation, it is only because of the great love she felt for Rochester's dead brother. Her penchant for arson arises, so the text improbably asserts, from her wish to "warm up" Rochester whom she mistakes for her dead husband (We 185). Wachler, following Birch-Pfeiffer, likewise transforms Bertha into Rochester's sister-in-law, Harriet Durham. Harriet abandoned Rochester for his older brother, Arthur, who married her. Later on she abandoned him too. Maddened by her hatred for her husband, she persists even after his death in hating Rochester whom she mistakes for him. To Jane's question as to whether she could not be housed elsewhere, the virtuous Rochester replies that he is duty bound to keep her at Thornfield.

The omission, diminishment, or redirection of Bertha's fury goes hand in hand with the reduction of Gothic elements. Reichhardt, true to his promise to minimize such sensation elements, continues in this vein. His Rochester tells Jane about his past up front and succinctly, eliminating mystery and menace.

No viewing of Bertha takes place, and thereafter Rochester's wife conveniently slips and falls on the stairs, breaking her neck and freeing him to propose to Jane. Reichhardt's version of the novel can therefore grant Jane her happy ending right after Mr. Rochester's proposal. No hidden madwoman or charismatic missionary intervenes to confront her with moral dilemmas, and the novel simply concludes with a view of Jane and Rochester's unproblematically harmonious marriage: their characters are exactly suited to one another; "folglich herrscht die vollkommenste Übereinstimmung zwischen uns" (Rt 240; consequently, the most perfect harmony prevails between us).

Eliding Bertha, repositioning her, or omitting her most deplorable aspects avoids compelling insights generated by her link to the narrator. Having lost her reason and possessing no interiority, Bertha exhibits unvarnished emotion on the surface in her tangled black hair, purple face, and frenetic scrambling on all fours. Pale Jane by contrast possesses well-cultivated feelings so delicate and guarded that Rochester must prise them from her. The German adaptations for girls appear reluctant to endorse either emotional woman—the dispossessed madwoman or the eloquently self-possessed, yet still angry, narrator. Instead, they tell a relatively simple, sometimes overtly didactic, story, in which good and patient Jane is ultimately rewarded either with an uncomplicated marriage to Rochester or in Reichard's version with a full life with the Rivers cousins or in Stieff's version with a virtuous life as a missionary's wife. Without Bertha, they avoid the near bigamy and the decision Jane makes to do what is morally right against her acknowledged feelings for Rochester, a decision she later reverses when she returns to Thornfield. In the aggregate, these plots invite more sentimentality and flirt less with the morally and psychologically suspect and the sexually charged, the "human and fallible" (126) so important to Brontë's original.

Of the two that retain Bertha, Hartung's handling of her deserves more attention, since this adaptation as a whole invests in delivering the full story to its young readers and tends overall not to retreat from sensitive material. In the matter of Bertha, however, through careful abridgment, omission, and rewriting, Hartung does avoid the issues that her presence and condition raise.

In keeping with her mitigated telling of Bertha's story, Hartung slightly reduces the shock value of the viewing of her. For one thing, she removes the word "bigamy" from the text, although the threat remains. For another, she somewhat humanizes and thus softens Bertha: Bertha wears "menschliche Kleider" (Ha 140; human clothes) rather than being described as "mit Kleidern behängt" (B 467; draped in clothes); instead of the "wilde Mähne" (B 467; wild mane), "menschliches Haar" (Ha 140; human hair) hangs from her head. While a "menschliche Hyäne" (Ha 141; human hyena) does throw itself on Rochester, Hartung writes, "Das tierische Weib, das zuerst auf allen Vieren herumgekrochen war, erhob sich und stand groß und gewaltig vor uns" (Ha 140; The bestial woman, who at first crawled around on all fours, raised itself up and stood great and powerful before us), making of her a "Weib" (woman), while Borch foregrounds only the raging animal: "Die angekleidete Hyäne erhob sich und stand groß und gewaltig auf ihren Hinterfüßen" (B 467; The clothed hyena raised itself up and stood great and powerful on its hind legs). While Borch's Rochester invites the viewers to compare Jane's clear eyes with Bertha's "rollenden Feuerkugeln" (B 468; rolling balls of fire), her face with the "graueneinflößenden Maske" (B 469; horrifying mask), her form with the "Klumpen" (B 469; clump) and then dare to judge him, Hartung's Rochester simply invites them to compare without naming grotesque features.

The Bartels edition, as does the entire Fort strain, also allows young readers a look at Bertha. This narrator opens the scene with the information that Bertha paced back and forth like a wild animal in its cage, a "Geschöpf, ohne menschliche Gestalt und ohne Namen" (creature without a human form and without a name); this was the "rechtmäßige Gebieterin des Schlosses" (Ba 217; legitimate lady of the manor). In this version, Jane stresses degeneration and lack of language while also referring to Bertha's being held prisoner and invoking her rights as Rochester's wife. This last statement brings to the surface the Bluebeard aspect of the story—the captive woman—and hence a note of Bertha's victimization. When, moreover, one of the Bartels versions for girls ends in the middle of the novel when Jane leaves Thornfield, it does not allow Bertha to unleash her full fury in a conflagration, making it more difficult to see her as purely evil.

When anger recedes or even vanishes on all these fronts, as it does in most of these versions for girls, readers encounter a narrative in which human relations involve much less struggle, disruption, and emotional ambiguity, one that permits the easy normalization of these fictional others—even Bertha. At the same time, adaptation that softens and in effect censors the original confirms its potential in this time period to unsettle and destabilize and thus construct and configure an Otherwise. The four translated versions of Brontë's novel, which for the most part retain the anger of the original, remained, however, for sale to accomplish precisely that re-vision.

Sadness

As the female protagonist of *Mellas Studentenjahr* suspects, her mother did not want her to read *Jane Eyre*. While her initial sighing over Rochester, as noted in Chapter 3, implies that her mother's likely prohibition has to do with sex, the book soon forgets Mella's fascination with the dark hero of Brontë's novel to worry over her general state of mind, her penchant for sadness—her tendency not just to experience it but, more alarming in this pedagogical context, to relish it.

Mella looks up from *Jane Eyre* to stare into space. Her reading inspires her to compose sad verses in her head, a pastime that she calls her "Wonne" (joy), only to have her mother reject it as piddling away time and her brother ridicule it as "geistige Trucksucht" (8; spiritual alcoholism). The beginning of a new poem paraphrases the tones of suffering of Heinrich Heine's "Mein Herz, mein Herz ist traurig/ doch lustig leuchtet der Mai" (1827; My heart, my heart is sad/ But May is shining gaily): Mella writes, "Mein Herz mein Herz ist dunkel/ Doch draußen leuchtet der Mai—" (8; My heart, my heart is dark/ But outside May is shining). She then stops short when she cannot find a word to rhyme with "dunkel." Another attempt at writing lachrymose verses meets a poetic impasse when she can only think of "Kohl" (cabbage) as a rhyme for "wohl" (well) and "hohl" (empty).[17] A pubescent appetite for melancholy, it seems, infuses both her writing and her desire for the gloomy Rochester.

Sadness shadows Mella throughout the year running up to her sixteenth birthday. A visit to Cologne Cathedral finds her articulating aesthetic experience in terms of sadness: "Siehst du, ich muß bei allem was ich am schönsten finde, immer etwas haben, was ich gar nicht begreifen kann, oder wonach ich mich sehne, bis zum Traurigwerden" (66; You see, with the things I find the most beautiful I always need something I can't comprehend or I long for to the point of becoming sad). Her friend Juliette worries that if this is so, Mella can never really be happy. Mella claims to manage her sadness and vague longings by writing poetry. But, as she also confesses, poems do not come easily to her. The text thereby raises the possibility that her sadness is superficial, transient, or misplaced.

Further down the Rhine, she must be coaxed from her lonely spot on a cliff where she weeps as she labors under an "unverstandene, ziellose Sehnsucht" (87; uncomprehended, aimless longing) like the lyrical subject in Heine's "Lorelei" who does not know the meaning of his sadness. The text never actually names the poem, but it clearly haunts the episode. The story proves slightly mean on the subject of such sadness when Mella is told here to put her faith instead in the potato fields that have grown over the spot where the Lorelei once sang.

While repudiating sadness, the pedagogical program of the book demands joy. Mella's mother, unaware of her daughter's surreptitious reading, rejoices at the sight of Mella and Juliette: both girls are "froh und glücklich" (cheerful and happy)—as they should be (17). When Mella disapproves of a smiling nun on board the ship, her mother remonstrates, "Das beste Christentum ist: gute Werke thun und einen fröhlichen Glauben haben" (71; The best Christianity is doing good works and having a cheerful faith). As readers learn over the course of the novel, young women are meant to be cheerful and happy—and not sad. Mella's reading and writing need to change to produce just such a young lady.

Schulze-Smitt was by no means a lone voice in prescribing cheerfulness for girls. The long-time editor and writer for children and adolescents Thekla von Gumpert, for example, underscored this sentiment in 1894, when she articulated the purpose of her annually appearing, religiously informed publication for girls: "Das 'Töchter-Album' möchte die Jugend frisch und fröhlich erhalten" (The "Daughters Album" would like to keep youth buoyant and cheerful).[18] Of course, romance could offer joy too, but Gumpert and others circumvent precisely those joys.

---

[17]   Here she may take inspiration from Nikolaus Lenau's poem "Die Mutter am Grabe ihres Kindes" (The Mother at the Grave of her Child), whose first line ends "wie kalt braust der Wind" (how cold the wind blows). Nikolaus Lenau, *Sämtliche Werke und Briefe* (Frankfurt am Main: Insel, [1971]), 1: 448.

[18]   Thekla von Gumpert, "Bilder aus dem Leben," *Töchter-Album: Unterhaltungen im häuslichen Kreise zur Bildung des Verstandes und Gemütes der heranwachsenden weiblichen Jugend* 40 (1894): 90.

In *Mellas Studentenjahr* reading *Jane Eyre* embodies the pedagogical problem involved in shepherding an adolescent girl into her seventeenth year. When Mella stuffs her diary along with *Jane Eyre* into the secret drawer of her desk, the novel marks the proximity of two elements of subject formation, reading and self-expression. By the end of the novel, the text and Mella have forgotten *Jane Eyre*, and diary writing reveals no secret feelings that would elicit the disapproval of Mella's mother. The book closes with Mella writing in her diary with her favorite doll, which she must soon give up, lying across her knees. Instead of sad poems, she composes a happy account of her sixteenth birthday, one that, since she can now write in a straight line, does not require lined paper. She has straightened her room and she and Juliet have happily amused themselves with her dolls: "Eigentlich sollte ich's wohl nicht mehr thun, aber ich kann's nicht helfen—ich mag es noch gar zu gern! Wir haben es hinter der verschlossenen Thür gethan, und es schadet doch auch wirklich nicht!—Heute bin ich ja erst sechzehn Jahr!" (302; Actually we probably shouldn't do it any more, but I can't help it—I so like doing it! We did it behind closed doors, and it really doesn't do any harm—I'm, after all, only [turning] sixteen today!). Twenty-nine dashes over two print rows follow, recalling the eighteen dashes that open the novel as Mella frets over the blank page of her first diary.

As amusing and charming as girls playing dolls on the cusp of adulthood may be for some readers, the text in the end has collapsed the melancholy imagination of this expressive girl into an account of giddy regression followed by silence. In the closing pages of the book, Mella does not reiterate the ideal she had once expressed in incipient rebellion: "Fertig sein, erwachsen sein, niemand mehr gehorchen müssen" (2; Being finished, being grownup, not having to obey anymore). Happily, on her sixteenth birthday, a sexless Mella must only conceal playing with dolls. She has no thoughts of disobedience; above all, she is no longer sad. The novel's pedagogy thus reduces Mella's initial expression of subjectivity *through* emotion, *in* affective language, and *as* feelings to approved conformity in mundane writing or outright regression.

The joy of romance comes with sadness. As Regis asserts of romance in general, such plots always reach a point of ritual death, when "the union between heroine and hero, the hoped-for resolution, seems absolutely impossible, when it seems that the barrier will remain, more substantial than ever."[19] We certainly reach that moment on Jane and Rochester's first wedding day when near bigamy comes to light and again when Jane returns to Thornfield to find it burned to the ground. But shades of sadness suffuse *Jane Eyre* from beginning to end, often interwoven with anger and proving the dominant register in signature episodes. We hear notes of sadness from the moment when the lonely child on a dreary November day withdraws from her miserable existence at Gateshead to lose herself in a book behind a curtain. Sadness persists to the very end, despite the happy marriage, when Jane writes of the solitary zealot St John who expects that he will soon be called to his Maker.

---

[19] Regis, *A Natural History*, 35.

When Jane is banished to the red room, even rebellious fury turns to sadness: "My habitual mood of humiliation, self-doubt, forlorn depression, fell damp on the embers of my decaying ire" (17). The four translators capture this comment, translating "forlorn depression" quite accurately as "trostlose Niedergeschlagenheit" (S 1:17) or "Trostlosigkeit und Niedergeschlagenheit" (G 1:16), and somewhat more distantly as "Drückendes meiner Lage" (H 1:17; the things in my situation that oppress me) or "hilflose Traurigkeit" (B 18; helpless sadness), and "ire" as "Zorn" (S 1:17, G 1:16, H 1:17) or "Wut" (B 18). A note of sadness also sounds upon the death of Mrs. Reed. As Jane reports, despite her own acquired self-control and good intentions, the riven relationship of aunt and foster-mother with niece and foster-child is not to be mended.

Sad events may sadden readers, but in this novel both Jane and Rochester struggle with a pervasive existential sadness; Howells speaks of Brontë's depiction of "mild depression" (160).[20] As Jane reflects on the injustice of her treatment at Gateshead, she seeks words to grasp her situation as a displaced orphan and thus invokes the anger and profound sadness that suffuse the novel. She feels a "consternation of soul," her "brain [is] in tumult" and her "heart in insurrection"—she fights a "mental battle" in "darkness" and "dense ignorance" (17). The four translators retain the passage in full, including the child Jane's inability to answer the question as to why she suffered.

Brontë's text offers many subsequent occasions for Jane to be sad as an unacknowledged displaced person. As she matures, occasions for sadness mount: her shaming at Lowood and Helen's death, the unexpected appearance of a beautiful rival in the form of Blanche Ingram, the death of Mrs. Reed and enduring estrangement, the departure from Thornfield and lonely trek across the moor, the discovery of the destruction of Thornfield and Rochester's maiming, and the news of St John's imminent demise. But the narrator also presents herself with a penchant for sadness, when she takes stock of her situation or the very fact of mortality. When Helen speaks to her of an invisible world beyond, it calms her, but with this peace comes an "inexpressible sadness"—"unaussprechliche Traurigkeit" (S 1:88; G 2:103), "unbeschreibliche Traurigkeit" (H 1:110), "unsägliche Traurigkeit" (B 104)—whose origins Jane cannot identify (65). The German translators faithfully reproduce Jane's struggle here and elsewhere to allow the adult Jane to give expression to what the young Jane can often only sense. Jane will again speak of "unaussprechliche Traurigkeit" (S 3:81; G 2:245)/ "unbeschreibliche Traurigkeit" (B 563) in connection with St John's inner turmoil and Calvinist leanings.

Jane's solitary reading in the opening chapter and her odd drawings likewise point to melancholy. Her peculiar enjoyment of the lugubrious illustrations of Bewick's *Birds* presages the three drawings of her own creation, drawings that tell of death and despair. When Rochester asks whether she was happy when she drew these pictures, she affirms, "I was absorbed, sir: yes, and I was happy" (116). Jane, it appears, does have something in common with young Mella in experiencing as a feature of the creative imagination a sadness that is also a joy;

---

20   Howells, *Love, Mystery*, 160.

indeed, this saturnine creative disposition underpins the romance of intelligibility and sympathy that drives this narrative.

A "distant reading" of the four principal German translations underscores this intertwining of sadness, imagination, and romance.[21] In all four, occurrences and repetitions of words expressing sadness, such as *Weh, Kummer, Traurigkeit, Klagen, Weinen, bedrückt, freudlos* (pain, worry, sadness, lament, crying, glum, joyless) cluster and spike in the middle section of the novel, which takes place at Thornfield and recounts Jane's growing attachment to Rochester, the discovery of the hidden first wife, and Jane's decision to leave. Sadness accompanies desiring; in romance generally and here particularly, desiring excavates what is "blocked, submerged, endungeoned." The "most wonderful thing" that would assuage sadness lies for long stretches of this novel beyond reach. Borch's repetitions of "hilflos" in both the "hilflose Traurigkeit" (B 18) that Jane experiences in the red room and "ohnmächtigen, hilflosen Zorn" (B 78) at Miss Scatcherd's treatment of Helen Burns captures precisely the frustration that the romance plot addresses.

While some readers may best remember the joyous moment when the narrator Jane declares, "Reader, I married him," the last three chapters of the novel also accumulate repetitions of words having to do with sadness—in Borch's translation, *Reue, Sorge, verlassen, allein, betrauern, jammern, weinen, Unglück, Kummer, trostlos, klagen, einsam* (regret, care, abandoned, alone, mourn, wail, cry, misfortune, worry, bleak, lament, lonely). There is every reason for the intradiegetic characters and readers alike to be sad even at this juncture since Rochester's damaged masculinity appears to have reached its tragic conclusion. Thornfield has burned to the ground and Rochester has lost a hand and his eyesight. He is vegetating without hope at Ferndean—so lacking in hope that he cannot believe his own ears when he hears that Jane has returned to him. Even on the very last page of the book, contrasting with the full life of Jane and Rochester that presumably delights readers who have succumbed to the charm of romance, St John casts a pall over such earthly delight when he writes of eagerly awaiting his impending death. His final words leave the reader not with Regis's "joy in the ending," but with a reminder of the finiteness of this life and the precariousness that accompanies attachment to it.

As observed in Chapter 3, unsanctioned emotion plays no small part in the affective life and self-expression of Rochester, a privileged thirty-seven-year-old man, miles apart in experience and prerogative from his female counterpart and presumably from most nineteenth-century female readers, especially distant from the teenagers who constituted the target audience of many of the German adaptations. In the original novel, Rochester's sadness mounts: the mistakes of his past and mistreatment by his father; his suffering as the husband of a madwoman; his aimless libertinage; his foiled plan to marry Jane and subsequent loss of her; and his physical debility. The narrator recounts his suffering

---

[21]   Franco Moretti coins the term "distant reading" for alternate procedures of textual analysis that, as here, for example, calculate repetitions or relative frequency of words in *Graphs, Maps, Trees: Abstract Models for Literary History* (London: Verso, 2005).

at length—and also allows him to express it in his own words—before granting him his happiness.

Jane in turn importantly digests what Rochester communicates to her of anger and sadness, making this shocking material part of her own reservoir of affective experience through reflection. In the unfolding of this romance, therefore, the sadness of both characters matters to their habits of being and their progress toward marital conversation. Adaptations handle this emotional current of the novel differently. *Jane Eyre, die Waise von Lowood, oder Gott führt die Seinen wunderbar* (1882), an adaptation for adults, in fact relishes Rochester's sadness. This religiously infused and otherwise much abridged version retold "für das Volk" (for the people) allows a repentant Rochester (not Jane) to speak of his regret at length. Sad words accumulate in the short final chapter. In the otherwise much pared down narrative, the happiness (*Glück*) of the restored manor house and Rochester's sight in one eye hardly counter the sadness of *trostlos*, *gedrückt, verlassen, hoffnungslos, einsam, gebrochen, düster, weinen, Qual, erduldet, Ruine, Unglück* (bleak, oppressed, abandoned, hopeless, lonely, broken, gloomy, weep, torment, suffered, ruin, misfortune).[22] Needless to say, the joyous liberation the text can offer is lost amid this lamentation.

German adaptations for girls, in turn, tend to curtail or alter the nature of sadness in *Jane Eyre*, making it less a ubiquitous emotion to be pondered and addressed as feeling, and more a simple reaction to an unfortunate chain of events. They, furthermore, attenuate the experience of sadness simply by leaving out plot elements and reducing interiority and reflection. When, for example, the words "hilflos" or "ohnmächtig" (helpless) appear, they modify "Mädchen" (girl) or "Kind" (child) and not sadness per se; in other words, they pertain to the fortunes of a type—the orphan—and not the specific character's subjective emotions and feelings, not her "hilflose Traurigkeit" (helpless sadness) and her "hilflosen Zorn" (helpless anger). Sadness has to do, that is, with external plot events rather than the central character's interior affective life. By way of exception, Hartung seems to have a feel for the existential sadness of the original when she notes that Rochester is sad by nature: "Traurigsein ... liegt so in seiner Natur" (Ha 62; Sadness ... is in his nature."

Some adaptations do permit Jane's reflection on sadness. Wedding, for example, allows the narrator to ponder at length her feelings in the red room, showing how she moves from anger to Howells's "low-level depression" (We 9–11). Nevertheless Wedding, as outlined in Chapter 3, subsequently ends her adaptation with the heroine falling silent in her happiness and so ending reflection altogether. Reichard, for her part, preserves "hilflose Traurigkeit" (R 15; helpless sadness) and "ohnmächtigen hilflosen Zorn" (R 62; powerless helpless anger) but does not allow her heroine to reach for the healing bliss of conjugal conversation. Reichhardt substitutes "einsame Traurigkeit" (Rt 17; lonely sadness) for "hilflose Traurigkeit" (helpless sadness). "Helpless" might, of course, reek of religiously forbidden despair. Reichhardt sees to it therefore that Jane's anger is

---

[22] *Jane Eyre, die Waise von Lowood, oder Gott führt die Seinen wunderbar*, 59–64.

not helpless. While his Jane does tremble with anger (Rt 61; "bebte vor Zorn"), the adaptation omits Borch's "ohnmächtig" and "hilflos" (B 78).

The combination of sadness and anger as a defining feature of Brontë's romance characterizes several chains of the diffusion of *Jane Eyre* in the German territories. Marlitt's works, as we shall see in Part Two, produce one angry heroine after another, female protagonists who are also sometimes sad. Yet with respect to depressive, world-weary sadness combined with anger one finds more compelling evidence for productive reception and transmission in Wilhelmine von Hillern's *Ein Arzt der Seele* (A Physician of the Soul), like *Jane Eyre*, a *Bildungsroman* that operates within the conventions of romance.

A Romance Remedy for the Sad and Angry Soul
Serialized in the *Deutsche Roman-Zeitung* and published as a book in 1869, *Arzt* displays sufficient affinities to Brontë to have figured in its time as a path of transfer. Its extensive engagement with its heroine's depressive sadness suggests both interest in female melancholy—and not merely sentimental sad events—and the discomfort of cultural conservatives with sadness.[23] Sadness, of course, potentially provided compelling evidence that something was amiss with women's lot in general and Hillern's novel can be seen to demonstrate just that. A brief look at *Arzt* as an episode of diffusion underlines the importance, in the wake of *Jane Eyre*, of this vocabulary of sadness combined with anger to romance plots intertwined with self-formation.

Wilhelmine Birch (1836–1916) was surely familiar with her mother's famous *Waise*. In 1853, the year in which Birch-Pfeiffer's play reaped applause in Berlin and Hamburg, seventeen-year-old Wilhelmine was preparing to try her own luck on the stage.[24] The writer Felix Dahn describes her in that period as temperamental, as "recht oft und fast niemals mit Grund zornig" (quite often and almost never justifiably angry) and passionately devoted to drama, lyric, epic, especially drama, which she read in both German and English.[25] In 1848, Birch had met the aforementioned actress Zerline Würzburg Gabillon who later famously played Jane.[26] Although her career never really flourished, despite her mother's connections and financial support, she starred in performances (1853–7), playing, among other female leads, Juliette, Griseldis, Maria Stuart, Viola in an adaptation of Shakespeare's *Twelfth Night*, Madame de Pompadour in Albert Emil Brachvogel's *Narziß*, and Fanchon in Birch-Pfeiffer's adaptation of George Sand's *La Petite Fadette* (Little Fadette) as *Die Grille* (The Cricket). In short, she knew the theater world and inhabited it until she married Hermann von Hillern, a man twice her age and superior in social rank.

---

23 I thank Lisabeth Hock who alerted me to the valences of nineteenth-century women's sadness or melancholy particularly with regard to this novel. On Hillern's novel more generally, see Hock, "Evolutionary Theory and the Female Scientist in Wilhelmine von Hillern's *Ein Arzt der Seele* (1869)," *German Studies Review* 37, no. 3 (2014): 507–27.
24 Ebel, *Das Kind ist tot*, 26–8.
25 Ebel, *Das Kind ist tot*, 22–3.
26 Bettelheim-Gabillon, *Im Zeichen des alten Burgtheaters*, 158.

As a bright and culturally literate young woman, Birch had by 1865 when she debuted as a novelist under her married name, Wilhelmine von Hillern, with *Ein Doppelleben* (A Double Life) likely also read a version of Brontë's novel. It was, after all, during the first seventeen years of its sojourn in the German territories easy to come by; besides its stage version, it existed in three German translations, two German adaptations for a general public, and two German adaptations for younger readers as well—not to mention its availability in English with Tauchnitz and British and North American publishers.

Hillern's novel stands out for its portrayal of sadness—not the sentimental, lachrymose sort that was legion in nineteenth-century fiction but instead an extended oppressive melancholy arising from constrictive and debilitating social and psychological conditions. *Arzt* is not a governess novel; rather, its similarities to *Jane Eyre* reside in its unfolding of romance coupled with an extended portrait of the development of an odd heroine, from her deeply unhappy lonely childhood to her hard-won happy marriage and new motherhood. While Hillern's novel ultimately appears to quash rebellion and freedom, it nevertheless ends by highlighting its heroine's intelligibility and acknowledgment, thus suggesting an affinity, even a debt, to Brontë.

Like Jane's, Ernestine von Hartwich's affective life is characterized by anger and especially sadness—and the novel itself, like Brontë's, gives off mixed signals. The plot, with its reliance on scheming avaricious relatives and deliberate isolation and mis-education of the heroine to make her unmarriageable, takes a cue from sensation fiction, but the extended depiction of the painful childhood of a physically abused, unloved, ugly, and socially awkward child who soon becomes an orphan also recalls *Jane Eyre*: "Sie war wieder das alte, verlassene, mißhandelte Kind, dessen Mark und Blut aufgezehrt ward von ohnmächtigem Grimm gegen seine Peiniger" (once again she was the erstwhile, abandoned, mistreated child, whose blood and marrow were consumed by helpless anger toward its tormentors), the narrator reports.[27] Repetitions of words of weary sadness such as "allein" (alone), "einsam" (lonely), "traurig" (sad), "verlassen" (abandoned), and "müde" (tired) accumulate. Ernestine's isolation and spiritual abandonment become central to her uncle Leuthold's noxious pedagogical program.

Ernestine, in her radical aloneness, has good psychological and sociological reason to be sad and angry and to wish her life were otherwise. As she grows older, thwarted desire provides new cause for sadness. For much of the novel, this desire revolves around scientific ambition encouraged by her uncle; later it is redirected toward the male protagonist, Johannes Moellner, at *his* wish. But as Ernestine confesses, she has loved Johannes since she was a child—he, like no one else, *saw* her, her "starke[n] Wille[n]" (strong will), her "wild schlagendes, ungestümes Herz" (1:61; her wildly beating, impetuous heart). He gave her the book of fairy tales that in her miserable childhood lent her hope. At times Hillern's driven Ernestine reads as a conflation of Jane and Bertha as she

---

[27]   Wilhelmine von Hillern, *Ein Arzt der Seele*, 4th ed. (Berlin: O. Janke, 1886) 1: 66–7, hereafter cited in text.

withdraws to a self-imposed captivity in her observatory, a converted tower. Multiple characters refer to the depressive, solitary seeker as a witch.

A surface reading of the plot must regard Ernestine's obsessive wish to pursue science, which is putatively against woman's nature, as maliciously implanted by her uncle to ruin her health and keep her from marrying. If this is so, then the ending, which depicts Ernestine, who has given up a scientific career for the sake of her health, as a wife and the proud mother of a new baby girl, constitutes an unambiguously happy normative outcome. In such a reading, the novel remains far from achieving the "love, freedom, and equality" that feminists have sought and sometimes found in *Jane Eyre*. The novel, however, leaves room for a less culturally conservative understanding of Ernestine's final circumstance, one that does not discount her intellectual ambition: romance has made both family and science possible for the heroine. In her foreword to the fifth edition of the book (1906), Hillern maintains that, although some had understood her novel to take a stance against the emancipation of women, this was not her intention; rather, she meant to work through the suffering imposed by cultural restrictions.[28]

In her own life Hillern had been confronted with the choice between a floundering but wished-for stage career and marriage hastened by an unwanted pregnancy. Supported by her mother, she chose the latter for the sake of propriety, turning to writing fiction only after bearing three more children and then forbidding her husband further marital relations. Her novel, attuned to the Woman Question of her day, begins to imagine somewhat broader possibilities and different alternatives for its heroine, even if its domesticated happy ending appears to curtail them.

Twenty-two years earlier, Brontë confronted her heroine with a choice between self-sacrificial missionary work yoked to a man she did not love, noble work that she also believed would kill her, and her desire for Rochester, which entailed both expression of self and the accompanying risk of returning to a man who was probably still married. Hillern, for her part, positioned her heroine between a brilliant career in science and fulfillment in marriage. Even when the novel ends conventionally with marriage, it has nevertheless in the preceding pages portrayed at length Ernestine's dogged pursuit of scientific ambition, raising the possibility that some women can and will choose this path. In the novel, social conditions (and not woman's nature per se, as the male protagonist initially asserts) force a choice between singlehood and science, on the one hand, and marriage and procreation on the other.

The novel realizes the requisite happy ending through the intervention of the male protagonist, the "physician of the soul," with whom Ernestine argues her case as a scientist for pages on end, reproducing Brontë's pattern of dialogue between protagonists destined to unite, the verbal battle that Oliphant recognized as a new kind of romance. Miraculously—and this "most wonderful thing" must be not be overlooked—Johannes does eventually recognize her

---

28   Wilhelmine von Hillern, *Ein Arzt der Seele*, 5th ed. (Berlin: Otto Janke, 1906), v. Her introduction proves, however, an exercise in ambivalence when, in an essentialist vein, she worries over changing gender roles and the necessity of sacrifice out of love which she sees as the "eternal feminine" (viii).

talent, despite his prejudices against the female mind. He thus acknowledges Ernestine in that powerful romance scenario which allows readers, in Radway's formulation, to identify with a heroine "at the moment of her greatest success, that is, when she secures the attention and recognition of her culture's most powerful and essential representative, a man" as "a sign of woman's attainment of legitimacy and personhood."[29] In the closing pages, readers learn that Ernestine has become her husband's assistant whom he needs in both his laboratory and his home: "Er kann über Alles mit ihr sprechen wie mit einem Manne ..." (4:180; He can talk about everything with her like a man), a liberal-minded male character declares. Through these words the conclusion sounds an idea of intellectual parity as expressed in continued marital conversation, here apparently a conversation all day long in the laboratory.

In naming chapter 2 "Das Märchen vom häßlichen jungen Entlein" (The Fairy Tale of the Ugly Young Duckling) and otherwise referring frequently and recursively to Andersen's fairy tales, particularly this one, the novel highlights its fairy tale pre-texts. But it also evinces shared plotting with *Jane Eyre* that renders it less a fairy tale and more a work, like *Jane Eyre*, teetering between romanticism and realism. In particular, the extended treatment of an abusive childhood, the narrative interest in Ernestine's (self-)formation, the investment in her affective life, the reproduction of tense dialogue between the male and female protagonists, and the romance pairing and trajectory resonate with Brontë's novel. Resolution requires that Ernestine own up to her love for an older, more experienced, and established man. Their conversations meanwhile force mutual recognition, although it is not clear that Ernestine here emerges as the verbal victor.

In the final scenario, the heroine has given birth to a daughter—not the conventional son with the eyes of his father of Brontë's telling. This recasting matters to the message. The 2014 stage adaptation of *Jane Eyre* repairs Brontë's ending for contemporary sensibilities in precisely that manner. This version concludes with Jane's giving birth. An unidentified voice and then Rochester proclaim—as the last lines of the play: "it's a girl."[30] Hillern's ending, 145 years earlier, rewrote romance for its times as well. Having begun with Ernestine's sad realization that she is "only a girl" and hence unimportant, Hillern's novel ends with the new family's future belonging to a girl, in whatever form it may take. It hints that the next generation, which will be raised by scientifically engaged parents, even if the mother is only her father's assistant, will walk a different path. This child shall in any case never envy men, Ernestine avers, as she delivers mixed messages for the future: "Es soll aufwachsen im Schooß der Liebe, es soll das jugendliche Haupt stolz erheben zu der geistigen Höhe, welche das Weib erreichen muß, um dem Manne eine würdige Gefährtin zu sein;—aber mit jeder Faser seines Herzens soll es in dem Boden wurzeln, aus dem wir doch die besten

29 Janice Radway, "Readers and their Romances," 243. For a fuller treatment of the possible progressive strains in this novel, particularly as highlighted in its American translation, see Tatlock, *German Writing, American Reading*, 102–11.

30 The Jane Eyre Company, *Jane Eyre, Based on the Novel by Charlotte Brontë* (London: Oberon Books, 2015), 101. This edition credits Sally Cookson as the director; the copyright is held by The Jane Eyre Company, which asserts itself as the author.

Kräfte ziehen: in dem alten geheiligten Boden der Familie!" (1:182; It [=child] shall grow up in the lap of love, it shall raise its youthful head proudly to the intellectual/spiritual heights that woman must reach to be a worthy companion to man—but with every fiber of its heart it shall be rooted in the soil from which we draw our best powers: in the ancient and holy ground of the family). Meanwhile, the final words of the novel, also spoken by Ernestine, invoke the harshness of the "therapy" she has undergone and the anguish she has suffered to reach this delicate balance of domestic life and scientific inquiry: "bitter" (4:183).

Given the euphoric centering of the once-ostracized odd woman and new mother within a community of well-wishers in this final scenario, historical readers might at this juncture have overlooked the bitter taste of that medicine. Still, as if worrying over the possible ambivalence of the original ending, the British Anglican priest Sabine Baring-Gould made certain that readers would never hear of it in his translation, *Ernestine, a Novel* (1879). Here he omitted these concluding words, banishing incipient doubt from paradise. In this version, Johannes speaks for her, concluding piously: "She is reconciled at last to the destiny of her sex."[31] Annis Lee Wister's American translation, *Only a Girl; or A Physician for the Soul*, by contrast, reproduced Hillern's original words in full.[32] While Baring-Gould's truncated version was last republished in 1881, Wister's translation remained in print through nine reprints from 1870 until 1898.

Subjectification: Taming Anger and Sadness

In her study of English Gothic fiction, Howells observes that, unlike previous fiction, *Jane Eyre* permits the Gothic mode to break through "into the world of everyday life and humane social awareness," which previous such fiction had "rejected or failed to realise."[33] Sadness surely belongs to and signifies this breakthrough. *Jane Eyre* may delight readers when it at long last briskly seals the match of Jane and Rochester, but full appreciation of its joy requires readers also to experience Jane's sadness and, through Jane's narration, also Rochester's, which increases near the novel's end when he is alone and disabled. Its joy also depends upon acceptance and integration of continuing melancholy even if the romantic coupling does hold sadness at bay. Sadness prompts, indeed signifies, the awareness that Jane achieves as she transforms inarticulate emotion into articulate feeling in the carefully chosen words of her autobiography. A contemplative sadness facilitates the achievement of what Howells sees as the "full realisation of the Gothic potential, where fact and fantasy can be fused into a statement about total human awareness."[34]

German adaptations for girls, in keeping with Mella's mother's pedagogy, eschew the sadness that permeates the original. Their avoidance of sadness becomes one more indicator of their tendency to elide the self-conscious verbal

31   Wilhelmine von Hillern, *Ernestine: A Novel*, trans. Sabine Baring-Gould (London: Thos. De La Rue & Co., 1879), 2: 299.

32   Wilhelmine von Hillern, *Only a Girl*, trans. Annis Lee Wister (Philadelphia: Lippincott, 1870).

33   Howells, *Love, Mystery*, 159.

34   Howells, *Love, Mystery*, 4.

integration of emotion as feeling as a salient feature of the narrative and thus to reverse the breakthrough that Howells describes as the "comprehensive view of feeling, imagination, and reason," a view treating even "irrational experience with full confidence in its value" and thus marking "significant progress beyond private fantasy and alienation back to the fully integrated personality."[35]

When the adapters reduced the depiction and contemplation of sadness and anger but retained the plot of familial strife, suffering, and cruelty along with new outlandish elements of their own invention, even indulging in a bit of fear-inducing sensation, they tended to forgo precisely such well-pondered integration of emotion and both rational and irrational experience. Their texts thus largely fail to offer Howells's "comprehensive awareness" or, in Pearce's terms, accession to the "relational selfhood" of modern romance. In other words, they miss or deliberately avoid a central point of the book—as autobiography and romance—and rely instead on simple accounts of human experience. Brontë's self-fashioning mustered emotion, and especially anger and sadness, and reflected on it, transforming it through language and conversation into feeling in the name of rebellion, self-possession, and a form of equality and freedom. It, moreover, allowed for sadness as its heroine absorbed loss, disappointment, shock, and suffering to live to tell at length of her experience and find resolution in a particular kind of marriage. By talking face to face with Rochester, Jane ultimately manages to remove herself from her binary behavior—simple sad acquiescence to the anger of others vs. rebellion out of her own anger. She learns to negotiate to a degree, to absorb and reflect with empathy on the feelings of another person in extended conversation.

In their role as mediators, all the adapters and editors of books for girls were surely among the novel's more attentive German-language readers. When they actively blunted the liberating force of anger and sadness as these emotions are reflected upon and integrated as feeling, Stieff, Spitzer, Reichard, Reichhardt, Wachler, Wedding, Hartung, and the anonymous editors who oversaw the Bartels editions presumably knew or at least suspected what the original offered readers, namely, emotions, thoughts, and possibilities to which young readers too were entirely receptive, but which those who watched over them preferred them not to know or experience, not even vicariously.

Gabriele Reuter's bestselling *Aus guter Familie: Leidensgeschichte eines Mädchens* (1895; From a Good Family: The Story of a Girl's Suffering) asserts this dynamic as a historical fact of the upbringing of bourgeois girls. It depicts precisely the tension between what girls want to read and what their concerned parents believe they should read. In the opening chapter, two confirmation presents excite young Agathe Heidling and both immediately reap adult disapprobation for they signal, on the one hand, love and sex and, on the other, radical politics: Friedrich Rückert's *Liebesfrühling* (Springtime of Love) and a poetry collection by the radical forty-eighter Georg Herwegh. Agathe reacts with anger and sadness. At the very end of the chapter she wanders out to the lake where she catches sight of a rotting skiff, now a miserable wreck, that had once fired romantic dreams of

---

[35]   Howells, *Love, Mystery*, 159.

adventure, unbounded freedom, indeed, the sublime—"Anfangs hegte Agathe romantische Träume über den alten Kahn: daß er draußen in Sturm und Wellen gedient—daß er das Meer gesehen habe und an Felsenklippen gescheitert sei" ("At first Agathe had cherished dreams of the old skiff: how it had served out there in the storm and the waves, how it had seen the sea and had foundered on the rocky cliffs").[36] The *Jane Eyre* reader might recall the young Jane pondering the "broken boat stranded on a desolate coast; to the cold and ghastly moon glancing through bars of cloud at a wreck just sinking" (10) and then relishing the accompanying words in Bewick's *Birds* that lend the image significance.[37]

After she has been told in the Confirmation ceremony that everything is hers, only to have that promise retracted as the disappointing day goes on, the sight of the skiff and the knowledge that it has never gone anywhere make Agathe sad. The text thus sounds the full chord of prohibited emotions and feelings— sadness, anger, passion—as they are tied to self-formation and liberation, in effect, the legacy and promise of the original *Jane Eyre* in the German reading world. The narrative proceeds to track the heroine from adolescence to adulthood, depicting her wishes for a full emotional and intellectual life, for greater experience and knowledge as both support individualization and, indeed, point the way to the "free individual," as it was then imagined. But beginning with the surveillance of her reading, Agathe's discovery of her desires is always followed by renewed prohibition—external or internalized—that blocks their articulation and fulfillment. The coda of this study will have recourse to Reuter's story of her heroine's colossal failure to survive as it takes a parting look at the purchase of romance in the manner of *Jane Eyre*. First, however, we turn in Part Two to the transmission and diffusion of *Jane Eyre* via Marlitt's serialized novels, their book publications, translations, and adaptations, 1865–1918.

---

[36] Gabriele Reuter, *Aus guter Familie: Leidensgeschichte eines Mädchens, Studienausgabe mit Dokumenten*, 2 vols., ed. Katja Mellmann (Marburg: Literaturwissenschaft.de, 2006), 1: 27; *From a Good Family*, trans. Lynne Tatlock (Rochester, NY: Camden House, 1999), 16–17.

[37] The four translators reproduce this passage, the three abridged editions of these translations retain it, Fort omits it.

Part Two: Variation on a Theme: Imitation and Adaptation as Reception and Diffusion

When the American novelist Sharon Pywell decided to experiment with the romance genre, she in the end wrote a "romance about romances," placing a "romance plot side-by-side with a 'real' story about love." Her *Romance Reader's Guide to Life* explores the role of struggle "to dominate or be subordinated" as a defining element of the genre.[1] Near the conclusion, the imperiled Neave, the heroine of Pywell's "real" story, picks up a used copy of *Jane Eyre*. "Some deeply stupid editor," she scoffs, "had decided to illustrate it with sighing maidens and flower-choked weddings."[2]

Neither of Pywell's principal heroines favors a sentimental idea of romance and both engage in struggle. Pywell pairs Electra, the beleaguered protagonist of a fictional bodice ripper set in the eighteenth century with Neave and her sister Lilly who eventually found a successful cosmetics business after the Second World War and thus profit from their female customers' wish for love, sex, and romance. Both plots consist of a romantic coupling that soundly defeats the male villain who abuses and exploits women. Both supply their respective heroines with an enigmatic and guarded male partner who eventually allows himself to surrender to his emotions and attraction to his female counterpart. While, however, Elektra and Neave, find their happy endings, Lilly fatally chooses the wrong man guided by her delusions of love.

Overall, Pywell's double, even triple structure, if we include the romance that the sisters are selling the public in their cosmetics business, confirms the idea that romance extends its purchase in different contexts and genres and through different means and media. But while women apparently are always ready to buy it, the text also advances the notion that they need to become smart consumers of it: some iterations and some brands are messy or outright toxic—as in the case of Lilly, whose abusive relationship ends with her murder and dismemberment, or one iteration of the lipstick the sisters are selling that turns into runny goo shortly after application.

These multiple takes on romance illustrate its mobility, polysemy, and protean nature. Marketing, historical conditions, and experience, including

---

[1] Sharon Pywell, *The Romance Reader's Guide to Life* (New York: Flatiron Books, 2017), 308.
[2] Pywell, *Romance Reader's Guide*, 283.

reading experience, matter to its realization and meanings. Pywell's discoveries via her own fiction writing rehearse what we now know occurred when *Jane Eyre* migrated across genres and languages and repeatedly transformed in the process—from translations more or less resembling itself to the theater, to girls' bookshelves to folk libraries to the sensationalist sequel, *Die Erbin der Waise von Lowood, nach dem Englischen der Lady Georgina Fairfax* (The Heiress of the Orphan of Lowood, after the English of Lady Georgina Fairfax), in which the heroine is drugged and held captive by villains wishing to steal her fortune.[3]

In examining Marlitt's novels and their adaptations in Part Two as yet another conduit of cultural transmission, we pinpoint the generative durability and mobility of the original *Jane Eyre* romance in Germany and Austria. Pywell's take on romance as a source of joy and freedom for its readers and a potential source of profit for its authors, as we shall see, applies to this set of novels too. As she, too, wrote novels suggesting that there were plenty of bad actors that women needed to learn to recognize and unmask, Marlitt all the while supported herself, her brother, and his family with her writing.

---

[3]　*Die Erbin der Waise von Lowood, nach dem Englischen der Lady Georgina Fairfax*, Bürgerliche Unterhaltungsbücher 8 (Heilbronn: Otto Weber, n.d.). The sensation elements in this plot, which concern Rochester and Jane's daughter, recall Wilkie Collins's *Woman in White* (1859).

Five Reinvigorated Gazing: *Das Geheimnis der alten Mamsell*

If anyone personally knew something about the desperate lives of the "proletariat of the mind" in its female variation, it was Eugenie John. After stage fright and likely psychosomatic hearing problems forced her to give up a promising career as an opera singer, John served for ten years (1853–63) as a reader and companion to her one-time patron, Fürstin Mathilde von Schwarzburg-Sondershausen. When the Princess's finances put an end to her services, she turned to writing and so launched a career as E. Marlitt, an international bestselling author.

Beginning with "Zwölf Apostel" (Twelve Apostles) in 1865 and quickly followed in 1866 by "Blaubart" and *Goldelse* and *Das Geheimnis der alten Mamsell* (1867), Marlitt's novels and novellas fascinated a broad German reading public to the consternation of many a male literary pundit. Ending with the posthumous *Das Eulenhaus* (The Owl House) in 1888, which was completed by W. Heimburg, all of Marlitt's fiction first appeared in serial form in *Die Gartenlaube* (The Garden Bower). Thereafter the same publisher (Ernst Keil) brought out the novels as individual books and by the late 1880s as an illustrated boxed set. Especially in the late 1860s and 1870s, Marlitt's fiction significantly contributed to the increased circulation of *Die Gartenlaube*, which peaked in 1875 at 382,000, each copy probably read by at least five people.[1]

Marlitt's much shorter and less complex fiction does not include governess novels in direct imitation of Brontë's original, and with the exception of *Das Heideprinzeßchen* (1871; The Little Moorland Princess), it is not narrated in the first person. Still, it perpetuates elements from *Jane Eyre* as its lively and intelligent heroines find acknowledgment via romance plots. When in 1870 Gottschall noted the resemblance of Marlitt's *Goldelse* to *Jane Eyre*, he recognized what any experienced recreational reader in that period might have discerned and come to desire from each new Marlitt serialization.[2] Yet Marlitt, according to her brother, Alfred John, had not read *Jane Eyre*, despite the fact that she was generally very well read.[3]

---

1   Kirsten Belgum, *Popularizing the Nation: Audience, Representation, and the Production of Identity in* Die Gartenlaube, *1853–1900* (Lincoln: University of Nebraska Press, 1998), 16.
2   Rudolf von Gottschall, "Die Novellistin der 'Gartenlaube,'" *Die Blätter für literarische Unterhaltung*, no. 19 (1870): 291.
3   [Alfred John], "Eugenie John-Marlitt. Ihr Leben und ihre Werke," *E. Marlitt's gesammelte Romane und Novellen*, 2nd ed. (Leipzig: Ernst Keils Nachfolger, n.d.), 10: 419.

Bachleitner has expressed skepticism with regard to John's statement, noting echoes of *Jane Eyre* in Marlitt's oeuvre.[4] Circumstantial and textual evidence indeed speaks against John's assertion and supports Bachleitner's skepticism. Marlitt's ten years' reading to the worldly Princess Mathilde coincided with the first proliferation of editions and adaptations of *Jane Eyre* and also Birch-Pfeiffer's staging of the novel. It is unlikely that of all the novels published in that period the well-read Marlitt missed precisely this very popular one. Furthermore, given the many respects in which her texts themselves overtly resemble it, it is next to impossible that Marlitt was unfamiliar with it. As will become clear in the following chapters, her works exhibit intimate knowledge of this English novel and a firm understanding of its romance dynamics. Her fiction reinvigorates its motifs, structures, plot turns, values, and social messages while also becoming its own brand. How Marlitt acquired this familiarity and in which of the myriad forms she or her informants encountered *Jane Eyre* must remain a mystery; that she perpetuated key aspects of *Jane Eyre* will not.

Secrets and Intelligibility

The high relative frequency of occurrences of *Auge/n* (eye/s) and *Gesicht/er* (face/s) numbers as one among many features that Marlitt's corpus shares with Brontë's *Jane Eyre*. Her narratives all rely heavily on gazing and construing faces (physiognomy), intradiegetic reading by the characters and extradiegetic reading by readers.[5] How, then, do gazes akin to those that inform Jane Eyre facilitate and figure in Marlitt's brand of romance? What functions does it have in narratives that, in overcoming (social) difference, entail 1) acknowledgment of the female protagonist as a thinking and feeling individual, 2) mutual intelligibility and trust between the members of the central couple, and 3) personal and social transformation toward freedom and equality? We turn now to interested active looking in Marlitt's *Geheimnis* as the protagonists find their way to one another via the inevitable obstacles of romance plots in the wake of *Jane Eyre*. Here traces of Brontë's novel inhere in a narrative of seeing and looking that give way to hearing and vocalizing as Marlitt's principal couple settle into the intimacy of domestic life—not among the landed gentry of Brontë's English countryside but in a German "hometown."

Representative of Marlitt's best and most Jane Eyrish work, *Das Geheimnis der alten Mamsell* was first serialized in 1867 (*Gartenlaube* 21–38), twenty years after the publication of *Jane Eyre*. Beginning with Annis Lee Wister's *The Old Mam'selle's Secret* (Lippincott, 1868), three North American English

---

[4]   In reviewing *Jane Eyre's* reception in Germany, Bachleitner, however, only reluctantly grants Marlitt's fiction the status of productive reception and turns instead to Amely Bölte's governess novel, *Elisabeth, oder eine deutsche Jane Eyre* (1873). Bachleitner, "Die deutsche Rezeption englischer Romanautorinnen," 189.

[5]   Marlitt indeed relies to some extent on the "science" of physiognomy, as Hamann has pointed out. *Zwischen Normativität und Normalität*, 144n236. In that sense too, Marlitt's novels participate in the discursive world of *Jane Eyre*.

translations, and one British translation, it circulated for at least fifty years, ultimately in over 100 issues in English alone, as the novel established itself as standard international leisure-time reading.[6] *Geheimnis* shares language and many features, motifs, and plot elements with its literary antecedent, including heavy reliance on gazing and reading faces for the purpose of constructing a love story tied to self-formation. Here, too, looking and talking inform a romance of sympathy and mutual intelligibility and fuel a general push toward freedom and equality. In rewriting and resituating it, Marlitt made this kind of romance appealing to the audiences that relied on *Die Gartenlaube* to deliver the stories of the day while also helping to create that reading public.

The fortunes of the novel's heroine, Felicitas, a foster child in the home of the wealthy merchant family, the Hellwigs, take a turn for the worse when Herr Hellwig dies, as did Jane's life at Gateshead upon the death of Mr. Reed. In her husband's absence, the bigoted Frau Hellwig sets the tone—like Mrs. Reed—closing one eye to her odious younger son's cruelty and finding fault with Felicitas at every turn. Felicitas, like Jane the product of a mesalliance, proves herself superior to those who tyrannize over her. The novel devotes substantial attention to the slow recognition of her qualities of mind by the male protagonist, Johannes Hellwig, the elder son who is also her legal guardian. Unlike Marlitt's subsequent male heroes but like Rochester, Johannes is not handsome—he is even outright "häßlich" (ugly); it will therefore be necessary in turn for Felicitas to see past the surface and her own prejudices to perceive his good character and qualities of mind.[7]

Marlitt invents a defiant Felicitas who becomes more vehement about freeing herself from the chains of obligation as her eighteenth birthday approaches. Johannes, who has long lived away from home in Bonn, first as a medical student and then a practicing physician, has given his revered mother a free hand with Felicitas. His failure to recognize the consequences of his decision makes him, in her mind, her chief malefactor and obstacle to freedom. To her dismay, as she comes to know him, he also becomes the object of her desire. Later on, as he tries to persuade her to accept his love, Johannes chides her for her refusal to give in to her feelings: "Wüten Sie nicht gegen sich selbst, wie ein kleiner ohnmächter Vogel, der sich lieber den Kopf einstößt, ehe er sich in das Unabänderliche fügt" (1:227; Don't rage against yourself like a helpless little bird that would rather break its neck before it would accept the unalterable). The Brontë reader cannot fail to hear an echo of Rochester's words: "Jane, be still; don't struggle so, like a wild frantic bird that is rending its own plumage

---

6   See Tatlock, "The One and the Many," 233–6, 252n8.

7   E. Marlitt, *Das Geheimnis der alten Mamsell, E. Marlitt's gesammelte Romane und Novellen* ([1888]; repr., Leipzig: Ernst Keils Nachfolger, n.d.), 1: 169, hereafter cited in text. The recent publication of *Geheimnis* as volume 1 is announced in *Die Gartenlaube*, no. 24 (1888): 408. The second reprint edition of Marlitt's complete works is announced in *Die Gartenlaube*, no. 35 (1891): 596. *Die Gartenlaube* is hereafter cited in text by volume and page number.

in its desperation" (228). Marlitt could have encountered the line in any of the three then extant translations:

> S 2:139: "kämpfen Sie nicht wie ein wilder, wüthender Vogel, der in seiner Verzweiflung sein eigenes Gefieder zerreist."
> G 2:81: "schlagen Sie nicht so um sich, wie ein wilder, wüthender Vogel, der in seiner Verzweiflung sein eigenes Gefieder zerreißt."
> H 1:100: "Schlagen Sie nicht so um sich, wie ein scheu gewordener Vogel der sich in der Verzweiflung sein eigenes Gefieder ausrupft."

Her paraphrase of Brontë insists on Felicitas's capitulation, but then Jane, too, who has from the start been associated with birds, soon capitulates: despite declaring herself "not a bird" and ready to leave, she accepts Rochester's marriage proposal. In Marlitt's scenario, Johannes promises that she will be free to think and act as she wishes, "nur beschützt und behütet, wie ein zärtlich geliebtes Kind" (1:227; just protected and shielded like a tenderly loved child). The text offers mixed messages when he simultaneously frees and infantilizes her. It appears to restore the role of male protector, yet Felicitas, like Jane, later becomes her beloved's protector when she vainly attempts to spare him the shame of learning of his family's crime. The parity of the conclusion of both works owes something to their heroines taking on the protector's role.

Among many similarities, Marlitt reproduces language having to do with detecting and feeling, including "Sphinx," "electric shock," and "machine without feeling." While Marlitt tends to make her characters relatively easy for experienced readers to understand, she renders them opaque to themselves and to one another. As in Brontë's novel, future spouses must here, too, become intelligible to one another; gazing plays a crucial role in a process that the text protracts.

In *Geheimnis*, religious bigotry, social prejudice, and human cruelty fuel misjudgment of others. Frau Hellwig is not disposed to welcome the half-orphan Felicitas into her home, for she views the world with the same stony eye with which Mrs. Reed regarded her orphaned niece: she looks at her "eisig" (icily) with her "starre[n] graue[n] Augen" (1:17; fixed gray eyes). The text underlines the noxious petrifying effects of the prejudicial stare with repetitions of words with the root "starr" in both the meanings "stare" and "petrify." The narrator even refers to Frau Hellwig's "Medusenaugen" (1:31; Medusa eyes). At a dramatic highpoint, Johannes's cousin, the hypocritical, outwardly beautiful Adele (a name recalling *Jane Eyre*) also takes on the appearance of a medusa—her disheveled curls "ringelten sich wie Nattern um die gerötete Stirn" (1:285; coiled like vipers around her flushed forehead). In a novel concerned with social mobility across class and estate, the objectifying look is anathema.

Geheimnis in fact opens with a spectacle that proves lethal. The beautiful Meta d'Orlowska, who married a Polish itinerate entertainer and was subsequently disowned by her aristocratic family, performs to the delight of an unidentified hometown in Thuringia. At the behest of her husband, she places her imposing figure on display only to be fatally shot in full view of a horrified public when the carnival trick goes awry. The narrator grants her an aestheticized death scene: with her thick blond tresses spread out over the white pillows and curling down to the floor, she begs her handsome but feckless husband to give up their daughter to be raised by "respectable people." Descended from these attractive social outcasts, parents who live by spectacle, the heroine takes a jaundiced view of the gaze. Objectively beautiful, but keenly aware of the social eye, she, like Jane, shrinks from high visibility and thus forgoes the ready charm that tends to accompany beauty and fuel romance in nineteenth-century fiction. In an erotically charged moment, Felicitas emerges, mermaid-like, from a brook after saving a child from being burned to death. Her thick hair frames her face and shoulders like a halo. When Professor Franck, a family friend, openly stares at the sight of her, she proudly blocks this objectification, refusing his thanks as well as Johannes's proffered medical treatment.

In *Geheimnis* spectacle is vulgar and beauty suspect—as in the case of both Felicitas's mother and Cousin Adele. Especially through the thoroughly unlikable Adele, the text repudiates surface beauty that does not bespeak deep-seated virtue and intelligence, both of which must be ascertained through intentional "forschendes" (searching), "durchdringendes," "durchdringliches," "eindringliches" (synonyms for penetrating), "prüfendes" (scrutinizing), and "unverwandtes" (fixed) looking.

Marlitt nevertheless allows her readers the pleasure of identification with a beautiful, misapprehended heroine, while the household conspires to erase her individuality and render her an obscure cipher of the serving class—plain, meek, and dull. While Rochester insists on naming plain Jane a fairy creature in keeping with his vision of her, Marlitt's text establishes Felicitas, aka Fee (fairy), as a fairy creature from the start through her parents' nickname for her. Johannes merely needs to recognize a truth obscured by social prejudice that should have long been evident to him. In an important scene in the developing romance, he does perceive Felicitas's physical beauty even though she is plainly dressed. Yet Marlitt ties this perception to his recognition of the heroine's intellect and virtue, for Johannes first notices that she can read French and suspects that there is more to her than meets the eye.

The romance plot requires Johannes to look at Felicitas so as to recognize and acknowledge her merits. He must apprehend the person—and not her social origins—to see beyond the prejudice that has led the family to rename her Caroline, dress her shabbily, and relegate her to servitude. Felicitas demands to be seen as a person and considers the Hellwigs' attempt to make her into a "willenlosen, dienenden Maschine" (serving machine with no will) and to destroy "das geistige Element" (the intellectual/spiritual element) in her, an unforgivable crime (1:154). She will not consent to be treated "wie eine Ware" (1:229; like a commodity). With the evocation of a machine, Marlitt paraphrases Jane's famous words, lines she also could also have heard Jane speak in Birch-Pfeiffer's stage adaptation.

Felicitas, for her part, must perceive and accept Johannes's remorse for his past misjudgment and acknowledge and trust his love. While the narrator endows her with a penetrating gaze, this gaze fails her for long stretches of the novel as she struggles with her hatred of Johannes, the surrogate for all the Hellwigs. Her willful blindness delays the happy ending for the sake of reader pleasure in the process of reaching it.⁸ Such misperception and retardation became in fact a signature of Marlitt's romance plots in general. As Kirsten Belgum observes of the general dynamic of Marlitt's novels, the male hero "comes into ever sharper relief as an appropriate and desirable partner for the morally upstanding heroine."⁹ In other words, desire, as in this novel, is linked to clarifying and clarified perception.

Reader pleasure, of course, also depends on belief in the mutual attraction of Felicitas and Johannes. The pair's looking offers insight into their feelings long before they confess them. Desire and admiration converge as both characters observe and approve of the other's socially benevolent acts. Felicitas rescues the neglected child, Ännchen, who thereafter falls ill. As she and Johannes nurse her, the two become "gute Kameraden" (1:152; good comrades) and so move toward the parity that will characterize their marriage. Johannes meanwhile ministers to the local community, among other things, by saving the eyesight of a local artisan and refusing payment. The investment of the romance plot in the observation of virtue leaves less space for the inwardness and subtle reading that constitutes Brontë's novel, but Marlitt by no means relinquishes emotion and feeling or mutual affect-laden looking and interpreting. Sympathy remains crucial and located in individual disposition; it too must be perceived and acknowledged.

Johannes characterizes his own change of heart as a "Wunder" (1:262; miracle), declaring that a "Wandlung der Dinge" (1:261; a transformation of things) has taken place—both formulations surprisingly anticipate Nora's words at the conclusion of *A Doll's House*. In Marlitt's novel, the miracle or change becomes manifest in Johannes's ability ultimately to admire and thus regard Felicitas as his social equal. As her subjective view of Johannes changes, Felicitas in turn recognizes that the steely, penetrating eyes he has inherited from his mother at times radiate their own "innere Befriedigung und Wärme" (1:132; inner satisfaction and warmth). But she has long since also noticed that Johannes's "unregelmäßige[s] Profil" (1:42; irregular profile) has lost its cold asceticism. A "mild light" emanates "von jener nicht schön geformten, jedoch bedeutenden Stirne" (from that forehead, which though not beautifully formed is distinguished); the doctor's eyes reveal "Mitgefühl" (sympathy). His "unschöne, eckige Bewegungen" (his unattractive, ungainly movements), his "abstoßendes Wesen" (repellent being) have been eclipsed by his "sittlich schöne Erscheinung" (morally beautiful aspect). Johannes "fühlt und denkt menschlich" (feels and thinks humanely); he has compassion (*Erbarmen*) with the most helpless of his neighbors (1:146).

As in *Jane Eyre*, sound eventually replaces sight, to aid cognition and establish intimacy, a development anticipated when Johannes audibly recognizes her individuality by addressing her by her true name rather than the name Mrs. Hellwig forced on her. This utterance stirs her like an "elektrischer Schlag" (1:134; electric jolt). But then the mere sound of his voice can confuse her normally well-ordered

---

⁸   Citing romance novelist Suzanne Simmons Guntrum, Regis makes the important point that since readers know that romance dictates a happy ending (traditionally in marriage) they read primarily for the process and not the ending. Regis, *A Natural History*, 14.

⁹   Belgum, "Narratives of Virtuous Desire," 265.

thoughts. His words touch her heart like "elektrische Schläge" (1:146; electric jolts), the narrator repeats. His newly mild and warm tone of voice "berührte jede Fiber ihres Herzens und machte es heftiger klopfen ..." (1:229; touched every fiber of her heart and made it beat faster). If Felicitas cannot believe her own eyes as Johannes's appearance becomes more attractive to her, she, like Jane, cannot mistake the truth of sound and her own somatic reaction to it. Sound remains important to this romance: in the end, Felicitas comforts Johannes every evening with her singing. Having acknowledged and embraced his desire for her, Johannes requires the sounds he once could not abide.

Unlike Brontë, Marlitt supplies the Hellwig household with two actively sympathetic characters: Cordula, the eponymous "Old Mam'sell" and the servant Heinrich. Both play an important role in the heroine's upbringing, choosing to care for her in keeping with their altruistic habits of being. The text figures their behavior, choices, and principles, too, through their manner of looking.

In the first chapter, his face brightly lit by the lantern he carries, Heinrich comes to the rescue of Herr Hellwig after a carriage accident and lights the way home. Shortly thereafter he witnesses Frau Hellwig's cruelty even as he recognizes Herr Hellwig's capacity for sympathy—like his own—with Meta and later with her child. Heinrich is present in the curiosity-seeking audience when Meta is shot and joins other concerned audience members to attend to her, crossing the line between passive voyeuristic pleasure and active assistance. The text pointedly includes him as one of the few adults to regard the orphan with sympathy from the beginning and preserves him in the novel's happy ending as an honored member of the couple's new household in Bonn. Our last view of the hypocritical Adele is colored by Heinrich's recognition of her true nature as the characters pass one another on the street. Although Adele refuses to acknowledge him, he grins to himself knowing that her efforts to entrap Johannes through ostentatious displays of sentimentality were for naught. With Heinrich, Marlitt, unlike Brontë, imagines a bourgeois household in which a servant does not, with his unacknowledged shadow labor, merely support the individualist existence of a master couple. Heinrich, respected as an individual in his own right, helps shape that household.[10]

During his years in the Hellwig home, Heinrich regularly tended to Cordula Hellwig, the eponymous "Old Mam'selle." As a counter-image to Brontë's Bertha, Cordula lives in the attic of the Hellwig mansion, where she has been banished along with her piano on account of her spirited playing of profane songs—German master composers including Bach—in the rigidly pious household shaped by Frau Hellwig's beliefs. Within the limits of this confined space she lives her life according to her own lights. She continues to play the German masters at full volume and to realize the values she believes they embody.

---

[10]   Two English theater adaptations of *Jane Eyre*—John Courtney's English theater adaptations of *Jane Eyre* as *Jane Eyre or The Secrets of Thornfield Manner* (1848) and John Brougham's *Jane Eyre: A Drama in five Acts* (1856)—both attend more to social class and highlight servants and peasants than does the novel itself. Patsy Stoneman, *Brontë Transformations: The Cultural Dissemination of Jane Eyre and Wuthering Heights* (London: Prentice Hull, 1996), 9, 15–16, 256–7.

This piano playing—and not mysterious laughter—attracts and enables young Felicitas to find her way into the marvelous hidden apartment, which for the child is a "Wunder, wie es die schönsten Märchenbücher nicht wunderbarer erzählen konnten" (1:66; marvel of a kind that the most beautiful books of fairy tales could not surpass). Gothic terror transforms into delightful spectacle. In a reversal of *Jane Eyre*, the attic harbors the virtue otherwise in retreat in the household. After Cordula's death, redemption occurs not through burning down the house, but airing out the attic and with it the family secret.

As her name indicates, Cordula has a heart; she looks upon Felicitas with kindness and interest, becoming foster aunt, teacher, and friend to her. While her years of educating Felicitas must remain secret until the latter reaches her majority, thereafter she plans to designate Felicitas as her companion and caregiver, thereby securing the orphan's livelihood. This tender female bond bears resemblance to Jane's attachment to the moribund Helen Burns, Miss Temple at Lowood, and the female Rivers cousins.

Nathaniel, the younger Hellwig son, however, labels Cordula the "alte Dachhexe" (1:45; old witch), and, before meeting her, Felicitas, suffused with terror, imagines her, in a Gothic vein, as a "schreckliches Weib mit einem großen Messer in der Hand" (1:45; terrible woman with a big knife in her hand). Cordula's secrets and solitary existence have in fact given her a somewhat peculiar and inharmonious appearance. In her youth, love for a talented but poor musician opened Cordula's eyes to her own father's part in keeping the musician and his impoverished aristocratic family from their rightful wealth, hidden from the enemy during the Thirty Years War in the foundations of their mansion, where the bourgeois Hellwigs now live. Her heated confrontation with her father over the swindle led to the latter's stroke. When Cordula later recalls the misdeeds of her family, her bitter lived experience marks her physiognomy: her expression is "unheimlich; es war ein Hohngelächter, wenn auch ein leises, gedämpftes, welches sie ausstieß; ihr sonst so stilles, liebes Gesicht hatte etwas Medusenhaftes, durch den plötzlichen Ausdruck unsäglicher Bitterkeit und einer namenlosen Verachtung" (1:126; uncanny; she emitted scornful laughter, even if it was soft and muted; her otherwise quiet dear face had a medusa-like quality resulting from the sudden expression of unspeakable bitterness and a nameless contempt). She struggles to overcome the horror of occasioning her own father's death and the burden of keeping the secret of the family crime. Still the monstrous self puts in an appearance—perhaps as a sign that she is an angry variation of Brontë's madwoman after all. Cordula differs, however, from Bertha as well as Frau Hellwig and the odious Adele with respect to self-awareness, regret, and compassion with the suffering of others.

Cordula numbers as one of several stigmatized women in Marlitt's corpus granted a voice and a plot. The text insists on this voice with the device of her diary. Cordula's voice resounds postmortem in Felicitas's reading of it; the narrative includes the entire text of the diary and its first-person narrator. It reveals the family's crime and prompts Johannes to bring about restitution to restore his family's honor. The pairing of Cordula with Felicitas ultimately repairs the split between heroine and stigmatized woman that Brontë reified. It constitutes this novel's most substantial innovation as productive reception of *Jane Eyre*. Still,

Cordula has to die in the logic of the narrative to free Felicitas to participate in the marriage script, a part the latter refuses to play early in the novel, when, insisting on her personhood, she rejects a loveless, arranged marriage.

A third of the way into the novel, Johannes tells the progressive Professor Franck that women bore him; he finds them a mixture of "Gedankenlosigkeit und Charakterschwäche!" (1:113; brainlessness and weak character). Franck counters that the fault is not in women but in their deficient education and possibilities: women's detractors should exhort them to serious thought and remove the limitations that they have imposed on them; with changed social conditions, women's "Eitelkeit und Charakterschwäche" (vanity and weak character) will quickly vanish (1:114). Johannes comes to recognize the truth of Franck's words through the example of the cultivated, articulate, and unfailingly reliable and honest Felicitas herself. Two years before Mill's treatise on women and three years before Lewald's *Für und wider der Frauen*, Marlitt, if clumsily, begins to recalibrate what romance in the wake of *Jane Eyre* can bring into view for the modern individual.[11] Education, which is so important to English Jane and so pitifully lacking in Norwegian Nora, is crucial to German Felicitas.

What, then, of the implicit response of Marlitt's text, after all the looking and talking, to Moi's question—"What will it take for two modern individuals to build a relationship (whether we call it marriage or, simply, a life together) based on freedom, equality, and love?"—the question that Brontë forcefully addressed in 1847? Felicitas has been liberated from the oppression of Frau Hellwig and her household and lives in a loving and respectful marriage. Yet the ending leaves twenty-first century readers, who may be hoping for a couple that talk all day long, with a disappointing picture of split gender roles within a marriage in which the spunky protagonist seems to have acquiesced to convention. She has given birth to her first child. In the evening she finds ways to soothe worry from Johannes's brow. While the couple may converse in the evening, husband and wife cannot during the day when Johannes, as a virtuous bourgeois professional, must tend to his patients.

Still, a transformation has occurred, one figured by the gaze. Not only has Johannes learned to admire Felicitas and she him, the wives of his colleagues in Bonn, too, admire the one-time social outcast. In Marlitt's world, a version of Rochester's intention to "make the world acknowledge [Jane] a beauty too" (232) has thus been accomplished. Marlitt's romance plot insists on the recast social regard as an element of its happy resolution. Felicitas, furthermore, has a "room of her own" furnished with the objects that had once graced Cordula's attic abode, including the grand piano and busts of famous Germans. With these reminders of her enlightened, accomplished, and charitable mentor, the novel encourages readers to picture another sort of continuing conversation, to

---

[11]   In advocating for women's education and a broader sphere of action, Marlitt's *Geheimnis* harmonizes with earlier impulses of the emergent bourgeois women's movement in the German territories. The year 1865 had seen the founding of the *Leipziger Frauenbildungsverein* and the *Allgemeiner Deutscher Frauenverein* in Leipzig, where Marlitt's liberal publisher was also located. Both organizations advocated for improved education and opportunity for women.

imagine Felicitas as she communes with Cordula's legacy and the values of the education she enjoyed under her watchful eye.

Jane merges with Rochester, becoming "bone of his bone and flesh of his flesh" as the couple happily converse on their country estate and she writes her autobiography (401). Twenty years later, in 1867, Marlitt, by contrast, imagines an urban middle-class companionate marriage not in terms of the couple blending but rather in terms of separate spheres in the everyday that leaves the heroine room to lay claim to a form of *Bildung* within the home and on into the future. In other words, Felicitas, unlike Ibsen's Nora, the ignorant plaything of men, has acquired an education and continues to call upon it. Marlitt's gloss on the happy ending, although hardly radical, does avoid submerging and silencing Felicitas in a sentimental idea of marital bliss in which, for all intents and purposes, the heroine becomes unintelligible to readers as an individual because she is "finished," silent, and blandly normalized. In this respect, Marlitt's conclusion differs from many *Jane Eyre* adaptations for girls and other German popular literature and hews to some of the progressive impulses of Brontë's novel, but within a different social imaginary. While Jane Rochester "makes noise," by telling and publishing the story of her younger self, Felicitas Hellwig or her children will likely make noise by playing Cordula's piano. This potential for noise—modern times and a new female self—may be the old mam'selle's real secret in plain sight.

But this is not where the novel finally ends. The text must attend to a second stigmatized female character, Marlitt's revival of Mrs. Reed. Unlike Brontë, she grants this bad mother figure, who herself was abused, the hope of reconciliation and redemption, among other things by allowing her, unlike Mrs. Reed, to live beyond the last page of the book. With a parting view of her knitting for her as yet unseen grandchild, the text supplies just enough information to enable readers to endorse the closing wish that the grandmother-to-be overcome her angry prejudice—"Hoffen wir, lieber Leser" (1:304; Let us hope, dear reader). In effect, it asks the reader who has learned to hate her to forgive her.

The Mam'selle's Secret on Stage

By the end of the nineteenth century, fourteen stage adaptations of eight of Marlitt's novels had appeared in print and these (and others that never reached print) had been widely performed over the course of approximately three decades, 1868–97, not only in the continental German-speaking world but also in the German Diaspora as far as Russia to the east and California to the west. A male contemporary later nastily recalled Marlitt's popularity as akin to an epidemic.[12] The metaphor, although unkind, captures the diffusion of the play productions, with Berlin and Hamburg usually serving as ground zero for the debut and multi-directional spread of each play production. Indeed, new productions of theater adaptations of Marlitt's first five novels peaked in the years 1868–75, having fanned out quickly from the locales of their premieres only to become

---

12   Felix Philippi, *Alt-Berlin. Erinnerungen aus der Jugendzeit*, n.s., 4th ed. (Berlin: Ernst Siegfried Mittler & Son, 1918), 75.

a matter for the provinces and beyond and then to disappear just as quickly. Calculated to entertain popular audiences and written with one, possibly two, exceptions by male authors close to the theater, these adaptations both preserve and distort Marlitt's originals. As productive reception via transmedial adaptation, they rely on Marlitt's cachet and the contents of her novels, but also alter these contents. They testify, moreover, not only to a culture in motion—materially, politically, socially—but also to the status and viability of Marlitt's novels and in turn to the relative vitality of some elements of *Jane Eyre* twenty to thirty years after its first appearance in the German-speaking territories.

Even in the case of Marlitt adaptations that hew closely to the original plots, theatergoers could not experience the same story as did readers; nor did they necessarily receive the same message, for that message was altered by the mere transition from prose and print to drama and theater spectacle. In the process of dramatization and theater production these plays in fact register the sociopolitical instability that Marlitt's fiction addressed, however tentatively. They also now serve as indicators of popular expectations of theater spectatorship. In comparison with Birch-Pfeiffer's *Waise aus Lowood*, which for nearly seventy years competed for attention in the German-language realm with iterations of Brontë's novel while also contributing to that novel's literary diffusion and survival, these plays experienced a much shorter performance life. Still, they document the historical reception of Marlitt and varied transmission and circulation of elements of *Jane Eyre*, indeed, the degree to which Marlitt's novels had become common property. We turn here to the three surviving theater adaptations of *Geheimnis*, all of which were first staged 1868–9, with the last performance recorded by the *Deutscher Bühnen-Almanach* occurring in 1886. The plays provide an index of the sturdiness of the romance plot described above as it moves via sympathy and intelligibility toward freedom, equality, and love.

In the process of pressing the *c.* 92,000 words of the novel into an evening's entertainment, much of what has concerned us in the analysis of the tentative searching, the slow unfolding of sympathy and intelligibility, was lost and with these aspects the tension that renders *Geheimnis* a pleasurable romance read. While the theater might allow for the performance of an array of looking practices, all three adaptations largely forgo this possibility and instead turn to other legible social gestures, in particular the hand—the hand extended, the hand refused. Furthermore, the printed scripts emphatically validate talk when they retain and enhance some of the confrontational dialogue between Johannes and Felicitas. Finally, despite alterations, they at least gesture toward Moi's "freedom, equality, and love" as well as ideas of acknowledgment and mutual intelligibility.

Staging *Geheimnis* for the theater meant re-investing in Felicitas, who would be played by a theater company's resident soubrette or by an attractive guest performer, actresses on whose hypervisibility the success of the production depended. A word count of dialogue and stage directions for Felicitas in all three plays confirms her enduring vocal centrality. Both Carl Mossberg and A. Jahn, for example, devote an entire scene to her reading Cordula's diary aloud and thus discovering the crime simultaneously for herself and the audience. In having Felicitas read Cordula's words, both plays also effectively double the female voice. All three adaptations in turn assign Johannes the second-most number of spoken words and stage directions. At a distance, these tallies suggest that the adaptations home in on verbal exchange as a constituent of romance. A closer look reveals, however, that the plays vary in their attention to this conversation.

Of the three surviving theater adaptations, Mossberg's play reached the stage first. After a trial run at the Schloßtheater in nearby Charlottenburg in August 1868, it opened on September 3, 1868, in Berlin at the Victoria-Theater with a Fräulein Le Seur playing Felicitas.[13] The large Victoria-Theater, where adaptations of Marlitt's *Die zweite Frau* and *Reichsgräfin Gisela* also premiered, boasted a seating capacity of 3,000. Ten performances with a full house thus comprised 30,000 spectators—this in a city whose population, including suburbs, numbered *c*. 800,000 in 1870. Theatergoers could buy tickets at varying prices, from standing room in the upper balcony at 5 Silbergroschen to a private box at 1 Thaler, 10 Silbergroschen, an evening in the theater thus being available to a range of socio-economic groups.[14] A single issue of the weekly *Gartenlaube* cost roughly the equivalent of standing room. For much less money than it cost to buy the serialization of the novel or the book publication and for far less an investment of time, spectators could learn how it all came out by the end of an evening's entertainment. The proximate delights of the theater replaced the pleasures of sustained engagement. What, then, did theatergoers actually see?

The *Gartenlaube* pronounced Mossberg's *Geheimnis* an unmitigated success and predicted that the play would become a box office draw and showpiece of the Victoria-Theater.[15] Noting the lively applause that accompanied the performance right to the end, the *Berliner Gerichts-Zeitung* too forecasted a long run: one was not bored for a single moment, and no one could ask for more.[16] Both the *Berliner Gerichts-Zeitung* and the *Vossische Zeitung* linked Mossberg's play to Birch-Pfeiffer's theater adaptations. As the *Gerichts-Zeitung* asserted, *Geheimnis*, "eine der reizendsten und effectvollsten Novellen, welche die Gartenlaube je enthalten" (one of the most charming and dramatic novels the *Gartenlaube* ever contained), had quickly found its Birch-Pfeiffer in a certain Carl Mossberg.[17] Both reviews point to paths of transmission that concern us here.

The anonymous review for the *Vossische Zeitung* especially merits attention, for it addresses the challenges of transmediation, connects the play to *Jane Eyre* via Birch-Pfeiffer, and enumerates reasons for the success of both the play and the novel. The reviewer stresses especially the psychological veracity of both as a feature of their appeal. Assuming that the novel was well known, the review points out the challenge of condensing the material and the resultant damage to

13   *Zweite Beilage zur Königl. Privilegirten Berlinisichen Zeitung*, no. 206, September 3, 1868, 2; *Berliner Gerichts-Zeitung: Tageszeitung für Politik, Rechtspflege* 16, no. 104, September 8, 1868, 2.

14   Ruth Freydank, *Theater in Berlin. Von den Anfängen bis 1945* (Berlin: Henschelverlag, 1988), 290.

15   *Die Gartenlaube*, no. 38 (1868): 608.

16   *Berliner Gerichts-Zeitung*, no. 104, September 8, 1868, 2.

17   *Königl. Privilegirten Berlinisichen Zeitung*, no. 210, September 8, 1868, 3.

the slow psychological development that is central to the plot. Yet while the compression of the material entailed loss of important details and made the drama somewhat disjointed, viewers could fill in the gaps and were likely not bothered by them; after all, they went to the theater mainly for the purpose of seeing a "zweite illustrirte Ausgabe" (second illustrated edition) of a novel they loved. In its psychological truth and topicality, the theme, for its part, the reviewer notes, recalls "*Jane Eyre, die Waise von Lowood.*"[18]

Of the three adaptations, Mossberg's play exhibits by far the most verbatim matches with dialogue from Marlitt's original and in that sense could satisfy audiences who wanted to see the novel they knew on stage. Its straightforward borrowings in turn make visible Marlitt's heavy reliance on dialogue—in the manner of Brontë. Yet in the process of adapting Marlitt, Mossberg muted the more progressive impulses while preserving the conservative elements that also haunt the original, particularly Johannes's paternalistic tone. He, for example, reproduces verbatim Johannes's protest against Felicitas's wish to free herself from her chains and his infantilizing promise to protect her like a child: she must not tear her own breast like a furious bird![19] In the play this speech hangs in the air as the authoritative point of view, since, in contrast with the novel, Mossberg does not provide the counterweight of Felicitas's vehement naming of the sins of the Hellwig family against her. The play contains no mention of "geistiger Tod" (intellectual/spiritual death) or of being raised to be an automaton without feeling. It barely mentions servitude. Without Felicitas's defiant and repeated articulation of the reasons for her anger, the struggle between the hero and heroine seems largely a matter of making a petulant Felicitas listen to reason and submit to a newly enlightened Johannes. The play does not dramatize the process by which Johannes comes to recognize her virtue, but does retain the *Jane Eyre*-word—"Sphinx"—invoking concealment and curious regard (27).

In the end, Felicitas proves reasonable. She acquiesces to Johannes's suit once he has demonstrated his virtue by acknowledging the wrongs of his family—all this in the vein of melodrama and virtue revealed. Assured of Johannes's worth, Felicitas is prepared to do everything she can to brighten the life of an honorable man. The play proclaims the world in order when Johannes declares that Felicitas, after all, possesses woman's "echte beseligende Liebe" (61; love that makes truly blissful). Seizing male prerogative, he then concludes the play by raising heavenward Cordula's revelatory diary, the prop that has enabled the desiring partners to make peace with one another and settle into their prescribed gender roles.

The words spoken in this final scene originate with Marlitt, but in staging them with Johannes's dramatic gesture, Mossberg loses sight of Marlitt's projection of a marriage informed by freedom and a form of parity. The reviewer for the *Vossische Zeitung* indeed understood Mossberg's ending in a gender-conventional vein as the heroine's deliverance from the defiance and anger that

---

18   *Königl. Privilegirten Berlinischen Zeitung*, no. 210, 3.
19   Carl Mossberg, *Das Geheimniß der alten Mamsell: Schauspiel in 3 Akten mit einem Vorspiel; Nach dem gleichnamigen Romane von E. Marlitt für die Bühne bearbeitet* (Berlin: August Gunkel, n.d.), 41, hereafter cited in the text.

threaten to destroy her by means of love's "magic word," spoken, of course, by the male protagonist.

Jahn's *Das Geheimnis der alten Mamsell* also evinces many overlaps with Marlitt's dialogue, but adheres more tightly to the romance plot, including its more progressive notes, than does Mossberg's.[20] Among other things, it devotes more energy to portraying Johannes's attempts to read Felicitas and the growing attraction accompanying these attempts. In two soliloquies Johannes broods on what he cannot understand and the strange feelings his incomprehension engenders in him; in a conversation with Frank, he, too, calls Felicitas a "Sphinx."[21] Felicitas, for her part, speaks in act 4, scene 7, a soliloquy revealing her love for Johannes (58–9).

In this play Felicitas repeatedly names the sins of the Hellwig family against her as she does not in Mossberg's version, namely, the deliberate decision not to educate her and instead to prepare her for servitude. She insists on the right of all human beings to education in words taken directly from Marlitt: no one has the right to condemn another "zu geistigem Tod"; she is by no means alone in knowing "wie ungerecht und strafbar es ist, einer Menschenseele die Berechtigung des Aufwärtsstrebens abzusprechen" (23; how unjust and criminal it is to deny a human soul the right of upward striving). These same words also appear in Anton Edmund Wollheim da Fonseca's adaptation.

Jahn, like Marlitt and Mossberg, includes Johannes's protest that Felicitas must be reasonable and not shred her own breast like a furious bird. Jahn's adaptation, however, makes more of bird metaphors in keeping with both Marlitt and Brontë. Felicitas, whose background has made of her a "Zugvogel" (18; migratory bird) in Frau Hellwig's derisive terms, at last finds a home in this play in Johannes's love. The birdcage that appears on stage in Aunt Cordula's apartment, as in the novel, suggests that being "caught" is not so terrible if one has a loving and nurturing home—as pointed out above, while Jane declares that she is "no bird" to be netted, she immediately allows herself to be caught.

Jahn works with the idea of voluntary submission found in both Brontë and Marlitt. The male protagonist asks in the final scene, "Ergiebt sich nun der junge, wilde Vogel für alle Zeiten?" (63; Does the young wild bird surrender for all eternity?). Felicitas answers in sentimental language: "Mein Herz war ja längst Dir entgegengeflogen" (63; My heart had long since flown to you). In the novel, Felicitas speaks both lines. Jahn makes of them instead a question and response and thus part of the romance dialogue, stressing free will and lending Johannes some humility. But Felicitas has more to say in the play; speaking the words of Marlitt's narrator, she declares that she will never again make the least effort to fly away: "Ach, es ist so süß, in starken Armen geborgen zu rasten" (63; It is so sweet to rest sheltered in strong arms). The effect of her speaking these words becomes clear when they are compared with Rochester's line in the closing

---

[20]   I have found only a trace of the performance of this adaptation in *Amts-Blatt für die königlichen Bezirksämter Forchheim und Ebermannstadt*, no. 44, April 13, 1869, 176, where a notice announces a performance on April 15, 1869, at the Stadt-Theater.

[21]   A. Jahn, *Das Geheimniß der alten Mamsell. Schauspiel in 4 Akten; Nach E. Marlitt's Roman bearbeitet* (Berlin: Eduard Bloch, n.d.), 27. Further references appear in the text.

scene of Birch-Pfeiffer's *Waise*. Here Rochester announces his intention to shelter Jane while Jane herself falls silent: "meine Braut, mein Weib, mein Kleinod, das meine starken Arme fortan wahren werden" (14: 147; my bride, my wife, my jewel, which my strong arms will keep safe from now on). It is unlikely that Jahn had not seen Birch-Pfeiffer's play; here he adjusts its romance conversation by allowing Felicitas to speak.

In his choreography of romance, Jahn furthermore calls upon two silver bangles, each inscribed with half a medieval love poem, "Stete Liebe" (constant love) by Ulrich von Liechtenstein. As in the original, the bangles serve as clues to the family crime and, once paired, they also convey an ideal of constancy and true love. In both the novel and the play, the lawyer Franck sees the matching bangles as "loyal comrades" united by the verses of the poem. Johannes repeats the epithet "treue Kameraden" (instead of "gute Kameraden" [good comrades] as in the novel) after he and Felicitas join forces to care for Ännchen (33). In the streamlined plot of the play the repetition stands out, linking the parity that the two achieve through collaboration to the love poem and the blissful life it promises. In the retention of this double function, Jahn makes full use of the theatrical possibilities of the bangles as stage props. Felicitas's closing vow—your loyal wife for all eternity until God calls me—invokes once more the constancy of Lichtenstein's verses and the companionate love relationship they foretell.

Wollheim da Fonseca's adaptation, by contrast with both Mossberg's and Jahn's, reproduces relatively little dialogue from the original novel. Yet its retention of key components of Marlitt's original makes it a reasonably progressive rendering. Its distribution of talk, however, results in a different emphasis. Wollheim assigns the servant Heinrich approximately the same number of words and stage directions as he does Felicitas and Johannes each. The couple, after talking less over all, thus reach their happy ending with a voluble third character in the mix. This re-weighted character impedes the streamlining of the play into a mere love story and gestures instead toward the more complex social world of the novel. At the same time, Heinrich is also a stock theater character and perhaps a sign of the pressure of theater convention on adaptation. Cordula, too—likely also played by a character actor—has a larger role in this play than in the other two and does not die until the end of the third act.

Das Geheimnis der alten Mamsell oder Hass und Liebe (The Old Mam'selle's Secret or Hate and Love) premiered at the Carl-Schultz Theater in Hamburg in November 1868, not long after Mossberg's adaptation debuted in Berlin.[22] While Mossberg's *Geheimnis* initially gained more traction across the German lands, Wollheim's evidences a longer afterlife. As one example, the latter script turns up in a miniature paper theater for home use.[23]

---

[22] A second adaptation was playing at the St. Georg-Theater as confirmed both by *Der deutsche Bühnen-Almanach* (1870), 150, and Theater Notice, *Hamburger Nachrichten*, November 8, 1868, 12. Neither source provides more than the title of the play and therefore it is not possible to determine whether it is Jahn's, Mossberg's, or yet another adaptation that has not survived in print form.

[23] Annegret Reizte, "Die Texthefte des Papiertheaters: Ein Beitrag zur Rezeption von populären Theaterstoffen und Kinder- und Jugendliteratur," PhD diss., University of Stuttgart, 1990, 114.

The cast of characters lists Heinrich as a former boatswain on a Hamburg "Galeaffe" (small sailing ship); in Hamburg he spoke his lines in Low German, to the delight of audiences.[24] He pops up in the second scene of the *Vorspiel* (prelude) and maintains a presence to the very last scene where he, Felicitas, and Johannes conclude the play with a vocal trio, as it were. Not only will Felicitas belong to Johannes forever, but Heinrich will also stay with them "until the end" (68). Ultimately the happy ending involves the union of upstairs and downstairs as well as of man and wife. Besides tailoring the play to the locale of its premiere, Wollheim endowed the mobile Heinrich with some of the functions and prerogatives of the original heterodiegetic narrator and some of the other characters: Heinrich provides exposition, pushes Herr Hellwig to adopt Felicitas and thus launches the entire plot; he advises Felicitas after Cordula's death and confronts the unpleasant Adele on Johannes's behalf. In act 4, scene 1, Heinrich also assumes the function assigned to Felicitas in the other two adaptations and in the novel, namely, the revelation of the "mam'selle's secret." Finally, he intervenes in act 5, scene 4, when Johannes, to his horror, learns of the family's crime; he in effect pushes the disoriented Johannes and Felicitas into one another's arms. In the end, Wollheim not only vindicates and empowers Felicitas but also lends Heinrich dignity and social worth in what is also a stock role: the lively servant.

Despite these new roles for Heinrich and many departures from the original, Wollheim does reproduce Marlitt's text verbatim in some exchanges that incorporate progressive aspects of a romance plot based in struggle. Marlitt's and Wollheim's Felicitas, for example, vehemently criticizes the limited education that the Hellwigs afforded her after Mr. Hellwig's death: no human being has the right to condemn another "zu geistigem Tod," Felicitas declares, as she also did in Jahn's version (36). Likewise, in yet another tense scene with Johannes, Felicitas objects, "Sie wollten mich zur willenlosen Maschine herabdrücken" (43; You wanted to debase me by making me a machine without a will). The insistence, true to Marlitt, on Felicitas's right to think and have a will is present in Jahn, although absent from Mossberg, but only Wollheim retains the *Jane Eyr*ish metaphor of the machine.

In addition to sporadic indications that Johannes's view of Felicitas is changing—his tone, for example, becomes "herzlicher" (42; more cordial)— Wollheim assigns Johannes an extended monologue in which he admits his family's error in attempting to kill her spirit (44; *Geist*). But when he discovers that she has been reading Dante (Wollheim's invention) and that Cordula has educated her in secret, he becomes less concerned with the sins against her and worries instead that he will give in to his attraction to her and contract a socially inappropriate marriage. Wollheim again emphasizes social stratification and prejudice.

In service of romance, Wollheim also reproduces Felicitas's inner moral turmoil as it arises from a love that itself is prohibited by the rules of the social

---

24 Anton Edmund Wollheim da Fonseca, *Das Geheimnis der alten Mamsell oder Hass und Liebe* (Hamburg: Berendsohn, 1869), 5, hereafter cited in the text.

order. Felicitas notes with dismay the fearful power of love: Johannes's every word penetrates her like an "elektrischer Schlag … elektrisch! Ja das ist's! kurz, gewaltig, schmerzlich und erschütternd" (41; electric jolt … electric! Yes, that's it! Short, powerful, painful, and shocking). Felicitas's repetition of "elektrisch" amplifies Marlitt's original formulation and also transmits another trace of *Jane Eyre* present in Marlitt. The language of the play—the machine and the electric jolt—suggests a direct transfer from Brontë through Marlitt to Wollheim. But the path of transmission is not quite that simple.

Wollheim's *Geheimnis* also evinces familiarity with Birch-Pfeiffer's *Waise*, where in act 3, scene 12, Jane also protests that she is not a machine. The migration of elements of Brontë's text to Wollheim's adaptation may, in other words, have occurred via multiple pathways—both through Marlitt's novel and theater productions of *Waise*. The structuring of his drama (unlike that of Mossberg and Jahn) appears to emulate Birch-Pfeiffer when it opens with a *Vorspiel* with the key scenes from Felicitas's childhood. Furthermore, Wollheim sorts the ensuing five acts into three "Abtheilungen" (sections) in the manner of *Waise*. In pushing the love story in the direction of social justice and the melodramatic gesture of "virtue revealed," Wollheim hews to the most notable innovation of Birch-Pfeiffer's *Jane Eyre* adaptation. As a popular play his adaptation of a run-away bestseller indebted to *Jane Eyre* thus supported the repetition, redundancy, and proliferation that matter to cultural transmission.

Six Goldelse: "A lighter-tinted Jane Eyre placed in somewhat different circumstances"

For some readers, Marlitt's *Goldelse* still more obviously displayed its genealogy. In his 1870 review, Gottschall especially emphasizes the resemblance of Goldelse to Jane; she is an "in etwas andere Verhältnisse versetzte, milder gefärbte Jane Eyre" (lighter-tinted Jane Eyre placed in somewhat different circumstances). A significant number of situations and episodes in *Goldelse* come across, he observes, as variations of the English novel, for example, Elisabeth's encounter in the forest with Rudolf, who arrives on horseback.[1] It is obvious, he concludes, that Marlitt wrote *Goldelse* under the influence of Brontë. Nevertheless, as he also emphasizes, important differences—particularly aspects of the "deutschen Gemüthes" (German disposition)—inform the novel. Nine years later, the literary historian Robert Koenig paraphrased this last observation and summarized the German author's debt to Brontë, asserting that she had both Germanized (*germanisiert*) and modernized (*modernisiert*) Brontë.[2] Lighter tinted, Germanized, and modernized—in what respects did Marlitt's first full-length novel, *Goldelse*, transmit *Jane Eyre* in these softened and altered tones, while also setting Marlitt on a course of novel writing that, as productive reception, generated its own rich reception history?

Over the course of the half century after its initial serialization, *Goldelse* inspired at least eight German-language adaptations and appeared as a deluxe edition illustrated by Paul Thumann (1871), in the illustrated collected works (1890),[3] and in many other German editions and reprints as well as in translation in at least six European languages. In the United States alone, it circulated in three

---

[1] Gottschall, "Die Novellistin der 'Gartenlaube,'" 291. In 1871, the Austrian *Neue Freie Presse* also noted the similarity between the two novels, condescendingly labeling Marlitt's novel a "thüringische Nachahmung der 'Jane Eyre' von der Currer Bell, verbrämt mit mondscheinumwobenen Schloßruinen und rauschendem Waldzauber" (Thuringian imitation of "Jane Eyre" by Currer Bell, lined with castle ruins and rustling forest magic bathed in moonlight) meant to delight a poorly educated female audience. P. E., "Die Rolle der Reminiscenz," *Neue freie Presse*, December 20, 1871.

[2] Robert Koenig, *Deutsche Literaturgeschichte* (Bielefeld and Leizpig: Velhagen and Klasing, 1879), 633.

[3] The publication of *Goldelse* as volume 8 of the illustrated series of Marlitt's novels is announced in *Die Gartenlaube*, Halbheft 13 (1890): 420.

translations and many reprint editions. The eight German adaptations include *Goldelschen* (1880) for the younger set; three printed theater adaptations; at least two additional stagings that never reached print; an abridged version by the children's author Else Hofmann (*c.* 1919); and a film adaptation from 1918 with National-Film, starring the Jewish, Hungarian-born Edith Meller (1897–1953), the "liebe Mädchen, dessen Blick aus den tiefgründigen Augen man sich nicht entziehen kann" (darling girl, who irrevocably captivates with the expression of her deep-dark eyes).[4] These instantiations of *Goldelse* exemplify the changing, splintered, and diffused legacy of *Jane Eyre* and the romance it delivered in the German-language domain. They bring into focus, through losses and gains, what *Jane Eyre* via Marlitt potentially offered readers in an era that began with the founding of the new German Reich and ended in a world war. As we shall see, unlike *Geheimnis*, which was published a year later, this first novel suggests that, even as she reproduced many key elements, Marlitt had yet to grasp some of the most compelling features of *Jane Eyr*ish romance.

* * *

Gottschall could have enumerated still more components shared with *Jane Eyre*. For one, both works name their female protagonist in their titles such that, in each case, speaking of the book invokes the character and vice versa. *Goldelse*, moreover, includes two characters whose first names duplicate character names in Brontë's novel: Helene von Walde, the male protagonist's ailing sister, and the servant girl Bertha in fact both display affinities to their English counterparts.[5] Like Helen Burns, Helene wastes away and dies in the female protagonist's arms, and Bertha, the "kleine Furie" (8:142; little fury), seems to be on the verge of actually biting Elisabeth in her rage, just as Bertha, labeled a "fury," bites her own brother.

Goldelse in fact exhibits many structural resemblances to its literary antecedent. These features produce romance as a verbal struggle between a powerful man and a much younger, relatively inexperienced but strong woman. This struggle is informed by sympathy through which the heterosexual partners, despite social inequalities organized around gender and class, achieve acknowledgment, a form of social parity, and relational selfhood realized within marriage. These structuring and equalizing elements, furthermore, share with *Jane Eyre* the prizing of the heroine's forthright speech, imagination, and aesthetic sensitivity as well as articulation of and reflection on emotion as feeling. This

---

4   Notice, *Der Kinematograph*, no. 605 (August 7, 1918), n.p. I thank Petra Watzke for alerting me to the existence of this and other promotional material regarding the filming of Marlitt's novels.

5   In her treatment of renunciation in *Goldelse*, Charlotte Woodford too, in passing, notes the echo of Bertha Mason in the servant's name. Charlotte Woodford, "Nineteenth-Century Sentimentality and Renunciation: E. Marlitt's *Goldelse* (1866) and Gabriele Reuter's *Liselotte von Reckling* (1904)," in *German Women's Writing of the Eighteenth and Nineteenth Centuries: Future Directions in Feminist Criticism*, ed. Helen Fronius and Anna Richards (Oxford: Legenda, 2011), 89.

romance with its interest in individual disposition, like its English antecedent, also falls under the broader rubric of domestic fiction, literature that, in Nancy Armstrong's formulation, represents the value of the individual "in terms of … essential qualities of mind" and "subtle nuances of behavior."[6] The reader comes to know and admire a great deal about the mind, heart, and behavior of both the male and female protagonists.

Tiny like Jane, Elisabeth is a gifted pianist; she plays Mozart and Beethoven and also improvises. Through music she lends form to her "Phantasien" (8:163; fantasies), her "eigenen Gedanken" (8:123; own thoughts). She has the power of giving expression to the subtle stirrings of her heart in her piano playing (8:124). Rudolf's perception and appreciation of this talent recalls the episode in which Rochester recognizes Jane's imagination and skill in drawings that the autobiographical narrator describes in ekphrastic detail. "Und wer lehrte Sie, den Wind zu malen?" (And who taught you to paint wind?) asks Rochester in all four translations (and the three abridged versions) as well as in Birch-Pfeiffer's play; the abrupt question admires Jane's quality of mind as much as her art.

Like Jane, Elisabeth expects to earn her own living. Having worked as a paid music teacher, she is preparing for a future as a governess when she meets Rudolf. Marlitt's novel operates with a keen understanding of Gottschall's "proletariat of the mind" in its depiction of the condescension of the snobbish Baroness von Lessen toward both Elisabeth and an actual governess, the long-suffering Miss Mertens. Her condescension echoes Blanche Ingram's rude disparagement of governesses. Miss Mertens's escape from the baroness's penurious employment through matrimony in turn recalls Miss Temple's departure from Lowood. With its female teachers—working women from the middle classes—*Goldelse* invokes its British literary antecedent (and governess novels written in its wake).

Recalling the Gothic turn of *Jane Eyre*, a woman lies hidden in Castle Gnadeck in *Goldelse*, secreted in a walled-off shrine. She is, however, not a living wife, but instead the long-dead Lila, the "gypsy" wife of the feudal lord Jost von Gnadeck. Marlitt musters this Gothic motif to address social inequality. Jost and Lila are the heroine's ancestors on her bourgeois father's side. Their story, one of social un-equals, took place during the Thirty Years War, the same historical event that plays a role in the eponymous secret of *Geheimnis*. After Lila's death in childbirth, the bereft Jost left for the war, never to return. With his death the story of his obsessive love fell into oblivion. Although the narrator does not comment further, German and Austrian audiences could have picked up immediately on the significance to a present-day family of the story of the war that devastated Middle Germany. Marlitt invokes this troubled history as a back story to present inequality, as does Brontë when she sets Rochester's back story in Jamaica, a site and symptom of British colonial capitalism—vividly embodied in the incarcerated mad Creole wife—and makes these the historical conditions underpinning Rochester's personal sufferings and failings. Marlitt, however, through the introduction of this past in *Goldelse*, offloads historical

---

6   Armstrong, *Desire and Domestic Fiction*, 4.

guilt onto Jost von Gnadeck who paid with his life. Two hundred years later, the now proudly bourgeois Ferbers can remain in the family castle, which they have restored with their own labor, and be mindful of the sins of feudalism without paying the price for them.

While the Ferbers reject their aristocratic lineage in keeping with the liberal outlook of the novel, this inheritance does matter to the happy ending—just as Jane's inherited riches from Madeira matter. In Elisabeth's case, the crucial element is not so much wealth as blood. Jost's story reveals that she is descended from nobility on both her mother and her father's side and also from a stigmatized minority. The aristocratic lineage preserves her from universal rejection by the local nobility when she becomes Rudolph's wife and at some level secures her equal footing in her marriage. At the same time her descent from Lila renders her one of the good, freedom-loving people of modern times—and thus morally superior to aristocrats who cling to privilege.

Meanwhile, the hidden coffin and its history number among several sensation elements that lend excitement to the romance. Sensation also characterizes such plot turns as the disgruntled bailiff Linke's attempt to kill Rudolph; Emil von Hollfeld's vicious scheming, sexual aggression and betrayal of both Helene and Bertha; and Bertha's imprisoning of Elisabeth in an abandoned tower. While no such scandal as bigamy sullies Rudolf's moral authority and no such moral scandal impeded the serialization of the novel in *Die Gartenlaube*, the sensation elements that are present are not exactly "lighter tinted." What did Gottschall mean when he spoke of a lighter-tinted Jane Eyre placed in somewhat different circumstances?

Intact Family as "Somewhat Different Circumstances"

With *Goldelse* and *Geheimnis* especially, Marlitt took cues from *Jane Eyre* to narrate a series of romantic couplings of a certain kind that brought her national and international success. In the first of these, *Goldelse*, she, however, mitigated her heroine's circumstances and embedded her in a happy family of origin, such as is not found in her own later novels or *Jane Eyre*.[7] The presence of the warm and close-knit Ferber family in *Goldelse* contrasts not only with the individualism of Brontë's original, but also Marlitt's subsequent novels which center on orphans, half orphans, feuding siblings, estranged spouses, second wives, irresponsible parents, even divorce. By ensconcing the heroine in her intact biological family, the narrative renders her less assailable while perforce also limiting the narrative adventures she can plausibly experience. The novel instead reproduces, in Gottschall's terms, "Gemüt," that sociable emotional disposition made visible in this family and perceived as particularly German. Minor characters instead bear the load of the troubled families that otherwise occupy the narrative center throughout Marlitt's oeuvre.

The principal troubled family of *Goldelse* resides off center at Lindhof. Here the extended family of the aristocratic von Waldes and their retainers perpetrate

---

[7]   Dingeldey likewise notes a loss in later novels of the "Heimelige" (homey coziness) present in *Goldelse*. Dingeldey, *Luftzug hinter Samtportiere*, 190.

deception, violence, and injustice.[8] Moreover, the unchecked sexuality of privileged men presents an enduring threat in the form of Emil at Lindhof.[9] Ultimately at fault is, however, the failure of Rudolf himself to exercise authority as the male head of the household, a failing he proceeds to address upon his return, starting with the firing of the bailiff. But the text does not dwell on Rudolf's fault and instead concentrates on his valiant attempts to repair the damage done in his absence. His recovery culminates in his love for and marriage to Elisabeth and the birth of their first son, who bears his features. This unlooked-for personal happiness, moreover, helps to restore the entire region, as Jane's marriage to Rochester does not.[10]

Elisabeth's happy ending does not, however, as Hamann has recently claimed, merely mark a complete return to tradition or normalcy.[11] Instead it necessitates a revised social imaginary, one in which noble birth matters less to a good marriage in the ruling classes than does noble character. To bring her novel to a close, furthermore, Marlitt does not exactly offer the series of like marriages and accompanying inward turn that conclude *Jane Eyre* to which Nancy Armstrong objects in *How Novels Think*. No double wedding or proliferation of cousins' marriages reproduces the same class-based household "as the collective body on which one can depend for care and protection."[12] Instead, the narrator attends to people of various groups who have been harmed by local power run amok—Bertha, Miss Mertens, the minister, Doctor Fels. Marriage per se does, however, present as a viable solution across social classes, when Bertha and Miss Mertens find refuge in marriage to appropriate men of their own social group. In its somewhat broader social vision, *Goldelse* initiates a trend that persists throughout Marlitt's oeuvre: the love story is situated in a conflicted social context and addresses social themes.

While social arrangements remain hierarchical in *Goldelse*, the final pages strongly hint that, with the banishment of aristocrats with bad character and bad intention, a more generous democratic spirit will inform the region. Following the departure of the baroness and her family and the death of his sister, only

---

8   The "Lind" of Lindhof invokes the heraldic dragon (as in *Lindwurm*), but it also has milder associations as in the adjective "lind" (mild, gentle) or the sentimental *Lindenbaum* (linden tree).

9   For a fuller account of Emil's sexual transgressions, see Woodford, "Nineteenth-Century Sentimentality and Renunciation," 89–90. Woodfield ferrets out a possible allusion to an unwanted pregnancy resulting from Emil's seduction of Bertha in the "few words" a doctor speaks to the forester after examining Bertha.

10   Laird notes, however, that early English-language stage adaptations of *Jane Eyre* attempt something similar: "Rochester and Jane's union creates a social bond with the community as a whole." Laird, *The Art of Adapting Victorian Literature*, 43.

11   Although he avoids dismissing Marlitt's works as kitsch, Hamann nevertheless sees Marlitt's novels as structured according to "Ein normativ-normalistisches Weltmodell" (a normative-normalistic model of the world) in harmony with broader trends in the literary system of the times, especially as constituted by popular magazines. He does not consider the more subtle textual indications of deviation. Hamann, *Zwischen Normativität und Normalität*, 143–72.

12   Nancy Armstrong, *How Novels Think: The Limits of Individualism from 1719–1900* (New York: Columbia Universitiy, 2005), 143.

Rudolf remains on the estate to represent the aristocrats. Although expected, even he is out of sight on the last page of the novel. From Gnadeck, the narrator reports, the Ferbers can see Lindhof, their daughter's new home. The novel thus closes by privileging the emphatically bourgeois Ferbers' point of view.

Ascent to Agency and Social Reintegration

One sign of Marlitt's re-positioning of *Jane Eyre*ish romance more generally resides in the narrative deployment and signification of the hand. "Hand/ Hände" and "Auge/n" rank consistently as the most relatively frequent nouns across Marlitt's entire oeuvre. The hand, of course, also figures in *Jane Eyre*, especially in the concluding chapters when Jane reveals that Rochester lost his left hand in the very process of using his hands in an attempt to rescue Bertha from the fire that she set with her own hands. When Jane first lays eyes on him after the accident, he repeatedly stretches out his remaining hand into emptiness in a histrionic gesture that continues until Jane reveals herself and seizes that hand. The narrative cannot replace his missing left hand except through Jane's actions on his behalf; as she puts it, "I am still his right hand" (401). Despite these significant plot events, the hand figures far less repetitively in *Jane Eyre* than in Marlitt's novels.

Goldelse does not muster the hand to narrate sad plot turns of maiming and permanent loss. Instead, from the start the hand helps to establish the worth and self-understanding of the musically gifted central female character. The hand also apportions agency and signifies connection. As the narrator remarks in the first chapter, the trials of a piano teacher consist in being forced to listen to the music of the unskilled hands of the pupil who tries to play a piece with fingers in the incorrect position. The same chapter will remark on the teacher Elisabeth's cold hands and her need for gloves. Later, when the Ferbers discover the mandolin that belonged to Lila, the narrator notes that the black fretboard bears the finger marks of the hands that once played it; what is more, the sound board is lightly indented where musicians usually place their little finger (8:24). These fingers, the narrator implies, were positioned correctly, and the special talent of this diminutive ancestor has resurfaced in the present day in the petite Elisabeth.

As the plot unfolds, hands signify social relations. A wave of an aristocratic hand dismisses social others. The spoiled Bella slaps her governess's extended helping hand. Elisabeth, for her part, holds her little brother's hand or takes his face between her hands. Her hand also becomes an object sought by both the villain and the hero. Emil, who has stalked Elisabeth for some time, finally lays his "schön geformte weiße Männerhand" (8:168; beautifully shaped white masculine hand) on hers and later forces a kiss of the hand upon her.

Chapters later, an agitated Rudolf asks a reluctant Elisabeth to wish him a happy birthday in the manner he desires. She must begin by offering him her hand, which he takes in his: although she trembles as she does so, she does not withdraw her hand. He then prescribes the words he wishes to hear from her, namely that it is her "eigener, unumstößlicher Wunsch und Wille" (8:218; own incontrovertible desire and will) never to leave him. Her proffered hand is to guarantee ineffable happiness. A guest interrupts the couple and Elisabeth is unable to speak the vow to the end. The romance does not reach resolution until

Elisabeth, at Rudolf's renewed entreaty, repeats its final words and pledges her troth with her extended hand. The crucial difference between this episode and the odious Emil's kissing her hand lies in the fact that Rudolf has Elisabeth's sympathetic ear and she chooses to let her hand remain in his. And with her hand she signals what Belgum considers the "most radical topic that Marlitt addresses in her novels": female desire.[13]

In the scene in which the two finally become engaged, Rudolf holds both her hands. When he speaks the next line for her to repeat—essentially the marriage vow—she bursts into tears. Assuredly cringe-worthy in our times, her next movement is to throw herself, wordless, into his arms in a pantomime of assent. When she pulls away, he begs her to leave her hand in his so that he can believe in his happiness. Her hand—the same hand that at the piano reveals her feelings to herself and her readers—and not her speech secures romantic union. Hands remain important to the end in performing human relations. Elisabeth's own hand serves as a sign of her agency and is hers to bestow on another. Marlitt returns to the female hand and its touch as a romance element many times in her subsequent novels, most notably in *Die zweite Frau*, when she invents two talented sisters, one who is an illustrator in the manner of the zoologist Ernst Häckel and one who wields a microscope to reveal a forgery.

In a final address to readers, Marlitt's narrator offers a hand to accompany them to the former ruins of Gnadeck where renovated living quarters and a parting look at Elisabeth await them. Unlike Jane's "Reader, I married him," which introduces the final chapter of Brontë's novel, this concluding scene, narrated in the present tense, imagines the reader not as the auditor of past events but as a mobile figure that becomes part of present events by entering the text via the helping hand of the narrator. Using the first-person plural pronoun ("an unsrer Hand") (8:333; [led] by our hand), the figural narrator serves as the reader's physical guide to the restored Gnadeck. The imagined hand thus performs the inclusiveness of the new community projected at the novel's end.

"Every inch a man"

Gottschall leaves no doubt that, for him, the virtuous Rudolf von Walde recalls Currer Bell's "Lord Rochester."[14] By pronouncing him "jeder Zoll ein Mann" (every inch a man), he implicitly compares him with Rochester, lightly suggesting that the latter falls short. Although in some respects hyper-masculine, Brontë's ambiguous protagonist does suffer vicissitudes that at times undermine his gender. Not only is he dependent at the end of the novel, but he also disguises himself as a female fortuneteller and later gives up his manly watch while continuing to wear Jane's necklace.[15] Marlitt's Rudolf shares many of Rochester's manly social markers and behaviors. Unlike Rochester, he displays no sign of deliberate blurring of those gender norms.

---

13   Belgum, "Narratives of Virtuous Desire," 275.
14   Gottschall, "Die Novellistin der 'Gartenlaube,'" 291.
15   Gottschall, "Die Novellistin der 'Gartenlaube,'" 291.

When Elisabeth meets her future husband on the forest path, she hears a powerful male voice. Rudolf then bursts on the scene, trying to master his skittish horse. As the horse attempts to throw him, he forces it to stop dead and remains firmly in the saddle—unlike Rochester who falls off his horse. Rudolf immediately takes advantage of his male seigniorial authority to quiz Elisabeth, recalling the dynamics of *Jane Eyre*. Yet Rudolf is a gentler man with none of the dark anger of a Rochester, and the scene takes place in broad daylight rather than by the light of the moon. A cheerful smile brightens his seriousness when he speaks with Elisabeth in this key scene. When she excuses herself for making his horse shy, he answers her not with curses but in friendly tones. Unlike Rochester, Rudolf has no guilty secrets to hide. While he has gained a reputation for scorning women and being somewhat too grave of manner as a result of his past history, that past has not scarred him irreparably.

With this protagonist, in other words, Marlitt does not investigate the damaged masculinity that figures so importantly in *Jane Eyre* and later in her own works. *Goldelse* invests instead in misreadings and misunderstandings to retard the romantic plot while heightening the tension of emergent desire. Separated by age, experience, and social station, Elisabeth and Rudolf find themselves easily misled and unable to read one another, even as they seek to do so. Marlitt thus retains the desire for sympathy and intelligibility that drives *Jane Eyre* without presenting the dilemma of an erotic union with serious moral impediments.

Overall, this remaking of Rochester as Rudolf avoids ethically and socially dubious complications. The above-described establishing scene, although in Gottschall's view reminiscent of *Jane Eyre*, unleashes a romance that is indeed "milder gefärbt" and thus more attune to bourgeois ideals of men who must become family men for the sake of women's happiness. If Marlitt's manly man originates in the Byronic model that Rochester inhabits, he also transforms in keeping with changing ideas of masculinity within the social classes for whom domesticity was paramount. While both Rochester and Rudolf ultimately forgo travel to stay at home, Marlitt does not have to wound Rudolf to achieve that end.

A Lighter Emotional Palette?

Goldelse deflects moral failings from her Rochester figure and confers them instead on the scheming, lustful, and mendacious Emil. Emil in turn pulls the sickly Helene and the overwrought Bertha in his wake and thus the text links other female characters with anger and out-of-control desire while sparing Elisabeth. Indeed, while Elisabeth experiences a relatively narrow palette of emotions, readers become privy to a broader array through Baroness von Lessen, Helene, and Bertha who, like Emil, carry the negative affective load. As a result, despite the reduced complexity of character overall, *Goldelse* does rely on a variegated if softened palette of emotion distributed over several characters.

In comparison with *Jane Eyre*, however, the novel traffics far less in the sensitive and integrative reflection that renders emotion as feelings. While sadness noticeably marks Jane's narration, happiness dominates Elisabeth's story, especially as it pertains to her family. Measured by repetitions of happy words, the happiest time in the novel occurs at the very beginning when the Ferber family is poor but united in B[erlin]. These opening scenes are the least complex of the novel as the text presents a heroine still enjoying a serene latency. Only later do growing desire and the idea that a woman could gladly leave her family for a beloved man trouble the hitherto still waters of Elisabeth's emotional life. Ultimately, her personal happiness in many respects resembles that of her parents, whose union (like that of Jane's parents) was a love match considered a mesalliance by her aristocratic relatives. It hardly bears repeating that the opening domestic scenes with the Ferbers contrast starkly with the Reed household. Yet this early novel does probe both sadness and anger as an enduring feature of Marlitt's story worlds. A closer look at the putative happy ending of this first novel reveals their presence.

As the final chapter makes clear, the local aristocrats are not amused and instead a little confused by the love match. The liberal Dr. Fels reports that news of the engagement has hit the town "wie eine Bombe" (8:332; like a bomb). But no major changes of heart have occurred. The snobbish Baroness von Lessen is tormented by the very idea of Elisabeth residing at Lindhof, and although out of sight on the final pages, she persists in her meanness and prejudice. At the ducal court, the Grand Court Mistress laments the engagement, only to hear the reassuring news from the snobbish duchess that Elisabeth in the end really is of noble birth.

Further undercutting any impression of untroubled happiness, the closing scenario evokes both sadness and anger. Readers do learn here of Elisabeth's happiness as wife and mother and of the disappearance of Rudolf's melancholy and severity. Nevertheless, sadness fissures the final scenario when Elisabeth's happy expression briefly darkens and her eyes cloud with tears as she recalls how Helene died in her arms. Anger, too, is present. The very last word in the novel is "grollt," a verb expressing enduring anger and resentment; its subject is the banished Emil, whom the narrator does not allow readers to forget even in the blush of happiness. This final instancing of mortality and anger echoes *Jane Eyre* where the last page veers from Jane's happy family and the marriages of her cousins to thoughts of the "stranger's hand" who will one day soon write of St John's death. Not all is well, not even in Marlitt's rendering of romance.

Narrative Mind Reading

Illustrated book editions and adaptations of *Goldelse* tend to ignore such sobering notes of realism within this romance narrative. Paul Thumann's saccharine illustrations for the 1871 deluxe edition of *Goldelse* in particular dispel any notion of disarray or strong emotion and pick up instead on harmony and happiness. Elisabeth appears in illustration after illustration, unfailingly serene and usually static, with her mouth closed.[16]

For decades a prolific popular classically trained artist with an academic appointment at the Academy of Arts in Berlin, Thumann routinely furnished *Die Gartenlaube* with illustrations and also illustrated German classics, religious books, fairy-tale collections, and advice books. His composed, decorative,

---

[16]   E. Marlitt, *Goldelse*, illustrated by Paul Thumann (Leipzig: Keil, 1871).

and idealized drawings tidily circumscribe his figures, especially women and children, within the markers of nineteenth-century bourgeois sentimentality. His illustrations for the deluxe edition for their part indicate the availability of the novel to simple interpretations, despite the more complex contents outlined above. With one exception, the theater adaptations, as we shall see, likewise lean in this direction. In fact, more is going on in the text below the surface than these facile (mis)readings suggest. Marlitt's narrative invests in Elisabeth's thoughts and feelings, not just in the serene facade suggested by Thumann's images. Distantly echoing *Jane Eyre*, *Goldelse* periodically allows the reader, in the terms of the narrative theorist Lisa Zunshine, to "read the mind" of her protagonist.[17]

Brontë's narrator tells a personal story that unfolds from moment to moment, each one colored by emotion brought to consciousness as feeling through narration. Marlitt's impersonal third-person narrator in *Goldelse*, by contrast, addresses emotion articulated as feeling only intermittently in descriptions of external actions and in moments of omniscience that permit reading characters' minds, principally Elisabeth's but also occasionally Baroness von Lessen's and Helene's.

When the narrator of *Goldelse* does permit a look into Elisabeth's mind, these instances of thinking and feeling can figure for readers as pleasurable discovery. The aforementioned scene in which Elisabeth improvises at the piano provides one such occasion. It involves the revelation of Elisabeth's inexplicable attraction to Rudolf whom she barely knows. Something has permeated the notes she plays that she herself cannot grasp, "denn es flog nur wie ein neuer, unbekannter Hauch über die Tonwellen. Es war ihr, als wandelten Schmerz und Freude nicht mehr nebeneinander, sondern flössen in eins zusammen ... Dies Suchen nach dem Wesen jenes unfaßbaren Klanges ließ sie aber immer tiefer in ihre Gefühlswelt hinabsteigen" (8:124; for it flew only as a new, unknown breath of air over the waves of sound. She felt as though pain and joy no longer walked next to one another, but flowed together ... This search for the substance of that unfathomable sound, however, led her to descend ever deeper into her world of feeling).

Through her playing, the assembled, like readers, gain access to the depths of her maidenly soul, the narrator avers. Alert readers can intuit the meaning of this unfathomable sound; they can recognize that the inexperienced Elisabeth is falling in love with a much older, ostensibly socially inappropriate man. Thus prompted, readers subsequently watch for further signs of attraction and thus small gestures become significant. In service of a plot of delayed recognition, Elisabeth herself, however, remains for many pages opaque to herself and other diegetic characters.

Later, Elisabeth, again seated at the piano, finally achieves clarity as to her feelings for Rudolf, but at the very moment when this "Wunderland voll goldener Verheißungen" (8:175; wonderland filled with golden promises) opens before her mind's eye, she finds herself separated from it by an unbridgeable gap—rather like Jane when she admits to herself that she loves Rochester, only to have Blanche

---

17   Lisa Zunshine, *Why We Read Fiction: Theory of Mind and the Novel* (Columbus: Ohio State University Press, 2006).

Ingram's arrival dash all her hopes. Elisabeth's hope is thwarted when Rudolf appears to harbor aristocratic prejudices that make him an impossible partner.

Hofmann's abridged version for Fock from *c*. 1919, apparently aimed at a younger reading audience, omits the above passage, as one among many of the occasional forays into characters' minds that it elides to streamline the narrative.[18] It thus loses much of what Marlitt preserves of Brontë's engagement with emotion articulated as feeling, accounts that enable readers to find themselves in the thoughts and feelings of fictional others. The abridgment yields an externally focused shallow story that depends on plot events rather than character development, one akin to the largely unimaginatively rendered, cognitively flattened German adaptations of *Jane Eyre* for girls. In his early review, Gottschall locates the appeal of Marlitt's novels in the author's ability to tell a story and her powers of description. In effect, he asserts what this abridged edition reveals through its omissions, namely, the weakness of the abridged edition arises from the elision of the detail and description that Marlitt manages so well.

Jane Eyre valorizes emotion as an element of individualization and probes and reflects on feelings. The reading effects of *Jane Eyre* urge a paraphrase of Iser that pairs feeling—the bringing to consciousness of emotion—with thinking: they make it possible for the feelings and thoughts of others to take place in readers so that they feel and think what they are not; feeling and thinking what they are not enables them in turn "to formulate themselves and so discover what had previously seemed to elude their consciousness."[19] That thing that had "seemed to elude … consciousness" especially for female readers and especially in a time of inequality was an idea of selfhood realized within a primary relationship and constituted via both the cognitive *and* the affective life. *Goldelse* offers a pale reflection of this aspect of Brontë's novel. Nevertheless, even in its pallor it preserves and transmits this reflective coming to consciousness of thought and emotion as an aspect of subject formation within social life. The adaptations of *Goldelse*, however, largely lose sight of that literary production of selfhood; these narrative losses bring into relief what the original novel offered nineteenth-century readers.

"Little Gold Elsie" for Girls

At just over half the length of Marlitt's original novel, Auguste Wachler's *Goldelschen* (1880; Little Gold Elsie), designated for girls between twelve and fifteen, circulated for at least three decades in ten editions.[20] Wachler, who, as we

---

18 Else Hofmann, *Goldelse. Für die weibliche Jugend bearbeitet* (Leipzig: Gustav Fock, n.d.). Also published around 1919 was Else Hofmann, *Das Geheimnis der alten Mamsell. Erzählung von E. Marlitt. Für die weibliche Jugend bearbeitet* (Leipzig: Gustav Fock, n.d.). A copy of this abridged edition owned by the author provides a clue as to its circulation and that of others in the series, namely, the dedication on the front flyleaf reads, "Meiner lieben Enkelin Hanna Goebel zum Gedenken an Weichnachten 1928 von ihrem Großvater Wolf" (My dear granddaughter Hanna Goebel in memory of Christmas 1928 from her grandfather Wolf).

19 Iser, *The Implied Reader*, 294.

20 By 1890, it was in its sixth edition. "Von unserem Jugendbüchertisch," *Deutsche Rundschau* 17 (1890): 480.

have seen, two years later adapted *Jane Eyre* for the same publisher, thoroughly rewrote Marlitt's text. Borrowing almost no language from the original, she took many liberties with the plot and characters, some of which signal the influence of other novels. Fifteen-year-old Elisabeth's teaching of knitting classes for local girls, for example, recalls not Marlitt's heroine but Brontë's Jane who, while living with the Rivers, teaches "farmer's daughters … knitting, sewing, reading, writing, cyphering" (317).

While she invents new pedagogical tasks for this model young woman in the vein of *Jane Eyre*, Wachler curtails the transmission of sensation elements. In *Goldelschen*, for example, the walls of the family castle merely contain a hidden coin collection and not Lila's corpse. Without Lila the text avoids invoking the past sins of the aristocracy. Instead, one learns of arbitrary fatherly authority: an ancestor hid her precious coins there before being sent away by her strict father to marry a man she did not love. Wachler also banishes threatening male sexuality by transforming the adult Emil into the child Emil. No adult Emil can betray Rudolf's invalid sister or Bertha or pursue Elisabeth and thus no desperate Bertha locks Elisabeth in a tower. Wachler's Bertha is, moreover, by no means insane, merely angry. A kind gesture from Elisabeth quickly dispels her anger and makes a friend of her. Wachler also eliminates the homicidal Linke. Elisabeth thus has no need to save Rudolf's life.

Conflicts in human relations generally turn out to be simple and easy to resolve, beginning with the disgruntled Bertha. The bigoted and malicious Frau von Hollfeld (=Baroness von Lessen) experiences a significant change of heart when Elisabeth rescues Emil. This Emil has not only replaced Marlitt's grown-up Emil but also his spoiled stepsister, Bella; in a less complex familial constellation, Wachler's baroness has only been widowed once. Rudolf's sister, here named Marie, does not die, but instead recovers and makes an appropriate match with a local aristocrat and friend of her brother. Negative emotions—anger, fear, and sadness—take up less space than in the original since Wachler has eliminated the episodes in which they signify. In short, as Wachler has it, the world is not a dangerous or frustrating place; it merely takes a kind word or deed to quell any turbulence that arises.

Romance is not necessary to happiness since there is little to thwart happiness to begin with. Elisabeth does in the end marry Herr von Walde. Yet readers learn of their union in a tacked-on page only *after*, as the narrator declares, the story has reached its conclusion with her "Eintritt in das Leben" (entry into life).[21] Readers have experienced none of the longing and sexual tension of the original. While the match may be generically dictated, the text has hitherto not invited readers to think much about it.

A comparison of Wachler's untroubled happy conclusion with Marlitt's original reinforces the contention that the latter is not as perfectly happy (and clichéd) as it may appear today. In the concluding chapter of *Goldelschen*, Elisabeth celebrates her sixteenth birthday and so supersedes the age of

---

[21]   Auguste Wachler, *Goldelschen*, 6th ed. (Berlin: Hermann J. Meidinger, n.d.), 215, hereafter cited in text as "WaG."

the book's designated target audience. By having her cross this threshold, Wachler can regale her young readers with the promises of adulthood. The text, however, works with a simple idea of this adulthood, beginning in the concluding pages with Elisabeth's birthday party.

The birthday party, always an occasion for familial joy, prompts all the pertinent characters to show their affection for Elisabeth. Her birthday table is piled high with small handmade gifts. Herr von Walde is not present; he still figures only as an older authority figure detached from Elisabeth's daily life and not as her future husband. Instead, in a fully feminized scenario, his sister, Marie, and Frau von Hollfeld, his aunt, bring Elisabeth birthday greetings. Frau von Hollfeld somewhat grotesquely heaps furs upon a grateful Elisabeth. While the narrator piously assures readers that the heroine values the modest handmade gifts from her family, the text also assures readers that she deserves these expensive, if inappropriate furs. The fur muff, collar, beret, cape, boots, and floor-length coat are to accompany her as she makes her way in the world as a governess. But it never comes to that. Instead, six weeks later Elisabeth is still at home. As the Ferbers celebrate the New Year, the forester-uncle pronounces this day the end of Elisabeth's childhood, yet insists that she remain as she is so that they can continue to call her proudly "Unser Goldelschen!" (WaG 215; Our little Goldelse). The meaning could not be clearer: Elisabeth should retain her guileless virtue even in adulthood and marriage. The text never seriously acknowledges the existence of social conflict, sadness, hypocrisy, sexual predation, and death. Rather, feminine goodness presides over untroubled social harmony in a benign world.

If Goldelschen is rewarded for her daughterly and sisterly virtue with a husband and a title at the end—as the text spells out, "Frau Baronin von Walde" (WaG 215)—this husband promises only a bland future. Rather like Jakob Spitzer's rendition of Rochester for girls, Wachler's Baron von Walde presents as a good provider. No passion fuels his proposal; it apparently arises from his brotherly attachment to his sister. Feeling isolated in his castle after his sister's marriage, the narrator reports, he asked Elisabeth's parents for her hand in marriage. Unlike Marlitt's *Goldelse*, the text does not mention a baby. The omission of the baby in this version for younger girls supports the idea that the baby in the original signals the fulfillment of mutual sexual attraction and that it is not merely a narrative sleight of hand to move a sexually innocent girl into the position of idealized (and sexless) mother by eliding what comes in between. Rather, a baby points to it.

Two years later no baby concludes Wachler's adaptation of *Jane Eyre*, either. Rather, Adele, in a sexless adoption, becomes the couple's official daughter, for on her wedding day Jane does not want to see the sad sight of another orphan in her immediate proximity. Harriet, Rowland's sister-in-law, has conveniently, quietly, and punctually died in Wachler's version, freeing Thornfield from danger and the male protagonist from further responsibility for caring for her. As it is in *Goldelschen* upon the arrival of the Ferbers in Thuringia, it is Pentecost when Wachler's Jane and Rowland marry in the church at Hay Lome. Christianity thus descends upon the setting of both.

The title page of this adaptation links *Jane Eyre* and *Goldelse* when it presents *Die Waise von Lowood. Für die reifere Jugend erzählt von Auguste Wachler, Verfasserin von Goldelschen, Preciosa* (The Orphan of Lowood. Told for More Mature Youth by Auguste Wachler, authoress of Goldelschen, Preciosa). This adaptation combines elements from multiple chains of the transmission of *Jane Eyre* in the German-speaking territories and also links Marlitt to Brontë. While, as outlined above, Wachler's *Waise* is palpably indebted to Birch-Pfeiffer, the first three chapters bear traces of Marlitt's signature insofar as they devote considerable space to an invented backstory of Jane's situation with the Reeds instead of beginning the story, as Brontë and Birch-Pfeiffer do, in medias res.

With her *Goldelschen* two years earlier, Wachler in any case had created a milder version of an already milder novel, even milder than her mild version of *Jane Eyre*. Her text neither permits the nastiness of Mrs. Reed an afterlife in the form of Baroness von Hollfeld nor entertains the possibility of abuse in a woman-controlled home. The three surviving stage adaptations, on the other hand, required a bit of villainy for the sake of dramatic conflict to meet popular expectation in the entertainment economy of the theater.

"Goldelse" on Stage

The proliferation of stage adaptations of *Goldelse* in the span of two years, 1868–9, responded to a perceived wish on the part of the public to see Marlitt's beloved characters on stage and in the flesh. When the well-seasoned Anton Edmund Wollheim da Fonseca in Hamburg, the team of Carl Wexel and Ringulph Wegener in Berlin, and Agnes Nesmüller in Dresden took on the staging of Marlitt's novel, theater adaptation necessarily overrode Marlitt's narrative voice. Yet these adapters had to assume that, given the popularity of the novel, theatergoers had probably read *Goldelse* or knew it secondhand and came to the theater expecting to see something of the bestselling novel they knew and loved and not an entirely new story. In this vein, the provincial *Kremser Wochenblatt* praised Wollheim's adaptation as "recht gut, wohl und deßwegen, weil es sich ziemlich an dem Marlitt'schen Roman hält ..." (quite good, probably and because it adheres fairly well to Marlitt's novel).[22]

The retention of the romance plot for stage entertainment confirms its importance to the generally positive reception of the novel. Yet the three published theater adaptations of *Goldelse* do take liberties and exhibit variety with regard to their resolutions and happy endings, endings that in turn reveal differing understanding of this romance and its relationship to broader social issues.[23]

---

[22]   "Lokal- und vermischte Nachrichten," *Kremser Wochenblatt: Zeitschrift für Unterhaltung*, October 16, 1869. The newspaper also reported (falsely) that Wollheim had staged the play with his own ending before the serialization was complete.

[23]   Evidence of two additional and now-lost stage versions from these same years, one in Munich attributed to the actress Emilie Schröder and one in Hamburg attributed to the dramaturg Haase-Pollnow, further testifies to the wide circulation and cachet of Marlitt's novel in the years just preceding the foundation of the empire and the eagerness of enterprising theaters to profit from that perceived interest.

As with *Geheimnis*, the staging of *Goldelse* invested in the charm of the actress who was to embody Marlitt's heroine. When Emilie Schröder's now-lost five-act adaptation debuted on May 31, 1868, at the Münchner Actien-Volks-Theater to a vicious review in the *Deutscher Theater-Correspondent*, the actress who played Elisabeth nevertheless reaped praise—she was, after all, even in this bad production, at the center of things: "Doch bewies die junge Dame [Fräulein Waschmitius], daß sie Talent, viel Talent, und ein hübsches Organ besitze. Sie sah sehr hübsch aus, so unschuldsvoll, wie nur Else immer sein mochte" (But the young lady proved that she has talent, a lot of talent, and a pretty voice. She looked very pretty, as innocent as only Else could be).[24] Haase-Pollnow's likewise-lost *Goldelse* was advertised as having four acts with a prelude entitled "Die Clavierlehrerin" (The Piano Teacher); the advertisement thus names the eponymous heroine twice, further highlighting her centrality.[25] The titles of the three surviving plays likewise feature the heroine and these plays deploy her variously.

Nesmüller (née von Leuchert), who in 1841 had married the actor, writer, and theater impresario Joseph Ferdinand Nesmüller, was a long-time theater professional by the time she adapted *Goldelse* in 1869.[26] In Dresden in 1854, she instituted the first "Familienvorstellungen"—performances to which children accompanied by adults were admitted for free—and in 1864 she founded a short-lived children's theater. Perhaps as a result of her interest in children and child-friendly theater, Nesmüller opts in her adaptation to make Marlitt's novel even more of a family story, with few scenes devoted to the mutual attraction and misunderstandings of Elisabeth and Rudolf. In her staging, the eponymous heroine has less to say but gains in symbolic significance.

As indicated in the dramatis personae, Elisabeth is sixteen and thus two years younger than Marlitt's original heroine. Nesmüller makes her more a child by placing her in the age group designated by booksellers as "die reifere Jugend" (more mature youth). Perhaps to offset Elisabeth's younger age, Nesmüller makes Rudolf thirty-three, four years younger than the original character. She apportions noticeably few lines to this younger Elisabeth, namely, 89 utterances as opposed to the 153 found in Wollheim's adaptation, 11.50% of the total words spoken as opposed to 18.91% in Wexel and Wegener and 21.53% in Wollheim. But in this play Rudolf has an even smaller role, namely, 7.33% of the total lines as opposed to 23.37% in Wexel and Wegener's version and 20.89% in Wollheim's. With 9.34% of the total lines, Elisabeth's uncle has more to say than

24 "München," *Deutscher Theater-Korrespondent* 13, no. 23 (June 14, 1868): [2]. The author of this review does not believe that E. Schröder can actually be Emilie Schröder, as has been reported. Another announcement of the play identifies Emilie Schröder as the author: *Neueste Nachrichten aus dem Gebiet der Politik* 21, no. 152 (May 31, 1868): 1815. The *Wiener Theater-Chronik* likewise identifies Emilie Schröder as the author in its report on theater in Munich; 10, no. 35 (July 6, 1868): 189.

25 *Hamburger Nachrichten*, November 29, 1868, 14. This now-lost version is advertised as playing at the St. Georg-Theater.

26 A[gnes] N[esmüller], *Gold-Else oder Das Geheimniß des Jost von Gnadewitz: Charakter-Gemälde in 5 Acten und 6 Bildern; Nach dem gleichnamigen Roman von Marlitt nebst einem Vorspiel: "In der Sylvesternacht"* (Dresden: n.p., [1869]), hereafter cited in text.

Rudolf. Bertha in turn has the longest speech in the play, for she recounts Linke's attempt to murder Rudolf.

These numbers alone indicate the diminished importance of the unfolding of the couple's attraction. Both characters age by two years over the course of the play, as a result of two temporal leaps of one year each, and thus Elisabeth does not reach the crucial age of eighteen until the play's conclusion. Meanwhile, although it is obvious that the two will eventually marry, the principal step in that direction takes place rather abruptly off stage between act 4, which ends with Rudolf beaming, and act 5, which opens with Elisabeth wearing her bridal gown. Act 5 then stages the wedding in both its private and public significance.

Mothers are in the end more important to this play than coupling. In the temporal gap between the prelude and the first act, when the journey from B. to Thüringen takes place off stage, Frau Ferber, Elisabeth's mother, dies. Her last spoken line refers to her own "seelige Mutter" (9; dearly departed mother) who left the family a piano as a memento of olden days. As in the novel, the family must leave the fragile piano behind, but the legacy of the (grand)mother endures.

Although the play omits the sensation element of a corpse secreted within the castle, this ancestral matriarch, buried near the Nonnenturm, figures symbolically. Nesmüller sets several key scenes near her grave. In one of these, Sabine recounts the story of Jost von Gnadeck's "gypsy" bride, which has been passed down in her own serving family from mother to daughter. Onstage we see the mound of a grave by a weeping willow near a tower covered in ivy. As she explains, Sabine weaves a wreath every Corpus Christi and lays it on the otherwise neglected grave. We later learn that the woman died in childbirth, in the very moment of becoming a mother.

In act 5, at the grave of the ancient mother, Elisabeth, does not waste words when she gives Rudolf her hand and assents anew on her wedding day to marrying him. Indeed, in the preceding speech, Rudolf has taken charge and seizes this moment to tell Elisabeth, as well as the audience, that a sudden "elektrische Funke" (63; electric spark) kindled his feelings. Nesmüller here employs the metaphor used in Brontë's original novel to characterize Jane's experience. As he further notes in his monologue, mutual feeling meanwhile lay dormant in the innocent Elisabeth until she saw his life endangered. At this point the spark of attraction "shot through" (*durchzucken*) her as well: "da wurdest du dir selbstbewußt ..." (63; in that moment you became conscious of yourself). Although here at last acknowledging desire, the play does not dwell on it. In act 4, even after she has rescued Rudolf from Linke's attempted murder, Elisabeth enters the stage only to fall into her father's arms and receive her uncle's kiss, while Rudolf stands to one side.

While the final act of the play rejoices in the marriage of Rudolf and Elisabeth, the scene is staged so as to render the wedding not personal and romantic but communal and conservative. In this moment, Elisabeth's symbolic importance becomes visible: as underscored by the dialogue and stage directions, she replaces her own mother and also assumes a maternal role vis-à-vis the greater community. In scene 3, Ferber calls his daughter the "Ebenbild deiner verklärten Mutter" (64; image of your exalted mother) and wishes her a happy marriage like his own. Thereafter, in scene 5, the minister stresses that they are standing at the grave of the matriarch on this occasion and exhorts the community not to forget its dead. The minister's sermon and the stage business of symbolic commemoration, including the placing of a wreath by the loyal servants on the grave of the mother-ancestor, conclude the play in communal harmony and celebration of eternity in God's love. Bertha, too, is dressed as a bride, for she is to marry Rudolf's sidekick, Reinhardt, on this day.

The stage directions preceding the final scene begin with the peal of church bells from nearby villages that introduces festival proceedings that result in a vivid tableau. Pairs of locals, wearing their best clothes and carrying wreaths, enter from all sides. Children dressed in white and carrying baskets of flowers likewise enter in pairs. The crowd parts for the entry of the silver-haired pastor of Lindhof and forms a semi-circle. At the right corner, Rudolf, Else, Helene, Ferber and Ernst form a group; at the left corner stand Reinhardt, Bertha, the head forester, and Sabine. The procession continues as four huntsmen in their Sunday best enter behind the children with four girls—the bridesmaids. Each bridesmaid wears and carries a wreath of a different color. The tableau thus elaborately performs communal harmony as a sermon concludes the play and church bells ring once again. With this emphasis on the recuperated mother and the restored local community associated with her, the play picks up on Marlitt's interest in the social. In this case, however, the social inheres in convocation of community supported by a conventional evocation of a ruling family. The wedding at the end restores the lost mother in the form of Elisabeth through the founding of a new family by the noblest the region has to offer.

Wexel and Wegner offer a different take on Marlitt's novel.[27] In their heavy borrowing of the language of the original—as characterizes their other adaptations as well—these adapters disproportionately include dialogue from scenes featuring Emil von Hollfeld and Baroness von Lessen who become the voluble villains of the drama. Together they speak 20.72% of the total lines, rivaling Rudolf's 21.40%. Emil in fact speaks an entire monologue, revealing his evil desires (9). With Linke's 2.54% of the whole, the three villains actually surpass Rudolf's part.

The first act takes place at Lindhof and unrolls the vexed relations there with no mention of Elisabeth's back story, which in this version has vaguely to do with being orphaned and coming to live with her uncle. In fact, the play does not invest in Elisabeth's prehistory or the Ferber ancestry. Gnadeck is never mentioned. Conflict in the drama arises largely from the two villains' machination with emphasis on Emil's betrayal of both Bertha and Helene and the bigoted Baroness von Lessen's mistreatment of underlings and support of Linke. Upon Elisabeth and Rudolf's first meeting at the forester's house in act 2, the play begins to unfurl their love story and remains steadily on course even as the two are repeatedly deflected from one another.

---

[27] Carl Wexel and Rhingulph Wegener, *Goldelse: Charaktergemälde in fünf Akten; Nach dem gleichnamigen Romane von E. Marlitt, für die Bühne bearbeitet* (Berlin: n.p., 1868), hereafter cited in text.

Wexel and Wegener display the feelings of both Bertha and Elisabeth especially through monologue. In act 2, Elisabeth reveals her first impressions of Rudolf and then, in a soliloquy in act 3, scene 7, reveals her knowledge of his feelings and her insight into his tightly guarded interior. In act 4, scene 8, she surrenders in a monologue to the "Zauber" (44; magic) that has possessed all her thoughts; she cannot resist Rudolf although he has deeply wounded her "Ehrgefühl" (44; sense of honor/pride). Taking a cue from the original, as do all the adaptations, including *Goldelschen*, the play rehabilitates Bertha. It grants her two monologues that present her in a sympathetic light. She soon comes to her senses after Emil rejects her. Unlike Marlitt who dispatches her in the concluding pages with marriage to a solid man from the appropriate class followed by emigration to America, Wegener and Wexel introduce a full-fledged character named Franz who loves Bertha from the start and tries in vain in several scenes to win her affection. The parallel love story of the secondary characters Franz and Bertha serves the harmonious conclusion.

Of the three adaptations, this one proves most interested in preserving the dialogic romance in key scenes. It, moreover, omits characters and side plots to foreground the love story. The movement of the play from singles to couples comes to fruition in the final scene. Pairing through stage blocking even Sabine and the *Oberförster*, who are not in a love relationship, contributes to visible symmetry and communal harmony. The two older characters stand in loco parentis to the orphaned Elisabeth. Miss Mertens, the long-suffering governess, returns in this adaptation to become the target of aristocratic bile only to be rescued by marriage, as in the original, to Reinhard, Rudolf's secretary. The two form the third couple and Bertha and Franz make up a fourth in the set of four pairs assembled for the final scene in which no character appears singly on stage.

Although it has provided the female protagonist with active scenes, the play has not given Rudolf a chance to confess his feelings. Therefore in the final scene of the final act, in the longest speech of the play, Rudolf recapitulates his own story, as does Rochester in Brontë's novel, the story of falling in love with Elisabeth only to be hindered by his own doubt and jealousy. As this confession nears its end, the three other pairs emerge from the forester's house and arrange themselves around Rudolf and Elisabeth, whereupon Elisabeth offers Rudolf her hand as guarantor of an "unaussprechlichen Glückes" (55; ineffable happiness). *He* promises to be *hers* in all eternity—a palpable reversal of the norms of romantic pairing, in the common language of the time, according to which the woman promises to be the man's property forever. She then throws herself into his arms, and the curtain falls.

Wollheim da Fonseca's adaptation, the longest lived of the three, includes relatively little language from Marlitt's novel. Nevertheless, its retention of some of its key elements yields a reasonably progressive stage version. Wollheim accords a third character, as he did in his adaptation of *Geheimnis*, in this case Elisabeth's uncle, the forester, approximately the same number of words as those spoken by each of the members of the romantic pairing. As in Wollheim's adaptation of *Geheimnis*, the couple achieves a happy ending with the garrulous participation of a third character. The re-weighted third character prevents this adaptation, too, from being reduced to a mere love story to evoke the more variegated social world of Marlitt's novels. At the same time, as becomes clear in his handling of Sabine, Wollheim operates with stock theater characters that acting companies were prepared to supply. The Carl Schultze Theater, where both adaptations debuted, apparently had the necessary resources.

The first performance of Wollheim's *Gold-Else oder die Egoisten* (Gold-Else or the Egoists) took place on November 29, 1868, in Hamburg.[28] Thereafter Wollheim's rendition premiered in Berlin in 1869 at the Woltersdorffer Theater and subsequently made the rounds across German-speaking Eastern Europe.

The casting of the perky Ernestine Wegner (1852–83) in the Berlin production as the title character suggests how she figured in Wollheim's version. Wegner was beloved in Berlin for her comedic trouser role as a Berlin newsboy in *Berliner Bauernfänger* (Berlin Con Artist), a role in which she had debuted eight months earlier and the first of many such roles she was to play.[29] The assertive and forthright heroine of Wollheim's adaptation repeatedly stands her ground, resisting and denouncing the scheming Emil, but also extending a merciful hand to the would-be assassin, the hard-luck Linke. As a thoroughly virtuous and likable heroine whose longest speech is, as indicated in the published script, to be accompanied by "Melodram" (66; melodrama), she claims center stage.

Wollheim, nevertheless, enriches the plot and dialogue to allow an array of characters to command attention. Besides foregrounding the folksy, true-blue forester, he also gives the two male villains, Linke and Emil, plenty to say. Together at 26.55% of the total words, they tally more lines than the heroine (21.53%). Wollheim also reinvents the forester's housekeeper, Sabine, as a comic figure prone to malapropisms.

With the attention to the ensemble and many omissions including the corpse in the walls of Gnadeck, Wollheim dulled obvious signs of *Jane Eyre* transmission. He did, however, retain some sensation elements including a scene in which Linke, not Bertha, locks Elisabeth in the Nonnenturm, one that permits the female protagonist a lengthy revelatory monologue. Wollheim's adaptation, on the other hand, plays up some salient aspects of Marlitt's original, particularly its anti-aristocratic sentiments. Adding new notes to *Goldelse*, he creates scenes broadly displaying the aristocrats' poor taste and social prejudice, including Emil's anti-Semitism. His play, moreover, not only retains Marlitt's messages of redemption and social justice, but also heightens them. It adds the new plot turn of a pardon for Linke, thus providing a happy ending even for one of the

---

[28] The *Wiener Theater-Chronik* reported that *Gold-Else* had debuted on the 29th of the previous month with extraordinary success at Carl Schultze's Theater. Notice, *Wiener Theater-Chronik*, December 17, 1868. Wollheim da Fonseca Dr. A. E. Wollheim, *Gold-Else oder Die Egoisten: Schauspiel in 5 Acten; Mit freier Benutzung des gleichnamigen Romans von E. Marlitt* (Hamburg: B. S. Berendsohn, 1869), hereafter cited in text. Notices of first-time performances of *Gold-Else* by the respective theaters appear in *Hamburger Nachrichten*, November 29, 1868, 14. The now-lost version performed at the St. Georg-Theater is listed here as consisting of four acts and a "Vorspiel," entitled "Die Clavierlehrerin" "nach Marlitt's Roman."

[29] "März," *Neuer Theater-Almanach. Theatergeschichtliches Jahr- und Adressen-Buch* 14 (Berlin: Genossenschaft Deutscher Bühnen-Angehöriger, 1903), 129; see also *Allgemeine deutsche Biographie*, s.v. "Wegner, Ernestine W."

villains. Wollheim's gender politics remain, however, conventional and out of step with both *Jane Eyre* and *Goldelse*, both of which valorize women's speech. This shortcoming becomes obvious when the final scene gives way to comedy at Sabine's expense.

A flash-forward on the final pages of the novel permits a view of the heroine, even allowing us to read her mind. The play, in contrast, is brought to a harmonious conclusion by the forester who re-integrates the would-be assassin Linke into the community with an offer of employment. Meanwhile his housekeeper, Sabine, cries out joyfully with her customary word salad, "das ist zu apoplektisch! … Diese Freude—ich juble, ich abonnire … ich werde schwach" (86; that's just too apoplectic … this joy—I rejoice, I subscribe … I'm getting weak) and thereupon faints. Praising God and reasserting male authority over female chaos, the forester heaves a sigh of relief, "so schweigt sie wenigstens still" (86; at least she's quiet now) and then exhorts everyone to celebrate the marriage by joining him in saying "Amen." The "Amen" serves the double purpose of celebrating not just the marriage but also Sabine's silence.

Imitation and adaptation register losses and gains. While it preserves liberating and appealing features of *Jane Eyre*, *Goldelse* also emits mixed messages, and nineteenth-century adaptations variously picked up on them. Wachler's *Goldelschen*, for one, does not perpetuate *Jane Eyre* in any thrillingly palpable manner, instead leaving its readers with normative messages about good behavior; in its softenings, omissions, and re-focusing on certain contents, it also anticipates Wachler's re-fashioning of Brontë for the same publisher and target audience, suggesting that contemporary cultural pundits and pedagogues believed that the "mature content" of both books needed to be retro-fitted for younger audiences. *Goldelse*, in its varied theater guises, in turn often slips into the simple modes and clichés of ensemble acting and family stories, even if Wollheim's play offers some of the feel-good liberal messaging of the original. Marlitt's novels themselves meanwhile became more complex over the following twenty years—and in some respects stranger and occasionally more sensational—and they continued to evince traces of Brontë's *Jane Eyre*. In these later novels, Marlitt also devotes more effort to realizing her female protagonists, rendering them as partaking of a somewhat more complex emotional and cognitive life. The messages do, however, remain mixed and subject to interpretation.

Seven Mixed Messages: Marlitt's *Little Moorland Princess*

The stubbornly enduring popularity of Marlitt's novels with female readers especially well into the twentieth century suggests that more is going on in and with these novels than their historical panning by a male-dominated punditry might indicate. The publishing industry successfully cultivated a (female) readership in the late nineteenth-century German-speaking world, one that, given its reading experience and social positioning, learned to read romance in a time of inequality and social transition for the plots, motifs, emotion, and possibility that (largely male) critics derided and that romance readers, on the other hand, apparently craved. Writers such as Marlitt in turn learned to negotiate this territory. Meanwhile, it appears that the more Marlitt's corpus was seen as "feminine" reading as the century waned, the greater hostility it provoked in a punditry imbued with prejudice against the popular, which itself was perceived as feminine. Koenig's *Deutsche Literaturgeschichte* (1879) may serve as a case in point.

In its earlier editions, this literary history borrows from Gottschall's generally positive assessment of Marlitt's works in his two reviews from the 1870s. Presumably Koenig (1828–1900), who for a decade and a half co-edited the family magazine *Daheim*, a rival to the *Gartenlaube*, saw Marlitt as the author of good reads for the middling classes that also read his magazine. By contrast, in his revised edition of Koenig's literary history, Karl Kinzel, pompously identified on the title page as "Prof. Dr.," cites in tones of outrage the *tendenz* that dominates Marlitt's oeuvre in keeping with that of the *Gartenlaube* itself. By *tendenz* he means Marlitt's opposition to aristocratic rule and her unrelenting criticism of religious hypocrisy, which he labels a veritable story of conversion to the so-called Enlightenment. Although he begins by grudgingly admitting her talent as a storyteller, by the end he has denied her "wirklich schöpferische Begabung, originelle Erfindung, psychologisische Vertiefung der seelischen Konflikte" (true creative talent, original invention, psychological deepening of spiritual-emotional conflicts) and any feeling for the burning questions of the day. Her sappy sentimentality and the wallowing of her fiction in forced emotion led gullible readers to overlook the dangerous tendency of her novels, he rages, pillorying both the works and their readers.[1] The transparently religious

---

[1] Karl Kinzel, ed., Robert Koenig, *Deutsche Literaturgeschichte* 13th rev. ed. (Bielefeld and Leipzig: Velhagen & Klasing, 1904) 2: 500–501.

and culturally conservative slant of this entry now communicates precisely the opposite of its original intention, namely, it suggests that Marlitt's novels did speak to historical readers of questions that mattered to *them*. Both Haas and Dingeldey have eloquently made that case.[2] Apart from Kinzel's obvious biases, this revised evaluation of Marlitt also testifies to changing fashion and varying sensibilities that respond differently to romance per se or particular historical expressions of it.

"Romance is unlikely to go away," Stacey and Pearce conclude in their summation of the results of interdisciplinary work on the romance genre in the mid-1990s. They stress its tough persistence as fashions and sensibilities change, due, they believe, to its marked "narrativity." Narrativity renders it "liable to perpetual *re-writing*." Its "capacity for 're-scripting,'" its adaptability, in other words, guarantees its survival.[3] It can and does adjust to new times. In the particular case of *Jane Eyre*, Beaty's study of mixed narrative signals brings into view the complex, dialogic transfer of literary material evidenced in Brontë's novel itself, showing how this novel carries obvious traces of its own literary antecedents to be received, rethought, and adapted by future readers and writers. As a result of mixed influences and composition, he demonstrates, *Jane Eyre* even "misreads" itself, responding as it unfolds variously (and sometimes misleadingly) to its own fluctuating genre signals. This dialogic composition is generative in its own right; over time and across cultures it allows readers a multitude of (mis)readings. Variable reading, as we have seen, is compounded in and confirmed by the rescripting involved in adaptation and imitation.

Mixed signals also characterize Marlitt's novels as they intermittently transmit elements of *Jane Eyre* refashioned for the 1860s, 1870s, and 1880s. In this popular and more formulaic literature they may, however, simply appear at first glance to be less the fascinating result of complex dialogic composition and more the inconsistency of weak writerly craft. Marlitt's fourth full-length novel, *Das Heideprinzeßchen* (The Little Moorland Princess), can serve as a case in point. Despite its innocuous title, this novel is neither mild nor simple. Its complexity arises in part from the ways it responds to, preserves, re-scripts, or ignores *Jane Eyre* elements and effects.

This chapter examines complexities of *Das Heideprinzeßchen* that make it too available to (mis)readings and (mis)understandings, some of which potentially delivered to its historical (female) recipients something akin to the hard-won relational selfhood of a Jane Eyre. Of all Marlitt's works, *Heideprinzeßchen* alone employs the fiction of autobiography and thus obviously places identity and self-formation at the narrative center of romance. This chapter will therefore play special attention to the ways in which the female protagonist's narration of self charts a course between individualization and normative subjectification. While the indebtedness of Marlitt's fourth full-length novel to *Jane Eyre* will become clear, we will also see how subsequent book illustration and adaptation pushed the material in different directions.

---

2   Dingeldey, *Luftzug hinter Samtportieren*, 16; Haas, *Eugenie Marlitt*, for example, 9.
3   Stacey and Pearce, "The Heart of the Matter," 12.

Angry Women *Redivivae*

Heideprinzeßchen first entered the pages of *Die Gartenlaube* (31–52) in 1871 in the year of German unification and the founding of the Second Empire. As the magazine complained a year later in three different notices, unauthorized translations had soon appeared in Paris, London, Philadelphia, and Hungary, reflecting, of course, Marlitt's growing international reach.[4] In 1872 the Leipzig-based German publisher Tauchnitz, which had published *Jane Eyre* in English in 1848, did its part toward making Marlitt available to English-language audiences when it published the novel as *The Princess of the Moor* in its Collection of German Authors. In the same year Annis Lee Wister's subsequently oft-reprinted translation *The Little Moorland Princess* appeared with Lippincott in Philadelphia—as the *Gartenlaube* complained.[5] Given its debt to *Jane Eyre*, the novel was in some sense born international. As Hugh Ridley has noted, furthermore, at some level popular literature "shows itself to be not only international in conception and production, but also both at home in and foreign to every culture in which it was read."[6]

As a sign of its affinity to *Jane Eyre*, this novel introduces the character Klothilde von Sassen, an angry, half-mad woman, who has withdrawn from society to a solitary farm on the North German heath. Long before Jean Rhys's *Wide Sargasso Sea* (1966) told Bertha's mother's story as one of abuse within the exploitative structures of gender, class, ethnicity, and coloniality, Marlitt gave a voice to a figure who recalls Rochester's first wife and who seeks justice—not as a colonial other—but as a Jew. In so doing, the narrator-granddaughter by no means prettifies the figure, whose flaming red face makes of her a "wilde, furchtbare Erscheinung" (2:25; wild, terrible apparition) and even in death elicits horror. Yet the text does demand respect for this "große, starkbeleibte Frau," a "wuchte Gestalt" with "energischen, kraftvollen Armbewegungen" (2:25; tall, corpulent woman; hefty figure; energetic, powerful arm movements). The narrator recalls her heavy tread and the rush of air that issued from her movements and is reminded of the powerful Cimbrian women of antiquity. She goes on to mention her thick gray braids and the "Braunrot" (2: 26; brownish red) of her face. When Klothilde breathes heavily, her dark bluish lips reveal her large white teeth (2:26). Her size, energy, hectic movements, heavy tread, thick gray hair, florid face, large white teeth, black eyes, and woman warrior qualities should recall for the *Jane Eyre* reader none other than Bertha Mason.

The two episodes that actually permit readers a look at the captive woman at Thornfield invoke these features, as faithfully reproduced by all three translations that were then available in German. Translated Jane describes the

---

4   "Blätter und Blüthen," *Die Gartenlaube*, no. 14 (1872): 236; "Blätter und Blüthen," *Die Gartenlaube*, no. 22 (1872): 366; "Blätter und Blüthen," *Die Gartenlaube*, no. 46 (1872): 764.

5   E. Marlitt, *The Princess of the Moor*, 2. vols., Collection of German Authors 23–4 (Leipzig: Tauchnitz, 1871); E. Marlitt, *The Little Moorland Princess*, trans. Annis Lee Wister (Philadelphia: Lippincott, 1872).

6   Hugh Ridley, *"Relations Stop Nowhere": The Common Literary Foundations of German and American Literature 1830–1917*, Internationale Forschungen zur Allgemeinen und Vergleichenden Literaturwissenschaft 109 (Amsterdam: Rodopi, 2007), 121.

vampire-like nocturnal invader who tears her bridal veil in lurid hues: "pur-purfarbig," "dunkelroth," "schwarz," "blutunterlaufen" (purplish, dark red, black, bloodshot; see S 2:179; G 2:130–1; H 3:149). When Rochester later leads the assembled company from the chapel to view his wife, German Janes char-acterize her, true to the English text, as a bestial creature that walks on all fours, wildly snapping and chewing. It has a "Masse dunkles graues Haar" (S 2:191; mass of dark gray hair) and the same swollen purple features of her night visitor (see S 2:191–2, G 2:146–7, and H 4:11–12). Jane stresses her large size and mascu-line strength when Bertha nearly overpowers Rochester.

Marlitt, however, reassembles these elements in *Heideprinzeßchen* to different effect and purpose. Unlike Brontë who allows us to hear Bertha's story only through Jane's recapitulation of Rochester's biased perspective, Lenore, in her autobiographical account, humanizes her solitary grandmother and makes cer-tain that readers know that this fearsome figure has good reason for her fury. Moreover, this woman is fully capable of telling her own story, unlike Bertha, whom the narrator reduces to grunts, gurgles, laughter, mutters, and screams. Lenore portrays her grandmother not as an animal but as a suffering woman.[7]

On her deathbed, Klothilde von Sassen, née Jakobsohn, dictates her final wishes. She observes that Lenore, her granddaughter from her second marriage to a gentile, has inherited the features of the Jewish Jakobsohns; forgives Chris-tine, her daughter from her first marriage to a Jew; and dies, despite her conver-sion to Christianity, with a German translation of the *Shema* on her lips. Lenore in her role as narrator repeats it in full (2:66) and confirms that her grandmother died a Jew but does not identify these words as a Jewish prayer.

Klothilde's mad fury stems from her experience of the harsh intolerance of Christians, especially that of a pastor, who, at a moment of family distress, informed her that, as Jews, her beloved, pious, and good-hearted parents were going to perdition. The portrait of the grandmother's suffering as a Jew may have drawn on contemporary popular literary sources such as Salomon Her-mann Mosenthal's play *Deborah* (1849), which in the 1860s had enjoyed a revival and continued for decades to occupy a place in the German theatrical reper-toire.[8] Unlike the defiant Deborah, however, the grandmother does not figure as a furious *belle juive*, but instead, as described above, replicates Bertha's unattrac-tive physical characteristics.

The novel subsequently pursues the philosemitic theme of (in)tolerance sounded in the portrait of the grandmother, through scenes of casual, sometimes naive, anti-Semitism that it invites readers to condemn. The theme culminates

---

[7]   Spivak characterizes Brontë's depiction of Bertha as rendering "indeterminate the bound-ary between human and animal" and thus weakening "her entitlement under the spirit if not the letter of the Law," that is, she is excluded from the soul-making that Spivak sees as central to the novel. Gayatry Chakravorty Spivak, "Three Women's Texts and a Critique of Imperialism," *Critical Inquiry* 12, no. 1 (Autumn 1985): 249. Marlitt does precisely the opposite with Klothilde.

[8]   On this play and its impact, see Jonathan M. Hess, *Deborah and Her Sisters: How One Nine-teenth-Century Melodrama and a Host of Celebrated Actresses Put Judaism on the World Stage* (Philadelphia: University of Pennsylvania Press, 2018).

in Lenore's public declaration that her grandmother was a Jew. Resonating with the self-revelation of the biblical Esther before King Ahasuerus, this declaration occurs in the presence of Princess Margarethe, the sister of the local duke, who is known for his anti-Semitic views. It reverses an earlier episode in which Lenore, newly self-aware and self-conscious, shamefully fails to acknowledge her origins.

The text also juxtaposes Lenore to Christine, Klothilde's estranged daughter from her first marriage to a Jew and Herr Claudius's first (and unfaithful) beloved. Unlike Lenore who is of mixed heritage and is marked by the darkness the text associates with Jews, Christine, the daughter of a Jewish father and mother, is markedly white of complexion. Jewishness has faded in the inauthentic Christine. With her pointedly Christian name, she instead functions as the embodiment of feminine fakery, hypocrisy, and treachery. Whitening her sets her up for her role as an irredeemable villain and ostensible rival for Claudius's affection. Romance, on the other hand, allows the dark-complexioned Lenore by contrast to become and accept herself.

As a feature of the acceptance of Lenore's Jewish heritage, Lenore as narrator enables the reader to picture her younger self as a Jew (according to contemporary philosemitic ideas), when she mentions a character's pronouncement that she resembles the French painter Paul Delaroche's depiction of Miriam observing baby Moses, *Moses in the Bulrushes* (before 1857). The narrator is, however, in the end not consistent in her characterization of herself as Jewish; in other reported scenes the diminutive Lenore figures more as an elemental spirit, a water sprite, an elf, with feet like quicksilver, and thus begins to sound like the Jane of Rochester's besotted imagining. We will return to her declaration of her ethnicity below.

As a half-mad, angry Jewish woman, Klothilde is unique in Marlitt's oeuvre, but only in her Jewishness and not in her insanity and fury. Marlitt's novels, counting on reader empathy, frequently, although not consistently, work toward repairing fictional families that confine or demonize inconvenient angry women by restoring their dignity. While she does not hesitate to populate her novels with villainous women and to traffic in the stereotypes of female villainy, Marlitt sympathizes with her Bertha Mason-related characters: madwomen (Bertha in *Goldelse*) and effectively captive women (Cordula in *Geheimnis*, Beatrice in "Blaubart," the Indian wife in *Die zweite Frau*, Lila in *Goldelse*, Blanca in *Die Frau mit den Karfunkelsteinen*). She even invites empathy with angry female characters that have hitherto played the role of villain, especially mother figures such as Frau Hellwig in *Geheimnis* and Frau Lucian in *Im Schillingshof*. *Heideprinzeßchen* for its part also rescues the angry Charlotte who attempts to turn Lenore against their benefactor, Herr Claudius. Having been given a second chance, Charlotte gains the capacity to wonder in dismay how it is possible that, when all human beings are born with the same right to exist, they can fall into two groups—the arrogant and the despised (2:415); she thus becomes the mouthpiece for Marlitt's liberal message.

Mixed Motifs in the Penumbra of German Unification

Angry women, particularly Lenore's grandmother, constitute one of many respects in which this novel bears the mark of *Jane Eyre*. The "madwoman" of *Heideprinzeßchen* is, however, in plain sight from the start and thus plays no role in the mystification of the home in Brontë's vein. Yet Marlitt's novel shares the sensation influence that informs *Jane Eyre*. As soon as Lenore enters the grounds of the Claudius firm, the text turns from its romanticized view of Lenore's relationship to the heath and begins to draw on Gothic motifs. Family secrets inhere in the walls of the so-called Karolinenlust (Caroline's Pleasure), a villa in the French Rococo style located in the grounds of the Claudius firm with blocked-off secret rooms that evoke former, yet now inaccessible, (sexual) pleasure. Meanwhile, just beyond the walls of the Claudius grounds lurks the debased Christine.

Jane Eyre worries over Englishness and Empire via Bertha, the colonial other; Rochester's sexual history with not only Bertha but also Céline, Giacinta, and Clara; Adele's Frenchness; and St John's missionary work in India. Marlitt, too, in 1871, the year of the Prussian victory over France, worries over Germanness in the portrait of the arrogant siblings, Charlotte and Dagobert.[9] The siblings have grown up understanding themselves as French and taking great pride in that fact. They disdain their "German uncle" for his allegedly plodding national character. The text, however, accords little attention to the immediate historical context, in fact pointedly ignores it. The story is set instead in the year 1861, and therefore the three wars leading up to unification can play no role in the plot; it focuses not on national unity but rather on social integration within a German hometown. The false pride of Claudius's adopted children in their Frenchness ultimately serves a different political message and is of a piece with their delusional pretentions to nobility.

Dagobert and Charlotte believe wrongly that they are the issue of a morganatic marriage between Claudius's older brother, Lothar, and the deceased sister of the local German duke, Princess Sidonie, and thus of noble birth (albeit German). Although evidence that this story may be true builds suspense and enlists Lenore's sympathy, it ultimately proves false. The novel thus undercuts the Gothic imagination—as does Marlitt's novella "Blaubart" and also *Geheimnis* with the benign Cordula—to reveal this alleged family secret as largely a figment of overheated imagination. In deflating delusion, *Heideprinzeßchen* does not, however, offer a satirical take on the Gothic genre, as, for example, does Jane Austen's *Northanger Abbey*; instead, the novel unfolds a plot of misapprehension and gullibility as a phase in Lenore's struggle to achieve adulthood and a place in the social world. As it turns out, a morganatic marriage did exist and the couple did from time to time occupy the secret rooms of the Karolinenlust. Dagobert and Charlotte are, however, the children of Christine—Claudius's former lover and Lenore's aunt—and a Frenchman, and thus connected to a different sort of family secret.

In addition to flirting with Gothic motifs, *Heideprinzeßchen* toys with the motif of the "gypsy," which it conflates with the perceived otherness of Jews. While Gottschall detects the influence of Annette von Droste-Hülshoff and Adalbert

---

9 On these contents, see Spivak, "Three Women's Texts," and, more recently, Sue Thomas, *Imperialism, Reform, and the Making of Englishness in Jane Eyre* (Houndmills, Basingstoke, Hampshire: Palgrave Macmillan, 2008).

Stifter in evocations of the heath, Emily Brontë's *Wuthering Heights* (1847; German, 1851) also haunts this text.[10] Lenore of the heath, with her brown feet, dark curly hair, and dark eyes, recalls Heathcliff, the "gypsy" boy.[11] Upon his first appearance in Chapter 1, Emily Brontë's narrator describes him as "a dark-skinned gypsy" ("dunkelfarbiger Zigeuner." 1:8); additional characters drive home Heathcliff's otherness by repeating this label five more times. In *Heideprinzeßchen*, Lenore is likewise several times labeled a "Zigeunerin" ("gypsy" girl). Once in town, she herself becomes aware that she looks a bit different; she describes her sunburned hands in the colonialist language of the times, as "kaffernbraun" (2:22; brown as a Kaffir [*sic*]). The evocations of the moor and Lenore's free-spirited life there also resonate with *Wuthering Heights*. Unlike Emily Brontë, however, Marlitt in the end offers a story of a successful socializing of a "wild child" when the novel briskly removes Lenore from the heath to the hometown where she will inhabit the house and grounds of the flower merchant, Herr Claudius.

Gottschall's review puzzles over a novel that initially celebrates the heath and then abruptly changes its tone along with its setting when Lenore moves to town to be educated; these two settings make a "verwirrenden Eindruck" (confusing impression).[12] Indeed, in town a focus on maturation, education, and socialization in a positive sense displaces the themes of the heath and wildness. *Heideprinzeßchen* thus moves away from *Wuthering Heights* and closer to *Jane Eyre* as both romance novel and *Bildungsroman*. In the process, Herr Claudius comes to the fore as Lenore's sparring partner. Although not the country gentleman of Brontë's imagining but instead a successful flower merchant in a bustling town, Claudius resembles Rochester.

Bildung in the Home of an Old(er) Man

The text marks an affinity to Rochester from the start when Claudius appears wearing disfiguring blue eyeglasses. Behind the eyeglasses, Claudius has very fine eyes—like Rochester. Each time he removes his glasses, Lenore, to her dismay, experiences a tug of attraction. As she eventually learns, his poor eyesight

---

10　[Emily Brontë], *Wutheringshöhe* (Grimma and Leipzig: Verlags-Comptoir, 1851). Gottschall's mention of the possible influence of Droste-Hülshoff is born out by the opening pages of the novel when Lenore refers to the evening wind blowing in "mein flatterndes Haar" (2:36; my flapping hair), in effect a paraphrase of the words of the lyrical subject in the final two lines of Droste-Hülshoff's "Am Turm" (1842; At the Tower), a poem that passionately expresses a desire for an autonomous self: "Und darf nur heimlich lösen mein Haar,/ Und lassen es flattern im Winde!" (And may only secretly let down my hair/ and let it flap in the wind). Lenore's subsequent slightly uncanny encounter with her own reflection in a stream may, furthermore, recall for some readers the face that children believe they see lurking below the surface of a pond in Droste-Hülshoff's evocative "Der Weiher" (1844; The Pond).

11　In yet another review, Gottschall invokes George Sand's Fanchon (*La petite Fadette*) and Goethe's Mignon (*Wilhelm Meister*) as possible literary antecedents. Sand does not label Fanchon a "gypsy" but rather a witch. Rudolf Gottschall, "Ein Urtheil Rudolf Gottschall's über E. Marlitt," *Die Gartenlaube*, no. 27 (1876): 480.

12　Rudolf Gottschall, "Neue Novellistinnen," *Blätter für literarische Unterhaltung*, no. 32 (1876): 500.

is the result of a duel he fought at the age of twenty-one over Christine. As with Rochester, past mistakes cast a pall over the present in the form of his wounded body, but our hero, unlike Brontë's, suffers no moral impairment. Instead, like Rudolf in *Goldelse* and Johannes in *Geheimnis*, he at first simply appears to be emotionally closed off and somewhat mysterious of manner. And although, like Rochester, Claudius for a time aimlessly traveled the world, he eventually found solace in work.

The narrative puts Claudius's virtues on display in dialogue with Lenore— his good sense and wisdom, his altruism, his conscientiousness and sense of responsibility as well as his connoisseurship and collectorship. Claudius eventually secures his moral standing (as does Rochester when Thornfield goes up in flames) with heroic acts undertaken amidst a disaster. Lenore's father, an eyewitness, affirms Claudius's fulfillment of a masculine norm, when he declares, "Was für ein Mann!" (2:300; What a man!). The duke shares his admiration not only for Claudius's sangfroid, but also the quiet dignity with which he accepts his misfortune when a flood destroys his property. Claudius proves his mettle yet again when he rescues Lenore's despairing father from a fire resulting from the latter's attempt to burn his own manuscript. As a result of his valor in this second dramatic episode, Claudius further damages his eyesight and also wounds his left arm—à la Rochester.

Gottschall characterizes the love between the young girl and the older merchant, the eventual center of the novel, as a "psychologisches Problem" (psychological problem).[13] In labeling it a psychological problem rather than an evolving romance convention, he overlooks Marlitt's recycling of plot elements from *Goldelse* and also German *Jane Eyres*. Readers familiar with these novels or Birch-Pfeiffer's play could reasonably expect love to blossom between the older man and the young girl. Still an enormous age difference does exist, and Lenore's consistent deference to "Herr Claudius" verbally widens it, invoking differences in age, power, and gender and recalling Jane's persistent address of Rochester as "Sir." Claudius's assumption of a paternal pedagogical role to tame Lenore highlights the gap yet again. The arrival at a marriage based in parity ultimately requires Lenore's rapid growth into self-confidence and self-awareness under Claudius's tutelage.

Lenore first appears on the heath with short hair, a short skirt, and bare feet. Two characters refer to her as the "wilde Hummel" (wild bumblebee), an epithet meaning "tomboy," and one of many occurrences of forms of the word "wild" to describe her.[14] These early chapters of *Heideprinzeßchen* operate with motifs that became standards of girls' books. Such books—most explicitly Käthe van Beeker's *Die wilde Hummel* (1899) and *Der Trotzkopf*, as discussed in Chapter 4—narrate stories of innocently charming and spirited "wild" heroines who must be tamed and groomed to gain a footing in bourgeois life. The move from the countryside to the city was also becoming a stock element of such pedagogical narratives in books for girls. Of these, Marlitt could have known the

---

13　Gottschall, "Neue Novellistinnen," 500.
14　*Vollständiges Englisch-deutsches und Deutschenglisches Wörterbuch*, 3rd ed., s.v. "Tomboy."

long-lived *Backfischchens Leiden und Freuden* (1863; The Sorrows and Joys of a Naive Young Girl) by Clementine Helm. Later, the 1880s brought, for example, Johanna Spyri's *Heidis Lehr- und Wanderjahre* (1881; Heidi's Apprenticeship and Journeyman's Years)—eight-year-old Heidi, too, has short black curly hair and cannot read or write when she arrives in Frankfurt to be educated. One wonders whether Spyri read Marlitt.[15] As we shall shortly see, *Heideprinzeßchen* may have eventually been read alongside such girls' books. In the early 1870s, Marlitt, however, created a text for the readers of the *Gartenlaube* that followed a program different from the mere taming of a charming young heroine to convention in the manner of these girls' books; she allowed her heroine to reach maturity through *Bildung* and romantic attachment and to reconfigure the new household over which she as matron will preside. Learning to write is critical to this development.

"Bildung," as the narrator terms it, begins with Lenore's learning to write a legible hand. As Claudius tells her, she does not yet know, "daß die Feder ein beseeltes und beschwingtes Wesen in unserer Hand wird, daß sie alles das, was Ihnen im Kopfe 'spukt und durcheinander quirlt', ausströmen kann ..." (2:183; that the pen becomes an animated and buoyant creature in our hand, that it can emit all those things that whirl around in your head ...). Yet the text also intimates that writing can disrupt family life. Lenore's parents were both writers. Lenore has mournful memories of her neglectful deceased mother, the poet and scholar, whose face she can barely remember because her mother paid her so little attention. Similarly, her father has immersed himself in his scholarly work and completely ignored his daughter. Not until the very end of the novel, however, does he actually publish a successful work that makes a splash in the circles that count. Through new scenarios of integration in which his grandchildren may be frequently found playing in his study or sitting on his lap, the narrator suggests that had he allowed her—his daughter—into his life from the start, his work would have achieved success sooner.

Bildung involves cultivating one's talents. When it is successful, such cultivation does not end with self-absorption but instead with socialization that sustains these talents, especially as they benefit the family, community, and nation.[16] What, then, does it mean for Lenore herself to pick up the pen and write her own story?

The Problem with "I"

The eponymous moorland princess opens her autobiographical account with descriptive narration in the third person, unlike Jane, delaying the use of the first-person pronoun for several pages. The narrative then advances to a harrowing rite of passage. The heroine, on her seventeenth birthday, should be on the verge of self-aware adulthood. Her isolated upbringing on the heath has,

15 The nineteenth-century English translation of the full title, *Heidi's Years of Wandering and Learning*, misses the reference to Goethe's *Wilhelm Meisters Lehrejahre* and *Wilhelm Meisters Wanderjahre* (Wilhelm Meister's Journeyman's Years) and thus the allusion to training for guild membership.
16 Tatlock, "Zwischen Bildungsroman und Liebesroman," 221–38.

however, rendered her less self-aware than even Brontë's ten-year-old Jane. On this day, Lenore not only confronts her own reflection as she wades in a stream, but also encounters the outside world in the form of the man, who by the novel's end has become her husband, and his adopted son, who will later show her unwanted sexual attention. The encounter on the heath unfolds in painstaking detail.

The as-yet unidentified narrator, still employing the third person, reminds readers that this young woman has operated free from the social and aesthetic norms that they know all too well: here on this loneliest of spots on the heath there is no measure for feminine beauty, no impetus to compare oneself to any sort of social norm. Her father's neglect and her grandmother's odd notions have left her barely touched by civilization and convention, "wild und lustig" (2:36; wild and merry) like the willows on the river. She is barely aware of herself as separate from nature. As the text shows, Lenore must learn to say "I" as she grows out of and separates from nature and moves toward adulthood and marriage.

Lenore the narrator, like Jane, in saying "I" will need to assert herself against the interpellations of others. She first becomes aware of others and how they position her when on her birthday amateur archeologists aggressively intrude on the heath to explore one of the many megalithic tombs to be found there. Since Lenore has perceived the heath as indistinct from herself, she experiences their intrusion as a personal violation. The text emphasizes her attachment to the landscape when she utters the word "mein" (my) four times in two consecutive sentences as she protests invasion: up to this, moment the hill has been "*mein* Garten, *mein* Wald, *mein* unbestrittenes Eigentum," the isolated Dierkhof was "*meine* Heimat" (2:13; *my* garden, *my* wood, *my* undisputed property; *my* home [my italics]).

The archeologists meanwhile wreak havoc on the landscape as they rip huge chunks of earth "aus dem Laibe des Hügels" (2:14; from the body of the hill) to gain access to a tomb. Lenore recalls seeing the "hochgeschwungene Hacke—wie ein feiner, schwarzer Strich hob sie sich vom flammenden Himmel ab, und so oft sie niedersank, war es mir, als schneide sie in das lebendige Fleisch eines geliebten Körpers" (2:14; raised pick axe—it stood out from the flaming sky like a fine black dash, and whenever it went down, it felt to me as though it cut into the living flesh of a beloved body). And since she has just pronounced this land-scape her own, the reader must see this "living flesh" as hers. The men continue to hack at the earth. Their removal of a huge stone block to gain access to the grave reveals a "dunkle, leere Höhle" (2:16; dark, empty cavity).

As yet another violation, the men crawl into the opening, exploring the tomb and indiscriminately hauling out objects. When the younger man, who turns out to be the offensive Dagobert, hastily and carelessly brings burial urns to the surface, they burst, scattering ash and charred human remains in all directions. The archeological dig, undertaken by men who seem oblivious to the beauty of the heath, provides a stark contrast to Lenore's naive attachment to every facet of the natural setting. When, however, Claudius praises the heath, the sudden affection she feels for him leads her, in an intimate gesture, to hand him the pearls she has received that day as proof of its beauty. Dagobert, on the other hand, as a sign of the sexual aggression he will display in town, comments flippantly on the shoes Lenore has left on the bank of the stream. For the first time Lenore experiences "Groll" (2:29; anger) and a wish for revenge. One hears echoes of her furious grandmother. Yet in Lenore's case anger will eventually be positively channeled.

By 1871, Marlitt readers had experienced such anger through the female protagonists of *Geheimnis*, "Blaubart," *Goldelse*, and *Reichsgräfin Gisela*. It would surface again in *Im Schllingshof* in Mercedes de Valmaseda. In all these narratives, anger spurs self-awareness, self-formation, and the discovery of desire when it is acted out vis-à-vis the romantic counterpart—as in *Jane Eyre*. The remainder of *Heideprinzeßchen* follows Lenore's rapid ascent to womanhood as she falls in love with Claudius and her necessary education and socialization into a previously alien world. The seventeen-year-old who had never even seen money comes not only (begrudgingly) to esteem the discriminating Claudius, the businessman *and* connoisseur, who can distinguish false currency from real, but also learns the value of money and the hard work connected with earning it.

This romance and Lenore's maturation are tightly interwoven with discovery of self as figured in mirrorings, be they outdoors on watery surfaces or indoors in actual mirrors. They bring Lenore (and her readers), as they do Jane as well, moments of alienation, reflection, and insight. A first such encounter occurs when Lenore gazes at her reflection in the stream on her seventeenth birthday. The girl's shadow darkens and deepens the waters so that the initially pleasing reflection generates in her a "heillosen Schrecken" (unholy terror). After noting two glittering, "übergroße entsetzte Augen" (2:7; outsized terrified eyes), the narrator startles the reader by using the first-person personal pronoun "mich" (me): "Hatte wohl die Welt solch einen Hasenfuß, wie mich gesehen?" (2:8; Had the world ever seen such a coward as me?) only to follow it two sentences later with "Zunächst schämte *ich mich* vor *mir* selber und dann vor *meinen* zwei besten Freunden, die Zeugen gewesen waren" (2:8; First of all *I* was ashamed of *myself* and then on account of *my* two best friends who witnessed it [my italics]). The four first-person German pronouns—*ich, mich, mir, mein*—evoking self-reflection and then subjectification based on the gaze of others, sound the central themes of self-consciousness/consciousness of self and social-integration.

Lenore's reflected image recalls the "strange little figure" that emerges when Jane looks into a mirror in the red room and first contemplates herself. Her "fascinated glance involuntarily explored the depth [the mirror] revealed. All looked colder and darker in that visionary hollow than in reality: and the strange little figure there gazing at me, with a white face and arms specking the gloom, and glittering eyes of fear moving where all else was still, had the effect of a real spirit ..." (16). In a moment of alienation, Lenore's own fascinated gaze reproduces the psychological and social valences present here in Jane's.

Mirroring persists in *Heideprinzeßchen* as Lenore negotiates emerging self-awareness. After penetrating the secret chambers of the Karolinenlust, she enters a room with walls covered in mirrors. A dark figure that turns out to be her own reflection elicits a scream. She again views her alienated image with the perplexity of the young Jane, noting in particular her dark features: "Die

Schwarze stand noch immer drüben auf der Schwelle und ließ ein Paar brauner Hände langsam vom Gesicht niedersinken, dann warf sie ein wildes, dunkles Haargewoge in den Nacken zurück—ei, das that ich ja eben auch!" (The black-haired girl was still standing over there on the threshold and lowered a pair of brown hands from her face; then she tossed back a wild wave of dark hair— oh, that was what I too had just done). She then laughs and moves forward to inspect the image—"war ich wirklich das Scheusälchen da drüben?" (2:111; was I really that little monster over there?).

Subsequently, as she readies herself for a social gathering, Lenore unexpectedly sees her mirror image in an unfamiliar social context. She has become the center of (male) attention and is ill prepared for it. As reflected in the mirror, behind her on the threshold of the parlor stands Dagobert and behind him appear "noch andere lachende Männergesichter" (still more laughing men's faces). Herr Claudius too rises up in the mirror (2:194).

A fourth mirroring requires the narrator to acknowledge her appearance and its deviation from social norms, namely, once again her dark complexion. She compares her "bronzefarbener Kreolenteint" (bronze creole complexion) unfavorably with her aunt's peach-colored cheeks and gleaming white brow (2:388). Immediately thereafter the statuesque Aunt Christine disparagingly labels the diminutive Lenore a "bräunliche Haselnuß" (brownish hazelnut) and marvels at her "samtene Zigeunerhaut" (2:388; velvety "gypsy" skin), effectively othering her and dismissing her as a rival for Claudius's affections, just as the imposing Blanche Ingram, in her designated whiteness and corporal grandeur, dismissed the little gray governess. Like Jane, for a time, Lenore believes that this sophisticated woman has won the affections of the man whom, as she at last acknowledges, she loves. As did Jane, Lenore turns her gaze from her inadequate self to admire the beauty and accomplishments of her perceived rival. Just as Blanche sang duets with Rochester, so Christine sings her signature song, Rossini's tarantella ("La danza") to command attention—it figures here as a seduction eight years before it also does in Ibsen's *Doll House* [1879])—in an attempt to win back his affections. Yet Christine soon vanishes from the purview of the narrative and the story reaches closure in a concluding scenario of looking and reflection centered on Lenore.

The concluding vignette occurring seven years after the couple's betrothal provides Lenore, in a final mirroring, with an affirmative image of self in the form of her own baby girl. As the narrator emphasizes, this moment is the "Sonnenblick des Glücks" (2:416; sunny look of happiness). With a neologism paralleling "Augenblick" (moment, blink of an eye) the text sustains the idea of Lenore as the object of a gaze—in this case, however, not Lenore herself, men, or society, but happiness looks upon her.

This concluding scene cuts two ways. Lenore, switching to the present tense, embraces interruption by her husband and family matters and commands herself to stop writing since the pen cannot paint the happiness that now shines on her. Marlitt's text here seems to anticipate Wedding's unsatisfactory adaptation of *Jane Eyre* which, as we saw in Chapter 1, allows Jane to run out of words since there is nothing to say once the blissful ending is reached. Lenore the narrator has apparently arrived at D. A. Miller's "non-narratable"—non-narratable because it "lacks the capacity to generate a story"; there is nothing left to tell.[17] With the conflicts set up by the romance narrative resolved, closure figures as the abiding present tense of family matters, of marital conversation beyond the book's horizon.

Like many of her female contemporaries who were earning their living by the pen, Marlitt appears to hew to domestic ideology based on inequality when she offers a happy ending according to which children and spouse take precedence. But as the principal emblem of social integration in the nineteenth century—and social integration is the destination of *Bildung* in the Goethean sense for both men and women—family should not be discounted as mere cliché or capitulation. More important to the messages and outlook of this novel is its depiction of the process of self-formation and the negotiations that make a new family possible. The concluding paragraph does not change the fact that the first-person narrator has been writing herself for over 400 pages and that had she not come to self-awareness, she could not have become the merchant's wife and the mistress of a differently configured household.

The text itself, the product of Lenore's successful education into literacy and written self-expression, embodies the agency of the "beseeltes und beschwingtes Wesen," the pen in one's hand (2:183). The mature Lenore can animate the pen to write her story, an undertaking that would have been impossible for the untutored seventeen-year-old moorland princess. Her self-aware life writing cultivates both individual disposition and social integration. Through Lenore's telling of her life story, the novel offers a take on individualization and subjectification that involves the acquisition of judgment and self-possession and also the discovery of desire for an unlikely partner as a feature of social integration. When she reports in the final chapter that it has taken her five years to complete this autobiography, the book itself figures as the crowning achievement of a girl who has advanced to self-aware literacy.

Lenore's confusions in the merchant's house circle around questions of character and identity. As she grows into selfhood, she realizes that she has misperceived Claudius and begins to worry that he misperceives her. Maturation involves learning to judge people and situations correctly, in particular her future husband and the household and business he runs. While the mysteries that the house harbors may have entertained some readers, the central plot involves a pair that move toward mutual intelligibility as the woman matures and finds a voice. As does *Jane Eyre*, Marlitt's novel only gradually reveals and cements Lenore's attraction to Claudius and his to her through dialogue. By thus intertwining love with maturation and the achievement of greater psychological sophistication and insight, it delivers something akin to Pearce's "gift of relational selfhood."

Whatever we may now think of this evocation of selfhood, this novel, in the wake of *Jane Eyre*, offered such a gift within the constraints of its day. The

[17]   D. A. Miller, "Problems of Closure in the Traditional Novel," in *Narrative Dynamics: Essays on Time, Plot, Closure, and Frames*, ed. Brian Richardson (Columbus: Ohio State University Press, 2002), 273.

education and maturation of the moorland princess does involve the gentling of Lenore's wild and defiant nature, but from the start Claudius insists that her "individuality" not be infringed upon; he means to keep her from "mechanical" work that could dull her spirit—no need for her to protest that she is not a machine. And, indeed, she retains something of her younger self. The enchanting "lizard with a crown" carries her native passion, sensitivity, and sympathy with her into a recalibrated bourgeois habitus. When Lenore sleeps for the first time in the main residence of the compound, she dreams of a matron in the Claudius family line, a figuration delicately balancing subjectification and individualization: "sie trug den Stirnschleier, wie die Hausfrauen der alten Claudius, und schritt durch die hallenden Gänge und die breite Steintreppe hinab; aber ihre Füße berührten die kalten Fliesen nicht, die ganzen Blumen des Gartens waren ja da hingeschüttet worden, und das kleine Wesen—ich wußte es unter einem unbeschreiblichen Glücksgefühl—war ich ..." (2: 329–30; She wore the veil across her forehead like the wives of the ancient Claudiuses and walked through the echoing corridors and down the wide stone staircase, but her feet did not touch the stone tiles, indeed all the flowers from the garden had been strewn there, and that little creature—I knew it as I was overcome by an indescribable feeling of happiness—was me ...).

Dressed in the traditional garb of the merchant wife, this oneiric Lenore retains her enchanting, elemental qualities. She floats over flowers, rather than prosaically grounding herself on the stone floor. The placement of "ich" in final position makes clear that through her newly acknowledged love for Herr Claudius, Lenore has attained the elusive "I" that she once heedlessly splashed away on the heath. Having done so, she at last summons the courage to announce to the local princess and all assembled that her grandmother was a Jew.

The formation and assertion of the self through writing enable the female protagonist's individualization and domestic happiness within the social imaginary of the novel; alterations in that social imaginary with broader implications for characters located at different points along the social spectrum accompany this individualization and this happiness. Like *Goldelse*, the novel ends not so much with a series of marriages as in *Jane Eyre*—although Charlotte does marry a man who has long loved her in vain—as with multiple configurations of happiness within and just beyond the Claudius grounds including Lenore's father's long-sought academic success, Dagobert's emigration to America, new management for the flower business, the resulting betterment of worker conditions, and the improvement in the fortunes of a family beyond the walls of the factory compound.

Illustrating the "Moorland Princess"

Illustration makes visible variable historical understandings of the discovery and formation of self in this romance narrative. A cheap edition printed in double newspaper columns (*c.* 1919) boasts, for example, a colorful cover illustration signed "Robert Sedlacek, Vienna."[18] Sedlacek, who later illustrated girls' books,

---

[18] E. Marlitt, *Das Heideprinzeßchen* [90-Pfennig Bücher] (Berlin: Globus, n.d.), copy owned by author.

created sexualized covers for this cheap series of Marlitt novels with Globus that anticipate those of later paperback "bodice-rippers." His covers depict women with bare shoulders and plunging necklines in moments of conflict or outright violence. That for *Geheimnis*, for example, transforms the physical tussle over Cordula's diary into a sexually charged scene in which the odious Adele throws back her head as though in ecstasy; the drawing threatens to expose her breasts as the sleeves of her dress slip off her shoulders.[19]

His cover for *Heideprinzeßchen* is tame by comparison, yet it entertains the possibility that a woman's self-discovery titillates. Sedlacek depicts Lenore gazing at her reflection in the stream, but not as Marlitt shaped it with her heroine laughing and splashing in the presence of Heinrich, the dog, and the cow (see Figure 7.1). Rather, a solitary Lenore, her knees parted, appears to slither toward the water, her body slightly twisted to emphasize her lithe figure. She leans over the water for a look at herself. Framed by wavy black bobbed hair, her face is highlighted with aqua eyeshadow extending from her eyelashes to her dark eyebrows. Through this lightly sexualized and reconfigured rendition of the scene, Sedlacek features the autoerotic pleasure of self-absorption.

Thirty years earlier, Erdmann Wagner had different ideas about the novel. In the 1880s, just prior to his illustrating *Heideprinzeßchen*, Wagner provided illustrations for two fairy-tale collections by Hans Christian Andersen, namely, *Dreißig auserlesene Märchen für den Familienkreis* (1884; Thirty Selected Fairy Tales for the Family Circle) and *Sechsundzwanzig auserlesene Märchen für die Kinderstube* (1887; Twenty-six Selected Fairy Tales for the Nursery). In *Heideprinzeßchen*, Wagner plays with motifs that recall these fanciful worlds, solidifying the latent connections in Marlitt's text with fairy tales and legends from the Germanic cultural reservoir, material that constituted for many German-language readers an element of their earliest reading socialization.

Motifs from legends, folk myth, and fairy tales of course also run through *Jane Eyre*, maintaining a mischievous presence in the form of Rochester's insistence on seeing his beloved as an airy creature. If Marlitt learned from Brontë to play off these elements, Wagner chose with his illustrations to tease out and highlight some of these associations and thus to help complete the communication circuit in which fairy tales and legends played an outsized role in the reading socialization of women writers and later on the fiction by these women and thus the audiences they addressed. Images of Lenore in the first and last chapters, which suggest that she belongs to a realm other than the one she finally inhabits, become interesting for a consideration of the reading effects of this *Jane Eyre* descendent and its gift of selfhood.

On the opening page, the illustrator supplies a picture of Lenore in a portrait box wedged in a forked flowering branch and surrounded by bees above a grassy field where a shy deer stands and stares at the reader. This beautiful child of nature wears a wreath, her long hair windswept and free—Erdmann had apparently overlooked the explicit description in the text of her hair as curly and cut rather short (2:7). In a three-quarter turn to face the reader, she tilts her

---

[19]   E. Marlitt, *Das Geheimnis der alten Mamsell* [90-Pfennig Bücher] (Berlin: Globus, n.d.).

Figure 7.1 E. Marlitt, *Das Heideprinzeßchen* [90-Pfennig Bücher] (Berlin: Globus, [*c.* 1919]). Copy owned by author.

head slightly up and to the left to look the reader in the eye, a half smile on her face. In the same chapter, a black-and-white plate depicts her standing in the stream and looking at her reflection, witnessed by her dog and Heinrich. It ends with a view from behind of a barefoot Lenore with her dog as she heads toward the men in the distance who are examining the burial mound (2:14). All three illustrations place the narrator's naive younger self out-of-doors and outside the domestic space that she will soon occupy.

The cameo illustration on the final page of the novel also draws upon Lenore's elemental quality, suggesting that the heroine is a hybrid or wild creature that has been tamed and integrated into bourgeois life (see Figure 7.2). Wagner here depicts the moment when the narrator puts down her pen in response to family demands. Wagner's has just a bit more to say than Marlitt herself or at least through his illustration clarifies the concluding situation. Here Claudius, as a doting, domesticated father, leans over the baby's crib, looking up at Lenore who has been sitting at her writing desk. She has jumped up; her flying pony-tail and outstretched arms express surprise, rather like the Virgin Mary inter-rupted in her reading by the angel Gabriel with the Good News in any number of European Renaissance evocations of the Annunciation. Lenore turns toward Claudius and away from the desk in a three-quarter twist, her back to the reader. Her concluding depiction thus provides a counterpoint to the three-quarter turn of the opening portrait toward the reader. Wagner's cursive signature shows up outside the cameo, as does the word "FINIS" in handwritten letters, thus pointedly asserting an authoritative role for the illustrator, as opposed to the narrator/author, in determining closure.

If the startled Lenore is called to her role as wife and mother in this scenario, Wagner nevertheless gives it a slightly unconventional turn with an extension of Lenore's dress that breaches the frame of the illustration. Her very long train curls, snakelike, to the left, to the right, and then to the left again. This train invokes Melusine, Andersen's "Little Mermaid," and related female water sprites from Germanic folklore. With the fairy-tale motif, the illustrator taps into the stuff of nineteenth-century women's reading and writing to offer a fanciful take on Lenore's bourgeois marriage.

Stories of female water sprites turn on the idea that such creatures can gain a soul only through marriage to a human. Attaining this goal always comes with conditions, sometimes not speaking or, as in *Melusine*, the husband's not looking in on her bath. In the tragic versions of these tales, the characters fail to meet the conditions. Lenore, who is after all not a water sprite, gains a self, not a soul, and manages the transition by virtue of pluck, good character, education, dialogue, and desire, all of which she has organized and processed through writing. With this cameo, Wagner invites the reader to recognize both her transition and the continued presence of her otherness.

Das Heideprinzeßchen for Girls
What could *Das Heideprinzeßchen* offer the late-century girl reader, who, like Charitas Bischoff, sought in her reading role models, alternate lives, and vicari-ous adventure? To what extent were adults ready to endorse the more progressive strains in the novel? The pretty illustrated book edition may have camouflaged

—◦§ 416 §◦—

getreten, er biegt sich über die Korbwanne und betrachtet sein schlafendes Töchterchen.

„Es ist erstaunlich, wie das Kind dir ähnlich sieht, Lenore."

Ich springe stolz auf; denn er sagt das mit einem entzückten Blick . . . Fort mit der Feder und dem Manuskript! Sie haben keine Farben für den Sonnenblick des Glückes über der Stirn des „Heideprinzeßchens".

FINIS

Figure 7.2 E. Marlitt, *Das Heideprinzeßchen*, illustrated by Erdmann Wagner, vol. 8 of *E. Marlitt's gesammelte Romane und Novellen* (Leipzig: Ernst Keil's Nachfolger, n.d.), 416. Copy owned by author.

the sensation elements and gained access to the book for some younger readers that the sexually suggestive Globus cover would have impeded.

An exemplar of this illustrated edition offers a clue as to what its makeup signaled to adults in the late nineteenth century. A plate pasted on the inside front cover reads as follows: "Prämium III'r Klasse/ verliehen an/ Emma Hempel/ für regelmässigen Besuch der Sonntagsschule/ der Zionskirche während des Jahres 1898/ Der Vorsteher: W. Theo. Schultze" (Prize of the Third Class/ presented to/ Emma Hempel/ for regular attendance of the Sunday School/ of the Zion Church during the year 1898/ The Principal: W. Theo. Schultze) (see Figure 7.3). The recipient of the book prize, Emma Hempel, born 1882, turns up in the 1940 census, age fifty-eight, single and living in Baltimore in Ward 8 with her sixty-one-year-old unmarried brother, Louis, and seventy-seven-year-old widowed mother, Matilda.[20] In 1898 she turned sixteen, close to the age of the protagonist. The "Zionskirche" is Baltimore's famous Zion Lutheran Church.

There are no marks in the book to indicate how or whether Emma read this book, but apparently the adults responsible for the book prize—ethnically German church members—thought it proper reading for a pious and conscientious sixteen-year-old, a gender-appropriate book from the Old Country that enforced the beliefs and ideals of the Sunday School. Presumably they were unaware of the novel's criticism of hypocritical Christian piety and missionary work, the *tendenz* that angered Kinzel; the sensation scenes; Gothic notes; and elements of *Jane Eyre*-flavored rebellion and independence.[21] Another volume from the same illustrated edition given as a gift in the United States in the same era likewise signals adult approval: "Grandma" presented "Eleanor Crosby" with a copy of volume 6 of the fancy illustrated set, Marlitt's *Die Frau mit den Karfunkelsteinen* (The Lady with the Rubies) on December 25, 1900.[22] Why did the sensation elements in Marlitt's novels not worry the adults who gave these gifts? One suspects that they knew Marlitt through the distorted lens of reputation, perhaps strongly associating her with *Die Gartenlaube*, understood, in the language of the time, as "wholesome" family fare. They may have associated the novels with other German-language reading for girls that had proliferated at the end of the century. In the case of *Heideprinzeßchen*, those responsible for the Sunday School prize might have thought they were presenting Emma with adolescent reading akin to Spyri's *Heidi*, sanitized adaptations of *Jane Eyre*, or Marie Otto's adaptation of the novel, *Heideprinzeßchen*.

20   1940 U.S. Federal Population Census, Genealogical Society No. 005461075, NARA Publication No., NARA Microfilm Roll 1512, Line No. 3, Sheet A, Sheet No. 61 https://www.archives.com/1940-census/emma-hempel-md-92788029(accessed August 14, 2021).

21   Katja Mellmann points out that early reception of Marlitt reacted to her perceived attacks on religion. Katja Mellmann, "'Detoured Reading': Understanding Literature through the Eyes of Its Contemporaries (A Case Study on Anti-Semitism in Gustav Freytag's *Soll und Haben*)," in *Distant Readings: Topologies of German Culture in the Long Nineteenth Century*, ed. Matt Erlin and Lynne Tatlock (Rochester, NY: Camden House: 2014), 302–4.

22   Inscription, E. Marlitt, *Die Frau mit den Karfunkelsteinen, E. Marlitt's Gesammelte Romane und Novellen*, 2nd ed. (Leipzig Ernst Keil's Nachfolger, n.d.), 6: front flyleaf, copy owned by author.

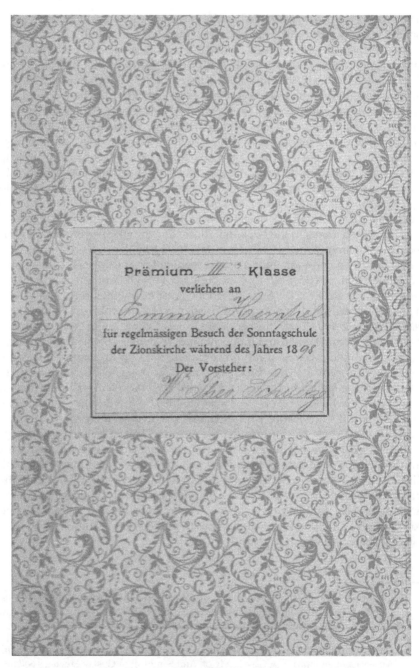

Figure 7.3 Book dedication, E. Marlitt, *Das Heideprinzeßchen*, illustrated by Erd-mann Wagner, vol. 8 of *E. Marlitt's gesammelte Romane und Novellen* (Leipzig: Ernst Keil's Nachfolger, n.d.).

As indicated by the designation "für die deutsche Mädchenwelt bearbeitet" (adapted for the German world of girls), Otto and her publisher must in
fact have believed revision necessary to make *Heideprinzeßchen* appropriate for
younger readers. First published in 1889 with the Norddeutsches Verlagsinstitut,
Otto's adaptation remained in print at least until 1910, when Globus reissued it
both under its own imprimatur and under the auspices of Meidinger's Jugend-
schriftenverlag, with which it had been combined in 1907. In the two and a half
decades preceding the First World War it circulated in at least 15,000 copies[23]
between decorative covers usually with a young woman at the visual center (see
Figure 7.4).

Like Wachler's adaptations of *Goldelse* and *Waise*, Otto's *Heideprinzeßchen*
omits the more sensational elements of the original plot, especially those involving sexual and social transgression and betrayal. The angry and vindictive Jewish grandmother has disappeared, as has her treacherous daughter. With them,
Lenore's mixed heritage, Claudius's fateful duel, and much of the angry animus
of the original have also vanished. Otto elides the opening scenes at the tomb
on the heath and its implied sexual violence by replacing the archeologists in
search of the ancient heathen past with bibliophiles piously seeking to view an
old family Bible on the farm.

The flower merchant's house has meanwhile lost its secret rooms, gates, and
passages, and thus its Gothic feel. There are no morganatic marriages to be dis-
covered. Charlotte registers as a charming but selfish brat, and the attractive,
sexually aggressive Dagobert here figures merely as an irresponsible young
man suffering from an inherited penchant for gambling. While in the original
he must leave the military to become a farmer in America, here he pulls himself
together to become a model military officer.

Lenore's move to town for the sake of her education happens at Claudius's
paternalistic urging and not Ilse's as in the original. Upon her arrival, an embrace
remedies fifteen years of estrangement from her father, and the novel blithely
proceeds to her "ganz weibliche Erziehung" (78; completely feminine education), which includes singing, cooking, sewing, and knitting. Like Mella, she
must also learn to write for everyday purposes and to care for her now-loving
but still-distracted father. Aside from these womanly occupations, she must
learn some life lessons, particularly, how not to conceal things from Claudius
who has her best interests at heart, how to read others, and how not to judge too
quickly by appearances. At Charlotte's prompting, however, she repeatedly misjudges the virtuous Claudius's actions until she recognizes the harm in doing so.

While the book makes room for love, there is no sexual tension. When Lenore
sings Goethe's "Heideröslein" (Little Dog Rose) at court, Princess Margarethe
remarks without irony that their "Heideröslein" would defend herself, "ehe es
sich brechen ließe" (107; before it would let itself be plucked). In a different context, the allusion to sex would be clear; here there is little indication of double
entendre. Otto does retain hints of Lenore's growing fondness for Claudius, but

---

[23]   Marie Otto, *Heideprinzeßchen. Mit teilweiser Benutzung von E. Marlitt's Erzählung "Heideprinzeßchen" für die deutsche Mädchenwelt* (Berlin: Globus Verlag, n.d.).

Figure 7.4 Cover image, Marie Otto, *Heideprinzeßchen. Mit teilweiser Benutzung von E. Marlitt's Erzählung "Heideprinzeßchen" für die deutsche Mädchenwelt* (Berlin: Globus Verlag, n.d.). Copy owned by author.

when he finally declares his love, their union is sealed not with a kiss but with an embrace and Lenore's weeping.

One alteration in particular highlights what Otto's adaptation denies the reader that the original supplied. Otto switches to a third-person narrator, as do Wachler and Reichard in their adaptations of *Jane Eyre* for girls, thereby affirming the difficulty of saying "I" and avoiding a central point of Lenore's story. In *Jane Eyre* the first-person narration invites readers to relish developing female subjectivity; in *Heideprinzeßchen*, Marlitt too creates a heroine whose acquisition of a sense of self the reader experiences intimately and pleasurably through first-person narration. Otto's avoidance of "I," like that of the two *Jane Eyre* adapters, suggests the dubiousness of that subjective point of view. In her *Töchter-Album*, Thekla von Gumpert tells us why.

In preaching self-effacement, von Gumpert's religiously flavored "Zwölf Freundinnen" (1896; Twelve Girlfriends) prescribes avoiding "I" even in autobiographical narration. Here twelve orphans promise to write their stories for one another ten years after leaving the orphanage. They also determine the form in which they will narrate, namely, in the third person: "das Ich, Ich, Ich würde uns peinlich werden" (the I, I, I, would become embarrassing to us).[24] In Gumpert's telling, these model women enter life striving for their ideals and intending to work, but they avoid putting themselves forward, even when telling their own stories.

Ignoring the achievement of the original Lenore, Otto's adaptation indeed avoids the "I, I, I" of Gumpert's warning. It shatters the subjective unity of the first-person narration by telling Lenore's story in the third person and interrupting it intermittently with Lenore's correspondence in the first person with Ilse, the farmwoman who raised her (chapters 4–7, part of chapter 10). This mix has several effects. First, the third-person narrator tends to unravel quickly any mystery or confusion that arises when Lenore misjudges a situation; it thereby imposes firm limits on her (and the reader's) speculative imagination. The letters, which include Lenore's misjudgments, constitute straightforward newsy communication of selected principal events. They collapse time and omit details, accelerating her education. Lenore's friendly prosaic letters foreclose entry into darker imagination, reflection, delusion, and desire. Ilse's letters, for their part, maintain a strong adult counter voice throughout much of the book. The adaptation does not include thoughtful narrative self-constitution, episodes of self-reflection, or literal mirroring. In short, Otto's version forgoes, in Light's above-quoted words, access to the "unified and coherent" subjectivity that can pleasurably distinguish romance reading.[25]

Sybille von Rhoden likewise adapted *Heideprinzeßchen*—through careful abridgment—"für die weibliche Jugend" (for female adolescents) around 1918. Although printed on cheap paper as an indication of wartime scarcity, the abridgment was furnished with four glossy plates. In A. Wimmer's frontispiece, the heroine, as a perky half-grown Heidi-like figure with short hair and one

[24]   Thekla von Gumpert, Part I of "Zwölf Freundinnen," *Töchter-Album* 42 (1896): 9.
[25]   Light, "'Returning to Manderley,'" 391.

arm around a garlanded cow, stands in the stream on the heath.[26] Wimmer's three additional plates depicting scenes that take place in the city portray Lenore wearing the fashions of 1918. Her short hair now reads as fashionably bobbed. Claudius has lost the nineteenth-century beard of the illustrated edition of 1888–90 and now sports a mustache and the knee-length frock coat, vest, and tie of a contemporary businessman. The cover, by contrast, depicts a timeless pastoral scene: her arm around a sheep and her legs outstretched, a young woman wearing loose-fitting clothes and a scarf around her hair sits on a flowery knoll.

This abridgment of *Heideprinzeßchen* retains the basic plot elements and the first-person narration, but omits many of the extended descriptions and thus the invitation to relish the detail of richly rendered interiors, social situations, opinion, taste, and personal reflection. Besides relentlessly making small cuts to trim detail, it drastically shortens chapter 4 to eliminate descriptions of Lenore's relationship to the heath, details of the violation of the tomb, her reflection on her life on the farm, and descriptions of her habits there. Chapter 7 likewise omits the long opening description of the farm and the heath, emotionally filtered through the narrator's mind. In contrast to Otto's much-altered and tamed version of 1889 for a younger target audience, this new-century version merely undertook shortening, flattening, and streamlining. As a shorter, less "literary" read, it perhaps reflected and accommodated popular reading habits of modern times.

Das Heideprinzeßchen on Stage and Screen

Two transmedial adaptations suggest the availability of the material to still other agendas and popular sensibilities—a play from 1872 and a film from 1918. Adolf Oppenheim's "arge Verstümmelung" (awful mutilation) of Marlitt's "charming" (*reizend*) novel, a "Charakterbild in 3 Acten nebst einem Vorspiel" (character sketch in three acts along with a prelude), the *Gartenlaube* reported, debuted in the summer of 1872 in Chemnitz.[27] The scant evidence of the play's performance thereafter suggests that it never gained traction, even as Oppenheim's one-act comedy *Eine Stunde Kaiser von Österreich* (One Hour Kaiser of Austria) was finding enthusiastic audiences.[28] Yet Max Kreutzer published this theater adaptation for the sake of its stage premiere, thus preserving it for posterity.

Oppenheim created a play that deviates sharply from Marlitt's novel.[29] Claudius, rechristened as Claudia, remains a merchant but has aged by nearly

---

26 Sibylle von Rhoden, *Das Heideprinzeßchen. Für die weibliche Jugend bearbeitet* (Berlin: Gustav Fock, n.d.), frontispiece.

27 "Blätter und Blüthen," *Die Gartenlaube*, no. 27 (1872): 446.

28 *Eine Stunde Kaiser von Österreich* debuted in Leipzig on October 1, 1871. "Ausländische Bühnen," *Blätter für Theater, Musik, Kunst* 17, no. 80 (October 6, 1871): 320. *Deutscher Bühnen-Almanach* lists new productions of 1871 at the Hamburg theater St. Georg-Theater, the Stadttheater in Leipzig, Damms Tivoli-Theater in Altona, the Carl Schultze Theater in Hamburg, Thaliatheater in Hannover, a theater in Marienbad, and the Stadttheater in Rendsburg. DBA 63 (1872): 9, 133, 136, 147, 183, 213 264.

29 Adolph Oppenheim, *Das Heideprinzeßchen. Characterbild in 3 Acten nebst einem Vorspiel; Seitenstück zu E. Marlitt's gleichnamigem Roman* (Hamburg: J. J. Nobiling, n.d.).

twenty years. At fifty-five he no longer figures as a love interest but instead plays the part of an angry father who must be reconciled to his children for the play to end happily. The play instead pairs the female protagonist with Claudia's age-appropriate son, Alfred, who is at odds with his father. The *Jane Eyre*-style romance of the novel between an older powerful man and a spirited, intelligent young woman thus gives way to the coupling of young people, impeded largely by the son's father to reproduce a New Comedy plot of conflict between fathers and sons. The "psychologisches Problem" that Gottschall once identified has vanished. Oppenheim deals here in stock elements of melodrama, sensation, and popular literature of the time—faithless lovers, disobedient children, illegitimate birth, a falsified signature, scheming Jesuits, disinheritance, profligate women, and family secrets—only some of which are present in Marlitt's original.

The Jesuit plot displaces Marlitt's education plot, and the play's final scene offers a scenario of familial reconciliation shaped by the patriotic turn in post-unification Germany. To this end Oppenheim moved *Heideprinzeßchen* forward in time from 1861 to 1871. Alfred returns from the front at this charmless play's end, wearing the uniform of a common soldier to prompt patriotism. His right arm in a sling, he proudly displays an iron cross which he has won for his capture of a French flag—a peculiar idea of warfare in the age of the Krupp six-pounder steel breech-loading cannons.

Nearly forty years later in 1918, when National-Film adapted the novel for the movies, Germany and Austria were again at war with France and its allies. As she had in *Goldelse*, Meller played the lead in *Das Heideprinzeßchen*. Promotional material for the "Marlitt- und Heimburg-Roman-Serie daher Klassenschlager [*sic*] ersten Ranges" (Marlitt-and Heimburg-novel-series, for this reason a box office smash of the first order) touts Meller as "die jugendlichste, schönste, eleganteste, übermütigste Filmdarstellerin" (the most youthful, most beautiful, most elegant, most high-spirited film actress), thus suggesting that audiences may have been enticed to go to the theater mainly to see the star of the film.[30]

Directed by Georg Viktor Mendel, the black-and-white silent film later received a *Jugendverbot* (adults-only rating) on July 9, 1921.[31] This designation signals a work different from the prize of 1898 for Sunday School attendance presented to Hempel by the Zionskirche or, for that matter, Fock's abridged edition for girls, which appeared at about the same time as the film. Without a copy of the film, we can only speculate as to what aspects merited that designation. Did the film capitalize luridly on the mad grandmother and the sexual undercurrents of the novel—Dagobert's aggressive pursuit of Lenore within the confines of the house; Aunt Christine's attempts to seduce Claudius, her former lover; the morganatic marriage of Princess Sidonie and Lothar; Lenore's own potentially erotic appeal as the othered moorland princess; the suggestive violation of the moor? As a silent film, it could certainly not reproduce, with intertitles, anything

---

30   Advertisement, *Der Kinematograph*, no. 605 (August 7, 1918): n.p.
31   "Das Haideprinzeßchen," filmportal.de https://www.filmportal.de/film/das-haideprinzesschen_854c96f2fbc047d7ab954d19985f15d7 (accessed April 21, 2018).

but the barest bones of the equalizing and humanizing conversation that leads to companionate marriage.

Like *Jane Eyre*, *Heideprinzeßchen* can be and was read in more than one way. Read only for its romantic resolution, it seems to offer a conventional happy ending. Read for the sensation elements, it offers moments of Gothic titillation. Read mindful of the complexities of Brontë's novel, its own attempt at psychological and narrative complexity becomes more readily visible, including the heroine's struggle with anger and self and her wish for acknowledgment and conversation, for words that are a "bridge thrown between myself and another."[32] Insofar as Marlitt's novel took on a bit of the fire of *Jane Eyre*, this fire diminished over the course of subsequent transmission via adaptation even as the book outlived its adaptations. Yet, as the adaptations suggest, its subtler shades—the psychological-emancipatory valences, the social criticism, the emphasis on language and literacy, the play with literary tropes, the very *Jane Eyre* elements—became less legible within the vicissitudes of the new century.

---

[32]   V. N. Voloshinov, (1929) *Marxism and the Philosophy of Language* (1929); qtd. by Stacey and Pearce, "The Heart of the Matter," 32.

Eight   The One and the Many

Unlike *Jane Eyre*, Marlitt's novels quickly acquired a profile as constituents of a single-author series. In this final chapter we turn to six of Marlitt's novels to read them as belonging to a set, as works born affiliated and thus always just a bit *Jane Eyr*ish. At first glance, four of these may appear to have little to do with this English antecedent. A closer look, however, identifies variations of *Jane Eyre*-indebtedness in each of them. In retaining these resonances, these novels remain true to their brand while also providing variety to loyal readers. What, then, are the ramifications of a book's belonging to a series rather than being one of a kind?

In the present day the casually curious reader can come across *Jane Eyre* in a number of modern editions and formats in German, but no longer in its myriad nineteenth-century variations. On the one hand, this novel presents in these editions as world literature and is marketed in German as a single, unique work, now uniformly titled *Jane Eyre*. On the other hand, the story is not quite that simple. In the summer of 2019, a visit to Dussmann KulturKaufhaus, a large, well-known Berlin bookstore, revealed that *Jane Eyre* in German was being sold on the floor as "klassische Literatur" (classic literature) in four different translations and five editions—a translation by Bernhard Schindler as a Diogenes paperback, a translation by Andrea Ott in both a Penguin paperback edition and a hardbound edition with Manesse, a translation by Melanie Walz with Insel, and an updated version of Marie von Borch's translation in a deluxe, illustrated, and enhanced hardbound edition from Coppenrath, Münster.[1]

This plurality of translations, each of which counts on title recognition—*Jane Eyre*—unambiguously connecting it to the English original, marks the status of this novel as the *one*, a unique novel with canonical standing. Yet publishers and booksellers also market it as one of the *many* by affiliating it with other English books in translation. In the summer of 2019, Dussmann, for example, displayed the novels of all the Brontë sisters alphabetically and next to one another, spines out. Coppenrath connected the novel, by means of its flowery cover and Marjolein Bastin's illustrations, with its edition of Jane Austen's *Stolz und Urteil* (Pride and Prejudice)—the resemblant makeup encouraged the common confusion of *Jane Eyre* with Jane Austen.

These similarly designed covers promise readers—in 2019 the publisher's use of flowers assumed these readers would be female—by association, that if they

---

[1]   Confirmed by author's visit on July 13, 2019. Dussmann das KulturKaufhaus, Friedrich-straße 90, 10117 Berlin.

like one, they will surely like the other. The blurb on the cover continues to affil-
iate the book with others by submerging Brontë's novel in genre fiction:

> Mittellos und als ungeliebtes Mündel ihrer hartherzigen Tante erfährt
> das Waisenmädchen Jane Eyre eine traurige Kindheit—und auch ihre
> Jugend im Internat bringt zahlreiche Entbehrungen mit sich. Aber
> trotz aller Widrigkeiten schafft sie es, sich von den gesellschaftlichen
> Einschränkungen des 19. Jahrhunderts zu emanzipieren und zu einer
> selbstbewussten und unabhängigen Frau heranzuwachsen. Jane lernt
> wahre Freundschaft und sogar die Liebe kennen, bis ein schreckliches
> Geheimnis dafür sorgt, dass sich erneut dunkle Wolken über ihrem Leben
> zusammenziehen.[2]

> [Without means and as the unloved ward of her hard-hearted aunt, the
> orphan girl Jane Eyre experiences a sad childhood—and her adolescence
> at boarding school is also accompanied by deprivation. But despite every
> adversity she manages to emancipate herself from the social restrictions of
> the nineteenth century and to grow up into a self-confident and independent
> woman. Jane comes to know true friendship and even love, until a terrible
> secret sees to it that once again dark clouds gather over her life.]

One scarcely recognizes *Jane Eyre* in this description; it sounds like a dozen other
popular historical romances available for purchase. Marketing thus appears
both to capitalize on the canonical status of the novel and also to tout it as utterly
accessible because not so very different from other novels readers may know
and love. In a similar vein, the algorithmically driven affinity analysis employed
by Amazon.de points a buyer of *Jane Eyre* in German to German translations of
Anne Brontë's *Agnes Grey*, Emily Brontë's *Wuthering Heights*, Thomas Hardy's
Tess [of the d'Urbervilles], Jane Austen's *Pride and Prejudice*, and her *Emma*, or to
an entire boxed sets of Austen's six best-known novels, "Die großen Romane"
(the great novels), one published by Reclam and one by Anaconda.[3]

   As outlined above, the nineteenth-century book trade treated *Jane Eyre* differently. It quickly decoupled it from Brontë's other novels and those of her sisters
so that it became, for a time, the one literary survivor of all these works. When
it did circulate in a series, it was as a member of a publisher's quality library
and not as a set of books whose contents resembled one another. Even when
published in a series, that is, it circulated singularly as "the one," like the world
literature it was coming to be.

---

[2]   Charlotte Brontë, *Jane Eyre, nach der Übersetzung von Maria [sic] von Borch* (Münster: Cop-
      penrath Verlag, 2018), back cover.
[3]   Search term "Jane Eyre" Amazon.de, https://www.amazon.de/Jane-Eyre-Roman-
      CharlotteBrontë/dp/3423143541/ref=sr_1_4?__mk_de_DE=ÅMÅŽÕÑ&keywords=
      Jane+Eyre&qid=1562824821&s=gateway&sr=8-4; https://www.amazon.de/,
      Jane-Eyre-Roman-CharlotteBronte/dp/332810285X/ref=sr_1_7?__mk_de_
      DE=ÅMÅŽÕÑ&keywords=Jane+Eyre&qid=1562824821&s=gateway&sr=8-7 (accessed
      July 11, 2019).

At the same time, given the vagaries of translation and adaptation, *Jane Eyre*, as we have also seen, proliferated in German as various versions of itself, versions that in some cases diverged widely from one another as well as from the original. It circulated as a plurality of texts that did not even share a uniform title and yet still registered as itself. Indeed, in her account of reading two significantly different versions, one of which did not even include Rochester, Charitas Bischoff did not express dismay at the disparities but rather joy in reunion and recognition when, as an older girl, she unwittingly came across a more mature and complex version of her life-changing childhood reading.

Marlitt too was adapted, but the reception history of her novels largely involves a plurality of a different sort. It consists of her serial production as it recycled *Jane Eyr*ish elements crucial to its appeal and power as romance. As Marlitt turned out ten novels and three novellas over approximately twenty years, readers came to know and love her brand. Encouraged by the *Gartenlaube*, they avidly anticipated each new serialization. Reading several or indeed the entire set of Marlitt's novels in turn provided even casual readers with a basis for more finely grained comparison of them beyond the obvious fact that they resemble one another. While critics disparaged these novels as formulaic, those who liked them could savor their sameness while appreciating the variations that distinguished them from one another. It almost goes without saying that this serial reading could occur in more than one language across the Western world. English-language readers, for example, could read all of these novels serially in at least two English versions, the most famous being Wister's translations for Lippincott. Lippincott, for its part, regularly marketed these translations as a set—both as Marlitt-authored novels and as members of a set of related German women's fiction, recognizable as Wister-translations.[4]

Marlitt herself must have understood serial reading quite well and have striven to meet expectations of both sameness and difference. Indeed, she experimented with the basic elements of her *Jane Eyre*-like love stories. This chapter examines the Marlitt-set with reference to *Jane Eyre*, aiming to offer a somewhat different perspective on what has been seen as their formulaic quality, one that illuminates the broader import of romance of a *Jane Eyr*ish kind, especially among German-speaking publics in the 1870s and 1880s. The first section of this chapter scrutinizes Marlitt's signature emphasis on troubled family and her lavishly evoked domestic spaces as these plots proliferate in the series and evince affinities to Brontë's novel. *Die zweite Frau* and *Die Frau mit den Karfunkelsteinen*, as we shall see, manifestly reproduce signature spatial motifs and structures alongside other *Jane Eyr*ish elements. The less immediately obvious affiliation of *Im Hause des Kommerzienrates* (In the Councillor's House) comes into focus through a consideration of precisely its spatialization of domestic tensions and struggle. The second section turns to three novels—*Reichsgräfin Gisela*, *Amtmanns Magd*, and *Im Schillingshof*—that feature reversals of motifs and plot elements that characterize the Marlitt set and still resemble or reference *Jane Eyre*. These variations testify to and fortify the continued appeal and power of novels

---

4   Tatlock, *German Writing, American Reading*, 225–33.

crafted in a similar vein, novels that in the nineteenth century supported the cultural transmission of *Jane Eyre* and its exhilarating messages.

Romance in Fraught Spaces

If, as Louise Otto, asserted in 1869, the foundation of the state was the family and everyone knew it, then something was rotten in the state of Germany as Marlitt repeatedly imagined it over the approximately twenty years of her serialized publication in the *Gartenlaube* in the wake of *Jane Eyre*.[5] After the idealized picture of the proudly bourgeois Ferbers in *Goldelse*, Marlitt created ever-more labyrinthine versions of broken families, some of whose pre-history took weeks to establish in serialized publication, most extensively *Im Schillingshof* (1879), whose exposition required eight of twenty-six installments. While romantic union in these novels never requires an overt confrontation with the state per se—nor does it in *Jane Eyre*—it does repeatedly entail struggle with its shaky foundation, the family. For all the family-friendly projections of the *Gartenlaube*, its most-touted author, from 1865 to 1888, offered extended accounts of familial corruption, tyranny, and vulnerability while withholding the possibility of happier arrangements until the very end when the sparring couple unites and the story dissolves into the non-narratable.

Jane Eyre depicts the damage to individuals wrought by family, from the accounts of Jane's time with the Reeds to Rochester's exploitation by his own father and brother. It involves an orphan's search for family, or rather, two orphans, for Rochester too has lost both parents. It gratifies Jane, after the torments, humiliations, and deprivation of orphanhood, with an embarrassment of family: cousins, a foster daughter, a husband, and biological children. The happy ending that the novel grants Jane and Rochester does not, however, require the restoration of or reconciliation with the old family, the Reeds, or even with Jane's generous uncle, John Eyre, as a member of the older generation. Rather it involves, after the catharsis of fire, the creation of a new family and a new conversation in a new location—Ferndean. Were the novel not structured by a romance plot and were it instead concerned with the restoration of the old family, Jane could remain happily single with her newly found paternal female cousins—as she does in Reichard's adaptation. As another alternative, she could have healed these fissures with cousin marriage; she could, that is, have married St John, as in Stieff's early adaptation, and headed off to India to do missionary work. Instead, when Rochester calls to her in the night, Jane acts on desire and thus puts her faith in creating something new.

The novel ends with the joy of conversation in relative isolation; recovery of extended family amplifies (but is not necessary to) the couple's happiness. To reach this ending the narrative moves Jane through five principal settings: Gateshead, Lowood, Thornfield, Moor House and environs, and Ferndean; each setting marks a different stage of development and movement toward romantic resolution. Especially Gateshead, with the red room, and Thornfield, with

---

5 Louise Otto, Excerpt from *Der Genius des Hauses. Eine Gabe für Mädchen und Frauen* (1869) in Häntzschel, *Bildung und Kultur*, 147.

Bertha's room upstairs, house hidden horror, but all the settings also contain spaces where Jane acquires an education in some fashion and exercises her imagination, where she reads behind the curtains, has tea in Miss Temple's quarters, climbs to the rooftop to survey the grounds, studies in the parlor with her cousins, and finally becomes Rochester's eyes and left hand. Over the course of telling, the text makes visible and shapes these largely indoor spaces with curtains, windows, doors, thresholds, stairs, and hallways as the characters move through them in scenic presentations. Of all these spaces, the unprepossessing Ferndean, which apparently harbors no family secrets, remains the least visible as the narrative comes to an end and the text privileges spousal conversation over looking and seeing.

Two decades later in her German context, Marlitt too invested heavily in the edifices and their surrounding grounds that house her plots. At the same time, she tends to recalibrate the narrative balance of individual and family tied to those spaces in order to expose and repair the family through romance—after all, it was the foundation of the state, as everyone knew. The presence of the old family in the old house upon the achievement of union varies. Sometimes the erotic union coupled with the heroine's achievement of self and a form of parity replaces the old family as in *Jane Eyre*; sometimes the narrative goes to some length to preserve what is salvageable of that old family.

Despite these variations and shifts in focus, the novels remain *Jane Eyre*ish, and this aspect potentially delivers liberating messages and reader pleasure. While family certainly matters to Marlitt's novels, romance rooted in self-formation and a push for female parity realized through conversation drives their plots. Marlitt, like Brontë, persists in telling stories focused on individual disposition and sees to it that the social does not silence individual yearning and that the female protagonist has a plot (even if predictable) that responds to her desiring. Family cannot force the coupling that ultimately constitutes the happy ending as a strategy to enhance wealth and status; instead, the errant desire of individuals culminates in a marriage that rids the home of violence and abuse to create a livable homespace. But the narrative does not merely speak metaphorically of homespace; like *Jane Eyre* it also spatializes romance within family configurations through domestic architecture.

Die zweite Frau

Its mothers either dead or mute, the Mainau family in *Die zweite Frau* (*Gartenlaube* 1–21 [1874]) is missing the feminine element. Juliane, the "second wife," is to address that lack. This novel, Marlitt's fifth, echoes Brontë's novel in a number of ways that were by no means lost on contemporary readers. Hugo Gottschalk's[6] review of Merlé's theater adaptation, for example, points to the

---

[6]   This print review is pasted in the back of the copy of the play held by the Staatsbibliothek zu Berlin: H. W. Merlé, *Liane, die zweite Frau: Charaktergemälde in 5 Aufzüge nach dem gleichnamigen Roman der E. Marlitt für die Bühne bearbeitet* (Berlin: Deutsch-österreichische Theateragentur, n.d.) signature Ys18459. The source is cut off. The play is hereafter cited in text. Gottschalk is listed as offering "dramatischen Unterricht" (drama training) in Berlin in Joseph Kürschner, *Jahrbuch für das deutsche Theater* (Leipzig: Hermann Foltz, 1879), 1:162.

affinity of all Marlitt's female protagonists—and particularly Liane—with their "Seelenstärke" and "Seelengröße" (strength and greatness of soul) to Jane. He summarizes their commonality in terms of a narrative of overcoming adversity through a toughness of spirit, taking Brontë's novel as the standard: "Sie gehen alle aus der Schule des Leidens und durch diese gekräftigten Erfahrungen, ähnlich wie Jane Eyre, die Waise aus Lowood, hervor ..." (All of them emerge from the school of suffering and through these strengthening experiences, like Jane Eyre, the orphan from Lowood). In recent times both Joeres and Yvonne Defant have traced vestiges of *Jane Eyre* in *Die zweite Frau*. I too have noted these.[7] Necessarily reiterating some of the findings of this earlier scholarly work, the following plot summary highlights key points of convergence.

In *Die zweite Frau*, the half-orphan Juliane marries the older, more experienced Raoul von Mainau under economic duress and pressure from her spendthrift mother. Despite aristocratic prejudice against working for pay, Juliane has sold paintings to supplement her aristocratic family's meager household income, but these efforts have not sufficed to keep her family out of debt. By marrying Mainau, whom she does not yet know, she seeks to repair the family's finances. Although not a paid governess, Juliane, as the second wife, occupies a comparable position within her marriage. Intending to pursue his own interests abroad, Mainau expects her, during his prolonged absences, to attend to Leo, his spoiled son from his first marriage.

Juliane has in effect consented to the loveless transactional marriage that Jane resisted. She sees the wrongheadedness of her sacrifice, just as she also realizes that she has fallen in love with the difficult Mainau under difficult circumstances. For Juliane, passion and conversation develop within a sham marriage that has not been physically consummated. This narrative tour de force—the marriage of convenience—as an alternative to the governess novel, allows Marlitt to confine two strong, intellectually and physically attractive strangers within the intimacy of a single dwelling. Not until Juliane determines of her own free will to leave that space does a union based on desire and freely proffered consent become possible. Meanwhile the sexual tension of an unconsummated marriage between two individuals who are falling for one another grows, rendering titillating the mere touch of an arm.

Apparently, this narrative conceit accomplished its purpose in its own time. Gottschall praised the novel for its "glaubwürdige und spannende Entwickelung" (credible and exciting development) and for Marlitt's portrait of the shift in Mainau's feelings toward Juliane: these lively depictions were informed by a subtle psychology, "die nie um beweiskräftige Züge verlegen ist" (that never wants for convincing evidence).[8] Many a nineteenth-century second marriage was in fact quietly contracted out of the need of the husband to have his household managed and his children cared for; such marriage

---

[7] See Joeres, *Respectability and Deviance*, 241–2; Yvonne Defant, "Le mystère du passé hante encore: l'influence de *Jane Eyre* sur *Die zweite Frau* d'Eugenie Marlitt," *Revue LISA* e-journal, https://journals.openedition.org/lisa/3510 (accessed May 1, 2020); Tatlock, *German Writing, American Reading*, 126–8.

[8] Gottschall, "Ein Urtheil Rudolf Gottschall's über E. Marlitt," 480.

bargains depended on the second wife's acquiescence to "woman's destiny," often coupled with her economic necessity. The premise of the Mainau marriage was in 1874 not as far-fetched as it may now sound and it offered a rewriting of that dire economic marriage script as a romance involving choice and parity.

The novel's opening gambit establishes the uncanniness of its setting in an unnamed German region, in effect, in Pyrhönen's terms, "relating material spaces to mental states."[9] The first chapter recounts the frivolities of the ducal court in a fake fishing village, reminiscent of Marie Antoinette's infamous *hameau* at Versailles, during which the recently widowed duchess hopes in vain to lay claim publicly to her once-jilted lover, Mainau. This unnatural location quickly proves to be the site of small cruelties licensed by social inequality when Mainau's son, Leo, strikes his dependent cousin Gabriel in the face with a riding crop.

The marriage of convenience places Juliane herself in a dependent relationship to a family with secrets in a region ruled by arbitrary whim. Marlitt thereby situates her novel within the Gothic genre, setting its heroine on a quest for knowledge that ultimately enables her to expose a will as counterfeit and to reveal the conspiracy that threatens to deprive Gabriel, the biracial son of the youngest of the three Mainau sons in the older generation and Mainau's first cousin, of his rightful inheritance. The scheming and bigoted middle Mainau son, the *Hofmarschall* (Lord Great Chamberlain), has, based on a forged document indicating his brother's dying wishes, disinherited Gabriel, his artistically talented nephew and is raising him to become a monk. At the mercy of his uncle, the sensitive boy has no say in his future. This plot twist draws on a nineteenth-century scandal, the Italian Mortara case from the 1850s and 1860s involving a kidnapped Jewish boy raised within the Vatican as a Catholic, a case the text names (7:72).

Juliane only slowly uncovers the family treachery as she explores the estate. Not far from the manor house, Gabriel's long-suffering, unjustly repudiated Indian mother lies mute in a pavilion in the "Valley of Kashmir," a simulacrum of India built for her on the estate by her deceased husband to ease her homesickness. As it turns out, the *Hofmarschall* attacked his sister-in-law years ago and is responsible for her vegetative state. Joeres and Defant rightly see traces of Bertha Mason in this character—like Bertha, she is an abused and displaced colonial other. The Marlitt reader might also recall Lila from *Goldelse* entombed in the family castle. Unlike Brontë, Marlitt demonizes neither character, but sets about recovering them.

The manor house itself constitutes an oppressive setting imbued with tense emotion and moral conflict. As the second wife, Juliane must inhabit the blue room, redolent with the perfume of Mainau's deceased first wife who was also his first cousin. With respect to the first wife's pervasive presence, *Die zweite Frau* anticipates Daphne du Maurier's *Rebecca* (1938), itself a *Jane Eyre*-influenced text. Marlitt is, however, less interested than du Maurier in the first wife as a rival to the second than in the religious bigotry and transgressions of the poisonous

---

9   Pyrhönen, *Bluebeard Gothic*, 2.

past that her haunting presence represents. Furniture and other features of the interior architecture loom large in the probing of the past: the writing desk, the fireplace, the locked chest. The *Hofmarschall* asserts authority over the interior spaces of the mansion from his wheelchair even as the wheelchair inhibits his movement through them. Meanwhile, the resident Catholic priest has free rein to dog Juliane with his sexual overtures.

When she finally acknowledges her love for her husband, Juliane joins forces with him to make the estate livable again, banishing the scheming priest, breaking the power of the *Hofmarschall*, and restoring Gabriel's rights. As in her other novels, Marlitt puts Juliane's mental toughness on display through verbal exchange; the heroine repeatedly proves herself the male protagonist's match, indeed his superior, in these confrontations. Her ringing indictment of the priest, who first pursues her sexually and then tries to murder her, makes the importance of the heroine's voice still clearer. She can speak for herself and on behalf of others.[10]

Insofar as it could be imagined in a time of inequality, shaped by separate spheres and starkly limited options for women, the struggle toward parity and union here, as in Marlitt's other novels, enables the projection of a marriage in which the educated wife will play a crucial role in determining the marriage's terms and conversations upon the sprawling estate. While Mainau may appear to have the upper hand, the novel concludes with Juliane's shaping the household, just as Jane does in the end. Even as Mainau declares that, as an incurable egoist, he has arranged everything to his liking, it is also obvious that the heroine has long since won him over to her views. Among other things, he has abandoned his plans for extended periods away from home.

When commissioned upon the author's death in 1887 to complete *Das Eulenhaus* (The Owl House), "in ihrem Sinne" (as she intended),[11] Wilhelmine Heimburg intuited precisely the importance of female-dominated conversation within the homespace to the conclusion of Marlitt's novels and honored it with an amusing variation.[12] In the final chapter the gossip of a secondary couple informs readers that the principal couple, Klaudine and Lothar, have been bickering. In this instance their argument has resulted in each of them trying to outdo the other in agreeing to do what the other wishes. But who won the argument? The answer is simple: "wer allemal recht behält, wenn ein Ehepaar zankt … Die Frau Baronin natürlich" (9:612; whoever is always right when a married couple squabbles … Naturally the Baroness).[13]

---

[10] For the role of religion in the early reception of Marlitt, see Katja Mellmann, "Tendenz und Erbauung. Eine Quellenstudie zur Romanrezeption im nachmärzlichen Liberalismus (mit einer ausführlichen Bibliographie zu E. Marlitt)," Habilitationsschrift, Ludwig-Maximilians-Universität, Munich, 2014.

[11] "E. Marlitt," *Die Gartenlaube*, no. 29 (1887): 476.

[12] On this collaboration, see Lynne Tatlock, "Death and Transfiguration in Installments: E. Marlitt and Das Eulenhaus (1887–1894)," *Colloquia Germanica: Themenheft: Periodical Literature in the Nineteenth Century* 49, nos. 2–3 (2016): 283–304.

[13] The *Gartenlaube* announces the availability of this volume in Halbheft 19 (1890): 612.

Extensive positive national and international reception of *Die zweite Frau* testifies to its importance in the *Jane Eyre*-Marlitt constellation.[14] Forty-three years later in 1917, full-page promotional material in *Der Film* for Robert Oswald's Marlitt film series touted *Die zweite Frau* as the "berühmste und meist gelesenste" (most famous and most read) of Marlitt's novels.[15] In the interim it had circulated in alternate print formats and adaptations in the German-language realm, including Fock's series, where it was reworked by Sybille von Rhoden for "female youth" and embellished with four illustrations. It also appeared, along with Marlitt's other novels, in the Globus 90-Pfennig series [1919]. While Fock's edition supplies a frontispiece emphasizing domestic virtue as Juliane tucks a babyish Leo in bed, the Globus cover features the lascivious priest's attempt to murder a revealingly clad Juliane.[16] In Alexander Zick's woodcuts for volume 7 in the illustrated collected works, in turn, the spirited Juliane appears for the most part in submissive attitudes, her head routinely bowed, Madonna-like. These extremes bear witness to the mix of the domestic and Gothic sensation that characterizes the entire series and *Jane Eyre* too.

H. W. Merlé's theater adaptation *Liane, Die zweite Frau: Charaktergemälde in 5 Aufzügen, nach dem gleichnamigen Roman von E. Marlitt für die Bühne bearbeitet* (Liane, The Second Wife: Character Portrait in 5 Acts, Adapted for the Stage after the Novel of the Same Name by E. Marlitt) debuted at the Victoria-Theater in Berlin on September 13, 1874, and ran through September 29 with "Fräulein [Marie?] Schröder" playing the female lead. *Liane* was at least the fourth stage adaptation of this novel. As the *Gartenlaube* complained in April 1874, adaptations by Karl Viereck, Hugo Busse, and Paul Blumenreich were currently playing in three different Berlin theaters, the Vorstädtische Theater, the Réunion-Theater, and the Belle-Alliance-Theater, even though the novel's serialization was not scheduled to conclude until late May or early June; indeed, a third of the novel had yet to appear.[17]

14 For its English translations, see Tatlock, *German Writing, American Reading*, 128–9.
15 Advertisement for *Die zweite Frau, Der Film* 43 (October 27, 1917): 3. I thank Petra Watzke for sharing this notice. For a description of the film, see Jürgen Kasten, "Dramatische Instinkte und das Spektakel der Aufklärung. Richard Oswalds Filme der 10er- Jahre," in *Richard Oswald, Kino zwischen Spektakel, Aufklärung und Unterhaltung*, ed. Jürgen Kasten and Armin Loacker (Vienna: Filmarchiv Austria, 2005), 42–6. Kasten notes the overlong intertitles required to sort out the complexities of Marlitt's plot (42–3).
16 Sybille von Rhoden, *Die zweite Frau. Erzählung von E. Marlitt. Für die weibliche Jugend bearbeitet* (Leipzig: Gustav Fock, n.d.); E. Marlitt, *Die zweite Frau* [90-Pfennig Bücher] (Berlin: Globus, n.d.).
17 Die Redaction der Gartenlaube, *Die Gartenlaube*, no. 14 (1874): 234. Notices in the *Vossische Zeitung* from April 1874 indicate that Blumenreich's adaptation played at least sixteen times in the Belle-Alliance-Theater and that Busse's adaptation played at both the Réunion-Theater and the Variété-Theater, in both cases advertised as "nach E. Marlitt's gleichnamigen Roman in der Gartenlaube" (after E. Marlitt's Novel of the Same Name). *Dritte Beilage zur Königl. Privilegirten Berlinisichen Zeitung*, no. 80, April 5, 1874, 2 (Réunion-Theater) and *Dritte Beilage zur Königl. Privilegirten Berlinisichen Zeitung*, no. 81, April 8, 1874, 2 (Variété-Theater) and *Zweite Beilage zur Königl. Privilegirten Berlinisichen Zeitung*, no. 90, April 18, 1874, 3. If these three stagings were ever published, these printed versions have not survived.

Merlé, who did wait to see how the novel ended, was, according to the pace set by his three fellow theater adaptors, late off the mark. Still, he turned out the play quickly, managing an 1874 premiere. While the few contemporary reviews that have survived do not testify to the play's success, a closer look at the published script reveals that Merlé produced a version that favors Liane, one that, unlike many of the other theater adaptations of Marlitt, does not significantly undercut the heroine's agency. Liane's strong voice in the play results from Merlé's decision to select key scenes and copy dialogue nearly verbatim from the original. He thus created a play with a density of scenes featuring confrontational dialogue involving Liane, beginning in the second act, where she stakes out her claims and voices her family pride and progressive views on religion and women's roles. The compactness of the play, which includes the major events of the novel, means that each scene brings Liane a new hurdle to clear and that she remains vocal and virtuous to the end, even uttering the final line of the play.

Merlé's play did not enjoy a long run on the German stage.[18] Despite the empowerment of the female lead, its dramatic architecture, which consists largely of "talking heads," founders. The fraught spaces of the Mainau estate are all but invisible in a play that focuses on character. In simply revealing virtue, it fails to reproduce the frisson of probing unsettling domestic spaces and the slow unfolding of romance within those spaces, the tentative mutual seeking across strangeness, that narrative allows.

Im Hause des Kommerzienrates

While the threads tying *Die zweite Frau* to *Jane Eyre* are many and obvious, at first glance, the possible debt of *Im Hause des Kommerzienrates* to this literary antecedent remains obscure. Its affinities to Marlitt's other novels are more readily discernable. Still, a closer look reveals many traces, especially in the mustering of architectural spaces and interior décor, revealing mental states and family conflict as constituents of an unfolding romance.

An inverse mirror to *Die zweite Frau* in its familial composition, Marlitt's sixth novel (*Die Gartenlaube* 1–26 [1876]) involves a nearly all-female blended family with no living biological fathers. It is the first of three of Marlitt's full-length novels—including *Im Schillingshof* and the co-written *Das Eulenhaus*—to name a house instead of a woman in its title. But in fact the narrative involves not a single house, but rather a complex of buildings. The Villa Baumgarten, the factory, the tower, the former farm building, and the mill spatialize family relations, with characters assigned to particular edifices and rooms therein. After the death of the "castle miller"—who owned the entire feudal estate—the property begins to break apart while the characters locate themselves in particular segments of it.

Kommerzienrat opens with the demise of the miller, the grandfather of the fourth and youngest Mangold daughter, Käthe, and thus the effective elimination of all male authority within the two intertwined *biological* families—the snobbish

---

18   The last performances of *Liane* recorded by the *Deutscher Bühnen-Almanach* occurred sometime before January 1, 1877. DBA 41 (1877), 277.

banker family, the Mangolds, and the more plebian miller family, the Sommers. The end of the male line in both families to a degree resonates with the family situation after the death of Jane's uncle at Gateshead, which leaves only the bratty John Reed who then dies young. In Marlitt's novel, the absence of biological fathers, too, enables the arbitrary rule of the matriarch in the day-to-day. The family housed in the aristocratic Baumgarten villa evince the ills of modern times. The maternal grandmother, Frau von Urach, asserts the authority of aristocratic etiquette and snobbery, while the oldest-living Mangold sister, Flora, tyrannizes the household with her egotism and opinions. Yet in this case female domestic tyranny is illusory, since Moritz Römer, the wealthy owner of the spinning factory, who married into the Mangold family, has long since stepped into the breach. The widowed Römer, the eponymous *Kommerzienrat*, functions as the head of the household, and after Grandfather Sommer's death, which he inadvertently causes, he also becomes the orphaned Käthe's guardian.

Römer, a parvenu who was initially an apprentice in the Mangold banking firm and once married to Klothilde, Flora's twin, has pursued—without the female family members' understanding or intervention—financial schemes that, in a novel serialized after the stock crash of 1873, must fail.[19] As the chief miscreant, the somewhat more complex Römer may for some readers prove more engaging than the tediously virtuous Dr. Bruck, the novel's love interest. Marlitt significantly locates Römer and his secrets not in the feminized villa but in the nearby tower, which itself bears the weight of local history as configured not only by the suits of armor lining the upstairs rooms but by two kegs of gunpowder left from the Thirty Years War in the basement. In Marlitt's novels, architecture, as in *Jane Eyre*, harbors secrets, in this case both concealing and revealing Römer's inner life. Outwardly a ruin belonging to a troubled past, the tower inwardly serves as Römer's richly appointed retreat, where he indulges his pretentions to grandeur and social ascendancy. In the end, his corruption revealed, he destroys that space—and its past—to make his escape.

Römer's financial scheming constitutes but one strand of the fraught relations in this household. His narcissistic sister-in-law, the pretentious and vain cigar-smoking Flora, pursues her own selfish agenda, spouting the emancipatory views of the budding women's movement whenever it suits her purposes.

---

[19] Belgum notes the seductiveness of the richly appointed interiors in this novel that prove emblematic of the pretentions of the parvenu. She sees the narration of interiors as "a strongly subjective strategy of narrative empathy," which first "serves to entice the reader into the text" and then to enable the reader to take a critical stance. Kirsten Belgum, *Interior Meaning: Design of the Bourgeois Home in the Realist Novel*, German Life and Civilization 91 (New York: Peter Lang, 1991), 114, 116. In their analysis of the evocation of social class in this text, Jochen Schulte-Sasse and Renate Werner trace the assignment of characters to particular locations in a dynamic that they characterize as "hüben und drüben" (over here and over there) by which clear-cut spatial positioning configures moral and economic difference. Jochen Schulte-Sasse and Renate Werner, "E. Marlitts 'Im Hause des Kommerzienrates': Analyse eines Trivialromans in paradigmatischer Absicht," in *Im Hause des Kommerzienrates*, by Eugenie Marlitt (Munich: Wilhelm Fink, 1977), 414–15.

Herself speculating within the local marriage economy, she attaches herself to the up-and-coming local favorite, the gullible Bruck. After the collapse of the household and her engagement to Bruck, she cynically contracts a marriage of convenience with a newly wealthy member of the old aristocracy. The narrative assigns Flora to the Baumgarten Villa, affording her a study, a red room—red from the carpet and the wall tapestries to the upholstery. This red room speaks not to the run-away imagination of an abused child, as in *Jane Eyre*, but instead to that of a demonized female figure. Indeed, Flora's red "room of her own" testifies to nothing but her tawdry pretension and viciousness.

As the chief impediment to romantic union, Flora plays the role of the first wife for most of the novel, keeping Bruck and eighteen-year-old Käthe apart for pages on end, even when she herself wishes to separate from Bruck, whom she does not love. The text twice labels her a vampire, suggesting once again that Bertha haunts Marlitt's narrative imagination. Bruck recoils as Flora's "unheimlich düstere Gestalt" (uncanny sepulchral figure) clings tightly to him, "so weich und geschmeidig und innig ... wie der Vampyr der Volkssage" (5:224; so soft and supple and fervent ... like the vampire of the folk legend). Käthe later speaks of her determination to free Bruck from her half-sister, the "Vampyr ... der nach seinem Herzblut trachtet" (5:358; vampire ... that seeks his heart's blood). Robert Sedlacek's lurid cover for the 90-pfennig edition of *Kommerzienrat* from 1919 picks up on precisely this demonization of Flora when it tries its best to sell the novel as a story of passion to a public in search of distraction around 1919. A blonde woman, certainly Flora, throws herself in a sort of orgasmic swoon into the arms of a handsome man while a distressed second woman, apparently also in the throes of passion, looks on.[20]

While the spiteful Flora refuses to release him from the engagement, Bruck, unlike Rochester who is prepared to commit bigamy in a more dire situation to attain the object of his desire, adheres for long stretches of the novel to an inflated sense of honor that dictates keeping his promise to marry Flora even though, as he later confesses, he has loved only Käthe since he first laid eyes on her. In the end, he castigates himself for his adherence to this false code of honor, thus slipping into the role of the male protagonist, who, like Rochester himself or Johannes in *Geheimnis* or Mainau in *Die zweite Frau*, comes to recognize his own error as a feature of the romance plot. Bruck's sudden self-awareness does not, however, have the force of a repentant Rochester. In fact, he is not the most interesting male figure in the novel; Marlitt splits her principal male characters into the virtuous professional man, Bruck, and the aforementioned ruthless capitalist, Römer, and thus forgoes the ambiguity and ambivalence that so powerfully fuel the romance plot of Brontë's novel.

The climax of the novel, the spectacular destruction of the tower, not only results in the death of a miller and physical damage to the aristocratic Baumgarten Villa, but also disperses and displaces all the inhabitants of the villa, echoing the cathartic burning of Thornfield. The good sister, Henriette, dies; Flora leaves for Zürich to study medicine, which she soon gives up; and

---

[20]   E. Marlitt, *Im Hause des Kommerzienrates* (Berlin: Globus, n.d.), cover image.

Grandmother von Urach is forced to leave the premises over which she once presided. The local authorities seal one room after another for the purpose of inventorying the contents for the benefit of Römer's creditors. As in *Jane Eyre*, disaster clears the way for a future built on more solid and less economically and socially overweening foundations. As always, Marlitt withholds outsize wealth from her heroine, lest she be loved for her money rather than her good character and, so it also appears, lest she be positioned outside of the comfortable upper middle classes and inadvertently bypass the social end point of most of these love stories.

After the catastrophe, young Käthe for a time assumes a place as head of the mill, all that remains of her once vast fortune, proving her intelligence, independence, and determination to enact social good. The delay of union in effect serves Käthe, like Jane, to complete her education and thus to gain greater autonomy. In the process she not only successfully runs the mill but also sees to it that workers in the nearby spinning factory have the means to build cottages on a strip of the mill property.

Acknowledging this success, even Bruck, who has suffered under Flora's hollow espousal of women's rights, approves of women's independence. Yet he does not want Käthe to waste her time with accounting, since he believes her to be destined for "Familienglück" (domestic happiness), the destination of all Marlitt's love stories. When he finally arrives at the mill to claim her as his bride, he proclaims the end of the career of the beautiful lady miller. Yet in the very act of claiming her he is nonplussed to discover the sacrifice she made to free him from Flora. The active role that Käthe has quietly played in his liberation in effect ensures that she is not merely an object to be claimed.

The discovery prompts the two, who have hitherto hidden their attraction to one another, to determine that there shall be no more secrets between them. As they talk, the companionate marriage that Marlitt typically envisions comes into view. They will start a new life together free from the aristocratic pretentions of Grandmother von Urach and the greed of the parvenu.[21] The final page depicts the couple entering yet another space, the aunt's house by the river, which has been completely renovated. If Brontë's isolated Ferndean with its unhealthy location was a bit suspect, Marlitt's renovated house by the river raises no such doubts; it glows in "Frische und Neuheit" (5:379, freshness and newness). In the closing scene Bruck's aunt greets the couple at the threshold, the village church bells ringing to proclaim Easter and attach this love match to an unambiguous message of resurrection. Heinrich Schlitt's final illustration for the edition of 1889 portrays the threshold as an enlarged keyhole through which the couple will pass into married life and thus expresses in spatial terms a final vision of marital harmony and closure.

---

[21]   Belgum contends that all of Marlitt's novels offer "extensive and undeniably liberating images of [women's] independence (both financial and intellectual)," and that it is wrong to think "that these strong women will cease speaking their minds, standing up for what they believe in, and fighting courageously for liberal causes as they have all along." Belgum, "Narratives of Virtuous Desire," 270.

As in this concluding image, Schlitt's illustrations for *Kommerzienrat* as volume 5 of the collected novels and novellas capitalize on the spatialization undertaken by the narrative itself. Woodcut after woodcut puts the characters before the reader in fully realized domestic spaces—both interiors and exteriors. A fullpage illustration depicts, for example, Flora in her study (5:25) calling attention to the description of Marlitt's version of a "red room." In another woodcut, Bruck appears at the window of the pretty little house surrounded by vines and flowers and a picket fence, his and Käthe's future home (5:97). Schlitt places Grandmother von Urach in the midst of a room in disarray as she wonders who will inherit Römer's money (5:320).

Schlitt's penultimate illustration visualizes Käthe, too, in her designated space, the mill, at the moment when Bruck enters to claim her for domesticity (5:385). The room is modestly appointed. Its heavy wooden beams, oldfashioned wooden chair in the so-called "altdeutsch" (old German) style, and wooden bench lend it a solid, bourgeois appearance. Wearing a work apron, Käthe, at her account books, pen in hand and the keys to the mill at her waist, hearkens to the sound of Bruck's entrance. The illustration recalls the interruption that concludes *Heideprinzeßchen* when Lenore puts down her pen to tend to her husband and child. While Wagner allows the moorland princess to retain some of her magical quality with the tail of her train, Schlitt, in this depiction, in keeping with the text itself, reproduces the levelheaded Käthe, whose rosy complexion and unpretentious middle-class ways signal goodness. Käthe simply ceases bookkeeping to turn to the everyday conversations of married life; her words are the last direct speech recorded.

This novel was repurposed in its own time for the theater in two unimaginative variations, both of which considerably alter the plot. Although dealing with a visual-spatial medium, neither manages to spatialize conflict and character in keeping with the conceit of the novel as it depicts the troubled family relationships emerging from the tangle of old feudal aristocracy and modern capitalist speculation.[22] Especially, the alternate versions of Römer—in Hugo Busse's adaptation he is the arch-villain; in Friedrich Wagener's version he aids the couple in unmasking Flora— put the weakness of the adaptations on display. Neither stage production manages to entertain the conceit of Römer as a mixed and possibly even arresting character. The contrast between the plays and the novel brings the strengths of the novel into view.

Die Frau mit den Karfunkelsteinen

Die Frau mit den Karfunkelsteinen (*Die Gartenlaube*, nos. 1–20 [1885]) features a snarled familial construction located largely in a single compound and invests anew in the hidden woman. In this case it is Blanka (duplicating Susemihl's name for Blanche Ingram), a secret second wife whose name features not dark otherness but pristine purity.

---

[22]   Friedrich Wagener, *Im Hause des Commerzienraths. Schauspiel in 4 Akten. Frei nach Marlitt's Roman in der Gartenlaube* (Berlin: Eduard Bloch, n.d.); Hugo Busse, *Im Hause des Commerzienraths. Schauspiel in 5 Akten nach E. Marlitt's gleichnamigem Romane* (Berlin: Bartels, n.d.).

Balduin's broken promise to his deceased first wife never to remarry serves as a tame substitution for attempted bigamy.[23] The sin of the present repeats the sin of the past: Great Grandfather Justus Lamprecht too broke his promise to his first wife, Judith, never to remarry when he fell in love with his beautiful ward, Dorothea, who lived in the same house. His marital bliss came to a bitter end when Dorothea died in childbirth. The ghostly presence of Justus's angry first wife as, in Brontëan language, a "graue Furie" (6:7; gray fury) in pursuit of the ghost of the second wife, the lovely Dorothea, and Dorothea's portrait as the eponymous "lady with the rubies" haunt the present. Meanwhile the entire family misapprehends what is right before their eyes. Not only does the family fail to recognize that Balduin, the current head of the household and the family firm, has married the painter's daughter, Blanka, who lives with her family in the warehouse, one of the back buildings of the compound, but they also later fail to recognize little Max, who is being raised by his grandparents, as Balduin and Blanka's son. Similarly, misreading hinders Margarete and Herbert over many chapters from discovering and expressing their mutual attraction and finding their way to a companionate marriage.

As she had in *Geheimnis*, *Gisela*, and *Heideprinzeßchen*, Marlitt devotes several opening chapters to her heroine's childhood. In so doing, she hearkens back not only to her own work but possibly also to its most important literary antecedent. A spirited nine-year-old, Margarete suffers in a household where her tyrannical and socially ambitious step-grandmother favors both her own son, Herbert, who is ten years older than Margarete, and Margarete's nasty younger brother, Reinhold, as the presumed heir to the family business. When carelessly thwarted by her preoccupied father, Margarete flees the household to take refuge with her grandfather who lives in a neighboring village separate from his domineering second wife. This attempt to escape the confines of the household turns out badly for a little girl, who loses her way and returns home only to fall into a feverish stupor. When she finally revives, her father leaves home, accompanied by Blanka—as we learn only later. Five years later, the increasingly uncontrollable Margarete, like Jane, is sent elsewhere for the sake of her education. Unlike Brontë's heroine, however, Margarete does not pursue a trajectory that leads outward from her traumatized childhood. Instead, she returns home after another five years, nearly unrecognizable as a nineteen-year-old.

Home, as a result of moral failing, social pretention, and cowardice, has long since become uncanny. Once again Marlitt attaches her characters to spaces in the home and makes penetration and transgression of concealed spaces a key plot element. In Margarete's childhood, the servants had already begun to whisper reports of sightings of the ghostly Dorothea, who walks the closed-off rooms of the house, and this rumor continues to haunt the household. The "red salon," where the portrait of the unfortunate Dorothea still hangs, functions literally and symbolically as the site of transgression and the container of secrets. Margarete's

---

[23] The *Gartenlaube* announced the publication of *Die Frau mit den Karfunkelsteinen* as volume 6 of the illustrated edition in 1890 (Halbheft 1 [1890]: 36). Haas, too, notes in passing the similarity of the hidden woman to the plot of *Jane Eyre*. Haas, *Eugenie Marlitt*, 170n322.

father, Balduin, had once made it his private quarters; later on he shut it up without explanation. It in fact holds the clues to unraveling the secrets of the past.

The ghostly sightings, fueled by superstition, once had a real cause, as the text slowly reveals. Balduin, who labors under the social pretentions enforced by his stepmother who is also his mother-in-law from his first marriage,[24] married the daughter of the humble painter but concealed the marriage. The "white lady" was actually Blanka, who traversed the wings of the complex from her parents' quarters through a closed-off passageway to be with Balduin. For one year the couple lived abroad, but when Blanka died, Balduin returned with their son, Max, whom he deposited within his purview with Max's maternal grandparents without publicly acknowledging him. Damage to the roof of the Lamprecht compound wrought by a powerful storm both figures and reveals the troubled state of the family, hastening Balduin's untimely death and eventually prompting Margarete and Herbert to ferret out the secret of Max's origins. For centuries "geheimnisvolles Dunkel" (mysterious darkness) has lived under the roof of the old house, the narrator observes. Now the stars are shining through and lighting up the floorboards so as to reveal the traces of those who once walked them (6:172). The storm provides the impetus for Margarete to enter the forbidden recesses of her own home eventually to unearth the secret in her deceased father's writing desk.

Marlitt intertwines Margarete and Herbert's budding romance with the revelation of this hidden marriage and the obtaining of justice for Max. Herbert and Margarete, who have lived as niece and step-uncle, must over the course of the novel come to regard one another with different eyes. Like Rochester, Herbert flushes out Margarete's feelings by fueling the rumor that he is courting the beautiful, rich, aristocratic, but intellectually inferior Heloise von Taubeneck. When the feisty Margarete capitulates, Herbert crows over his success at drawing her to him, but then cries, "Nun aber genug des Kampfes!" (6:321; But now enough with the struggle!), thus confirming the antagonistic dynamic that has propelled the love plot.

The romantic coupling is nothing if not claustrophobic. In chapter 1, Herbert has an adolescent crush on Blanka, at whom he gazes longingly across the interior courtyard of the compound. Blanka, as the text specifies, later became Margarete's second mother for the one year of her father's second marriage. When Herbert and Margarete finally openly express their love, Herbert again raises as much as dispels the specter of incest when he declares, "er ist begraben, der alte Onkel! Und du bist fortan nicht meine Nichte, sondern—" (6:320; He is buried, the old uncle! And from now on you are not my niece, but instead—), and she interrupts him, "Deine Grete—" (Your Grete—).

The oppressive and confined textures of the plot in general and the incestuous feel of the romance of uncle and niece bring into full view the degree to which the combination of elements that powered Marlitt's eight previous novels, in the

---

[24]   The text leaves underexplained how it is that Grandmother Lamprecht is both Balduin's stepmother and his mother-in-law. The reader must infer that at some point she married Balduin's father, as his second wife, bringing two children into the marriage: Fanny, who married Balduin, and Herbert who eventually will marry Margarete, her granddaughter and his niece.

manner of *Jane Eyre*, relies on creating and policing an existential homespace, one that integrates those who do belong and guards against and expels those who do not. Herbert's mother (Margarete's maternal grandmother) leaves the compound soon after the revelation of Balduin's marriage and Max's patrimony while her husband, Margarete's paternal grandfather, moves back in to occupy the "red salon," where the generations gather daily as an "enger Kreis von Menschen" (6:325; close circle of people) bound by ardent love. While the novel mentions this fact only in passing, Julius Dreßler's theater adaptation of *Karfunkelsteine*—announced as having been undertaken with the permission of the author—used the relocation to milk the uncanny doings of the red salon for the stage.[25]

Dreßler borrows slavishly from Marlitt's dialogue to produce a play that brings out some of the spatial aspects. His adaptation supplies markedly more detailed descriptions of the sets than do the other Marlitt theater adaptations. He thus appears to have had a good sense of the Gothic notes that inform her narrative. He particularly picks up on the possibilities of the red room. Over the course of the fifth act, set entirely in the red salon, the room transforms from an uncanny space, the terrain of ghostly wives and the keep of family secrets, to one in which the grandfather and Herbert in the final scene do most of the talking. If the red room at Gateshead was haunted by the dead father, this one is haunted by the dead mothers. Dreßler makes certain that the patriarch has repurposed this feminine space by the time the curtain falls. In enacting this restoration, he misses the fact that Marlitt's novel lands elsewhere—indeed, in the kitchen where the servants worry that the house may still be haunted. The novel concludes, in fact, with a bit of sympathy for the errant human heart disposed to irrationality: "Der Glaube an dunkle Mächte wird nicht sterben, solange das schwache Menschenherz liebt, hofft und fürchtet!" (6:326; Belief in dark powers will not die as long as the weak human heart loves, hopes, and fears!) Marlitt perhaps also meant therewith to signal that she had more stories to tell.

Sameness and Difference: Variations on Romance and Self-Formation

Even when Marlitt's romantic formula presents somewhat differently, her novels nevertheless preserve elements of *Jane Eyre*. The successful serial recycling of these features suggests that her oeuvre addresses an enduring need in her readers for reliably repetitive yet varied reading. Repetitions, however, figure differently with different readers. A disdainful review of Marlitt's first five novels, titled "Marlitt und ihr Leserkreis" (Marlitt and her Circle of Readers) from 1876 typifies the dismissive criticism launched at the perceived formulaic quality of Marlitt's novels and at the readers who sought it. Despite the scorn and condescension, points raised concerning variety and repetition merit attention in the present context.

---

[25] Julius Dreßler, *Die Frau mit den Karfunkelsteinen, Schauspiel in 5 Akten und 1 Vorspiel, nach dem gleichnamigen Roman in der "Gartenlaube"* (Leipzig: Leopold & Bär, n.d.), title page. The *Neuer Theater-Almanach* records a production of Dreßler's play, staged to celebrate the opening of the Julius Dreßler-Theater in Leipzig on February 7, 1897. *Neuer Theater-Almanach. Theatergeschichtliches Jahr- und Adressen-Buch* (Berlin: Genossenschaft Deutscher Bühne-Angehöriger, 1898), 9:437.

This review correctly identifies features of *Reichsgräfin Gisela* shared with *Goldelse*, *Geheimnis*, and *Heideprinzeßchen*. B.W., the anonymous reviewer, sees similarity especially in the principal characters and the situations in which they find themselves. Gisela displays Felicitas's rebellious pride and self-control, Elisabeth's intuitive wisdom, and Lenore's naiveté. The male protagonist of *Gisela*, Berthold Ehrhardt, in turn is the same misunderstood, mysterious man. The "heroischen kleinen Mädchen" (heroic little girls) scold these tyrannical men until they fall into their arms, the mystery having readily revealed itself, B. W. sneers.[26] The review also notes Marlitt's reversal in *Gisela* of gendered patterns from previous novels: while in *Geheimnis* Felicitas must lay out for Johannes the injustices to which his mother has subjected her, in *Gisela* Berthold awakens the young countess to the injustices in which she has unwittingly played a part. At bottom, these variations, B. W. maintains, cannot mask the fact that Marlitt always delivers the same story.

After establishing the formulaic quality of the novels, the author turns to the second target of the essay—readers themselves—to disparage them for returning repeatedly to this same unconvincing story. Marlitt, B. W. avers, uses her narrative talent to take advantage of the weaknesses (*Schwächen*) of the general public.[27] She includes decorative, titillating details that do not contribute to the coherence of the plot, using them simply to appeal to the need for excitement on the part of shallow audiences in search of light reading.

Some men, B. W. speculates, read these novels on account of the heroine, who possesses a piquant mixture of primness and vivacity. In 1885, Hermann Friedrichs asserted in this same vein that Marlitt stirred up passions in her readers in a "hysterisch-krankhafter Weise" (hysterical-sick manner); her "versteckte Sinnlichkeit" (hidden sensuality) had an extremely powerful effect on readers *because* it was hidden.[28] Aside from their moralizing, these two critics are not exactly wrong on this point. These same descriptors might be applied to Jane, too, as could the notion that reading *Jane Eyre* stirred readers' passions. The cagey conversations of Jane and Rochester, as governess and master, in particular, build sexual tension. Finally, B. W. objects, Marlitt fascinates her audiences through "Effekthascherei" (sensation).[29] One need only think of the madwoman plot at the center of *Jane Eyre* to see the proximity of what B. W. deplores in Marlitt to a work now regarded as world literature.

Even if some nineteenth-century readers, like B. W., were impervious to its charms, the continued wide circulation of Marlitt's fiction indicates that many contemporaries were not. In 1885, on the occasion of the serialization of *Die Frau mit den Karfunkelsteinen*, a different Austrian reviewer praised Marlitt's "wahre

---

[26]   "Marlitt und ihr Leserkreis," signed B. W., *Die Presse*, April 1, 1876, 1.

[27]   "Marlitt und ihr Leserkreis," 3.

[28]   Hermann Friedrichs, "Die Clauren-Marlitt," *Das Magazin für die Litteratur des In- und Auslandes. Organ des Allgemeinen Deutschen Schriftsteller-Verbandes* 54 (1885), no. 10 (March 7, 1885): 14. On the controversy unleashed by Friedrichs' view of Marlitt, see Katja Mellmann, "Die Clauren-Marlitt: Rekonstruktion eines Literaturstreits um 1885," *Archiv für Sozialgeschichte der deutschen Literatur* 39, no. 2 (2014): 285–324.

[29]   "Marlitt und ihr Leserkreis," 2.

Erzählerkunst" (true narrative talent), describing the new serialization as captivating the reader in the first four installments so powerfully that one anticipated the ones to follow with burning impatience.[30] In this concluding section, we examine the ways in which three of Marlitt's novels play off some of the *Jane Eyre*-shaped clichés of the entire series to satisfy readers with pleasurable variation within sameness.

Reichsgräfin Gisela

Reichsgräfin Gisela (Heft 1–32, 1869) features an orphaned female protagonist abused by two preceding generations of four scheming aristocratic families. The opaque familial relationships of the Volderns, Fleurys, von Zweiflingens, and the ducal family are difficult to sort out. The disguise of the male protagonist, Berthold Ehrhardt, further complicates the plot. A local bourgeois claiming to be Herr de Oliveira, a newly immigrated Brazilian entrepreneur, Berthold pursues his intention to avenge his brother's betrayal, even as he establishes worker-friendly iron works in the region and a home for orphans that welcomes Jews and Christians alike.

In particular due to its aristocratic characters, passionate anti-aristocratic messages, championing of (male) enterprise, and pleas on behalf of the downtrodden, Marlitt's third serialized novel may seem removed from Brontë. Indeed, its setting within the ruling houses of a fictitious corner of Thuringia and the ramifications of the love story for the local populace suggest an outright departure from Brontë's tight focus on her female protagonist. The embourgeoisement of the eponymous countess, her real decline in social station, also runs counter to the upward rise that Jane experiences. In fact, Marlitt does not stray far from her *Jane Eyre*-flavored brand.

Like *Jane Eyre*, *Gisela* pairs two articulate individuals of unequal social station and experience with troubled pasts; the narrative tantalizes the reader with the slow revelation of their developing feelings and the delayed expression of them to one another. As in the other novels, the text spatializes difference, with the "white castle" and its grounds serving as the locus of scheming corruption and the refurbished forester's house the site of hope for a different future.

The plot of *Gisela*, like *Jane Eyre*, moreover, evinces affinities to sensation fiction. The wealth of the protagonist and her step-parents, Baron Fleury and Jutta (née Zweiflingen), rest on the shaky ground of a crime. Fleury, a consummate diplomat and power broker at the local princely court, has long schemed to get his hands on Gisela's wealth that, as he knows, is ill begotten because he himself played a part in the swindle. With the aid of his wife, a governess, and a doctor, he subjects the orphaned Gisela to an abusive regimen in the hope that she will never marry and will die before she has control over her own destiny and her grandmother's wealth.[31]

---

[30]   "Vom Büchertisch," *Mährisches Tagblatt*, February 7, 1885, 6.
[31]   Hillern's *Ein Arzt der Seele* and *Reichsgräfin Gisela*, which both appeared in 1869, have in common an extended account of their respective orphaned female protagonist's childhood and abuse at the hands of her guardian. This overlap suggests a common pre-text.

An ugly and sickly child, Gisela is kept ignorant of her circumstances—from her own health to local affairs—and spoiled so as to become unlovable and unfeeling. Removed from the view of the aristocratic circles to which she belongs by birth, she is repeatedly told that she is ill and incapable even when it is obvious that she has grown into a ravishingly beautiful and strong woman. Her awakening to the poverty and suffering of others, prompted by her budding desire for the mysterious Portuguese, leads her to discover that she has not only a heart but also a voice. Near the conclusion, in a paraphrase of Jane's words to Rochester in the Thornfield garden, she not only declares herself free of her stepfather but excoriates him for trying to educate her to be a heartless machine: "daß ihr ganzes Bestreben darauf gerichtet gewesen ist, mich zu einer herzlosen *Maschine* [my italics] zu erziehen!" (3: 376; everything you've done was aimed at making a heartless machine of me).

Motifs and props abound that recall Brontë's novel and perhaps any number of other novels written in its wake. A large dog, Hero, precedes the appearance of his master, Berthold. Berthold's bronzed face, athletic build, and dark anger conjure Rochester, although the narrator assures readers that all the ladies find him handsome. Marlitt does not as a rule deny her protagonists beauty. Berthold has secrets including his concealed identity, his knowledge of corruption in high places, and his determination to seek revenge on those he holds responsible. He also carries some of the load normally assigned in Marlitt's fiction to female characters and assumed by both Bertha and Rochester in the English setting. In his disguise as Herr von Oliveira, that is, he introduces the exotic other and a whiff of colonialism into the German province.[32] His deeply tanned face, which is nevertheless white where his hat has covered his forehead, vividly invokes the European colonial enterprise that is reshaping, unsettling, even undermining the status quo in this imagined corner of Thuringia. While Brontë invokes colonialism as an obscure secret lying at the foundation of English wealth and property, Marlitt, in the German context of 1869, when there are no official German colonies and not yet a history of state-sponsored colonial abuse, presents such enterprise as an opportunity for men oppressed at home.

Religious hypocrisy, marked by outright cruelty, a recurring theme in Marlitt's novels, pervades this Thuringian setting as it does Lowood. Here Marlitt locates it largely in an unfeeling aristocracy that is all too ready to condemn a local pastor for his interest in astronomy and his inclusiveness in his parish while it sees the poverty of the local population as the just deserts of the underclasses and leaves it unmitigated. Both hypocritical Catholics and Protestants reap criticism in the novel. The text also devotes space to petty social prejudice, particularly as expressed by aristocratic women, and thus amplifies some of the social nastiness of Brontë's Blanche Ingram episode.

In a turn worthy of sensation fiction, Fleury menaces Gisela with life in a convent to silence her opposition forever. The text does not, however, pursue this threat. Instead, whenever the narrator raises reader expectation that the evil

---

[32]   For an incisive overview of the ways in which Marlitt's oeuvre is informed by colonialism and empire, see Kontje, "Marlitt's World," 408–26.

Fleury will attempt to kill the eighteen-year-old Gisela, put her in a convent, steal her inheritance, or otherwise thwart her, Gisela obstructs these conventions of sensation fiction through her defiant speech.[33]

Misunderstandings, the inability to read faces and gestures, hinder the course of romance, even as both Gisela and Berthold inspect one another searchingly, laboring under the pull of attraction yet seeking all the while to conceal their feelings. For a time the narrator only hints at Gisela's emergent love for Berthold. Gisela, like Marlitt's Felicitas and Elisabeth, initially has little insight into her own heart even if the reader is not long in doubt. Nevertheless, once desire has been established, the text does attend to it—as does Brontë once the narrator Jane allows desire for Rochester to surface in explicit language. In Gisela's case a total change of heart accompanies her recognition that she loves Berthold; it banishes the aristocrat she has been reared to be and enables her not only to feel empathy for others but also to act on their behalf. In a dramatic scene, Gisela rides her Arabian steed saddled only with a light blanket to sound the alarm for the burning village, interrupting the frivolities of the court and subjecting herself to derision.

In the text's sentimental understanding of improved and recalibrated power relations, Gisela declares her wish to be loved—as opposed to being obeyed— by those dependent on her. After this epiphany, the text nevertheless retards romantic union by introducing Gisela's mistaken notion that the lady-in-waiting Esmeralda Sontheim has captured Berthold's heart and thus here too reproduces elements of the Blanche Ingram episode. As if signaling this literary antecedent, Esmeralda, dressed like a "gypsy," reads Berthold's palm during an elaborate outdoor court festivity. The Brontë reader might recall Rochester's "gypsy" disguise.

These aspects might be dismissed merely as nineteenth-century clichés not necessarily related to *Jane Eyre* were they not galvanized to reproduce its romance dynamic. Love for an older, established angry man with a secret, a relationship born in conflict and struggle, is for the eighteen-year-old heroine intertwined with personal moral and emotional education, achievement of a kind of parity, and the ability to speak for herself. The isolated and abused orphan finds enduring human connection through that relationship in speaking, gazing, and even touching—a kiss of the hand, Gisela's protective seizing of Berthold's arm, and the surreptitious extension of her hand through the back of a bench to signal her solidarity with him. The union requires not only struggle but mutual acknowledgment, in this case Gisela's acceptance of Berthold's true identity as a bourgeois and his recognition that Gisela has freed herself from aristocratic entitlement. The marriage promises to be exclusive and enduring as the couple retreat to the remote forester's house, which recalls the isolation of Ferndean. Yet

---

[33] Versions of Wilkie Collins's sensation novel *The Woman in White* (1859) had been available for some years in the German territories, as a Tauchnitz edition in English (2 vols., 1860); as a theater adaptation, *Die Frau in Weiß*, by Charlotte Birch-Pfeiffer (Reclam, 1866); and in Marie Scott's translation *Die Frau in Weiß* (1861). The reader, expecting victimization like that which befalls Collins's heiress, Laura, likely anticipated the worst given the signals in Marlitt's text.

in this case—as the concluding pages hint—home will not impede an active life bettering the community.

Some of the language employed to characterize this union bespeaks nineteenth-century retrograde norms, suggesting more conservative impulses and certainly not sitting well in our day. Berthold pronounces himself an "egoist," as does Mainau in *Die zweite Frau*, declaring his intention to make Gisela his sole property forever (3:380). But then Rochester, too, displays an overweening possessiveness—which he does not relinquish even in his blindness—to which Jane eventually submits, apparently confident that she can hold her own. Not to be silenced, Gisela, for her part, takes charge, commanding, "Nehmen Sie mich hin— ich bin Ihr Eigentum!" (3:381; Take me—I'm yours [literally, your property]!). Gisela's moment of assent lacks the active, aggressive force of "Reader, I married him" as does her overwrought declaration in yet another dramatic scene that she wishes to die with him rather than abandon him. At this earlier juncture, however, he has not yet asked her to stay with him, but instead told her to leave. Gisela thus seizes the prerogative to reveal her wishes and literally to give herself away.

If Marlitt lacks the subtly of Brontë and overly indulges in sentimentality, the conclusions of the two novels are nevertheless not so far apart. In 1869, the union entered into constituted not only an "oasis" for the happy couple (3:399), but also a respite for the hungry reader as well, even as the world outside the text continued its evil ways. The text by no means offers a simple normative ending; rather, it offers hope that a marriage based on mutual affection and respect can provide refuge and support self-realization.

The final pages mark Gisela's salutary embourgeoisement with a description of the transformed tower room of the forester's house. As a room of Gisela's own, this space signals domesticity with its white muslin curtains and its sewing table (apparently the aristocratic Gisela now knows how to sew). Nevertheless, for all the markers of normative class allegiance, much in this space, as in Felicitas's room in *Geheimnis*, marks individuality, restructuring, and integration. For example, it contains a bronze cage with two bright Brazilian birds[34] and, facing one another, oil paintings of Gisela's aristocratic mother and Berthold's bourgeois brother, the foreman of the iron foundry, both of whom died tragically young, each representing a different social stratum reconciled through this marriage. Both paintings emanate a persistent sadness that is also acknowledged and integrated into this new beginning, like Jane's cognizance of mortality on the last page of Brontë's novel. A final detail indicates that within this restructured domesticity Gisela, the "poor little rich girl," has been acknowledged. Berthold's parrot, which once squawked "Rache ist süß" (revenge is sweet), has been re-trained to say her name: "Gisela" (3:400).

Marlitt's popularity prompted immediate adaptation. In late August 1869 the *Gartenlaube* excoriated an unauthorized theater adaptation of *Reichsgräfin Gisela* that had not even waited for the serialization to end and the outcome of

---

34   While these caged exotic birds might in a different context signal the oppressiveness of the colonial project or a future underwritten by coloniality, in a text published in Germany in 1869 they likely registered instead, in the optimistic thinking of the time, as the penetration of a beautiful "wide, wide world" into the everyday.

the novel to be known: the play had already garnered a dozen full houses, the magazine complained, the "Plagiarius hat den klingenden Erfolg im Beutel, die Dichterin das Nachsehen für eine etwaige eigene Dramatisirung ihres Werkes!" (plagiarist has clinking success in the bag, the female writer is at a disadvantage should she wish to adapt her work for the stage herself).[35] The adapters, Carl Wexel and Rhingulph Wegener, had with their four-act play interfered with Marlitt's storytelling, profited from her name, and then impeded her ability to profit from her creative labor. Yet in their expedient refashioning and staging of *Gisela*, Wexel and Wegener too served cultural transmission. The play, to paraphrase Stoneman on the subject of *Jane Eyre* theater adaptations, made "common cultural property" of Marlitt's novel,[36] putting it in circulation in new ways.

Wexel and Wegener's adaptation endured on German-speaking stages until at least 1880 and conforms in many scenes to Marlitt's original, tallying over one-third more verbatim matches of four-word sequences than a second surviving adaptation of the novel by Emil Hildebrand, aka Fritz Volger.[37] Yet Wexel and Wegener's version takes a conservative turn restoring power to the local prince and sidelining Gisela. Hildebrand's four-act play better captures key elements of Marlitt's novel, some of which place it in proximity to *Jane Eyre* and its presentation of female subjectivity via a romance plot. It enables Gisela to find both her heart and voice. Indeed, often literally center stage, she speaks 33.65% of the total lines, including several monologues that voice her thoughts and feelings. "Nehmen Sie mich hin, Berthold!" she cries in the final scene, "Ich bin ganz Ihr Eigenthum: ja, nur für Sie will ich leben! Für den einzigen Menschen, welchen ich achte und liebe!" (Take me, Berthold! I am entirely yours [your property]: yes, I only want to live for you! For the only person I respect and love!).[38] As she repudiates the hierarchical social differentiation of the feudal estates and her aristocratic rank on stage, she also seals the union in rapid-fire declarations of attachment, in essence "marries him." If Gottschalk saw affinities to Brontë's female protagonist in the "Seelenstärke" and "Seelengröße" of Marlitt's characters, then Hildebrand recognized these qualities in Gisela and attempted to convey them in his adaptation.

Reichsgräfin Gisela became a "90-pfennig book" with another of Sedlacek's titillating covers at approximately the same time as it became available as a silent film. Although dressed in innocent white, Sedlacek's Gisela, her blond hair flying, is caught in a moment of high drama and erotic tension as Bernard masterfully reins in her runaway horse. The director Georg Viktor Mendel's silent film

---

[35]   *Gartenlaube*, no. 36 (1869): 576.

[36]   Stoneman, *Jane Eyre on Stage*, 1.

[37]   Max Schneider identifies Fritz Volger, writing under the pseudonym Emil Hildenbrand, as the author. *"Von wem ist das doch!?" Ein Titelbuch zur Auffindung von Verfassernamen deutscher Literaturwerke* (Berlin: Eugen Schneider, 1907), 123. Franz Brümmer alternatively confirms this synonym as "Ed. Hildebrand" and "E. Hildebrand." *Lexikon der deutschen Dichter und Prosaisten des neunzehnten Jahrhunderts* (Reclam: Leipzig, 1885), 351, 432. The catalog of the Staatsbibliothek incorrectly lists Emil Hildebrand as a pseudonym for Martin Böhm, while also including "Emil [sic] Volger" as a co-author.

[38]   Emil Hildebrand, *Reichsgräfin Gisela. Schauspiel in 4 Akten. Nach E. Marlitt's Roman bearbeitet* (Berlin: Bloch, n.d.), 52.

version with National Filmgesellschaft (1918), by contrast, does not sexualize Gisela but instead trains the erotic gaze on Jutta von Zweiflingen.

Reichsgräfin Gisela provides insight into the limitations and possibilities of early movie adaptation, 1918–19, and suggests how it privileges sensation over subtlety of mind and tentative seeking.[39] The film evokes many high points of the novel, but does not reproduce this convoluted plot as a comprehensible narrative. While it delivers a happy ending that unmasks and overthrows the villains and pairs the virtuous Gisela and Berthold, it devotes little attention to the delicate unfolding of the romance. Instead, it favors easily readable broad gesture and facial expression and simple motivation. In one scene, for example, Gisela's beaming face communicates her joy when she learns that Berthold has not perished in the burning village after all. Her decision to renounce her inheritance, furthermore, does not register as stemming from an overall change of heart and moral maturation brought about by her growing love for Berthold; instead, the film suggests that she has always been virtuous and simply requires the revelation of wrong to do what is right. For his part, the prince unambiguously figures as a benign presence whose interest in and subsequent visit to Berthold's iron works signal his progressive thinking and concern for the prosperity of the land. His full white beard and dignified bearing project male authority.

The story underlying the sequence of weakly linked episodes introduced by short intertitles might have been better grasped by a spectator who had read the novel. Like theater adaptations of Marlitt's novels, this film adaptation in effect illustrates the text; those in the know can fill in the gaps. On the other hand, its choice of scenes offers a different slant on Marlitt's material. It underplays the dynamics of romance based on conversation and searching struggle and invests instead in the visual pleasure of screen villainy and the joy of seeing Gisela's tormentors get their comeuppance.[40] Close-ups feature the eye-shifting histrionic villainy of Fleury and Jutta. Else Roscher plays Jutta as a self-absorbed, ruthless, dark-eyed, and black-haired sexually attractive beauty. Film audiences likely knew Roscher from the twenty-six films in which she had previously played a role, including National Filmgesellschaft's adaptation of *Die Frau mit den Karfunkelsteinen* (1917).[41] Her appearance in *Gisela* was presumably an attraction for some filmgoers.

---

[39] *Reichsgräfin Gisela*, directed by Georg Viktor Mendel (Berlin: National Filmgesellschaft, 1918). The film is held by the Deutsche Kinemathek—Museum für Film und Fernsehen, SDK00222–A. The International Movie Database lists the date as 1919. International Movie Database, s. v. "Reichsgräfin Gisela," https://www.imdb.com/title/tt5860370/?ref_=nm_flmg_act_11 (accessed September 2, 2020). The screenwriter is Josef Richards. My film analysis could not have been completed without the aid of Tobias Feldmann. In 2020 Covid-19 prevented me from making the trip to Berlin to screen the film at the Berlin Filmmuseum. Feldmann stepped in for me, viewed the film, and took notes to answer a list of questions I provided. We discussed his findings at length.

[40] Kasten notes the same of Oswald's *Die zweite Frau*, in which the machinations of Ernst Deutsch's villainous Jesuit priest significantly overshadow the depiction of the love story and Marlitt's assertive heroine ("Dramatische Instinkte," 46).

[41] See her film credits as listed in the following entry: International Movie Database, s.v. "Else Roscher," https://www.imdb.com/name/nm1339846/ (accessed September 2, 2020).

As the annotation in the opening credits suggests, film audiences by contrast probably did not know Grete Reithofer, the actress who played Gisela. The credits list Reithofer without a first name as "Frl. Reithofen [*sic*] v. Wiener Volkstheater" (Miss Reithofen from the Vienna Folk Theater).⁴² Reithofer's Gisela presents as a round-faced ingénue. Emphasizing her youth, she wears her hair in a long ponytail and dons beribboned, wide-brimmed hats, sailor collars, and shirtwaists, occasionally with a prim tie. Her white party dress in a later scene preserves her virginal naiveté. The film does not overtly entertain the idea that her developing love for Berthold might be intertwined with both sexual and moral maturity.

Long, half-long, and medium shots taken by a stationary camera dominate the film, blunting any gesture toward revelation of subtle and hidden or repressed feelings. Instead, the camera and the scenic presentation favor depictions of social relations as configured by the blocking. The characters are, as it were, on stage. The final shot of the film displays the nefarious Fleury holding a gun to his head. The novel, by contrast, evokes his suicide after he has disappeared into the forest of the palace park with a simple statement: a shot rang out.

In 1918, the Richards-Mendel team distanced their film from Marlitt's original and in the process effectively reduced its debt to the romance values and structures of Brontë's novel. And without these values and structures, this film, insofar as it still tells a love story, has little of the power of the original romance. Any force or fascination for contemporaries likely lay instead in the dramatic gestures of its villains. Overall, this adaptation, while indeed calling upon the polysemy of the original and circulating in its own Marlitt set, figures as an ephemeral offshoot from the transmission chain that has concerned us here. Nevertheless, announced as "nach dem gleichnamigen Roman" (after the novel by the same name), it did, in 1918, keep Marlitt's novels in the public eye and thus tangentially Marlitt's literary forebears. Ultimately, the novel, which can still be purchased through amazon.de in multiple formats—from antiquarian copies to Kindle editions to reformatted modern editions—long outlived its silent film adaptation.⁴³

Amtmanns Magd

At twenty chapters and 199 pages in volume 10 of the illustrated edition of 1888–90,⁴⁴ *Amtmanns Magd* (*Gartenlaube* 1–13 [1881]), claims just under half the length of Marlitt's two longest novels, *Gisela* and *Heideprinzeßchen*. In this edition, it

---

42   The IMDB lists Grete Reithofer as playing Gisela with one additional film credit from 1918. It also credits a "Frau Reithofer," who may or may not be the same actress, as playing in a single film from 1919. International Movie Database, s.v. "Grete Reithofer," https://www. imdb.com/name/nm8266304/?ref_=fn_al_nm_5 and s.v. "Frau Reithofer," https://www. imdb.com/name/nm2057953/?ref_=fn_nm_nm_3 (accessed September 2, 2020). Neither entry testifies to Reithofer as having figured as a familiar film star in her time.

43   Search term "Reichsgräfin Gisela," Amazon.de, https://www.amazon.de/s?k=Reichsgr% C3%A4fin+Gisela&ref=nb_sb_noss_2 (accessed September 2, 2020).

44   The publication of *Thüringer Erzählungen* as volume 10 is announced in *Die Gartenlaube*, Halbheft 26 (1890): 836.

appears together with Marlitt's three much-shorter works, "Blaubart," "Zwölf Apostel," and "Schulmeisters Marie," as *Thüringer Erzählungen* (Thuringian Stories). Yet it is of sufficient length to unfold a romance plot entangled in family finances and property. *Amtmanns Magd* provides variety to Marlitt's brand through inversion, while recalling the governess novel and by extension *Jane Eyre* itself. Marlitt assigns a male figure, Herr Markus, the epistemological quest otherwise undertaken by Brontë's female protagonists and the Jane Eyre avatars of her own invention, or rather reproduces and reweights the parallel quest that Rochester undertakes as he seeks to fathom Jane's well-concealed feelings. In contrast, however, to Brontë's first-person narrative, which allows entry into Rochester's point of view only when he speaks, Marlitt's third-person narration focalizes the narrative so as to privilege Markus's point of view. Frequent use of free indirect speech makes transparent emotions that he often refuses to acknowledge even to himself.

Markus's search involves determining the eponymous maid's true identity even as he settles into his new role and responsibilities as a large landowner. This quest, however, transforms into the discovery of his own self and his hitherto unacknowledged desire. The possibility that Markus has depths that he himself cannot fathom becomes clear early on when he stands before the youthful portrait of his deceased female benefactor, his heart inexplicably expanding in a peculiar feeling of longing. The narrative eventually parses this feeling, but in service of the pleasurable torment of delayed gratification, it prolongs his acquisition of self-knowledge and his misperception of his female counterpart.

A sense of obligation to his benefactor requires Markus to fulfill her wish to aid her long-suffering friend, the bailiff's wife, whom she failed to include in her will. Markus would not know of it had he not found a letter in a knitting bag, in which she wrote of her plan to leave a piece of her property to Agnes Franz, the bailiff's niece, who could be entrusted to stand by her aunt. Despite his good intentions, Agnes, a former governess, whom he has never met, figures unpleasantly in his imagination: given his ingrained prejudices against governesses, he is reluctant to make good on his obligation. Archly invoking the "governess novel," Marlitt has Markus rehearse all the detestable aspects of governesses. Of course, he will ultimately marry Agnes—as any habitual Marlitt reader knows he must when the narrative establishes a tense repartee between this male heir to property and a determined young woman, who declares that no man will ever tell her what to do.

Their initial encounter, when both have yet to receive a name, unfolds as a variation on the first meeting of Rochester and Jane. On his way to claim the estate he has inherited, Markus fails to mind his step and foolishly puts his foot through the slats of the ramshackle bridge that he must cross to reach his property. As in the case of Rochester, the first words from his lips are curses, as he tries in vain to remove his leg from the bridge. In this very moment his female counterpart, likewise newly arrived in the region, also makes her way toward the bridge. He does not hesitate to order the girl, whom he takes for a peasant, to hurry to his aid. She prepares to help him, but when he tries to lean on her, she places a handful of grass between her shoulder and his arm. This gesture of modesty, which he takes for prudishness, suggests that she is not what she appears to be. With her assistance and further angry curses, he frees himself.

Despite his coarse male language, he briefly slips into the position of Brontë's female protagonist in her initial meeting with Rochester, when he searches the "maid's" half-hidden face. It requires sixteen of the nineteen remaining chapters for him to discover that she is one and the same as his bailiff's niece. The experienced reader, however, quickly solves the mystery.

Even as the text privileges Markus's point of view, it also makes obvious his flawed sense of himself and others. He blunders for pages on end. Assuming class difference, he condescendingly addresses Agnes with the familiar you-form, "du." Class prejudices and masculine prerogative allow him, moreover, upon a second meeting impulsively to push back her hat and kerchief so as to see her face. When she recoils in fury, he rationalizes his misstep by recalling that his male friends never hesitate to impose themselves on pretty women of the serving classes. Who could have even considered finding anything about this uninvited attention reprehensible, even if the woman in question resisted? he scoffs. And yet as he continues to rationalize and also to wonder what possessed him to touch her in the first place, he knows—and the reader knows—he has wronged her.

For long stretches, Agnes remains, on the one hand, merely the "junge Mädchen" (young girl), a type submerged in the underclass, and, on the other hand, only a name, imagined as a member of a professional group Markus cannot abide. In an encounter with the putative maid, he asks her about "Fräulein Agnes Franz," only to receive the ambiguous reply, "Die werden Sie nicht sehen" (10:70; You won't see her). For reasons he cannot explain to himself he now addresses her with the formal "Sie," even as she assures him again that he will never see what is behind the facade since of course there is nothing to see that he could not have already seen had he been more perceptive.

Eventually he is able to take in not a type but a whole person. The text signals this attainment of insight when Markus addresses the heroine four times as Agnes over the course of his plea for understanding and forgiveness. To underline the transformation that he undergoes and his newfound ability to acknowledge Agnes, he recalls what he had come to know through his deceased benefactor, the felicitous mixture of tenderness, charm, power, and energy in an ostensibly weak woman.

In recounting the process by which Agnes becomes intelligible to Marcus, *Amtmanns Magd* reproduces some of the structures and motifs of Marlitt's more obviously *Jane-Eyr*ish romances, starting with the assertive female protagonist and her verbal fencing with the male protagonist, within yet another iteration of fraught domestic arrangements. Marcus closes, via searching looks and highly charged conversations, the distance between himself and Agnes as he falls for a woman with a mind of her own. The novel ends playfully in the voice of the garrulous Frau Griebel, as she busily contemplates a match for her young daughter as well. This humorous deviation into the talk of others differs from the closing scenarios of most of Marlitt's novels. It suggests that Marlitt may have been having a bit of fun when she replaced her signature searching female heroine in this novel with an obtuse and slightly arrogant young man seeking answers.

B. W. underestimated Marlitt in scorning her remixes of romance elements. *Amtmanns Magd*, for one, consists of more than simple-minded repetition of narrative clichés and instead reveals a practiced storyteller at work. But in fact her second publication in *Die Gartenlaube*—"Blaubart"—makes clear that she had range: Marlitt could tell it straight or she could play with the romance conventions she absorbed and perpetuated. For much of "Blaubart," Lilli foolishly believes that her mysterious neighbor, Dorn, holds a woman captive like the eponymous Bluebeard, only to learn that she has completely misread the situation and thereby made her own path to recognizing and acknowledging her future life partner thornier than it should have been. Near the novella's conclusion, Dorn, for his part, finally reveals his feelings for Lilli but then backs off. Not to be put off at this juncture, Lilli firmly announces her intention to marry Dorn to her disapproving aunt with the words "ich gehe mit ihm!" (10:337; I'm going with him) in a faint echo of "Reader, I married him."

Im Schillingshof

Im Schillingshof (*Die Gartenlaube* 14–39 [1879]) moves the stigmatized woman from the hidden recesses of domestic space to the narrative center—not in the form of a madwoman from the British colonies but a determined woman from the defeated state of South Carolina after the American Civil War. As it develops the romance between the former slaveholder, Mercedes de Valmaseda, and the unhappy Arnold von Schilling, these morally compromised representatives of two feuding families that live in adjoining houses, the narrative places the blame for family troubles on the fathers. The narrator speaks of Arnold as a "second Isaak," a son sacrificed by his father not at God's command but on account of property—like Rochester (4:432).[45] Once Marlitt's seventh full-length novel is viewed in relation to the entire Marlitt set, its affinity to the more obviously *Jane Eyre*-informed novels as well as to *Jane Eyre* itself comes into focus. Indeed, *Im Schillingshof* rests on similar romance elements and premises while also introducing variations of them. This novel, most notably in its depiction of Arnold, works the territory of morally damaged masculinity that figures in *Jane Eyre*. But Mercedes herself issues from the second marriage of the divorced Major Lucian to a Spanish-American woman and thus also finds herself on shaky footing in Thuringia where her appearance, her origins, and her slaveholding past render her morally suspect.[46]

Im Schillingshof relies on Marlitt's signature conversational dynamics, what an American reviewer described as "an agreeable and lively game of fencing."[47]

---

[45] Its availability as volume 4 of the collected works is announced in *Die Gartenlaube*, no. 21 (1889): 356. Spivak notes that Jean Rhys's *Wide Sargasso Sea* insightfully depicts the compromised circumstances of the second son who, subject to entailment, is sent in the context of European imperialism to the colonies to find a rich bride. "Three Women's Texts and a Critique of Imperialism," 253.

[46] The two freed slaves accompanying Mercedes suggest at the very least Marlitt's poor understanding of the American context. For a discussion of the sentimentalizing of the master-slave relationship and the association of Mercedes as an othered woman with her slaves, see Lynne Tatlock, "Eine amerikanische Baumwollprinzessin in Thüringen: Transnationale Liebe, Familie und die deutsche Nation in E. Marlitts *Im Schillingshof* (1879)," in *Amerika und die deutschsprachige Literatur nach 1849. Migration—kultureller Austausch—frühe Globalisierung*, ed. Christof Hamann, Ute Gerhard, and Walter Grünzweig (Bielefeld: transcript, 2008), 105–25.

[47] Review of *Im Schillingshof*, *The Nation* 29 (December 25, 1879): 443–4.

As in *Jane Eyre*, it still takes pages for the tussling interlocutors to own up to their desire for one another. The married Arnold can neither admit his feelings nor fully recognize the immorality of his marriage of convenience until he beholds Mercedes defending his artwork and covered in blood. With this moment of clarity also comes the long-awaited acknowledgment that cements their future marriage.

Marlitt amplifies the motif of the first wife in this story by introducing two first wives, one of whom she redeems and one of whom she eliminates from the new order established at the end of the novel. Klementine, Arnold's fanatically Catholic and jealous first wife, is not locked up, but instead roams the mansion freely. Her fury casts a pall over the entire household; in the aforementioned scene, in a jealous rage, recalling Bertha, she stabs Mercedes, while attempting to shred her husband's masterpiece. The second angry first wife, Frau Lucian, tyrannizes over the adjoining household until she learns the secret of both houses, including her own brother's treachery. The novel spares her undue scrutiny by leaving the circumstances of her divorce vague and buried in the past.

Divorce here replaces bigamy as a less offensive nineteenth-century social taboo. Still, the plot surely presented uncomfortable moments for historical readers when it became clear that the married Arnold was falling for Mercedes next door, the divorced Major Lucian's daughter from his second marriage. If the story is to conclude happily, Arnold must divorce Klementine; therefore, to justify this drastic step, the novel highlights the circumstances under which the marriage was contracted, including the Schillings' financial necessity and Klementine's deceit. Arnold, who, like Rochester, was forced into a marriage of convenience by his father, earns his happiness by proving himself in both the Austro-German and Franco-Prussian wars. In the end, religious differences justify annulment rather than outright divorce, softening the rupture necessary to romantic union.

The complex of the two adjoined buildings harbors the sins of the respective male owners—the avaricious Franz Wolfram and the spendthrift Krafft von Schilling. Marlitt does not, however, purge wrongdoing, as does Brontë, by burning down the house. Instead, the Wolframs' home is torn down and the adjoining Schillingshof remodeled to reveal the grace of its original Italian design. The marriage of Mercedes and Arnold provides the occasion for reconfiguring family relations overall. While this milder ending does not reproduce the force of the cathartic event in *Jane Eyre*, Marlitt's concluding pages have a salutary force of their own. Whereas *Jane Eyre* eliminates Bertha, *Schillingshof* makes the dark othered woman a part of the projected future. Furthermore, while *Heideprinzeßchen* makes a first sally into this territory by taking up the socialization and triumph of the innocent seventeen-year-old, brown-skinned Lenore, *Schillingshof* puts Mercedes, a full-grown foreign woman with a dubious past, at the center and more obviously makes her otherness count significantly for the rehabilitation of the entire community. Otherness arms the Spanish-German-American cotton princess for sexually charged verbal dueling with Arnold and enables her to play a critical role in restoring the denizens of the divided property (herself included) to their better selves. Those who disparage Mercedes's sallow skin and black hair, black servants, and foreign ways reveal themselves as unworthy of the new community that forms around the erotic union of Mercedes and Arnold and thus the text unceremoniously eliminates them.

The concluding pages do send mixed messages. In the process of bringing Mercedes into the family the text in effect whitens her, turning her sallow complexion pink. Furthermore, in a domesticating vein, Mercedes promises Arnold to separate herself from her wealth and to run his household according to his wishes. Nevertheless, she also plans to use her money to support a second household in her own name, the "Villa Valmaseda" where the displaced and redeemed Frau Lucian is reestablishing her life on her own terms with her dying daughter-in-law, Lucile Fournier, and her grandchildren. But Mercedes also makes demands with regard to the Schillingshof, namely, that she have access to Arnold's studio at all times: given that she is the wife of a famous man, she must be allowed to say with pride, "daß ich auch geistig neben him auf seiner Bahn schreite—" (4:430; that I walk intellectually side by side with him on his path). The novel again makes clear that in the most important things the heroine will prevail. While from the vantage of the present, Marlitt's resolution remains wanting, the placement of the dark, strong-minded woman from the New World at the center constituted a perhaps unsettling and provocative variation in its historical context. While we cannot know exactly how nineteenth-century readers received it, we do know that they likely encountered this novel as one of a set and thus did have the possibility of comparison.[48] If they did compare texts, they could have recognized Mercedes's difference both as a character and as a literary device.

Each subsequent publication of Marlitt's fiction as a set carried *Schillingshof* forward through the decades. The novel, for example, appeared in the higher-end illustrated series in 1889 as volume 4 and around 1919 in the lower-end set of 90-Pfennig books with Globus and in sets in between. In 1919, *Im Schillingshof* reached film audiences as one in the series of Marlitt films produced by National-Film, both under its original title and alternatively titled *Liebe, Haß und Geld* (Love, Hate, and Money).[49] This new title signals the penchant of the early film industry to milk Marlitt plots for their sexual, sensational notes. Given the fact that the ubiquitous Edith Meller plays the frivolous French dancer Lucille—and not Mercedes de Valmaseda—one suspects that the film adaptation lost track of what made *Schillingshof* a significant variation of *Jane Eyre*-flavored romance in the nineteenth-century context.

If *Goldelse*, *Geheimnis*, *Heideprinzeßchen*, and *Die zweite Frau* encourage readers to empathize with the stigmatized Lila, Cordula, Klothilde, and the Indian wife, but keep them on the margins of the romance plot, *Schillingshof* places

---

48   According to the *Wiener Theaterzeitung*, Hugo Busse adapted the novel for the stage as *Im Schillingshof, Schauspiel in 3 Acten nach Marlitts Roman* (In the Schillings Court, Play in Three Acts after Marlitt's Novel). "Aus unserem Bühnen-Verlage," for K. K. conc. Theater-Agentur J. Wild, *Wiener Theaterzeitung*, April 1, 1882, 4.

49   "Liebe, Haß und Geld (1919)," International Movie Database, https://www.imdb.com/title/tt0130080/?ref_=nv_sr_2?ref_=nv_sr_2 (accessed March 1, 2020).

Mercedes at its center. In the context of the Marlitt set, this novel constitutes a feat of the imagination when it makes an otherwise disparaged literary type the heroine of a love story set in Germany. In this regard, *Schillingshof*, placed side by side with *Jane Eyre* and Marlitt's obviously *Jane Eyre*-informed novels, displays the persistent protean vitality of this romance configuration in a time of inequality.

Epilogue: "Relations stop nowhere": The Purchase of Romance in a Time of Inequality

It's odd, this youthful desire to write, because it is born from the pleasure of reading. For once—and perhaps once and only once—the desire derives from the pleasure.[1]

Over the seven decades after the first appearance of *Jane Eyre* in the German lands, more girls and women than ever before were reading, and much of this reading was fiction. More women were writing than ever before, too, and much of this writing was fiction.[2] Writing begins in reading. Charlotte Brontë's fictional Jane begins as a reader and ends as a writer. Eugenie John, too, began as a reader and later became E. Marlitt, a bestselling author who serially reproduced elements of the story Brontë tells via Jane.

As we have seen, in late-century Germany, Amalie Baisch ridiculed women who aspired to write professionally, even when, in her view, women by nature loved to tell stories. In fact, the enduring purchase of *Jane Eyre* and romance in that vein in Germany and Austria, 1848–1918, surfaces precisely in the published works of generations of women who came to maturity in these years, women who read and later wrote, as the fictional Jane did. The historical Charitas Bischoff recounts such a story according to which reading *Jane Eyre* in two different iterations at two pivotal points in her life inspired her to write. In Bischoff's case fiction shaped a real life and also engendered fiction. Later on, the German popular authors Else Ury (1877–1943) and Hedwig Courths-Mahler (1867–1950) turned to Marlitt, as an author, and her novels, as reading, as inspiration for their own fiction writing.

In finding a path into paid labor and financial independence, these historical women writers constitute the clearest examples of an actualized *Jane Eyre*- or Marlitt-effect in a time of inequality and social movement toward its remedy,

---

1   Alyson Waters, "A Conversation with Éric Chevillard," trans. Jeffrey Zuckerman, *Music & Literature* 8 (2018), https://www.musicandliterature.org/features/2017/10/26/a-conversation-with-eric-chevillard (accessed May 1, 2020).

2   See, for example, Sophie Pataky, *Lexikon deutscher Frauen der Feder*, 2 vols. (Berlin: Carl Pataky, 1898). Pataky remarks in the preface of her two-volume lexicon on the "riesiges Anwachsen" (gigantic increase) in works by and about women of the preceding thirty years that inspired her ground-breaking lexicon of works by women since 1840 (1:v).

of the impact of this brand of romance fiction on real lives. Marianne Brentzel's biography of Ury, a beloved children's author, presents Marlitt's serial writing as a model for Ury's imagining of a professional life as a fiction writer for herself. While she does not want to believe that happiness and fulfillment lie only in marriage, Ury, in this telling, wishes she could write like Marlitt: "Ja, wenn ich einen Roman wie die Marlitt schreiben könnte! Der wird von Tausenden in der Gartenlaube gelesen." (Yes, if I could write a novel like Marlitt! It would be read by thousands in the *Gartenlaube*.)[3] The unmarried Marlitt could, as here, serve as a role model for girls who needed to face the fact that the marriage urged upon them by social norms was not necessarily within their reach or in the end something they desired for themselves; alternatives lay in professional writing.

Fränze, a character in Ury's novel *Wie einst im Mai* (As Once in May), set in the late 1860s and 1870s, has apparently been reading the *Gartenlaube* (and, we can infer, also Marlitt) and has submitted a poem to the magazine under a flowery pseudonym, "Rosa Immergrün" (Rosa Evergreen).[4] At various points, the narrative smiles at her vain attempts to write a novel. Her brothers taunt her with her pseudonym. Unlike Schultze-Smidt's Mella who has her wings clipped when she tries to write sad, sentimental poetry, Ury's Fränze, however, eventually realizes her writerly aspirations and achieves domestic bliss too. Ury concludes the novel by imagining Fränze not only as a wife and mother but also as the author of eloquent essays advocating women's education published by women's magazines. She proudly signs them with her *Gartenlaube*-pseudonym, Rosa Immergrün.[5]

But what of ordinary historical readers, thoughtful readers who may have picked up these books with no intention of writing themselves, but who still relished the words they found there. As the British author Mary Stewart in *Nine Coaches Waiting* (1958; *Das Jahr auf Valmy* [German trans. 1966]), a *Jane Eyre*-influenced romance mystery, formulates it, those who relished "the best words in the best order ... always got the same shock of recognition and delight when someone's words swam up to meet a thought or name a picture."[6] What, then, took place when historical readers encountered the words of others and so began to formulate themselves in Iser's sense?

The Austrian feminist and Viennese modernist Rosa Mayreder (1858–1938) in fact had her doubts about such words, about the subject-formation of ordinary readers that might occur via romance. In a pedagogical vein, she viewed the possibility raised by such reading as unrealistic and hence harmful to girls and women who had to live in the real world. Finding pernicious much of what passed for appropriate reading for girls at the turn of the twentieth century, she rejected "Familienliteratur" (family literature) as a "Puppenbühne" (puppet

---

3   Marianne Brentzel, *Mir kann doch nichts geschehen ... Das Leben der Nesthäkchen-Autorin Else Ury* (Berlin: ebersbach & simon, 2015), 31.

4   Else Ury, *Wie einst im Mai: Vom Reifrock bis zum Bubikopf; Eine Erzählung für junge Mädchen* (Stuttgart: Union Deutsche Verlagsgesellschaft, [1930]), 28.

5   Ury, *Wie einst im Mai*, 218–19.

6   Mary Stewart, *Nine Coaches Waiting* (1958) (Chicago: Chicago Review Press, 2006), 93.

theater; literally: doll stage),[7] the literary equivalent of Mella's play with dolls or Nora's impoverished life as a wife and mother. Mayreder especially objected to the tendency of romance, which invests so heavily in the relationship between the sexes, not to investigate marriage:[8] while the heroines of romance novels inevitably advance toward marriage, she complains in *Zur Kritik der Weiblichkeit* (1905; Toward a Critique of Femininity), the reader never learns what happens next. Romance cheats women by giving them false ideas about what lies before them as wives and mothers. On this point, Mayreder and conservative bourgeois parents, such as Mella's mother, apparently agreed: girls needed to learn to be sensible. Mayreder would surely have objected to being placed in this company, but in the interest of instilling realism, she does similarly, if inadvertently, support limits on women's options and experiences.

Mayreder does not name specific authors in her essay; she might have given *Jane Eyre* a pass, but she certainly must have had Marlitt in her sights or at least Marlitt as she was by 1905 regarded in modern German literary circles that had left the *Gartenlaube* and its fictions behind them. Yet given her sense for the ironies of social ideals and gendered social arrangements, revealed in such stories as "Sein Ideal" (1897; His Ideal), Mayreder may have had a more nuanced understanding of the empowering pleasures of reading romance than she displays in this essay.

Mayreder's principal point would in any case be difficult to dispute if the purpose of leisure-time reading were solely to learn to accept and acquiesce to reality as it is no matter how disappointing and oppressive or, conversely, to recognize the social wrongs of the Real and then systematically change things. Romance, however, operates in a different vein and serves different purposes. It invites readers to play, to imagine alternate possibilities in the process of subject formation, and to take deep pleasure in them—even if only within the limited freedom of reading. In this vein, Pamela L. Cheek, on the subject of eighteenth-century European women's romance writing, conceives of romance as "offering an escape clause to the contract of an emerging realism: romance becomes a woman's interior resource for defending herself against external cultural claims."[9] Similarly, we recall, Light insists on the ability of romance to offer readers the experience of a "subjectivity that is unified" in the context of the difficulties of negotiating femininity in real life. Such experience, she also points out, does not "explain away politics."[10] One might both enjoy romance and be alert to the inequities of the Real.

Romance in the particular vein of *Jane Eyre* allows for discernment, intelligibility, and affective choice and in the process delivers not only pleasure but also a form of (at least temporary) liberation from things as they are—and need not be. It provides the reader with "joy in the ending," in Regis's terms, when the heroine "undergoes two great liberations," the "cheating of ritual death and the

7   Rosa Mayreder, *Zur Kritik der Weiblichkeit* (Jena: Diederichs, 1905), 189.
8   Mayreder, *Kritik*, 193.
9   Pamela L. Cheek, *Heroines and Local Girls: The Transnational Emergence of Women's Writing in the Long Eighteenth Century* (Philadelphia: University of Pennsylvania Press, 2019), 87.
10   Light, "'Returning to Manderley,'" 391, 372, respectively.

freedom to live."[11] It addresses Moi's modernist "freedom, love, and equality." *Jane Eyr*ish romantic union delivers the vicarious experience of intelligibility and acknowledgment in Cavell's sense; it functions, in Radway's formulation, as "a sign of a woman's attainment of legitimacy and personhood."[12] It bestows the gift of "relational selfhood" that Pearce sees in twentieth-century novels, one that consists "in an on-going exploration of the other's unique difference and peculiarity," in essence Brontë's conversation all day long.[13] In sum, in a given historical moment, romance in the vein of Brontë's novel may lead readers—as it apparently did many readers in nineteenth-century German lands—to discover something for which they do not yet have adequate words, not the least of which may be the wish for their own voice and will. Indeed, in the nineteenth century, German *Jane Eyre*, when translated in full, and various German novels written in its wake made the vague wish for meaning and purpose articulate via the conversations, plots, and characters of romance. Moreover, they made it transitive through the invention of an exciting male partner capable of acknowledging the heroine in all her complexity.

In late-century Germany and Austria, girls, as modeled in the story of the fictional Mella, were, however, to be discouraged from longing for that partner and the promise of such romantic union and to be redirected to the unadorned prose of life. As we have seen, German adaptors of *Jane Eyre* elided or reframed Brontë's Rochester to make him more appropriate marriage material and much less alluring. These very alterations suggest that pedagogues, publishers, and parents recognized the radical possibility that Brontë's novel and sometimes its less radical heirs raised in telling love stories tightly entwined with female subject formation, stories that did not shy away from strong language, unsanctioned emotion, morally unsettling plot developments, and ostensibly risky but in the end felicitous and empowering pairings.

By Mayreder's time, of course, new options beyond husband and family for the women of some social classes were beginning to top the horizon. In Austria the first women matriculated in the university in 1897. In Germany women began to be admitted to the *Abitur* (university qualifying exam) in the 1890s; between 1900 and 1901 individual German states began, furthermore, to admit women students to the university on the basis of the exam.[14] Yet if a woman chose to pursue a profession, it generally meant forgoing a husband and family, and late-century advice books, such as Baisch's above-quoted *Aus der Töchter- schule*, continued to warn against the consequences of relinquishing this most cherished hope. At the same time, with increased leisure time, in the middle and upper classes, the gap in social roles widened. Women's special obligations focused on the family's aesthetic and affective life while the male family members carried on a full and demanding life elsewhere, outside the home.

---

[11]   Regis, *A Natural History*, 15.
[12]   Radway, "Readers and their Romances," 243.
[13]   Pearce, *Romance Reading*, 153.
[14]   Patricia M. Mazón, *Gender and the Modern Research University: The Admission of Women to German Higher Education, 1865–1914* (Stanford, CA: Stanford University Press, 2003), 14, 117.

At mid-century the *Grenzboten* had invoked the "gute Herz des Deutschen" (German's good heart) when it reviewed Birch-Pfeiffer's *Waise* and about twenty years later Gottschall had seen *Goldelse* as a rewrite of *Jane Eyre* infused with aspects of the "deutschen Gemüts" (German disposition). Over the course of the decades the cultivation of this national affect had become ever more the responsibility of middle- and upper-class women, whereas their men upheld national ideals through active pursuits outside the home. In the complementary gendered arrangements of those decades, love—the heart—shaped women's sphere in these social classes; it colored the social tasks that the very same readers, discouraged from sighing over Rochester, were expected to shoulder as grownups. Women were charged with managing the emotional life of the family, expected to bond intensely with their children and to love their husbands even if reality little supported this imagined affective community. In a chapter addressing separate spheres in this period titled "Kulturfrauen und Geschäftsmänner" (women of culture and businessmen), the historian Ute Frevert cites Hermann Helmholtz's letter from 1877 to illustrate the gendered fissures of domestic life. Here Helmholtz speaks of the presence and love of his wife as the "beste Schmuck meines Lebens" (most precious jewel of my life), but he also notes that his wife's love only superficially touched his actual existence, given that his work and his office prevented him from spending time at home.[15] As Jennifer Askey has shown, girls were taught to cultivate a sentimental attachment to empire and its rulers too.[16] It is not hard to imagine that this emotion, once valorized and harnessed to imagination, could, through reading, develop a secret life of its own, could support an education of a quietly oppositional sort.

Gabriele Reuter's above-cited *Aus guter Familie*, a milieu study of the German bourgeoisie in the vein of the French naturalists that ends in the heroine's incapacitation, indicates that it could and did. The novel repeatedly takes up girls' and women's reading and at illuminating points depicts that hidden life of emotion associated with it. Its heroine, Agathe Heidling, reads Byron, the Bible, dirty books, the zoologist and evolutionist Ernst Häckel, and radical political tracts. In this account of failed *Bildung*, the sensitive and suggestible heroine seeks in her reading alternatives, escape, answers to questions that she is hardly able to formulate. Reuter's treatment of Agathe's histrionic fantasies in *Aus guter Familie* is equivocal, inviting readers both to sympathize with the thwarted passion and rebellious spirit behind them and to wince at their childishness and failure to evolve.

We do not know whether Reuter ever encountered *Jane Eyre* directly, yet Brontë's by-then nearly fifty-year-old novel appears to haunt this bestselling anti-*Bildungsroman* as its female protagonist seeks but does not find the selfhood that *Jane Eyre* and romance written in its wake promised and delivered. Agathe is not an orphan but a well-brought-up daughter from the eponymous "good family," yet she too suffers. Our first glimpse of her—like *Jane Eyre*, the book

---

15 Ute Frevert, *"Mann und Weib, und Weib und Mann": Geschlechter-Differenzen in der Moderne* (Munich: Beck, 1995), 159.

16 Askey, *Good Girls, Good Germans*.

begins in medias res—is not of a girl reading behind a curtain, but it amounts to something of the same. This girl finds herself divided against herself on her Communion Day. She imbibes the norms of her social class even as she questions and sometimes rebels inwardly against them. The novel follows Agathe's failure to thrive within the bourgeois milieu while registering her wishes, dreams, desires, impulses—an interior life at odds with the restrictive and conventional life to which she is conditioned and, insofar as she is able, outwardly conforms. Reuter appears to have learned something from Brontë when, for example, she employs ekphrasis to put Agathe's aesthetic sensibility on display and charts her course via two paintings as a martyr of bourgeois mores.

Agathe's vague longings materialize recursively as narratives of romance—her love of Jesus; her crush on the long-dead Byron; her love for the socially inappropriate artist, Adrian; her attempt to turn a sensible bourgeois marriage with the much-older Raikendorf and its domesticity into a happy ending; and finally her unrequited love for her cousin Martin, the former radical and champion of individualism. The narrator invites readers to be critical of a culture that denigrates women for wanting love. Even in allowing Agathe occasionally to appear silly or overwrought, it does not suggest that it is wrong for her to imagine Nora's "most wonderful thing" or to hope for Jane's conversation "all day long." Rather, it shows that the cultural conditions of Imperial Germany favor none of these outcomes—not even with men who fancy themselves political radicals and revolutionaries. And unfortunately, as the text also makes clear, Agathe herself, like Nora, is not up to them anyway because she has not been educated to be so; she remains subject to and dependent upon her parents. But the novel is not primarily about failed love stories; rather it concerns most of all the inhospitality and inhabitability of this milieu, one that prevents the protagonist from thriving. It depicts Agathe's failure to realize selfhood in a purpose of any kind, be it love, marriage, motherhood, religion, charity, an intellectual life, a profession, or a cause. The most passionately emotional, sexually charged moment in the novel, one that operates in the register of romance, takes place not as an element of one of the aborted love stories, but instead when, after reading revolutionary political tracts, Agathe, alone in her girlhood bedroom surrounded by knickknacks, expresses a wish for meaning: "Ein kurzer schluchzender Schrei und das Mädchen warf sich lang auf das kleine Sofa nieder—die Arme weit hinausgebreitet in dem hilflosen Begehren nach etwas, das sie an die Brust drücken konnte—nach der Empfängnis von Kraft, von dem befruchtenden Geistesodem, der im Frühlingssturm über die Erde strömt." ("A short sob. The girl threw herself down full length upon the little sofa, her arms spread wide in helpless desire for something that she could embrace, in the desire to be impregnated with strength, to receive the fructifying breath of spirit and intellect that streams over the earth in a spring storm").[17]

What commences with Confirmation, appearing to promise a female novel of formation, ends in dull failure. The once imaginative and curious Agathe acquires neither a voice nor a purpose. After shock treatments, moreover, she

---

[17]   Reuter, *Aus guter Familie*, 133; Reuter, *From a Good Family*, 102.

has no chance for the social integration that is the end point of the *Bildung* of the *Bildungsroman*—this despite her surprisingly resilient serial attempts to achieve self-realization through passionate embrace of a person or cause. The closing picture of Agathe's blighted affect leaves readers with a crushing sadness; the text raises the expectation that her brother and sister-in-law will eventually place her in a rest home. The voice that in the beginning chapters was sometimes hoarse has simply petered out.

* * *

Given her perceptive account of Agathe's imaginative flights and her suffering and her criticism of some of the middle-class prejudices that her heroine has internalized, one may then be taken aback to read Reuter's easy condescension in her autobiography, *Vom Kinde zum Menschen* (1921; From the Child to the Person), on the subject of romance reading by a household retainer. The anecdote concerns the merchant family's Austrian cook in Alexandria, Egypt, *c.* 1869. The cook, she recounts, was willing to stay with the family to be able to read the installments of the *Gartenlaube* that arrived weekly by steamship: "solange die 'Goldelse' oder die 'Reichsgräfin Gisela' nicht glücklich in den Armen der Liebe gelandet waren, hatten wir unsere Marietta sicher. Bedenklich blieben nur die Zwischenzeiten in denen andere Dichter mit weniger Anziehungskraft in dem Blatte ihre Feder tummelten ..."[18] (as long as "Goldelse" or "Countess Gisela" had not yet landed in the arms of love, we could be sure of keeping Marietta. Only the times in between were cause for concern, times during which the pens of other less attractive writers romped in the paper). In 1921, fifty years after the fact, it was perhaps easy to treat the fantasies of ordinary people from long ago with arch snobbery. Still, Reuter's sneer at the cook's taste in this flattened misrepresentation of Marlitt resembles the view transmitted in the 1854 send-up of Birch-Pfeiffer's audiences. As we saw in Chapter 2, the fictitious housemaid, Friederike Badeker, writes by candlelight to the playwright to learn how *Waise* ends, for she sees her life reflected in Birch-Pfeiffer's Jane. Such condescension to domestics whom romance inspires to wish for something different and something more suggests precisely the power of romance to unsettle the social order. In denying domestics reading fantasies, it also echoes the class prejudices of Brontë's Ingrams who believe that governesses should know their place and of Marlitt's fictional Frau Hellwig and her son who believe that Fee should not be educated because people of her class must resign themselves to their economic lot. Both Brontë and Marlitt assert through romance that this is not necessarily so.

Around 1882, approximately thirty years after the fictitious Friederike thrilled to Birch-Pfeiffer's *Jane Eyre* and thirteen years after the Reuter's cook thrilled to

---

[18]   Gabriele Reuter, *Vom Kinde zum Menschen: Die Geschichte meiner Jugend* (Berlin: S. Fischer, 1921), 88–9. Reuter invokes the well-known *Goldelse* to make her point, but the cook could hardly have been reading "newly delivered" weekly installments of *Goldelse* as it had been serialized three years earlier in 1866. *Reichsgräfin Gisela*, however, was serialized in 1869, corresponding to Reuter's timeframe.

Marlitt, the illegitimate fifteen-year-old serving girl Hedwig Courths-Mahler, for her part, was also eagerly reading by candlelight, in this case Marlitt.[19] If she wished for something different and something more, it turned out to be far from vainly foolish for her to do so. Commencing with her first serialized publication in 1904, Courths-Mahler went on to write over 200 romance novels that eventually circulated in over 80 million copies. Many of them remain in print.[20] The contents of these novels suggest that Courths-Mahler missed many of Brontë's and Marlitt's most important and interesting dynamics and messages; nevertheless, there are points of contact.

Courths-Mahler made no secret of the importance of Marlitt to her life; it became part of her own self-presentation, according to which her life resembled Marlitt's. As she later claimed, even when she was a serving girl, she was also her employer's lady's companion and reader—just like Marlitt before she began to publish her fiction.[21] The romance writer's younger daughter, Friede Birkner, claimed that when Courths-Mahler died at eighty-three, she had one of Marlitt's novels in her lap. While both stories may be apocryphal and merely part of the family's attempt to burnish the Courths-Mahler myth, the point is that the author herself never hesitated to cite her debt to and love of Marlitt's novels.[22] In some respects her voluble reverence for Marlitt and her determined public attachment to her did her idol a disservice; in the popular imagination books by these two authors are understood to be cut from the same cloth, and the academy long accepted that view. Cementing the affiliation, National-Film, 1917–19, for example, adapted both authors for the movies and in the process no doubt made them more like one another—in a manner similar to the German book blurb for *Jane Eyre* cited in Chapter 8.[23]

The prolific Courths-Mahler in the end churned out genre fiction, frequently set in an aristocratic milieu that the author could only have known from books. She offered simple plots—often straightforward Cinderella stories—and little prompting to (self-)reflection. Marlitt, on the other hand, aspired to art, worked slowly and painstakingly, and if she did not achieve art, she did manage craft. And she operated fairly consistently and insightfully in the wake of Brontë's classic novel with stories that spoke in related terms to her own time and audiences, spoke to middle-class aspirations almost within reach. Yet chains of transmission and diffusion likely run from Brontë to Marlitt to Courths-Mahler as well. The romance fantasies of Courths-Mahler, too, deserve a critical look within this romance complex, but such investigation exceeds the bounds of the present study.

Could reading pleasure be translated into real-world action? Charitas Bischoff's autobiography suggests that it could and was. Emma Goldman's *Living*

[19]   Andreas Graf, *Hedwig Courths-Mahler* (Munich: dtv, 2000), 32–3.
[20]   Graf, *Courths-Mahler*, 8–9.
[21]   Graf reports that Courths-Mahler's daughter Friede Birkner rejected this account, since Courths-Mahler's employer was not interested in novels to begin with and since Courths-Mahler herself was after all an uneducated serving girl. *Courths-Mahler*, 32–3.
[22]   Graf, *Courths-Mahler*, 135–6, 139.
[23]   Graf, *Courths-Mahler*, 101.

my Life offers a still more compelling example of a woman who, unlike Reuter's fictional Agathe, found her causes and calling. In 1931, the Lithuanian-born anarchist (1869–1940) fondly recalled reading Marlitt together with her female German teacher during her years in the *Realschule* in Königsberg (c. 1878–81). Her account indicates that for her the romance plot has retained its purchase. First, in its narration of her early years, it testifies to girls' need in their reading for both enjoyment and something more than the bitter everyday life they knew. In recollecting her sentimental reading, it suggests how romance reading could inform the habits of being of girls and the women they would become. Young Emma and her teacher bonded over Marlitt's "unhappy heroines."[24] Yet all these "unhappy heroines" in the end found their happy endings, and Emma herself led her own life not as a tragedy but as if happy endings were possible. As she tells it, more than sympathy emerged from reading romance with the consumptive teacher. This same teacher encouraged her pupil to continue her education in Germany, thus fueling dreams of studying medicine and a romance of self-formation.

Emma's real world, however, proved harsh. The teachers beat the children regularly. One teacher abused the girls sexually. A male religion teacher shamed her before her entire class, declaring that she was "a terrible child and would grow into a worse woman." This same teacher then denied her the certificate of good character that she needed to enter the Gymnasium.[25] Goldman does not mention Brontë, but the entire episode sounds familiar, akin to Jane's shaming at Lowood. Life, as Goldman produces it in her autobiography, imitates literature.

This recollection of reading Marlitt and of disappointed dreams occurs in the same chapter in which Goldman affirms passion and offers her own gloss on romance narrative in terms of her political activism.[26] Here she recounts her love for Ed Brady, in whose arms she "learned the meaning of the great life-giving force."[27] When, however, he became possessive and protective, Goldman, unlike her literary counterparts, after a long struggle gave her political mission and her ideas, which Brady did not share, precedence over love, even though she continued to love him.[28] In political activism, Goldman ultimately found that elusive selfhood, a public voice, and the purpose that informed both. Yet fifty years later in 1931 in a new world, she was still writing her life as a romance, one in which she took center stage as a notorious, passionate, and committed political player. While she claims, "I would live and work without love," she apparently did not

---

[24]   Emma Goldman, *Living my Life* (New York: Alfred A. Knopf, 1931), 116.
[25]   Goldmann, *Living*, 117–18.
[26]   In the English context, Flint cites the case of Alice Foley (b. 1891) who, as Foley recalls in *A Bolton Childhood* (1973: 25), avidly read *Jane Eyre*, because it was "an enchanting experience in a new romantic world, and it aroused a girlish passionate yearning for the ultimate union of the demure, yet indomitable little heroine with her frenzied and strangely dark lover." Later, at age fifteen, she was "enthusiastically imbibing socialist doctrines arising out of family readings … ." As with Goldman, the passion remains but it has been transferred to other kinds of reading, to the romance of a cause. Flint, *The Woman Reader*, 232.
[27]   Goldman, *Living*, 120.
[28]   Ibid., 195. See also where Goldman again describes how, in the balance she sought between life and politics, politics always took precedence (234).

give up on love either. In this account she remains attached to Brady to his death, appearing at his funeral to the dismay of the woman he had meanwhile married.[29] Patrick Colm Hogan, in his study of nationalism, also notes her imagination of politics in general "through a romantic narrative prototype"; Goldman, he writes, "imagined happiness, first of all, as romantic union."[30]

In 2007, Hugh Ridley, quoting the preface from the New York edition to Henry James's *Roderick Hudson*, titled his comparative study of the formation of German and American national literature *Relations Stop Nowhere*. That phrase also speaks to the transmission and purchase of *Jane Eyre* and *Jane Eyre*-like romance among German-speaking writers and readers. James's artist, who is invested in the related state of things, must both attend to continuity and ignore it to carve out "a geometry of his own, the circle within which [relations] shall happily appear" to stop.[31] Unlike the present study, which must stop within its geometry, the purchase, transmission, and diffusion of German *Jane Eyre* and *Jane Eyre*-indebted romance, as Goldman's autobiography implies, by no means came to an end in 1918.

As a case in point, Irmgard Keun's (1905–82) *Das kunstseidene Mädchen* (1932; The Artificial Silk Girl) deftly deconstructs tropes of popular romance as they figure in Weimar Germany across the media, unmasking the false hope they offer ordinary people. Yet the novel also allows the imaginative but naive, undereducated, and rootless first-person narrator, Doris, some moments of almost-real felicity in her serial romances, which, as the text makes clear, affect her differently from her one-night stands or transactional, economic arrangements. Near the end of the novel she ensconces herself temporarily in a happily-ever-after domestic setting, which she forsakes when she sacrifices her happiness for her lover's. But for the present context, it is more telling when Doris becomes the eyes of the blind (and married) Brenner on the evening before he is to go into an asylum. In so doing, the narrator reenacts Jane's function as the "apple of Rochester's eye" and her happiness in "putting into words the effect of field, tree, town, river, cloud, sunbeam—of the landscape before us; of the weather round us—and impressing by sound on his ear what light could no longer stamp on his eye" (401). As Patrizia McBride describes the experience, while "vision grants Doris access to a heightened sense of her incarnated self, the same is true of hearing for Brenner"; his "sense of intoxicating beauty relates to hearing rather than seeing."[32] Keun's text, in this formulation, invokes something akin to the sensory regime of seeing and hearing advanced in the present study as a quintessential feature of *Jane Eyr*ish romance. For this one evening, translating sight into sound or rather words, Doris insists on shepherding the blind Brenner through Berlin,

29   Goldman, *Living*, 244. Her account of the final days and the funeral reads much like a novel, complete with dialogue. See *Living*, 337–42.

30   Patrick Colm Hogan, *Understanding Nationalism: On Narrative, Cognitive Science, and Identity* (Columbus: The Ohio State University Press, 2009), 314.

31   Henry James, preface to *Roderick Hudson* (New York: Charles Scribner, 1907), vii.

32   Patrizia McBride, "Learning to See in Irmgard Keun's 'Das kunstseidene Mädchen,'" *The German Quarterly* 84, no. 2 (Spring 2011): 234.

experiencing in her capacity as interlocutor and guide moments of awkwardness and dispiritedness but also intimacy and giddiness as she begins despite herself to develop feelings for him, even to find words for them. As she cautiously allows, "es kann nämlich auch sein, daß ich ihn doch etwas lieb gehabt habe" (In fact it may be that I actually sort of loved him).[33]

---

[33] Irmgard Keun, *Das kunstseidene Mädchen* (Cologne: Ullstein, 2004), 118.

Acknowledgments

For this project I have relied on the assistance, encouragement, and good will of more friends, colleagues, and students than I can possibly name here—some of them have been cited over the course of the book. I am deeply grateful to all of them, named and unnamed. A few must, however, be mentioned at this juncture. I would like to thank Simone Pfleger whose unflagging interest, efficiency, and energy yielded the better part of the curated texts that form the searchable text archive that I mined for the purpose of analysis and comparison. Brooke Shafar too was ever ready with advice and assistance over the many years involved in the assembly of the corpus. At Washington University in St. Louis, Stephen M. Pentecost, Senior Digital Humanities Specialist, sometimes in tandem with Douglas Knox, Assistant Director, Humanities Digital Workshop, in turn created tool after tool to expedite this analysis and to visualize the results. Without the dedication, expertise, and interest of these four, this book would have been much harder to write; the texts and tools remain available for future experimentation. Tobias Feldmann provided valuable assistance in viewing the silent film version of *Reichsgräfin Gisela* in my stead in Berlin when I had no hope of getting there myself during the pandemic of 2020. Grace Klutke patiently conferred with me to create the diagram of the genealogy of translations and adaptations that appears in the introduction. I owe thanks to Olin Library at Washington University, especially our former German subject librarian, Brian Vetruba, who aided me in procuring digitized copies of rare plays, and to the Staatsbibliothek Berlin where I was able to conduct research during short visits over several summers. Arts & Sciences at Washington University supported my work with a year-long leave and a generous research account, and those funds went in part toward the purchase of eight of the nine adaptations of *Jane Eyre* for girls, which are otherwise nowhere collected in a single place. I thank the two external readers for invaluable feedback on the original version of the manuscript. I would also like to express my appreciation to Imke Meyer, who presides over New Directions with wisdom and humanity. It has been a pleasure working with her, as it has likewise been with Haaris Naqvi and Rachel Moore at Bloomsbury Press. I would also like to express my gratitude to Lisa Eaton and Linda Fisher at the Press for their meticulous attention to the mechanics and format of the manuscript and for their patience throughout the process.

Matthias Göritz read chapters in progress and encouraged me with his infectious enthusiasm to keep at it, and Michael Sherberg, as so often over the many years we have known one another, offered moral support throughout. Finally, I thank Joe Loewenstein, my husband and university colleague, for all the conversations and adventures we have had since we arrived as singles long ago in St. Louis on nearly the same day.

Bibliography

Translations, Editions, and Adaptations of *Jane Eyre* Published in Nineteenth-Century Germany and Austria

Bauernfeld, Eduard von. *Jane Eyre, die Waise von Lowood*. Halle an der Saale.: Otto Hendel [1904].

Berger, Otto. *Jane Eyre, die Waise von Lowood, oder Gott führt die Seinen wunderbar. Für's Volk erzählt*. Reutlingen: Enßlin & Laiblin, 1882.

Birch-Pfeiffer, Charlotte. *Die Waise aus Lowood. Schauspiel in fünf Akten, mit freier Benutzung des Romans von Currer Bell; Als Manuscript gedruckt und Eigenthum der Verfasserin*. Berlin: Druckerei von F. W. Gubitz, 1853.

Birch-Pfeiffer, Charlotte. *Die Waise von Lowood*, 33–147 in vol. 14 of *Gesammelte Dramatische Werke*. Stuttgart: Philipp Reclam jun., 1876.

Birch-Pfeiffer, Charlotte. *Die Waise aus Lowood. Schauspiel in 2 Abteilungen und 4 Aufzügen*. Bibliothek der Gesamtlitteratur des In- und Auslands 1229. Halle an der Saale.: Otto Hendel [1899].

Birch-Pfeiffer, Charlotte. *Die Waise aus Lowood. Schauspiel in zwei Abteilungen und vier Aufzügen. Mit freier Benutzung des Romans von Currer Bell von Charlotte Birch-Pfeiffer*. Universal Bibliothek 3928. Leipzig: Verlag von Philipp Reclam jun. [1899].

Birch-Pfeiffer, Charlotte. *Die Waise aus Lowood. Schauspiel in 4 Akten (2 Abteilungen)*. Edited by A. Ziegler, Danner's Volksbühne 26. Mühlhausen i. Th.: G. Danner [1913].

[Brontë, Charlotte]. *Jane Eyre: An Autobiography by Currer Bell*. Leipzig: Tauchnitz, 1848.

[Brontë, Charlotte]. *Jane Eyre*. Translated by Christian Friedrich Grieb. Stuttgart: Franckh, 1850.

[Brontë, Charlotte]. *Jane Eyre. Memoiren einer Gouvernante*. Translated by Ludwig Fort. Leipzig, Grimma: Verlags-Comptoir, 1850.

[Brontë, Charlotte]. *Jane Eyre: Die Waise von Lowood*. Translated by G. A. Volchert. 6th ed. Stuttgarter Ausgabe. Stuttgart: Franckh [1912].

[Brontë, Charlotte]. *Jane Eyre, die Waise von Lowood. Nach dem Englischen der Currer Bell*, 2 vols. Altona: E. M. Heilbutt, 1854.

[Brontë, Charlotte]. *Jane Eyre, die Waise von Lowood: Eine Autobiographie*. Translated by Marie von Borch, Reclams Universal-Bibliothek 2376–80. Stuttgart: Reclam [1887–90].

[Brontë, Charlotte]. *Jane Eyre oder die Waise aus Lowood*. Translated by A. Heinrich, 5 parts in 2 vols. Pest, Vienna, and Leipzig: Hartleben's Verlags-Expedition, 1854.

[Brontë, Charlotte]. *Johanna Ehre* [sic]. Translated by Ernst Susemihl, 3 vols. Berlin: Duncker & Humblot, 1848.

[Brontë, Charlotte]. *Johanna Eyre, die Waise von Lowood von Currer Bell*. Die besten Romane der Weltliteratur in neuen Ausgaben, 3 vols. Vienna, Leipzig: Karl Prochaska [1892].

[Brontë, Charlotte]. *Johanna Eyre. Die Waise von Lowood*, Klassische Romane der Weltliteratur. Ausgewählte Sammlung Prochaska in 32 Bänden, 3 vols. Vienna: Prochaska [1902].

[Brontë, Charlotte]. *Die Waise aus Lowood.* Collection Hartleben, 3 vols. Vienna: A. Hartleben [1894].

[Brontë, Charlotte]. *Die Waise von Lowood.* Weißensee bei Berlin: Bartels [*c.* 1905].

[Brontë, Charlotte]. *Die Waise von Lowood.* In *Aus der Pension ins Leben: Erlebnisse dreier Backfische, mit fünf feinen Farbendruckbildern nach Aquarellen von Ränicke und Pasedach,* by William Forster [Marie von Felseneck], 106–224. [Berlin: Bartels, n.d.].

Die Erbin der Waise von Lowood, nach dem Englischen der Lady Georgina Fairfax. Bürgerliche Unterhaltungsbücher 8. Heilbronn: Otto Weber, n.d.

Hartung, Ilka von. *Die Waise von Lowood, Eine Erzählung von Currer Bell, Aus dem Englischen übersetzt und für die reifere Jugend bearbeitet.* Berlin: A. Weichert [1911].

Morton, Harry. *Die Mission der Waise: Schauspiel in 3 Abtheilungen und 5 Akten.* Berlin: [C. Lindow], 1854.

Reichard, Gertrud. *Die Waise von Lowood von Currer Bell.* Berlin: Jugendhort [1905].

Reichhardt, Rudolf. *Jane Eyre, die Waise von Lowood. Nach Currer Bell aus dem Englischen übersetzt und für die Jugend bearbeitet.* Berlin: Globus [1906].

Spitzer, Jacob. *Die Waise aus Lowood, frei bearbeitet nach Dr. Grieb's Übersetzung.* Vienna: A. Pichler's Witwe & Sohn, 1867.

Stieff, Henriette. *Johanna, oder: Durch Nacht zum Licht. Eine Erzählung für die reifere Jugend.* Besonders abgedruckt aus der Jugend-Bibliothek von Gustav Nieritz. Leipzig: M. Simion's Verlag [1852].

Wachler, Auguste. *Die Waise von Lowood. Für die reifere Jugend erzählt.* Leizpig: Carl Ziegler, 1882.

Wedding, Anna. *Jane Eyre, die Waise von Lowood von Currer Bell. Aus dem Englischen für die reifere weibliche Jugend bearbeitet,* 5th ed. Berlin W: Leo [*c.* 1890].

Adaptations and Spoofs of Charlotte-Birch Pfeiffer, *Die Waise aus Lowood*

"An Frau Charlotte Birch-Pfeiffer bei der fünfundzwanzigster Aufführung der 'Waise von Lowood,'" *Carnivals-Scherz des Kladderadatsch* 5 (22 February 1854): 7.

Görner, C. A. "Die Waise aus Berlin, oder: Ein Mädchen für Alles, Parodistische Posse mit Gesang in 2 Abtheilungen und 3 Akten," 223–95. In *Possenspiele.* Altona: Verlags-Bureau, 1862.

"The Orphan of Lowood a Play in two Parts and 4 Acts dramatized from Charlotte Bronte's Novel 'Jane Eyre' / written and adapted from the German by John Schlesinger," US Library of Congress, PS635 Z99 S44 (Drama Deposits).

"Die Waise von Lowood. Dritter Theil. Fastnachtsspiel in 3 Acten. Frei nach dem noch ungedruckten Manuscripte aus dem Englischen bearbeitet von Hans Sachs dem Jüngeren," *Carnivals-Scherz des Kladderadatsch* 5 (22 February 1854): 6.

"Die Waise von Lowood, ein wunderbor schönes Stück von de Birch-Pfeiffer." In *Die Waise von Lowood,* 107–20. Berlin: Eduard Bloch, n.d. Staatsbibliothek zu Berlin, Call number: 20 ZZ 202a.

"Die Waise von Lowood. Offner Schreibebrief an Frau Charlotte Birch-Pfeiffer hierselbst," *Kladderadatsch* 6, no. 55 (November 27, 1853): 218.

Selected Editions and Adaptations of the Fiction of E. Marlitt

Busse, Hugo. *Im Hause des Commerzienraths. Schauspiel in 5 Akten nach E. Marlitt's gleichnamigem Romane.* Berlin: Bartels, n.d.

Dreßler, Julius. *Die Frau mit den Karfunkelsteinen, Schauspiel in 5 Akten und 1 Vorspiel, nach dem gleichnamigen Roman in der "Gartenlaube."* Leipzig: Leopold & Bär, n.d.

Hofmann, Else. *Das Geheimnis der alten Mamsell. Erzählung von E. Marlitt. Für die weibliche Jugend bearbeitet.* Leipzig: Gustav Fock, n.d.

Hofmann, Else. *Goldelse, Erzählung von E. Marlitt. Für die weibliche Jugend bearbeitet.* Leipzig: Gustav Fock, n.d.

Jahn, A. *Das Geheimniß der alten Mamsell. Schauspiel in 4 Akten; Nach E. Marlitt's Roman barbeitet*. Berlin: Eduard Bloch, n.d.

Marlitt, E. *Das Geheimnis der alten Mam'sell* [9 Pfennig Bücher]. Berlin: Globus, n.d.

Marlitt, E. *Goldelse*. Illustrated by Paul Thumann. Leipzig: Keil, 1871.

Marlitt, E. *Im Hause des Kommerzienrathes* [90-Pfennig Bücher]. Berlin: Globus, n.d.

Marlitt, E. *Das Heideprinzeßchen* [90-Pfennig Bücher]. Berlin: Globus, n.d.

Marlitt, E. *The Little Moorland Princess*. Translated by Annis Lee Wister. Philadelphia: Lippincott, 1872.

Marlitt, E. *E. Marlitt's Gesammelte Romane und Novellen*, 2nd ed., 10 vols. Leipzig Ernst Keil's Nachfolger, n.d.

Marlitt, E. *The Princess of the Moor*, 2 vols., Collection of German Authors 23–4. Leipzig: Tauchnitz, 1871.

Marlitt, E. *Reichsgräfin Gisela* [90-Pfennig Bücher]. Berlin: Globus, n.d.

Marlitt, E. *Die zweite Frau* [90-Pfennig Bücher]. Berlin: Globus, n.d.

Mendel, Georg Viktor, dir. *Reichsgräfin Gisela*. Berlin: National Filmgesellschaft, 1918. Deutsche Kinemathek—Museum für Film und Fernsehen, SDK00222–A.

Merlé, H. W. *Liane, die zweite Frau: Charaktergemälde in 5 Aufzüge nach dem gleichnamigen Roman der E. Marlitt für die Bühne bearbeitet*. Berlin: Deutsch-österreichische Theateragentur, n.d.

Mossberg, Carl. *Das Geheimniß der alten Mamsell: Schauspiel in 3 Akten mit einem Vorspiel; Nach dem gleichnamigen Romane von E. Marlitt für die Bühne bearbeitet*. Berlin: August Gunkel, n.d.

Nesmüller, Agnes. *Gold-Else oder Das Geheimniß des Jost von Gnadewitz: Charakter-Gemälde in 5 Acten und 6 Bildern; Nach dem gleichnamigen Roman von Marlitt nebst einem Vorspiel: "In der Sylvesternach."* Dresden: n.p. [1869].

Oppenheim, Adolph. *Das Haideprinzeßchen. Characterbild in 3 Acten nebst einem Vorspiel; Seitenstück zu E. Marlitt's gleichnamigem Roman*. Hamburg: J. J. Nobiling, n.d.

Otto, Marie. *Heideprinzeßchen. Mit teilweiser Benutzung von E. Marlitt's Erzählung "Heideprinzeßchen" für die deutsche Mädchenwelt*. Berlin: Globus Verlag, n.d.

Rhoden, Sibylle von. *Das Heideprinzeßchen, Erzählung von E. Marlitt. Für die weibliche Jugend bearbeitet*. Berlin: Gustav Fock, n.d.

Rhoden, Sibylle von. *Die zweite Frau, Erzählung von E. Marlitt. Für die weibliche Jugend bearbeitet*. Leipzig: Fock, n.d.

Wachler, Auguste. *Goldelschen*, 6th ed. Berlin: Hermann J. Meidinger, n.d.

Wagener, Friedrich. *Im Hause des Commerzienraths. Schauspiel in 4 Akten. Frei nach Marlitt's Roman in der Gartenlaube*. Berlin: Eduard Bloch, n.d.

Wexel, Carl and Rhingulph Wegener. *Goldelse: Charaktergemälde in fünf Akten; Nach dem gleichnamigen Romane von E. Marlitt, für die Bühne bearbeitet*. Berlin: n.p., 1868.

Wexel, Carl and Rhingulph Wegener. *Reichsgräfin Gisela. Schauspiel in vier Akten, frei bearbeitet nach dem gleichnamigen Marlitt'schen Romane*. Berlin: R. Bittner, 1869.

Wollheim da Fonseca, Anton Edmund. *Das Geheimnis der alten Mamsell oder Hass und Liebe*. Hamburg: Berendsohn, 1869.

Wollheim da Fonseca, Anton Edmund. *Gold-Else oder Die Egoisten: Schauspiel in 5 Acten; Mit freier Benutzung des gleichnamigen Romans von E. Marlitt*. Hamburg: B. S. Berendsohn, 1869.

Works Cited

Short unsigned nineteenth- and early twentieth-century reviews, notices, and advertisements are documented in the notes only.

Armstrong, Nancy. *Desire and Domestic Fiction. A Political History of the Novel*. New York: Oxford University Press, 1987.

Armstrong, Nancy. *How Novels Think: The Limits of Individualism from 1719–1900*. New York: Columbia University Press, 2005.

Askey, Jennifer Drake. *Good Girls, Good Germans: Girls' Education and Emotional Nationalism in Wilhelminian Germany*. Rochester, NY: Camden House, 2013.

Bachleitner, Norbert. "Die deutsche Rezeption englischer Autorinnen des neunzehnten Jahrhunderts, insbesondere Charlotte Brontës." In *The Novel in Anglo-German Context: Cultural Cross-Currents and Affinities*. Edited by Susanne Stark, Internationale Forschung zur Allgemeinen und Vergleichenden Literaturwissenschaft 38, 171–94. Amsterdam and Atlanta: Rodopi, 2000.

Bachleitner, Norbert. *Quellen zur Rezeption des englischen und französischen Romans in Deutschland und Österreich im 19. Jahrhundert*. Studien und Texte zur Sozialgeschichte der Literatur 31. Tübingen: Niemeyer, 1990.

Bachleitner, Norbert. "'Übersetzungsfabriken': Das deutsche Übersetzungswesen in der ersten Hälfte des 19. Jahrhunderts." *Internationales Archiv für Sozialgeschichte der Literatur* 14, no. 1 (1989): 1–49.

Baisch, Amalie. *Aus der Töchterschule ins Leben. Ein allseitiger Berater für Deutschlands Jungfrauen*, 5th ed. Stuttgart: Deutsche Verlags-Anstalt, 1890.

Beaty, Jerome. *Misreading* Jane Eyre: *A Postformalist Paradigm*. Columbus: Ohio State University Press, 1996.

Beecroft, Alexander. *An Ecology of World Literature from Antiquity to the Present Day*. Brooklyn, NY: Verso, 2015.

Belgum, Kirsten. "E. Marlitt: Narratives of Virtuous Desire." In *A Companion to German Realism 1848–1900*. Edited by Todd Kontje, 259–82. Rochester, NY: Camden House, 2002.

Belgum, Kirsten. *Interior Meaning: Design of the Bourgeois Home in the Realist Novel*. German Life and Civilization 9. New York: Peter Lang, 1992.

Belgum, Kirsten. *Popularizing the Nation: Audience, Representation, and the Production of Identity in Die Gartenlaube 1853–1900*. Lincoln: University of Nebraska Press, 1998.

Belting, Hans. "The Gaze in the Image: A Contribution to an Iconology of the Gaze." In *Dynamics and Performativity of Imagination. The Image between the Visible and the Invisible*. Edited by Berndt Huppauf and Christoph Wulf, 93–155. New York: Routledge, 2009.

Bentley, Eric. *The Life of the Drama*. New York: Atheneum, 1965.

Berlant, Lauren. *Cruel Optimism*. Durham, NC: Duke University Press, 2011.

Bettelheim-Gabillon, Helene. *Im Zeichen des alten Burgtheaters*. Vienna: Wiener Literarische Anstalt, 1921.

Birnbaum, Gustav. "Die Waise aus Lowood." In *Dramaturgische Blätter aus Oesterreich*, 39–42. Vienna: Prandel & Meyer, 1857.

Bischoff, Charitas. *Bilder aus meinem Leben*. 1912; repr. Berlin: G. Grote, 1914.

Blackbourn, David. *The Long Nineteenth Century: A History of Germany 1780–1918*. New York: Oxford University Press, 1998.

Boes, Tobias. *Formative Fictions. Nationalism, Cosmopolitanism and the Bildungsroman*. Ithaca, New York: Cornell University Press, 2012.

Bolton, Philip H. *Women Writers Dramatized: A Calendar of Performances from Narrative Works Published in English to 1900*. London: Mansell, 2000.

Bonifer, M. Susan Elizabeth. "Like a Motherless Child? The Orphan Figure in the Novels of Nineteenth-Century American Women Writers, 1850–1899." PhD diss., Indiana University of Pennsylvania, 1995.

Brennglas, A. [=Adolf Glaßbrenner]. *Komischer Volks-Kalender mit vielen Illustrationen von Jul. Peters für 1853*. Hamburg: Verlags-Comptoir, 1853.

Brentzel, Marianne. *Mir kann doch nichts geschehen … Das Leben der Nesthäkchen-Autorin Else Ury*. Berlin: ebersbach & simon, 2015.

Brontë, Charlotte. *Jane Eyre: An Autobiography*. Edited by Deborah Lutz. Fourth Norton Critical Edition. New York: W. W. Norton & Company, 2016.

Brooks, Peter. *The Melodramatic Imagination: Balzac, Henry James, Melodrama, and The Mode of Excess* (1976), 2nd ed. New Haven, CT, and London: Yale University Press, 1995.

Bruny, Martin. "*Die Verlagsbuchhandlung A. Hartleben. Eine Monographie*." MA thesis, University of Vienna, 1995.

Cavell, Stanley. *Contesting Tears: The Hollywood Melodrama of the Unknown Woman*. Chicago: University of Chicago Press, 1995.

Cavell, Stanley. *Pursuits of Happiness: The Hollywood Comedy of Remarriage*. Cambridge, MA: Harvard University Press, 1981.

Cheek, Pamela L. *Heroines and Local Girls: The Transnational Emergence of Women's Writing in the Long Eighteenth Century*. Philadelphia: University of Pennsylvania Press, 2019.

Damrosch, David. *What is World Literature?* Princeton/Oxford: Princeton University Press, 2003.

Davis, Natalie. "Women on Top." In *Society and Culture in Early Modern France: Eight Essays*, 124–51. Stanford, CA: Stanford University Press, 1975.

Defant, Yvonne. "Le mystère du passé hante encore: l'influence de *Jane Eyre* sur *Die zweite Frau* d'Eugenie Marlitt," *Revue LISA* e-journal, https://journals.openedition.org/lisa/3510.

Devrient, Eduard. *Geschichte der deutschen Schauspielkunst*. Edited by Rolf Kabel and Christoph Trilse, 2 vols. Munich/Vienna: Langen Müller, 1967.

Dingeldey, Erika. *Luftzug hinter Samtportieren: Versuch über E. Marlitt*. Bielefeld: Aisthesis, 2007.

Doyle, Christine. *Louisa May Alcott & Charlotte Brontë: Transatlantic Translations*. Knoxville: University of Tennessee Press, 2000.

Ebel, Gisela. *Das Kind ist tot, die Ehre ist gerettet*. Frankfurt am Main: tende, 1985.

Eitler, Pascal, Stephanie Olsen, and Uffa Jensen. Introduction to *Learning How to Feel: Children's Literature and Emotional Socialization, 1870–1970*. Edited by Ute Frevert et al., 1–20. Oxford: Oxford University Press, 2014.

"E. Marlitt." *Die Gartenlaube*, no. 29 (1887): 472–6.

Evans, Catherine Anne Evans. "Charlotte Birch-Pfeiffer: Dramatist." PhD diss., Cornell University, 1982.

Ewbank, Inga-Stina. "Adapting Jane Eyre: Jakob Spitzer's Die Waise aus Lowood." In *Beiträge zur Rezeption der britischen und irischen Literatur des 19. Jahrhunderts im deutschsprachigen Raum*. Edited by Norbert Bachleitner, Internationale Forschungen zur Allgemeinen und Vergleichenden Literaturwissenschaft 45, 283–92. Amsterdam: Rodopi, 2000.

Ewbank, Inga-Stina. "Reading the Brontës Abroad: A Study of the Transmission of Victorian Novels in Continental Europe." In *Re-Constructing the Book: Literary Texts in Transmission*. Edited by Maureen Bell, Shirley Chew, Simon Eliot, Lynette Hunter, and James L. W. West III, 84–99. Aldershot. UK: Ashgate, 2001.

Felsenstein, Frank and James J. Connolly. *What Middletown Read: Print Culture in an American Small City*. Amherst: University of Massachusetts Press, 2015.

Flint, Kate. *The Woman Reader 1837–1914*. Oxford: Clarendon Press, 1993.

Fontane, Theodor. "Königliche Schauspiele." *Dritte Beilage zur Königl. privilegirten Berlinischen Zeitung*, no. 251, October 26, 1876.

Fontane, Theodor. "Königliche Schauspiele." *Vierte Beilage zur Königl. privilegirten Berlinischen Zeitung*, no. 117, May 21, 1878.

Fraiman, Susan. "Jane Eyre's Fall from Grace." Chapter 3 in *Unbecoming Women: British Women Writers and the Novel of Development*. New York: Columbia University Press, 1993.

Frevert, Ute. "Defining Emotions: Concepts and Debates over Three Centuries." In *Emotional Lexicons: Continuity and Change in the Vocabulary of Feeling 1700–2000*. Edited by Ute Frevert, Monique Scheer, Anne Schmidt, Pascal Eitler, Bettina Hitzer, Nina Verheyen, Benno Gammerl, Christian Bailey, and Margrit Pernau, 1–31. Oxford: Oxford University Press, 2014.

Frevert, Ute. *Emotions in History—Lost and Found*. Budapest and New York: Central European University Press, 2011.

Frevert, Ute. "*Mann und Weib, und Weib und Mann*": *Geschlechter-Differenzen in der Moderne*. Munich: Beck, 1995.

Freydank, Ruth. *Theater in Berlin. Von den Anfängen bis 1945*. Berlin: Henschelverlag, 1988.

Friedrichs, Hermann. "Die Clauren-Marlitt." *Das Magazin für die Litteratur des In- und Auslandes. Organ des Allgemeinen Deutschen Schriftsteller-Verbandes* 54, no. 10 (7 March 1885): 145–7.

Fuhr, Lina. *Von Sorgen und Sonne. Erinnerungen, bearbeitet von Heinr[ich] Hub[ert] Houben*, 2nd ed. Berlin: Berlin Behr, 1908.

"Genée, Ottilie." In *Ludwig Eisenberg's großes biographisches Lexikon der deutschen Bühne im 19. Jahrhundert*, 316–17. Leipzig: Verlagsbuchhandlung Paul List, 1903.

Gensichen, Otto Franz. *Marie Seebach—Memoiren*. Charlottenburg: Max Simson, n.d.

Gilbert, Sandra M. and Susan Gubar. *The Madwoman in the Attic: The Woman Writer and the Nineteenth-Century Imagination*. 1979. New Haven, CT: Yale University Press, 1984.

Gold, Tanya. "Is Jane Eyre the Sexiest Book Ever Written?" *Daily Mail*, September 28, 2008, https://www.dailymail.co.uk/femail/article-407404/Is-Jane-Eyre-sexiest-book-written.html (accessed May 25, 2019).

Goldman, Emma. *Living my Life*. New York: Alfred A. Knopf, 1931.

Gottschall, Rudolf [von]. "Der Gouvernantenroman." *Blätter für literarische Unterhaltung*, no. 1 (1854): 14–16.

Gottschall, Rudolf [von]. "Neue Novellistinnen." *Blätter für literarische Unterhaltung*, nos. 32–3 (1876): 497–500; 517–21.

Gottschall, Rudolf [von]. "Die Novellistin der 'Gartenlaube.'" *Blätter für literarische Unterhaltung*, no. 19 (1870): 289–93.

Gottschall, Rudolf [von]. Review of *Die Waise von [sic] Lowood*, etc." *Blätter für literarische Unterhaltung*, no. 2 (1858): 32–3.

Gottschall, Rudolf [von]. "Ein Urtheil Rudolf Gottschall's über E. Marlitt." *Die Gartenlaube*, no. 27 (1876): 480.

Graf, Andreas. *Hedwig Courths-Mahler*. Munich: dtv, 2000.

Guillory, John. *Cultural Capital: The Problem of Literary Canon Formation*. Chicago: University of Chicago Press, 1993.

Gumpert, Thekla von. "Bilder aus dem Leben." *Töchter-Album: Unterhaltungen im häuslichen Kreise zur Bildung des Verstandes und Gemütes der heranwachsenden weiblichen Jugend* 40 (1894): 84–179.

Gumpert, Thekla von. " Zwölf Freundinnen," pt. 1. *Töchter-Album. Unterhaltungen im häuslichen Kreise zur Bildung des Verstandes und Gemütes der heranwachsenden weiblichen Jugend* 42 (1896): 6–17.

Günter, Manuela. *Im Vorhof der Kunst. Mediengeschichten der Literatur im 19. Jahrhundert*. Bielefeld: transcript, 2008.

Haas, Caroline. *Eugenie Marlitt–eine Erfolgsautorin des 19. Jahrhunderts*. Leipzig: Edition Hamouda, 2009.

Hamann, Christof. *Zwischen Normativität und Normalität: Zur diskursiven Position der "Mitte" in populären Zeitschriften nach 1848*. Diskursivitäten 18. Heidelberg: Synchron, Wiss.-Verl. der Autoren, Synchron Publishers, 2014.

Haug, Christine. "Kunst, Bibliophilie und Warenhaus. Kultur als Element professioneller Reklametechnik um 1900." In *Parallelwelten des Buches. Beiträge zu Buchpolitik, Verlagsgeschichte, Bibliophilie und Buchkunst*. Edited by Monika Estermann, Ernst Fischer, and Reinhard Wittmann, 413–34. Wiesbaden: Harrassowitz, 2008.

Heinrich, A. *Deutscher Bühnen-Almanach*. Berlin: Comissions-Verlag von Leopold Lassar, 1854–1901.

Hes, Else. *Charlotte Birch-Pfeiffer als Dramatikerin, ein Beitrag zur Theatergeschichte des 19. Jahrhunderts*. Breslauer Beiträge zur Literaturgeschichte, n.s., 38. Stuttgart: J. B. Metzler, 1914.

Hess, Jonathan M. *Deborah and Her Sisters: How One Nineteenth-Century Melodrama and a Host of Celebrated Actresses Put Judaism on the World Stage*. Philadelphia: University of Pennsylvania Press, 2018.

Hevesi, Ludwig. *Zerline Gabillon: Ein Künstlerleben*. Stuttgart: Adolf Bonz & Comp., 1894.

Hillern, Wilhelmine von. *Ein Arzt der Seele*, 4th ed. Berlin: O. Janke, 1886.

Hillern, Wilhelmine von. *Ein Arzt der Seele*, 5th ed. Berlin: O. Janke, 1905.

Hillern, Wilhelmine von. *Ernestine: A Novel.* Translated by Sabine Baring-Gould. London: Thos. De La Rue & Co., 1879.

Hirsch, Franz. Introduction to the 2nd ed. (1885). In *Der Trotzkopf. Eine Pensionsgeschichte für erwachsene Mädchen,* by Emmy Von Rhoden, 10th ed., v–vi. Stuttgart: Gustav Weise, 1891.

Hirsch, Franz. "Neue englische Romane." *Blätter für literarische Unterhaltung,* no. 28 (1869): 441–5.

Hock, Lisabeth. "Evolutionary Theory and the Female Scientist in Wilhelmine von Hillern's *Ein Arzt der Seele* (1869)." *German Studies Review* 37, no. 3 (2014): 507–27.

Hogan, Patrick Colm. *Understanding Nationalism: On Narrative, Cognitive Science, and Identity.* Columbus: Ohio State University Press, 2009.

Hohenhausen, Elise von. *Die Jungfrau und ihre Zukunft in unserer Zeit* (1854). Exerpt in *Bildung und Kultur bürgerlicher Frauen 1850–1918.* Edited by Günter Häntzschel, 377–80. Tübingen: Max Niemeyer, 1986.

Hohn, Stephanie. *Charlotte Brontës Jane Eyre in deutscher Übersetzung: Geschichte eines kulturellen Transfers.* Tübingen: Günter Narr, 1998.

Howells, Coral Ann. *Love, Mystery, and Misery: Feeling in Gothic Fiction.* London: Athlone Press, 1978.

Hurrelmann, Bettina. "Was heißt hier 'klassisch'?" In *Klassiker der Kinder- und Jugendliteratur.* Edited by Bettina Hurrelmann,, 9–20. Frankfurt am Main: Fischer Taschenbuch Verlag, 1995.

Hutcheon, Linda (with) Siobhan O'Flynn. *A Theory of Adaptation,* 2nd ed. London: Routledge, 2008.

Ibsen, Henrik. *A Doll's House.* In *The Complete Major Prose Plays.* Translated and introduced by Rolf Fjelde, 120–96. New York: Farrar Straus Giroux, 1979.

Ibsen, Henrik. *Et Dukkehjem: skuespil i tre akter.* Copenhagen: Gyldendal, 1879.

Ibsen, Henrik. *Ein Puppenhaus: Schauspiel in drei Akten.* Translated by Marie von Borch. Berlin: Fischer, 1890.

Iser, Wolfgang. *The Implied Reader; Patterns of Communication in Prose Fiction from Bunyan to Beckett.* Baltimore, MD: Johns Hopkins University Press, 1974.

Jäger, Georg. "Reclams Universal-Bibliothek bis zum Ersten Weltkrieg: Erfolgsfaktoren der Programmpolitik." In *Reclam. 125 Jahre Universal-Bibliothek 1867–1992,* 28–45. Stuttgart: Philipp Reclam jun., 1992.

James, Henry. Preface to *Roderick Hudson,* v–xx. New York: Charles Scribner, 1907.

Jane Eyre Company, The. *Jane Eyre, Based on the Novel by Charlotte Brontë.* London: Oberon Books, 2015.

Janns, Christian. "When Nora Stayed: More Light on the German Ending." *Ibsen Studies* 17, no. 1 (May 2017): 3–27.

Joeres, Ruth-Ellen Boetcher. *Respectability and Deviance: Nineteenth-Century German Writers and the Ambiguity of Representation.* Chicago: University of Chicago Press, 1998.

[John, Alfred]. "Eugenie John-Marlitt. Ihr Leben und ihre Werke." In *E. Marlitt's gesammelte Romane und Novellen,* 2nd ed., vol. 10, 399–444. Leipzig: Ernst Keil's Nachfolger, n.d.

Kaplan, Carla. "Girl Talk: Jane Eyre and the Romance of Women's Narrative." *Novel: A Forum on Fiction* 30, no. 1 (Autumn 1996): 5–31.

Kargau, Ernst D. *St. Louis in früheren Jahren. Ein Gedenkbuch für das Deutschthum,* St. Louis: self published, 1893.

Kasten, Jürgen. "Dramatische Instinkte und das Spektakel der Aufklärung. Richard Oswalds Filme der 10er- Jahre." In Richard Oswald, *Kino zwischen Spektakel, Aufklärung und Unterhaltung.* Edited by Jürgen Kasten and Armin Loacker, 15–139. Vienna: Filmarchiv Austria, 2005.

Kellen, Tony. "Einleitung. Aus der Geschichte der Verlagsbuchhandlung Franckh zu ihrem 100jährigen Bestehen, 12. Juni 1922." In *Die Bücher der Franckh'schen Verlagsbuchhandlung Stuttgart,* iii–xxiii. Stuttgart: Franckh, 1922.

Keun, Irmgard. *Das kunstseidene Mädchen*. Cologne: Ullstein, 2004.

Kinzel, Karl, ed. *Deutsche Literaturgeschichte*, by Robert Koenig, rev. 13th ed., 2 vols. Bielefeld and Leipzig: Velhagen & Klasing, 1904.

Kirilloff, Gabi, Peter J. Capuano, Julius Fredrick, and Matthew L. Jockers. "From a Distance 'You might mistake her for a man': A Closer Reading of Gender and Character Action in *Jane Eyre, The Law and the Lady*, and *A Brilliant Woman*." *Digital Scholarship in the Humanities* 33, no. 4 (2108): 821–44. https://doi-org.libproxy.wustl.edu/10.1093/llc/fqy011.

Klapp, A. *Unsere jungen Mädchen und ihre Aufgaben in der Gegenwart*. Berlin: L. Oehmigke, 1892.

Klotz, Aiga. *Kinder- und Jugendliteratur in Deutschland 1840–1950: Gesamtverzeichnis der Veröffentlichungen in deutscher Sprache*, 4 vols. Stuttgart, Weimar: J. B. Metzler, 1990–1996.

Koenig, Robert. *Deutsche Literaturgeschichte*. Bielefeld and Leipzig: Velhagen & Klasing, 1879.

Kontje, Todd. "Marlitt's World: Domestic Fiction in an Age of Empire." *German Quarterly* 77, no. 4 (2004): 408–26.

Kord, Susanne. *Ein Blick hinter die Kulissen: deutschsprachige Dramatikerinnen im 18. und 19. Jahrhundert*. Ergebnisse der Frauenforschung 27. Stuttgart: J. B. Metzler, 1992.

Kühne-Harkort, Henriette. "Der Ärger: Vortrag, gehalten im Frauen Gewerbsvereine in Dresden." *Die Dioskuren* 7 (1878): 159–65.

Kümmerling-Meibauer, Bettina. *Kinderliteratur, Kanonbildung und literarische Wertung*. Stuttgart: J. B. Metzler, 2003.

Kürschner, Joseph. *Jahrbuch für das deutsche Theater*. Vol. 1. Leipzig: Hermann Foltz, 1879.

Laird, Karen E. *The Art of Adapting Victorian Literature, 1848–1920: Dramatizing Jane Eyre, David Copperfield and The Woman in White*. Surrey, UK: Ashgate, 2015.

Lewald, Fanny. *Für und wider die Frauen. Vierzehn Briefe. Zweite durch eine Vorrede vermehrte Auflage*. Berlin: Otto Janke, 1875.

Light, Alison. "'Returning to Manderley': Romance Fiction, Female Sexuality, and Class." In *Feminism & Cultural Studies*. Edited by Morag Shiach, 371–94. Oxford: Oxford University Press, 1999.

Losano, Antonia. "Reading Women/Reading Pictures: Textual and Visual Reading in Charlotte Brontë's Fiction and Nineteenth-Century Painting." In *Reading Women: Literary Figures and Cultural Icons from the Victorian Age to the Present*. Edited by Janet Badia and Jennifer Phegley, 17–52. Toronto: University of Toronto Press, 2005.

Maas, Liselotte. *Das Friedrich-Wilhelmstädtische Theater in Berlin unter der Direktion von Friedrich Wilhelm Deichmann in der Zeit zwischen 1848 und 1860*. Berlin, Munich: Dissertations-Druckerei Charlotte Schön, 1965.

Maltitz, G. A. von. "Die Dichterin." *Der Gesellschafter oder Blätter für Geist und Herz* 8, no. 43 (March 15, 1824): 209.

Manguel, Alberto. *A Reader on Reading*. New Haven: Yale University Press, 2010.

"Marlitt und ihr Leserkreis," signed B. W. *Die Presse*, April 1, 1876, 1–3.

Martino, Alberto. *Die deutsche Leihbibliothek: Geschichte einer literarischen Institution (1756–1914)*. Wiesbaden: Harrassowitz, 1990.

Mayreder, Rosa. *Zur Kritik der Weiblichkeit*. Jena: Diederichs, 1905.

Mazón, Patricia M. *Gender and the Modern Research University: The Admission of Women to German Higher Education, 1865–1914*. Stanford: Stanford University Press, 2003.

McBride, Patrizia. "Learning to See in Irmgard Keun's 'Das kunstseidene Mädchen.'" *The German Quarterly* 84, no. 2 (Spring 2011): 220–38.

McGann, Jerome (with Lisa Samuels). "Deformance and Interpretation." Chapter 4 in Jerome McGann, *Radiant Textuality: Literature after the Word Wide Web*, 105–35. New York: Palgrave, 2001.

Mellmann, Katja. "Die Clauren-Marlitt: Rekonstruktion eines Literaturstreits um 1885." *Archiv für Sozialgeschichte der deutschen Literatur* 39, no. 2 (2014): 285–324.

Mellmann, Katja. "'Detoured Reading': Understanding Literature through the Eyes of Its Contemporaries (A Case Study on Anti Semitism in Gustav Freytag's *Soll und Haben*)." In

Distant Readings: Topologies of German Culture in the Long Nineteenth Century. Edited by Matt Erlin and Lynne Tatlock, 301–31. Rochester, NY: Camden House: 2014.

Mellmann, Katja. "Tendenz und Erbauung. Eine Quellenstudie zur Romanrezeption im nachmärzlichen Liberalismus (mit einer ausführlichen Bibliographie zu E. Marlitt)." Habilitationsschrift, Ludwig-Maximilians-Universität. Munich, 2014.

Milde, Caroline S. J. *Der Deutschen Jungfrau Wesen und Wirken.* Leipzig: C. F. Amelang, 1869.

Miller, D. A. "Problems of Closure in the Traditional Novel." In *Narrative Dynamics: Essays on Time, Plot, Closure, and Frames.* Edited by Brian Richardson, 272–81. Columbus, OH: Ohio State University Press, 2002.

Miller, Lucasta. *The Brontë Myth.* London: Jonathan Cape, 2001.

Moi, Toril. *Henrik Ibsen and the Birth of Modernism.* Oxford: Oxford University Press, 2006.

Moretti, Franco. *Atlas of the European Novel 1800–1900.* London: Verso, 1998.

Moretti, Franco. *Graphs, Maps, Trees: Abstract Models for Literary History.* London: Verso, 2005.

Morgenstern, Lina. *Die Frauen des 19. Jahrhunderts: biographische und culturhistorische Zeit- und Charactergemälde,* 3 vols. Berlin: Verlag der Deutschen Hausfrauenzeitung, 1887–8, 1893.

Morin, Olivier. *How Traditions Live and Die.* Oxford: Oxford University Press, 2015.

Mukherjee, Ankhi. "What is a Classic?" *International Literary Criticism and the Classic Question. PMLA* 125, no. 4 (October 2010): 1026–42.

Nies, Fritz. "Superlativ in Serie: Französische Buchreihen mit besonderem Wertanspruch (1875–1921)." *Romanistische Zeitschrift für Literaturgeschichte. Cahiers d'histoire des littératures romanes* 16 (1992): 227–36.

Oliphant, Mrs. [Margaret]. "Modern Novels—Great and Small." *Blackwood's Magazine* 77, no. 475 (May 1855): 554–68.

Otte, Marline. *Jewish Identities in German Popular Entertainment, 1890–1933.* Cambridge: Cambridge University Press, 2006.

Otto, Louise. *Frauenleben im Deutschen Reich: Erinnerungen aus der Vergangenheit mit Hinweis auf Gegenwart und Zukunft.* Leipzig: Moritz Schäfer, 1876.

Otto, Louise. *Der Genius des Hauses: Eine Gabe für Mädchen und Frauen* (1869), excerpt. In *Bildung und Kultur bürgerlicher Frauen 1850–1918.* Edited by Günter Häntzschel, 147–63. Tübingen: Max Niemeyer, 1986.

Pargner, Birgit. *Charlotte Birch-Pfeiffer (1800–1868): Eine Frau beherrscht die Bühne.* Bielefeld: Aisthesis Verlag, 1999.

Pargner, Birgit. *Zwischen Tränen und Kommerz: Das Rührtheater Charlotte Birch-Pfeiffers (1800–1868) in seiner künstlerischen und kommerziellen Verwertung.* Bielefeld: Aisthesis Verlag, 1999.

Pataky, Sophie. *Lexikon deutscher Frauen der Feder,* 2 vols. Berlin: Carl Pataky, 1898.

Pearce, Lynne. *Romance Writing.* Cambridge, UK: Polity, 2007.

Philippi, Felix. *Alt-Berlin. Erinnerungen aus der Jugendzeit,* n.s., 4th ed. Berlin: Ernst Siegfried Mittler & Sohn, 1918.

Polko, Elise. *Unsere Pilgerfahrt von der Kinderstube bis zum eignen Heerd. Lose Blätter* [1865], 5th ed. Leipzig: C. F. Amelang, 1874.

Pritchett, Rinske van Stipriaan. *The Art of Comedy and Social Critique in Nineteenth-Century Germany: Charlotte Birch-Pfeiffer (1800–1868).* North American Studies in 19th-Century German Literature 35. Oxford: Peter Lang, 2005.

"The Prize Question in Fiction." *The Publishers' Weekly,* no. 227 (1876): 633–6.

Prutz, Robert. *Die deutsche Literatur der Gegenwart. 1848 bis 1848,* 2nd ed. Leipzig: Voigt & Günther, 1859.

Pyrhönen, Heta. *Bluebeard Gothic: Jane Eyre and Its Progeny.* Toronto: University of Toronto Press, 2010.

Pywell, Sharon. *The Romance Reader's Guide to Life.* New York: Flatiron Books, 2017.

Radway, Janice A. "Readers and their Romances." In *Reception Study: From Literary Theory to Cultural Studies.* Edited by James L. Machor and Philip Goldstein, 213–45. New York: Routledge, 2001.

Radway, Janice A. *Reading the Romance: Women, Patriarchy, and Popular Literature*. Chapel Hill: University of North Carolina Press, 1991.

Regis, Amber K., and Deborah Wynne, eds. *Charlotte Brontë: Legacies and Afterlives*. Manchester, UK: Manchester University Press, 2017.

Regis, Pamela. *A Natural History of the Romance Novel*. Philadelphia: University of Pennsylvania Press, 2003.

Reizte, Annegret. "Die Texthefte des Papiertheaters: Ein Beitrag zur Rezeption von populären Theaterstoffen und Kinder- und Jugendliteratur." PhD diss., University of Stuttgart, 1990.

Reuter, Gabriele. *Aus guter Familie: Leidensgeschichte eines Mädchens. Studienausgabe mit Dokumenten*, 2 vols. Edited by Katja Mellmann. Marburg: Literaturwissenschaft.de, 2006.

Reuter, Gabriele. *From a Good Family*. Translated by Lynne Tatlock. Rochester, NY: Camden House, 1999.

Reuter, Gabriele. *Vom Kinde zum Menschen: Die Geschichte meiner Jugend*. Berlin: S. Fischer, 1921.

Rhoden, Emmy von. *Der Trotzkopf. Eine Pensionsgeschichte für erwachsene Mädchen*, 10th ed. Stuttgart: Gustav Weise, 1891.

Richter, Daniela. *Domesticating the Public: Women's Discourse on Gender Roles in Nineteenth-Century German*. Oxford: Peter Lang, 2012.

Ridley, Hugh. "Relations Stop Nowhere": The Common Literary Foundations of German and American Literature 1830–1917. Amsterdam: Rodopi, 2007.

Rubik, Margarete. "Jane Eyre on the German Stage." In *Anglo-German Theatrical Exchange: "A sea-change into something rich and strange."* Edited by Rudolf Weiss, Ludwig Schnauder, and Dieter Fuchs, 283–304. Leiden: Brill Rodopi, 2015.

Schlittgen, Hermann. "In der Leihbibliothek." *Fliegende Blätter* 90, no. 2285 (1889): 165.

Schneider, Max. *"Von wem ist das doch!?" Ein Titelbuch zur Auffindung von Verfassernamen deutscher Literaturwerke*. Berlin: Eugen Schneider, 1907.

Schulte-Sasse, Jochen, and Renate Werner, "E. Marlitts 'Im Hause des Kommerzienrates': Analyse eines Trivialromans in paradigmatischer Absicht." In Eugenie Marlitt, *Im Hause des Kommerzienrates*. Edited by Jochen Schulte-Sasse and Renate Werner, 389–35. Munich: Wilhelm Fink, 1977.

Schulze-Smidt, Bernhardine. *Mellas Studentenjahre*. Bielefeld and Leipzig: Velhagen & Klasing, 1892.

Seelye, John. *Jane Eyre's American Daughters: From The Wide, Wide World to Anne of Green Gables; A Study of Marginalized Maidens and What They Mean*. Newark: University of Delaware Press, 2005.

Spiekermann, Uwe. *Basis der Konsumgesellschaft. Entstehung und Entwicklung des modernen Kleinhandels in Deutschland 1850–1904*. Schriftenreihe zur Zeitschrift für Unternehmensgeschichte 3. Munich: C. H. Beck, 1999.

Spivak, Gayatry Chakravorty. "Three Women's Texts and a Critique of Imperialism." *Critical Inquiry* 12, no. 1 (Autumn 1985): 243–61.

Stacey, Jackie, and Lynne Pearce. "The Heart of the Matter: Feminists Revisit Romance." In *Romance Revisited*. Edited by Lynne Pearce and Jackie Stacey, 11–45. New York: New York University Press, 1995.

St Clair, William, and Annika Bautz. "Imperial Decadence: The Making of the Myths in Edward Bulwer-Lytton's *The Last Days of Pompeii*." *Victorian Literature and Culture* 40 (2012): 359–96.

Stewart, Mary. *Nine Coaches Waiting* (1958). Chicago: Chicago Review Press, 2006.

Stoneman, Patsy. *Brontë Transformations: The Cultural Dissemination of Jane Eyre and Wuthering Heights*. London: Prentice Hull, 1996.

Stoneman, Patsy. *Jane Eyre on Stage, 1848–1898: An Illustrated Edition of Eight Plays with Contextual Notes*. Aldershot: Ashgate, 2007.

Sydow, Johnna von. *Behalte mich lieb! Mitgabe beim Eintritt in die Welt und das gesellschaftliche Leben* (1881). Reprint, Quellen und Schriften zur Geschichte der Frauenbildung 5. Paderborn: M. Hüttemann, 1989.

Tatlock, Lynne. "Eine amerikanische Baumwollprinzessin in Thüringen. Transnationale Liebe, Familie und die deutsche Nation in E. Marlitt's *Im Schillingshof.*" In *Amerika und die deutschsprachige Literatur nach 1848*. Edited by Christof Hamann, Ute Gerhard, and Walter Grünzweig, 105–25. Bielefeld: transcript, 2009.

Tatlock, Lynne. "Canons of International Reading: Jane Eyre in German around 1900." In *Die Präsentation kanonischer Werke um 1900: Semantiken, Praktiken, Materialität*. Edited by Philip Ajouri, 171–46. Berlin: de Gruyter, 2017.

Tatlock, Lynne. "Death and Transfiguration in Installments: E. Marlitt and Das Eulenhaus (1887–1894)." *Colloquia Germanica: Themenheft: Periodical Literature in the Nineteenth Century* 49, nos. 2–3 (2016): 283–304.

Tatlock, Lynne. "Domesticated Romance and Capitalist Enterprise: Annis Lee Wister's Americanization of German Fiction." In *German Culture in Nineteenth-Century America: Reception, Adaptation, Transformation*. Edited by Lynne Tatlock and Matt Erlin, 153–82. Rochester, NY: Camden House, 2005.

Tatlock, Lynne. *German Writing, American Reading, 1866–1917*. Columbus: Ohio University Press, 2012.

Tatlock, Lynne. "Jane Eyre's German Daughters: The Purchase of Romance in a Time of Inequality (1847–1890)." In *Vergessene Konstellationen literarischer Öffentlichkeit zwischen 1840 und 1885*. Edited by Katja Mellmann and Jesko Reiling, 177–200. Studien und Texte zur Sozialgeschichte der Literatur 142. Berlin: de Gruyter, 2016.

Tatlock, Lynne. "The One and the Many: *The Old Mam'selle's Secret* and the American Traffic in German Fiction (1868–1917)." In *Distant Readings: Topologies of German Culture in the Long Nineteenth Century*. Edited by Matt Erlin and Lynne Tatlock, 229–56. Rochester, NY: Camden House, 2014.

Tatlock, Lynne. "Romance in the Province: Reading German Novels in Middletown, USA." In *Print Culture Beyond the Metropolis*. Edited by James J. Connolly, Patrick Collier, Frank Felsensten, Kenneth R. Hall, and Robert G. Hall, 304–30. Toronto: Toronto University Press, 2016.

Tatlock, Lynne. "Zwischen Bildungsroman und Liebesroman: Fanny Lewalds *Die Erlöserin* im literarischen Feld nach der Reichsgründung." In *Der Bildungsroman im literarischen Feld. Neue Perspektive auf eine Gattung*. Edited by Elisabeth Böhm and Katrin Dennerlein. Studien und Texte zur Sozialgeschichte der Literatur 144, 221–38. Göttingen: de Gruyter, 2016.

Thomas, Sue. *Imperialism, Reform, and the Making of Englishness in Jane Eyre*. Houndmills, Basingstoke, Hampshire: Palgrave Macmillan, 2008.

Townsend, Mary Lee. *Forbidden Laughter: Popular Humor and the Limits of Repression in Nineteenth-Century Prussia*. Ann Arbor: University of Michigan Press, 1992.

Ury, Else. *Wie einst im Mai: Vom Reifrock bis zum Bubikopf; Eine Erzählung für junge Mädchen*. Stuttgart: Union Deutsche Verlagsgesellschaft [1930].

Vicinus, Martha. "'Helpless and Unfriended': Nineteenth-Century Domestic Melodrama." *New Literary History* 13, no. 1 (1981): 127–43.

Waters, Alyson. "A Conversation with Éric Chevillard." Translated by Jeffrey Zuckerman. *Music & Literature* 8 (2018): 92–107.

Weilen, Alexander von. *Charlotte Birch-Pfeiffer und Heinrich Laube im Briefwechsel*. Schriften der Gesellschaft für Theatergeschichte 27. Berlin: Gesellschaft für Theatergeschichte, 1917.

Weitemeier, Bernd. "Deutschsprachige Übersetzungsserien 1820–1910." In *Die literarische Übersetzung in Deutschland: Studien zu ihrer Kulturgeschichte in der Neuzeit*. Edited by Armin Paul Frank and Horst Turk, 329–44. Berlin: Erich Schmidt, 2004.

West, Russell. "English Nineteenth-Century Novels on the German Stage: Birch-Pfeiffer's Adaptations of Dickens, Brontë, Eliot and Collins." In *Beiträge zur Rezeption der britischen und irischen Literatur des 19. Jahrhunderts im deutschsprachigen Raum*. Edited by Norbert Bachleiter, 293–316. Amsterdam: Rodopi, 2000.

"What Middletown Read?" Muncie Public Library. Center for Middletown Studies, Ball State University Library. http://www.bsu.edu/libraries/wmr/.

Wildermuth, Ottilie. *Die Heimat der Frau*. Stuttgart: Union Deutsche Verlagsgesellschaft, 1859.

Williams, Carolyn. "Melodrama." In *The Cambridge History of Victorian Literature*. Edited by Kate Flint, 193–219. Cambridge, UK: Cambridge University Press, 2012.

Williams, Carolyn. "Moving Pictures: George Eliot and Melodrama." In *Compassion: The Culture and Politics of an Emotion*. Edited by Lauren Berlant, 105–44. Routledge: New York and London, 2004.

Woodford, Charlotte. "Nineteenth-Century Sentimentality and Renunciation: E. Marlitt's *Goldelse* (1866) and Gabriele Reuter's *Liselotte von Reckling* (1904)." In *German Women's Writing of the Eighteenth and Nineteenth Centuries: Future Directions in Feminist Criticism*. Edited by Helen Fronius and Anna Richards, 84–98. Oxford: Legenda, 2011.

Zunshine, Lisa. *Why We Read Fiction: Theory of Mind and the Novel*. Columbus: Ohio State University Press, 2006.

Index

Page numbers followed by "f" refer to information in figures. Those followed by "n" refer to notes. The abbreviation "trans." has been used to indicate a translator and "dir." for "director."

For the sake of brevity, English translation for repeated German titles does not appear within the index entries for the individual titles. Readers should note that the German word "Waise" translates as "orphan"; "Memoiren einer Gouvernante" as "Memoirs of a Governess" and "Mission der Waise" as "orphan's mission." For other German titles, readers can find the English translation against the index entry for the German title.

The initial entry term for the names of fictional characters is the surname, unless none is given.

Names including "von" appear in the index with the name following "von" as the entry term.

Articles "der," "die," "das," and "ein" have been ignored in the alphabetical arrangement of the index which is based on the word following the article.

Printed in the USA
CPSIA information can be obtained
at www.ICGtesting.com
LVHW010259240823
756133LV00010B/540